MICRO
TO
MAINFRAME DATA INTERCHANGE

MICRO TO MAINFRAME DATA INTERCHANGE

MICHAEL SIMON BODNER, Ph.D.
Bodner, Hutchins & Associates, Inc.
Houston, Texas

TPR
TAB Professional and Reference Books
Division of TAB BOOKS Inc.
P.O. Box 40, Blue Ridge Summit, PA 17214

This book is dedicated to my parents, Nathan and Marsha Bodner, who gave me the power to achieve my dreams.

FIRST EDITION
FIRST PRINTING

Library of Congress Cataloging in Publication Data

Bodner, Michael Simon.
Micro to mainframe data interchange.
Includes index.
1. Microcomputers. 2. Electronic digital computers.
3. Computer networks. I. Title.
QA76.5.B567 1987 004.16 87-18006
ISBN 0-8306-2940-8

Questions regarding the content of this book should be addressed to:

Reader Inquiry Branch
Editorial Department
TAB BOOKS Inc.
P.O. Box 40
Blue Ridge Summit, PA 17214

Contents

Trademark Recognitions

1-2-3, HAL and Symphony are registered trademarks of Lotus Development Corporation.
3COM +, Ethershare, and Etherprint are registered trademarks of 3COM Corporation.
Accountmate is a registered trademark of Sourcemate Information Systems Inc.
Apple II and Macintosh are registered trademarks of Apple Computer, Inc.
Baler is a registered trademark of Brubaker Software.
Boeing Calc is a registered trademark of Boeing Computer Systems.
Business BASIC Extended is a registered trademark of Basis, Inc.
Clipper is a registered trademark of Nantucket, Inc.
CP/M is a registered trademark of Digital Research, Inc.
DAC-EASY is a registered trademark of DAC Software, Inc.
Datamation is a registered trademark of Technical Publishing Company.
dANALYST is a registered trademark of Transec Systems.
DataEase is a registered trademark of Software Solutions, Inc.
DataFlex is a registered trademark of Data Access Corporation.
dBASE II, dBASE III PLUS, and Multimate are registered trademarks of Ashton-Tate.
DBSQL and Quicksilver are registered trademarks of Wordtech Systems, Inc.
DSBACKUP is a registered trademark of Design Systems, Inc.
Fastback is a registered trademark of Fifth Generation Systems, Inc.
Focus, PC-Focus and Foccalc are registered trademarks of Information Builders Inc.
IBM, IBM-PC/XT/AT, PC-DOS, BASICA, DB2, IBM BASIC Compiler, OS/2, DisplayWrite, Personal Editor 2, MVS, SAA, CICS and TSO are registered trademarks of International Business Machines Corporation.
Informix is a registered trademark of Relational Database Systems, Inc.
IRMA is a registered trademark of Digital Communications Associates, Inc.
Megacalc and SuperCalc 4 are registered trademarks of Computer Associates International, Inc.
MS-DOS, Windows, MS-Word, GWBASIC, QuickBASIC, Microsoft C, Xenix and Multiplan are registered trademarks of Microsoft Corporation.
Norton Utilities is a registered trademark of Peter Norton Computing Company.
Omnicalc is a registered trademark of Tower Systems International.
Open Systems is a registered trademark of Open Systems, Inc.
Oracle, SQL*Plus, SQL*Report, SQL*Calc, SQL*Forms, SQL*Star and SQL*Plus are registered trademarks of Oracle Corporation.
Paradox is a registered trademark of ANSA Software.
PFS:File is a registered trademark of Software Publishing Corporation.
PC/T is a registered trademark of Tallgrass Technologies.
Quickcode III Plus, Quickindex, and Quickreport are registered trademarks of Fox & Geller, Inc.
R:base 5000 is a registered trademark of Microrim, Inc.
Reflex is a registered trademark of Borland International, Inc.
SYLK is a registered trademark of Daybreak Technologies.
Solomon is a registered trademark of TLB, Inc.
Twin is a registered trademark of Mosaic Software Inc.
UI is a registered trademark of WallSoft Systems Inc.
Unix & C are registered trademarks of AT&T Bell Labs.
Viewgen is a registered trademark of Software Tools.
VisiCalc is a registered trademark of Software Arts Inc.
VMS is a registered trademark of Digital Equipment Corporation.
VP-Planner is a registered trademark of Paperback Software.
Words & Figures is a registered trademark of Lifetree Software Inc.
WordStar is a registered trademark of Micropro International Corporation.

Acknowledgment

In this, our second work for TAB BOOKS, I wish to acknowledge my colleague and best friend, Pamela Kay Hutchins, without whose inspiration, help and guidance I would be incapable of producing such things. Her hard work, organizational skills, and kind hand were all essential to the completion of this work. My thanks are small payment for all you have done.

Introduction

The computer age is, as of this writing, less than forty years old. Our society has, in this relatively short period of time, been completely transformed by these electronic wonders. The curious behemoths of the 1950s are dwarfed in power, speed and capabilities by the desktop workstations of today. The microcomputers used in today's applications are not only much more powerful than their ancestors but also far lower in cost. The result is an exponential growth in the number of computers on the planet. The low cost and high performance of this technology has resulted in a proliferation far in excess of what even the most optimistic proponents of high technology might have predicted even as recently as 1970.

The early computer systems were large, expensive, and difficult to operate. The number of uses that could justify the expense, in time, people, resources, and money, were very few. Indeed, even early IBM predictions are reputed to have foretold the need for less than one hundred computers by the end of the century. After all, it was only large corporations, financial institutions, and government agencies that could even remotely justify the ante.

As the years passed, the rules changed. Driven by advances in the laboratory, the computer's very fabric underwent radical redefinition. While the first great "electronic brains" used vacuum-tube switching circuitry, the discovery of the solid-state switching device called the transistor in the physics groups at Bell Labs gave birth to a new framework within which to design the next generations. The horror stories of the down times involved in finding a dead vacuum tube in the ENIAC days faded into historical curiosity. The solid-state devices lent themselves elegantly to the design of smaller (although still quite large by modern standards) computing machines, with higher reliability.

It is difficult to find a more symbiotic relationship between science and technology as that which occurred between solid-state physics and the computer industry. Almost every new discovery was rushed to market to improve the quality, power and integrity of computing.

While the early machines were hand-wired (or wire-wrapped), engineering and manufacturing technologies came into existence to replace the nightmare of wire "rat's nests" with printed circuit board technologies that were simple to make and support. Suddenly it became feasible to mass-produce complex electronics at competitive prices with the promise of higher quality.

The offshoot of these technological advances benefited the general society as well. Transistor radios, color television, calculators, and home hi-fi stereo/video systems—all appeared in the last few decades. While the consuming public developed an appetite for high technology, the wonders poured into the market place. "More bang for the buck." Calculators, in less than a decade, went from three hundred dollar simple four-function models to models so complex that you need a math degree just to turn one on.

The race to the moon created even more intense pressure on the creative side of the high-technology wellsprings. As more and more functions were demanded in smaller and smaller spaces, transistors gave way to integrated circuits. Electronic subsystems that filled boards several square feet in surface area were replaced by unimaginably complex microstructures in silicon, measuring less than one-sixteenth of a square inch. Such advances helped us get to the moon, calculate our tax bills, and watch "Laugh-In." What the world was not aware of was that generations were passing in the computer world. Intelligent machines were getting faster, smaller and cheaper. More and more users could afford such devices. More applications could be placed on computers and remain cost-effective.

First DEC, then Data General and PRIME arose and became Fortune 1000 level companies in those years. Competition in the minicomputer world continued the cost/performance wars.

In the 1970s the component density on the silicon surfaces of integrated circuits reached the point where all of the components needed to build a computer could be fabricated in microstructure. These first microprocessors were little more than a laboratory curiosity. Small groups of hobbyists and "hackers" built primitive four- and eight-bit computers from these early chips. The national press handled stories about these devices as news fillers. Still, behind the scenes, there were visionaries who dreamt of low-cost personal computing. If you had asked the average businessman in 1976 if he thought that he would ever use/afford/need a personal computer, he would probably have changed the subject.

The great surprise of this past decade is the explosion in this low end of the market. Microcomputers, driven by applications like electronic spreadsheets and word processing, have become an integral part of the very fabric of institutional, corporate, and even social life. Millions of desktop workstations are now in place, with millions more on the way. The power at the desktop level has grown continuously as the cost of this power has declined. After four years, the standards based on the Intel 8088 microprocessor chip that forms the basis of the IBM PC and its clones are giving way to new performance standards using the far more advanced 80286 and 80386 chips. The hardware is arriving before the true multitasking operating systems needed to make complete use of these new chips.

Indeed, there is an interesting economic "Catch-22" in this industry. Manufacturers, previously driven to deliver the latest high-technology wonders to market, now must try to maintain downward compatibility across a true generational boundary. The strategy has been to cripple the new machines rather than alienate the multimillions of users of the older machines. Thus, while users purchase 1987 generations of machines, they are still running operating systems designed to run on machines built in 1981. From the industry's point of view, however, the introduction of full-featured operating systems for the 32 bit microprocessors would cleave the user base into two incompatible groups. Historically, users have moved along with the technology, gaining the advantages of the new generations while justifying the "junking" of the previous generations. In this case, there is an unusual resistance to change, because the installed base is so large, and the power of this obsolete generation is more than enough to fulfill the needs of a large percentage of current users.

As of this date, IBM has introduced its strategy for the next generation of personal computers, the PS/2 line. By and large the major divergence in this announcement is the return of IBM to proprietary chips and architectures, specifically the "Micro-Channel" bus that bears a similarity to the System/370 architecture. These announcements place the new line of microcomputers as an integral component of the Systems Applications Architecture (SAA) around which IBM plans to build its future systems.

SAA, which IBM has paralleled in importance to its Systems Network Architecture, will provide application developers with a framework under which future applications programs will be able to run across hardware lines. SAA defines protocols and other conventions that enable developers to write for IBM microcomputers, System/3X and System/370 products. The four elements of SAA encompass common user access, programming interface, communication support, and applications. There is also to be a new operating system, OS/2, which will take full advantage of all of the advanced features of the 80386 chip. This operating system is the first product that IBM has announced within the SAA framework. It will allow for the addressing of up to 16 megabytes of memory, a great improvement over the 640 kilobyte limits that the current DOS imposes in its very definition.

The clone manufacturers are hard at work and promise PS/2-type clones by early 1988. The reaction of the marketplace to this coming schism between the old PC and the new PS/2 system architectures is hard to predict at this time. It is safe to say that the emergence of an advanced multitasking, multiuser operating system in the microcomputer world is bound to be a major factor in obliterating the distinctions between microcomputers, minicomputers and small mainframes.

The outcome will thus be unique in the history of technology. The rift will develop as new advanced DOS and application systems arrive, but the older technologies will continue to thrive as well. The 8088-based machines will continue to be more than adequate for word processing, small spreadsheets, database applications and as workstations in communications systems. These older machines offer spectacular cost/performance results. At their current pricing, desktop workstations based on the IBM PC design offer users far more functionality then mere terminals, which might cost more than the microcomputers. Linking PCs into local area networks on or as part of mainframe communications systems is not only a good idea technically, but structurally, inasmuch as such systems can be used to form the basis for efficient information exchange within organizations.

Not too many years ago corporate and institutional users of technology were resigned to manually extracting specific data from large printouts, then entering them into other reporting systems. When electronic spreadsheets arrived, the user demands for data grew. As more and more users gained more and more access to ever increasing amounts of data, a new set of problems arose. The inefficiency involved in rekeying became monumental. Users were becoming aware of the issue of *interapplication data interchange.* MIS directors were deluged with questions about how to deliver the mainframe data into any one of an ever increasing number of new formats. As a concerned data processing community watched, a "Tower of Babel" effect emerged. The proliferation of microcomputers and their attendant applications only exacerbated the problem. Each new departmental user group came on-line with a new set of demands. Each new "whiz-bang" software package made the situation worse.

While it can be argued that the computer industry never has been strong on standards, the current situation is made more acute merely by the magnitude and diversity of the demands of the end-user groups.

The problem is a major one in modern technology. Data and information are essential to the operation of almost every organization in existence. The efficient interchange of this information, while addressing issues of security and error control, is a necessary component of the successful operation of these organizations. This book attempts to address the issues involved in the information distribution process. Topics include data communications, file structures, interapplications file interchange methodologies, data security and the maintenance system. A number of popular applications software packages and hardware subsystems are evaluated as well.

It is my hope that this work will provide you with an adequate base from which to address the issues and problems involved in what promises to be one of the most exciting periods in the high-technology age: the complete availability of information to the widest possible number of users.

Chapter 1

The Data Processing Universe

There are surprisingly few standard components common across the entire computing spectrum, from the tiniest microcomputer to the largest super-mainframe. It is usually man's orientation to anthropomorphize machines, so it is convenient to use words describing parallel functions in human thought to describe processes in computers. This is why terms like memory, logic, and intelligence are in the lexicon of modern computing. In the next few decades, as computer science delves further into the very functionality of thought, artificially intelligent machines will arise.

THE CENTRAL PROCESSING UNIT

The heart of any computer is its central processing unit (CPU). This, as the name implies, is where much of the "brain work" is accomplished. At the microcomputer level chips, called *microprocessors,* are often described interchangeably with the entire system. Thus, when you refer to an 8088 or 80286 machine, what you really mean is a computer based on an 80xxx CPU microprocessor chip.

The CPU contains the circuitry needed to perform logical and arithmetic operations on bit pattern. A bit is a binary number, either a zero or a one, used in base-two arithmetic. Base two is a natural for electronic devices, because it corresponds to the on/off or plus/minus states associated with switches. The number of bits that a CPU can process at once is the basis of its power rating. Early microprocessors, like the 6502 that ran the Apple II and the 8080 that formed the architecture of the CP/M machines, were all eight-bit devices. They were limited to addressing a maximum of sixty four thousand bytes (64K—eight bits are a byte) of random access memory (RAM), which in those days seemed like a huge amount. The eight-bit machines were also severely limited in the size of numbers they could handle. The term "precision" is used in this context. When a number had too many places, the eight-bit machines were forced to round the least significant data. An accounting system on such a machine might not be able to handle numbers larger than say, 9,999,999.99 without dropping its accuracy in the cents position. While some clever methodologies were developed to handle higher precision in some of these early microcomputers, it was widely conceded that they would never be adequate in any number-crunching tasks.

Eight bits were, however, more than enough to describe characters, punctuation, and graphics, allowing for 256 different patterns. A standard was created by which each pattern was correlated to a specific letter and punctuation mark. The lower numbers were given over to control codes and the higher values to graphics and special characters. This became known as the ASCII standard, and is the most widely used character standard in use today.

Mainframes, driven by the IBM machine architectures of the past few decades, used a character methodology called Extended Binary Coded Decimal Interchange Code (EBCDIC). Users have had to deal with ASCII-EBCDIC conversions in trying to move data between systems. In the current industry, many mass-marketed software and hardware systems exist that handle these conversions.

Users of computer-based information should consider themselves lucky to merely have to deal with two major standards. It might have been worse, as would have been the case if each system manufacturer had invented their own "better" character codes. Consider the confusion caused by the use of varying printer control codes in the fuzzy definition areas of the ASCII standard. Depending on the type of printer the user has, a bit pattern of say, 28, can perform different functions. This ambiguity requires major canned software vendors to include printer driver installation programs. One need only look at such products as WordStar (release 4) to realize what a mess this lack of strict definitions has generated.

On the positive side, the market drives the standards. As millions of Epson-compatible parallel printers find their way into the workspaces of the user community, the strength of the standard increases, and the ambiguities dissolve.

As mentioned earlier, the eight-bit representations are more than adequate to handle character- and graphic-based tasks, but fail in number-crunching. Sixteen and 32 bit CPU systems are now becoming the standard in the microcomputer world. There are extremely complex differences in the ways these superchips operate. They can either use their wider data bit architectures to process lower precision numbers faster, or slowly calculate very high precision data. Some CPUs can actually do some tasks while other tasks are in process. This is called *parallel processing*. Some CPUs have hardware memory management function, enabling multitasking in different protected regions of memory.

The range of microprocessor CPUs in use is broad, crowned by the latest Intel wonder, the 80386. This class of processor is in many ways functionally a minicomputer. In years to come, users will see microprocessors with CPUs garnering power on the order of today's mainframes. Recent technological breakthroughs in superconductivity and solid-state physics increase the possible component density on microchips, while lowering the raw power requirements. These discoveries almost guarantee major generational enhancements in CPUs in the next decade.

RANDOM ACCESS MEMORY

A second major component of all computer systems is memory, which defines a class of devices that hold data. CPUs process data, memory stores the data. Early computers used magnetic rings suspended in matrices of wires, in which bit status was determined by magnetization states. This was called *core memory*. It was expensive, large, very susceptible to failure, and difficult to repair and maintain.

Data storage can be accomplished by a variety of devices. Modern computers make use of solid-state components called random access memory (RAM) as the prime workspace for applications. RAM can be eight, 16 or even 32 bits. The main computer circuitry includes memory address decoding devices that help manage where data is as it is processed. The IBM PC has a 16-bit microprocessor that uses an eight-bit data bus to its memory. It takes nine 64-kilobit DRAMS (dynamic RAM) to make up a row of PC memory on the motherboard. Each chip holds one bit of each memory data and uses the ninth bit as a parity check for internal data integrity utilities. Thus, a single memory location exists physically as one bit in each of the nine chips. Sixteen-bit memory chips would require 16 chips to each physical row, not including parity.

This type of solid-state memory device is called dynamic RAM because it quickly loses its memory state (either a one or a zero) unless it is periodically "refreshed," which implies that energy must be expended to keep the memory states stable. There is a certain time window, called the *refresh cycle*, after which the memory bit states begin to drift. Thus, each bit of each memory chip in the entire addressable memory must be worked on within each of these refresh cycles. Typically, this refresh procedure is controlled by special integrated circuits on the motherboard so that they do not take central processor overhead.

Another class of microcomputer solid-state memory devices, called static RAM (SRAM), exists, which does not require such constant attention to retain its memory bit state. These devices are made up of thousands of circuits called *bi-stable multivibrators*, or *flip-flops*. SRAM devices are stable in either the one or zero state, and require energy to change state, rather than to maintain it. As long as enough power is supplied to keep the chip in operation, the memory states are preserved without the intervention of the CPU or any refreshing support chip subsystem. Recently, a number of manufacturers have released battery packs attached to large banks of static RAMs, which are being touted as portable backup/high-speed mass-storage devices. These products, known as BatRAMs, can keep their memory states as long as there is power in the batteries. This is an excellent, nonmechanical storage device technology, and might become very popular in the future. While it might seem that static RAMs would be the devices of choice for existing, on-board computer memory systems, economic considerations have driven almost all of the modern computer systems to use the less expensive DRAM chips.

If you could see the workings of a computer, you would be aware that the processor runs through a very orderly sequence of steps under the strict cadence of the system clock, which defines the machine cycle. A typical operation might include fetching some data from one memory location, bringing it into the processor's registers for computation, and then sending the output data to some other memory location. These memory locations can be anywhere in the addressable space, can be accessed in any order (hence the term "random access") and are volatile. When the power goes off, or is interrupted in some unclean fashion, the detail in RAM is lost or corrupted. Thus, RAM is only useful as a temporary workspace for applications in process.

READ-ONLY MEMORY

A type of solid-state memory that does not lose its data when power is removed is called read-only memory (ROM). ROM devices actually have the data "burned in" to the silicon micro-circuitry. Many computers have their Basic Input/Output Systems (BIOS) on ROMs. The ROMs are unchangeable by the user. They are, thus, only useful for system programs and static data.

A new type of technology has recently been added to the ROM world, the optically based CD-ROM. These systems use laser light to read data from a compact disk that has been "burned" by the manufacturer. While solid-state ROMs might be limited to 64K bytes, CD-ROMs can hold gigabytes (one gigabyte is one billion bytes). Such large amounts of read-only memory open new possibilities in information processing, and CD-ROMs will most certainly become a major component of systems as standards are defined and data is made available.

Recent advances in larger optical disk technologies will offer users incredibly large on-line memory capability. Kodak has released its Optical System 6800, which stores 6.8 gigabytes of data on a 14-inch optical disk that is read by a laser technology not unlike that used in home video laser disks. Up to 150 of these disks are stored in an automated disk library that acts as a kind of juke box. The total storage is 1020 gigabytes, a truly mind-boggling number, but one that will be much appreciated by organizations that need access to such large amounts of data in real time. Applications include electronic imaging and storage of x-rays and CAT scans in medical centers, computer-aided design graphics libraries, electronic publishing systems, and ultralarge governmental databases. Smaller versions of these systems will become available in the next few years to provide this type of on-line data storage to small to medium size organizations.

There is also a fuzzy class of ROMs that can be written by a process and then act as a ROM. In the solid-state world, there are Erasable Programmable ROMs (EPROMS), that can be burned, used, erased by exposure to ultraviolet light, then reprogrammed. An optical device also exists, called a Write Once, Read Many times (WORM) drive. It is hard to delineate a class for such devices because they function as both ROMs and disk drives. The optical technologies can be useful for large, relatively static databases, such as encyclopedias and government list, but also offer the possibility of "pseudo read/write" functionality, in which updated data is burned in onto unused optical tracks, while the earlier versions are marked as archival (or erased). This is feasible because there is so much data space on the media. The directory of the disk would maintain a listing of the track and sector locations of the most current data so that the user applications would not be involved in data retrieval any more than it already is in magnetic storage technologies. The advantage here is that the optical memory is nonvolatile; it does not lose data during power glitches or system crashes. There is the additional advantage of having the earlier data sets available on-line in case there is some need for that data. While not as easy to write to as RAM, such optical WORM devices might offer great utility to users needing massive on-line capacity and nonvolatility in their data systems.

DISK STORAGE METHODS

Once the data processing is complete, the data needs to be placed in a nonvolatile, high-speed, long-term storage device. These devices are based on magnetic technologies, and there are general classes: floppy disks, hard disks, and tape. In modern systems, the disk technologies have become standard.

Floppy disks now come in three sizes. The oldest, eight-inch, disks were part of many minicomputer and early microcomputer systems, as well as most of the dedicated word processing systems. With the advent of microcomputers, a new format was created, the 5¼-inch microfloppy. Early units, like those created for the Apple II nearly a decade ago, stored a little over a hundred thousand bytes per disk. As the years passed, density grew to meet user demands. The first IBM PCs used 160K, single-sided drives. Later, double-sided 320K drives were released, along with a new disk operating system (DOS 2.0) to handle the new devices. Later DOS releases upped the capacity to 360K on 5¼-inch diskettes.

When the IBM AT was introduced, a new drive mechanism (using higher density media) brought the 5¼-inch floppy to its current zenith, 1.2 megabytes per disk. This seems to be about as far as magnetic media technology will go for now, but it is questionable as to how popular this format will be in the future. The millions of PCs with 360K drives would need new hardware to use these higher density diskettes, with the cost/benefit equation not really justifying the upgrade.

A new floppy technology has been added in the past few years, first on the Apple Macintosh, then on most of the IBM compatible "laptop" computers. This is the so-called 3½-inch technology. These smaller diskettes offer high density (720K bytes) in a strong, hard, plastic case with a metal slide top covering the media when not in use. The major problems with public acceptance of this new format are momentum (most people have 5¼-inch drives, programs, and media), and the fact that most of the copy-protected mass-marketed programs cannot be purchased in the new format. This latter point will certainly change. Recently, Microsoft has begun to offer inexpensive upgrades for users wishing to convert their 5¼-inch programs to 3½-inch media.

The newly announced PS/2 computers from IBM are based on this smaller floppy drive as well, which will link the fate of the acceptance of this drive technology to the success of the PS/2 itself. If the market goes to this new standard, there will no doubt appear "retro-fitting" packages to allow owners of the older style systems to add these drives and easily transfer data to and from their 5¼-inch diskettes. (I would like to offer a theory as to the choice of sizes like 5¼-inch and 3½-inch. I think that 5¼-inch is just the right size to slip a floppy into the pocket of my sports coats, while 3½-inch is exactly the width of my shirt pockets. Ergonomics at its best!)

There are also indications that smaller, denser floppy technologies are in the offing. One major microcomputer magazine has reported the introduction of a 2-inch microfloppy cartridge and drive at the 1987 Comdex show in Japan. This tiny disk is said to be able to store over a megabyte of data. It is hard to imagine a smaller package ever being developed. One of the uses for such tiny diskettes might be to store digital images in some yet-to-be-invented optical camera system, replacing the film technology now used.

Hard disks come in many sizes and styles as well. Mainframes and minicomputers use 14-inch disks or "disk packs" that look like a stack of long-playing records on a cylinder. Some minicomputers and super microcomputers use 8-inch disks. The vast majority of microcomputer hard disk systems employ winchester technology in a 5¼-inch format, with densities from 10 megabytes up to 130 megabytes in the IBM AT generation. There are also hard disks using the 3½-inch winchester technology, sometimes in a "hardcard" configuration, in which the drive and its support electronics exist on a single plug-in card. These small hard disks are in the 10-40 megabyte range.

The driving force in the winchester technology development is the user hunger for more space at a lower access time. Thus, the modern user is bombarded by a broad set of technical specifications in choosing a new hard disk.

The major point to be aware of is that the disk might often be the bottleneck in a high-power processing system. Thus, you should pick a drive with the lowest possible access time, which at the time of this writing is 28 milliseconds. A high-density drive with slow access can be a frustration in a microcomputer system, because the larger amount of data that formed the justification for the upgrade can also be its operational downfall.

Many users need to purchase larger disks merely because they are sloppy housekeepers, rarely discarding unneeded data or backing any archival information onto floppies. This, however, is why the market in add-on hard disks is so lucrative, and why the prices continue to drop.

TAPE BACKUP SYSTEMS

Speaking of backup, one rarely plans for disaster until it is too late. Tape backup systems exist in a remarkably low percentage of modern microcomputer-based installations. Often users perform spotty floppy backups or no backups at all. Excellent tape technologies exist, in which tape drives closely emulate standard disk commands. Such a system is the PC/T system from Tallgrass Technologies, a major supplier of tape backup systems.

A number of floppy-based backup systems also exist, such as Fast Back and DS Backup, which will perform high-speed backups to floppies.

Other methods for backup include removable winchester disks (10-20 megabytes) and Bernoulli cartridge drives (5-20 megabytes), the latter being a hybrid floppy technology in which a cartridge contains several magnetic surfaces. The recent release by Leading Edge of an "Infinite Capacity" computer makes use of a Bernoulli drive as its data storage device. In such a system, when you fill up one disk pack, you can merely pop it out and insert a new empty one. Hence the designation of "Infinite Capacity."

INPUT/OUTPUT

A computer system consists of a central processing unit, memory, and storage. How does the user interact with these internal processes of the computer? Through a function known as I/O (Input/Output).

In the old days, humans communicated with the "brains" of the computers using teletypes. Then, IBM Selectric typewriters were invented as consoles. Eventually, cathode ray tubes (CRTs) replaced print, and the computer terminal was born. Terminals contain keyboards for input and screens for output. A large variety of vendor-specific communications protocols exist, but the basic map is one in which each user gets a terminal and shares the computing resources of the mainframe or minicomputer system. This is known as *multiuser* or *multitasking* system architecture.

Personal microcomputers have been designed and constructed as single user systems. Their I/O architecture is one in which the console is an integrated system component. The video display is actually a part of the computer memory, and the keyboard is an interrupt-driven device. This is structurally extremely different from using a mainframe or minicomputer "dumb" terminal over a communication channel. This fundamental architectural difference between microcomputers and their older brothers is a direct outgrowth of the difference in their respective design philosophies and operational missions.

In modern systems, the microcomputer can be configured as a super-smart terminal on a mainframe data communication network. In such cases, the microcomputer can emulate mainframe data protocols and "trick" the host into thinking that it is communicating to just another terminal.

SUMMARY

Data communications protocols manage data traffic between systems as well as error checking and translation procedures. Here, as in no other area of the industry, the standards are very strict and well-defined. A misbehaving data communication device can bring down an entire system, such as a bank or airline computer, and great pains have been spent to minimize such failures.

Users can purchase hardware and software for microcomputers to interface with nearly every species of minicomputer or mainframe, both as terminal emulations and file interchange devices. While the terminal emulations are fairly straightforward, the file interchange problem is a multifaceted, complex entity. Users of microcomputers have little understanding of the texture and complexion of the mainframe, nor do they feel the need to decipher its complexity just to download a file. This is a nontrivial problem, and a major component of this book. The need for information residing on different systems is the central issue in data communications. The various system architectures and operating system software involved in these procedures will be defined, and methods of data file interchange will be developed in later chapters.

Chapter 2

The Major Types of Applications

The desktop microcomputer workstation has come from being a rare and expensive high-technology toy to being a major component of modern corporate and institutional operation in less than seven years. It is of value to discuss the kinds of things that most of the millions of users are doing with their microcomputers, and how these applications can benefit from the types of services offered by data communications that enable the efficient interchange of data between users, both at a peer-to-peer and host to-user level.

WORD PROCESSING

Perhaps the most obvious use for a desktop workstation is the production of printed words. In nearly every conceivable organization there is a pressing need to produce reports, letters, memos, charts, manuals, and tables. The invention of the typewriter in the last century revolutionized the office, and played a major part in the information flow in the industrial revolution. As the industrial societies grew, advances in the processing of words became more necessary as the need for greater information flow increased.

Computers came from this need for data, and early in the computer age it became apparent that these devices could help in the area of word processing. Microcomputers, even in their eight-bit incarnations, were ideally suited to the processing of words. All of the characters and punctuation could be represented in a relatively small processor. The standard ASCII set requires only seven bits. This meant that the microprocessor could store, print and move blocks of text with far less difficulty than the methods available to the typewriters.

Even the more advanced, self-correcting models of electric typewriters could not compete with the CRT-oriented electronic word processor. A user could type a document into the computer, see the words on the screen, correct errors easily, and type the resulting documents at inconceivable speeds (right justified and perfect each time). Documents could be saved to magnetic storage, retrieved later, changed slightly and reprinted at will. Shell letters could be merged with mailing lists to produce thousands of "personalized" letters, much to the dismay of all of us who receive junk mail. Because this form of business activity is so common and universal, it is often the entry point for a company into the new technologies. It is also the easiest way to "computerize" a corporate staff, because processing words is far less difficult to understand than processing numbers in formulae.

As it turned out, thousands of firms did go into automation initially by purchasing dedicated word processors, and they began to wish that they could total columns, calculate percentages, and in general compute more things. Because microcomputers could word-process so well, and offer an upward path for computing, some of the more adventurous companies chose to use them instead of the dedicated systems. An early microcomputer program was WordStar. It has evolved, along with the microcomputer chips themselves, into an industry-wide standard with an estimated four million users. Other packages such as MultiMate (which is a Wang word processor look-alike), IBM's DisplayWrite, and Microsoft's Word, round out the top of the market.

Corporate users demanded high-quality printed output, and the industry responded. The dot matrix printers of a decade ago have been replaced by more exotic technologies such as ink-jets and laser printers. Speed, graphics and near-typeset letter quality are now the norm. Again the technology price/power curve is active in the printer market, with more power being offered at progressively lower prices.

In years to come, the economic benefits of mass production and tight competition will bring the laser printer technology down to the price levels of current dot matrix models. The introduction of ultra-high-resolution color laser printers will bring the quality of in-house document production to meet or exceed that of current graphics service output. The other major breakthrough on the horizon is the voice typewriter, a word processor link with an artificially intelligent computer that is capable of recognizing speech patterns. While this might seem to be straight out of science fiction, current IBM television commercials display the precursor of this very device.

It is probably safe to say that electronic word processing is now a standard in corporate America, with typewriters existing only for quick little jobs like single envelopes or labels. In fact, many modern office typewriters are thinly disguised microcomputers with dedicated word processing programs.

Thus, a large number of users who own microcomputer-based word processing systems are now beginning to want more.

DESKTOP PUBLISHING

As of this writing, a new area of microcomputer usage is developing—desktop publishing. Over the last two years, the laser printer market has become extremely competitive, and as a result, the costs have been dropping while the features have been increasing. Software has been written by a number of companies to make use of the high quality printed output of the new laser printers. It is now possible, using microcomputers and these laser devices, to produce camera ready art in-house. Thousands of companies are using such systems to do work that had to be sent out to typesetting houses in the past. The linking of the Apple MacIntosh to the laser printer has resulted in the primary market for that machine. Now that high-resolution bit-mapped graphics programs are available on the IBM PC type machine, many users will use this application to justify bringing microcomputers into their companies.

While some might consider these processes to be an extension of word processing, the graphic orientation demands a different type of expertise, and should thus represent a large area of growth and opportunity for the manufacturers of desktop publishing hardware and software as well as those users who will become proficient in this area.

ELECTRONIC SPREADSHEETS

Electronic spreadsheets may be considered the major area of microcomputer usage. In the late 1970s when VisiCalc was invented, it gave the microcomputer the applications base it needed to be embraced by corporate "number" people. These folks had been using manual spreadsheets for decades to do budgets, planning and analysis. VisiCalc was an excellent answer to the "what can it do for me" question, and is credited with being the impetus for the microcomputer revolution. Many analysts claim that VisiCalc was the reason that Apple computer hit the Fortune 500 list in only five years (a record until Compaq beat it), and subsequently brought IBM into the microcomputer market to compete with Apple. Even today, there are hundreds of thousands of users who continue to justify the expense, in time and money, of their microcomputers because of its electronic spreadsheet.

Spreadsheets are a cross between word processing and calculators, in which a user can label a column, enter a list of numbers, and use a formula to calculate the sum, average, percentage or whatever. The complexity of the calculation is limited in most cases to your imagination, because the spreadsheets included extensive mathematical and arithmetical functions. If you later need to change one or two numbers, the sheet can recalculate in seconds, a time saver of immeasurable value on a large sheet. Financial analysts, bankers, realtors and others have found that they can increase their efficiency many times, and that the cost for this increased productivity is minuscule in relation to its value.

When the IBM PC arrived Lotus created the next generation of spreadsheet, 1-2-3, which combined a more powerful function set with graphics and a database system, and made use of the PC's 16-bit capability. It rapidly became the industry standard. With products like 1-2-3, analysis and number-crunching can be accomplished without programming, and high-quality output reports and graphics can be produced by users without computer backgrounds. While a number of excellent competing products, such as SuperCalc 4, MultiPlan, and a variety of 1-2-3 clones, have tried to topple 1-2-3, Lotus continues to dominate the market. Even Lotus' Symphony, a "next generation" spreadsheet, has had little impact on the multimillion member user base for 1-2-3.

In recent months, the marketplace has seen the introduction of a number of 1-2-3 add-ons. One such product, HAL, is an English language front-end for 1-2-3, making it easier for users to take advantage of the power of 1-2-3 without needing to learn the 1-2-3 command set. Word processors, data communications packages, and preprogrammed application templates are all now available for 1-2-3 users. It is safe to say that 1-2-3 will continue to dominate the spreadsheet market, and will be the standard by which all contenders are going to be measured. The latest release of 1-2-3, Version 2.0, has a broad file import/export/translate utility, indicating a long-range commitment on the part of Lotus to keep 1-2-3 at the top of the best-seller list.

The spreadsheet is no longer solely a microcomputer application. In recent years, a number of products have begun to appear on mainframes and minicomputers. This is most interesting because the interactive nature of such products more closely align them to the architectural aspects of microcomputers, specifically the single-user, screen mapped, heavy computational nature of the PC. However, the larger machines can be programmed to emulate microcomputers in such cases, and the spreadsheet moved up. It is important to note that this is probably the only application that has moved up the computer family tree. All of the others follow the more natural downward migration, as in the case of database management systems.

Products on mainframes include BoeingCalc, from Boeing Computer Systems, which is a three dimensional spreadsheet with consolidation capability, that runs under IBM MVS. Another major mainframe entry is MegaCalc, by Computer Associates. This is a spreadsheet that incorporates a decision support system (DSS), and has complete upload and download capability to microcomputer spreadsheet file formats. It runs under IBM MVS/TSO, CICS, and VM/CMS.

Oracle Corporation has a mainframe spreadsheet that is a part of an integrated environment called SQL*Calc. It is Lotus 1-2-3 compatible and has the same interface as its PC version. The Oracle environment, which includes a full database management system that runs on both microcomputers and mainframes, is discussed in Chapter 6, as one of the products that span the microcomputer-to-mainframe gap.

A second product discussed in that chapter also has a spreadsheet as a part of its integrated fourth generation language/DBMS environment. It is FOCUS, by Information Builders. The spreadsheet product is called Foccalc, and runs on IBM mainframes under VM, CMS, MVS/TSO, and DOS/VSE. It also exists in a version that runs on the VAX minicomputer architecture under VAX/VMS and Microvax. There is even a Wang VS version. It is totally integrated with the FOCUS DBMS, and can make direct access of FOCUS data using standard report syntax. Recent announcements describe the enhanced ability to interchange data with other DBMS systems and spreadsheets.

The microcomputer competitors to 1-2-3 are SuperCalc 4 from Computer Associates International, MultiPlan from MicroSoft, Silk by Daybreak Technologies, and a number of microcomputer versions of mainframe spreadsheet packages like Boeing Calc, OmniCalc, SQL*Calc and Foccalc. A number of Lotus 1-2-3 clones also exist, such as VP-Planner from Paperback Software, Twin from Mosaic Software, and Words & Figures by Lifetree Software. A large legal battle is brewing between Lotus and these clone manufacturers over the issue of the power to copyright the "look and feel" of software. These clones so closely emulate the functionality of 1-2-3 that the files and macro programs are interchangeable. Lotus is seeking to prevent such programs from infringing on its design philosophies. This issue is a major one, and any decisions made will be sure to influence the future of the software industry.

ACCOUNTING

Often a major reason for computerizing a business is to aid in accounting. Because computers make excellent number-crunchers, and competition in the mass market has made a large number of canned accounting systems available at a reasonable cost, many small firms have purchased microcomputer systems specifically for this task. In the early days of the microcomputer revolution accounting applications were severely limited by the relatively low precision and memory capabilities of eight-bit chips. In the 16-bit machines with large memory and a hard disk, accounting becomes an acceptable use for the system.

Out of a large number of available products, only a few are in wide use. The spectrum is wide, from the inexpensive, totally integrated system like DAC-EASY to the expensive, modular packages like Solomon, AccountMate, and Open Systems. The latter, which is a minicomputer application down-sized to the PC, runs under its own Business Basic. These packages are often sold and supported by accounting firms that charge for setting up and customization of the package. Because few existing companies can use a canned accounting package as is, the after-market customization business is quite lucrative for developers and accountants with expertise in one of the major systems.

Although many of these packages contain report writers and profess to be easy to install and modify, this is often as much of a misleading concept as the "of course it can do it" idea expressed by the unscrupulous salesman. Because the most popular systems have nonstandard file and data structures, it is also a nontrivial task to send data to a spreadsheet or any other application, an issue which becomes more important as the automation process follows its course.

The multiuser issue is most critical in this area. The power of 80286/80386-level microprocessors are luring larger firms into the use of such machines to do their accounting. The larger firms cannot operate with all of the work being done on one machine, no matter how powerful it is. This often forces such users into multiuser alternatives, such as local area networks (LANs). There is also the need in such firms to move accounting data to and from other systems and other applications. The term "departmental computing" is often used in these situations, in which the corporate mainframe still maintains the responsibility for corporate accounting and number-crunching, but the departmental LAN needs to extract accounting and other data pertinent to the operation of that department. Such situations are often the ones in which the issues of data file interchange methodologies are most problematic. Departmental computing is also often a hotbed of ad-hoc conversion schemes and custom translation programs, which usually do the job, but suffer from the lack of quality control and the verification of data integrity.

Several years ago, a story was told of a board meeting at a major oil company in Houston at which several division heads presented reports created on their departmental workstations. The quality of the documents was high; graphics, slides, charts and tables all looked spectacular. Each group had extracted sales, production and research data from the corporate mainframe, then used tools like 1-2-3, dBASE III, and various word processors to produce the results. The only problem was that none of the reports agreed with any others, and management was confused to the point that none of the information was of any value to them. This is not an uncommon scenario, and is a problem that must be overcome.

DATABASE MANAGEMENT SYSTEMS

The last standard type of application is perhaps the broadest and most important—the database management system (DBMS). A DBMS makes use of both the character-handling and number-crunching power of the computer to do almost any task. Simple applications might be the maintenance of a customer mailing list, an inventory system, or a file of telephone numbers. Linking databases, through relations, allow for the development of large application systems, such as accounting, which are customized by design rather than by modification.

The flagship of the microcomputer DBMS type software is dBASE by Ashton-Tate. From its early days (when it was known as Vulcan) dBASE evolved into its present version, dBASE III PLUS. It has its own procedural language and a much simplified user-friendly interface. Using the dBASE procedural language, a large community of application developers have written thousands of varied systems. Several analysts are now claiming that dBASE is more a language than a database product. With the advent of compilers like Nantucket's Clipper, and a host of tools and utilities, dBASE forms a rich development environment. Other contenders in this area include MicroRims's R:Base 5000, Paradox by Ansa, and DataEase by Software Solutions Inc. The combination of database functions and a procedural language make these products attractive as the basis of application development.

Many of the microcomputer DBMS packages include applications generators that enable nonsophisticated end-users to construct simple applications, often from a forms based screen-painting scheme. A number of add-on packages exist for dBASE, such as UI from WallSoft, Genifer from Bytel, QuickCode III Plus from Fox & Geller, and Viewgen 2.0 from Software Tools, that offer more advanced application generation tools.

PROGRAMMING

The microcomputer environment also offers the programmer a full complement of languages, including C, Fortran, Pascal, COBOL Ada, Modula and trusty old BASIC. It is unlikely, however, that unsophisticated end-users would make use of these to develop custom applications. It is also unlikely to find a programmer custom-writing a word processor, spreadsheet or database management system when such industry standards as WordStar, 1-2-3 and dBASE exist. The use of standard packages keeps development and support costs down, and frees the end-user from a possibly crippling dependence on a single programmer. In the mainframe and minicomputer eras, it was not unusual for a company to spend hundreds of thousands of dollars developing code that later became difficult (if not impossible) to support or transport to other hardware configurations.

The cost of time on the mainframe is often much higher than that on desktop workstations, so it has become feasible to write code on microcomputer versions of the mainframe language, edit, test and debug, and then transport the source to the host system for final compilation and debugging. Programming languages like COBOL, Fortran, and C exist in compatible versions in both environments, and can use this scheme in the development process. This is a very efficient use of the microcomputer's editing, compilation, and execution capabilities, and minimizes the negative impact on the host. The code that is finally sent to the host is usually free of syntax errors, and hopefully logically sound. In any event, the edit, compile, link, execute, and debug cycle on the microcomputer is often much faster than can be achieved on a mainframe network of any size. There is also a much lower probability of a fatal crash of the host system by some really serious bug in newly written code.

CONCLUSION

In this chapter a number of major application areas and end-user needs have been defined and discussed. These are by no means the only things that people do with computers, but represent the main types of functions. The computer is the center of the information interchange process, and applications are the functional methods by which this process works. It should be evident that these applications drive the need for the efficient exchange of data between themselves, ultimately resulting in the fulfillment of the end-user requirements for the reporting of this information.

Chapter 3

Data Communications

Information is much more valuable if it can be shared. This is true in almost any imaginable situation and forms a fundamental driving force in the computer age. In the early days of computing, there was little need and basically no efficient method for moving large amounts of information around. Data was entered on large, clunky, mechanical teletypes, processed by the central processing unit, and output was printed to paper. The use of punch cards and paper type allowed for a batch processing mode of data entry, as well as a form of output that could be read by machines for use as input in subsequent processes. The very technology of punch cards was borrowed from the wonders of the early industrial revolution; machines like looms were programmed to do repetitive patterns by reading the holes on a chain of punched paper cards. This scheme was invented by J. M. Jacquard in the late 1700s. Charles Babbage, a British mathematician and mechanical engineer, used this punch card concept in his "Analytical Engine" in the late 1800s, widely considered to be a precursor to the modern computer.

The process of reading, in an electromechanical way, the holes in punched cards is credited to Herman Hollerith, and in the Fortran language today his name is used to denote character representations. In 1911, Hollerith formed, with two other companies, the Computing Tabulating Recording Company, whose name was later changed to International Business Machines.

The punch technology was an ingenious way to record large amounts of data for later computation. Sequences of commands, called programs, could be punched into the paper tape or punch cards as well, relieving the operator of having to retype the commands each time the programs ran.

These primitive console input and output devices were eventually replaced by magnetic storage media and CRT display devices, which are ubiquitous today. Still, there was often data in one file or site that would be useful in some other applications at some other site. It thus became necessary to set up methodologies that would allow data processing devices to communicate. This was not a trivial task, given the complexity of the systems involved. This chapter defines and describes the communications universe as it pertains to data interchange.

FUNDAMENTAL CONCEPTS

All communications systems have three physical components: transmitters, receivers, and transmission media. This media can be copper wire, fiber optics, air, vacuum, and even string. (Remember paper cup telephones?) The systems also need a protocol, a way in which things will be done. There are also three methods of transmission. The first, and most primitive, is called *simplex.* This is communication in one direction only. The transmitter sends and the receiver can only get the message. The sender cannot know that the message was received. When Paul Revere used the "one if by land, two if by sea" signal, that was simplex. The person in the church steeple sent the message, and had no way of knowing if it was received. Television and radio broadcasts are other examples.

Two-way radio, like citizen's band, is an example of *half duplex* communication. First, one person presses a "talk" button, speaks a message, then ends with "over." During the time a person is transmitting, the receiver can only receive. The sender "owns" the channel. The person at the other end can then press the "talk" button to respond. That person is now the sender, and the first person receives the reply message. They have reversed roles. Each device can be called a *transceiver,* because it can act as both a transmitter and a receiver. Half duplex systems can thus provide a method of acknowledgment unavailable in simplex systems, because the sender can say things like "did you get that?"

The third, and most natural, method is one in which both the sender and receiver can talk and listen at the same time—kind of like holidays at your parent's house. This is called *full duplex* communication, and is the way in which telephones work. Both the speaker and earphone are active at once, and signals can go in both directions at the same time. Even though both parties can speak and listen at the same time technically, such an information exchange could be confusing, so it is still customary to wait until the other person has finished before you begin to talk. This "custom" can be thought of as a *protocol.* This protocol of when to talk, when to listen, and when to say "I did not understand what you just said" must be defined before computers can "talk" on the phone. There is more about protocols later in this chapter.

Another consideration in communication systems is the *configuration.* When two parties are talking, they can be connected in a straight line (Fig. 3-1), just like the paper cup and string telephones of our childhood.

Fig. 3-1. Simple point-to-point connection (two sites).

Connecting three kids could be accomplished with three cup-string sets, as in Fig. 3-2.

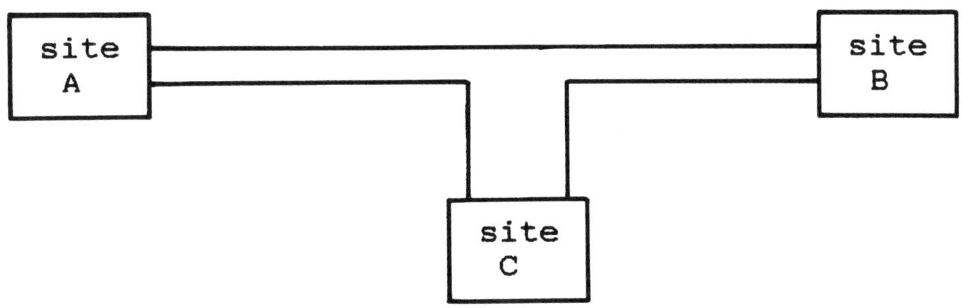

Fig. 3-2. Simple point-to-point connection (three sites).

Four kids need six sets, as shown in Fig. 3-3, and so on. Point-to-point com-

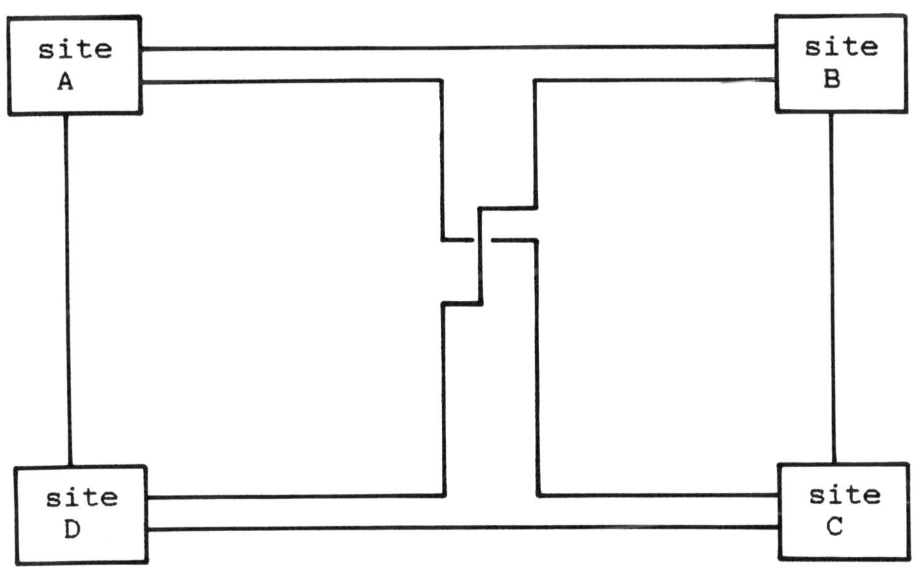

Fig. 3-3. Simple point-to-point connection (four sites).

munications get exponentially complex, and are therefore impractical in systems of any size. Early telephone networks addressed this problem via the use of "star" configurations (see Fig. 3-4), in which thousands of phones linked into a central switching center, with the switching centers linked.

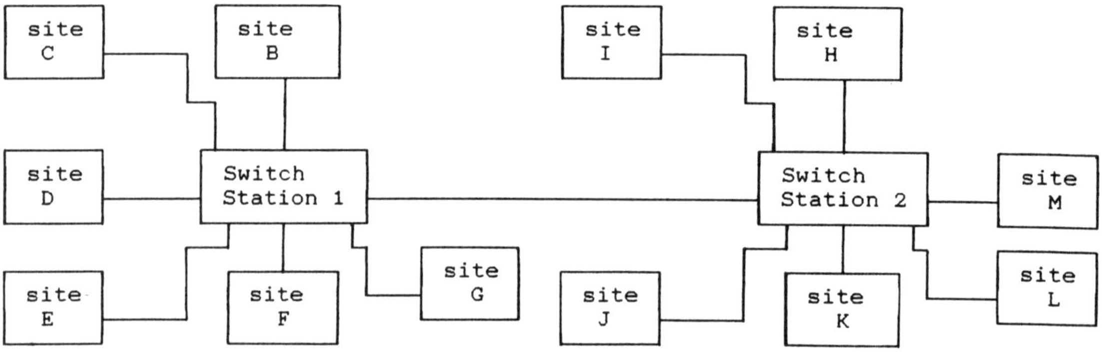

Fig. 3-4. Central switching network—multiple point-to-point.

If a person at home "C" wants to call a person at home "E," the call is routed through switching station "1," then back out to "E," creating the "C-E" point-to-point required. If "C" wants to call "K," the call goes to switching station "1," then to switching station "2," then to "K." The worldwide telephone network is just a superset of this system, in which hundreds of millions of phones are interconnected.

In some cases where user demand is not high, "party" lines might be adequate. Here, a radial line can "multi-drop" as shown in Fig. 3-5.

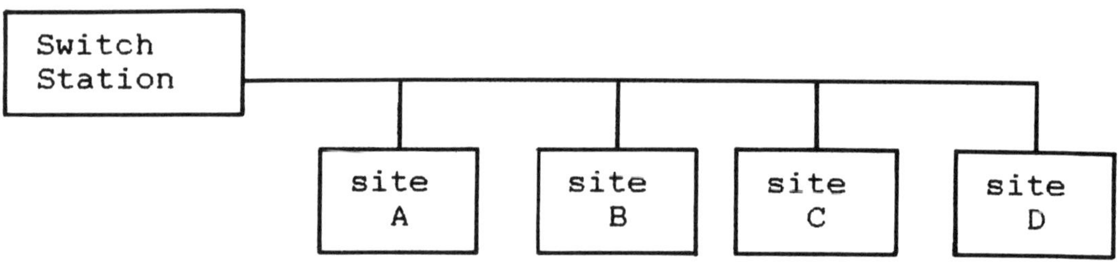

Fig. 3-5. Multidrop communication line (telephone party line).

In this configuration, either "A," "B," "C," or "D" can make a call. If two of them tried to talk at the same time, the messages would collide. A protocol would need to exist to let the other three phones know that one of the party line sets is in use.

As this applies to computers, a method would need to be established by which the host could communicate with each of the data sets in an unambiguous manner. One method, used by early airline reservation systems like PARS, is called *polling.* In this protocol, the host asks each terminal in turn, "Do you have anything to say?" If the terminal does, it sends its request, then waits quietly for either a response or a request for more data. Each terminal waits its turn, and each has an "address" so that it can recognize its own messages. There is a lot of protocol overhead, but the terminals can effectively share the party line.

Finally, there is a method available to data communications that would be unusable in voice. It is called *multiplexing.* The two most widely used types are *time division multiplexing* (TDM) and frequency division multiplexing (FDM). Time division gives each party a share of time as shown in Fig. 3-6, while frequency division multiplexing divides users with different frequencies on a data line.

Message Fragment 1 User A	Message Fragment 1 User B	Message Fragment 1 User C	Message Fragment 2 User A	Message Fragment 2 User B

← Data Stream —

Fig. 3-6. Time division multiplexing.

Message Channel for User A.......(Frequency 1)
Message Channel for User B.......(Frequency 2)
Message Channel for User C.......(Frequency 3)
Message Channel for User D.......(Frequency 4)

← Data Stream —

Fig. 3-7. Frequency division multiplexing.

Multiplexing allows for several users to "share" a high-speed data line. The host can have four ports, each 1200 baud, then these four signals can be multiplexed and sent out at 4800 baud on one line. At the other end the signal can be demultiplexed and routed to four terminals. The terminals each act as if they have a point-to-point full-time data link (Fig. 3-8).

DATA COMMUNICATIONS HARDWARE

There are several standard components of data communications systems. The two that have previously been discussed are the CPU and the user con-

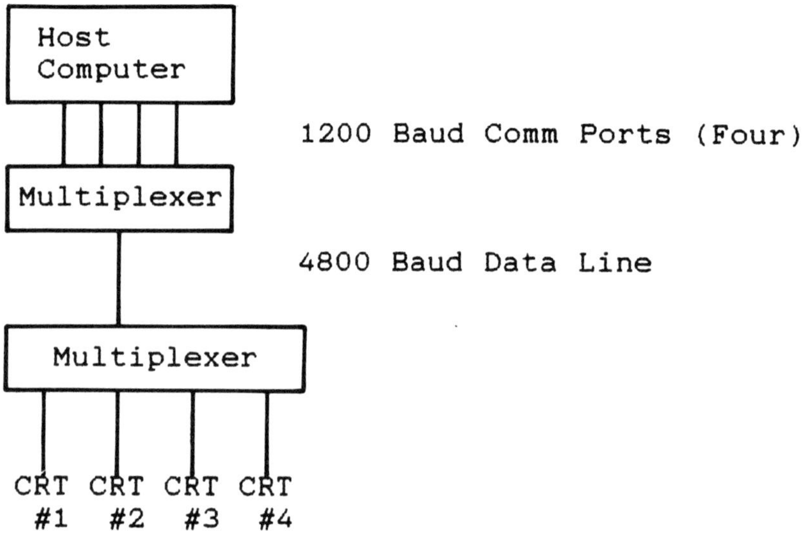

Fig. 3-8. Multiplexed system (four ports on one high-speed line).

sole. The requirement that the CPU simultaneously give access to a large number of terminals imposes the need for additional hardware to implement the protocol and manage data traffic.

In order not to burden the CPU itself with data communication overhead, many manufacturers have developed what are known as *front-end communications processors.* In the IBM mainframe world, these are Model 37x5 devices. They sit between the CPU and the data communications devices. Data is actually transmitted on telephone lines in two frequencies, representing ones and zeros using a device called a *modem,* (*mo*dulator-*dem*odulator). Modems take a digital data stream and convert the bits to audible pulses on the telephone line. At the other end, a modem demodulates, converting the audible pulses back into digital electric bits.

Modem speeds are measured in baud rates, roughly ten times the character speed. Thus, a 1200 baud modem sends roughly 120 characters per second on to the line. Most modern microcomputers use 1200 or 2400 baud asynchronous modems on dial-up telephone lines.

Asynchronous Communications

The word "asynchronous" means something that is not synchronized, or timed. In a data stream, the term implies that character codes can be sent and received with various random lengths of time in between them. Because the receiver has no way of knowing how long to wait for the next character, as is the case in synchronous communications, there must be some way of letting it know that a character is coming.

The process of identifying a character as a valid data stream is called *framing.* A special "start" code is at the beginning of a bit stream, and a "stop" code at the end. Once the bits begin, they will be moving at the baud rate (1200, 2400, etc.), but there might be long periods of time during which no bits move at all. Only when the receiver sees a start code does communication begin, and it continues until the transfer is ended with a stop code.

Because the data in this type of communication marches down a single wire one bit at a time, it is called "serial" communication. Ones and zeros are represented by minus (−15 to −5) and plus (+5 to +15) dc voltages. The standard interface, the RS-232, uses +5 to +15 as "on" for interface control signals such as handshaking.

When there is no transmission of data, the line is said to be idle and has a constant one or "mark," state. When transmission is about to begin, there is a state transition to a zero, or "space," condition. This is what the receiver calls a "start." The duration of this startstate is the same as that of any data bit, and would be 1/2400th of a second for a 2400 bit-per-second line.

The stop condition is a return to "mark" after the set number of data bits has been received. If there is any problem with the stop, such as it not arriving after the 7th bit, or not being long enough, a framing error is reported and the packet is bad.

Thus, an asynchronous port must be told the number of bits for the character, the number of stop bits, and the parity of the packet.The diagram in Fig. 3-9 shows the asynchronous data stream for the letter "L" (8-bit, one stop).

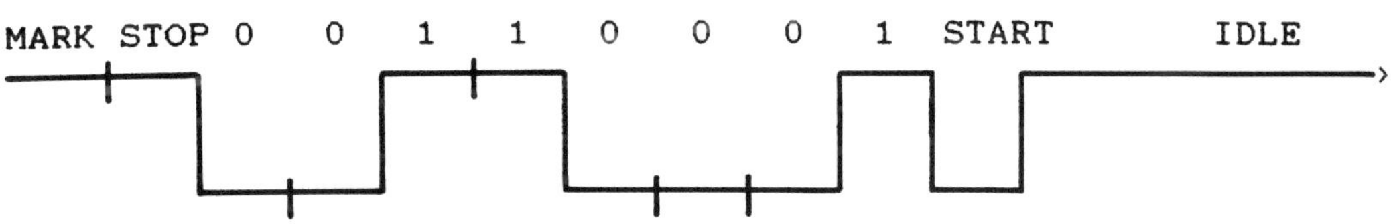

Fig. 3-9. Asynchronous data stream ("L", 8-bit, 1 stop).

In most modern systems, there are hardware interfaces that take care of most of the asynchronous port overhead. These are called *UARTs* (universal asynchronous receiver/transmitter) or *USARTs* (universal synchronous/asynchronous receiver/transmitter), and are usually fabricated into single integrated circuit chips. USARTs also have the capability to handle synchronous data communication. The transmitter takes each character from its input buffer, serializes it into a data stream, wraps it in start and stop bits (as programmed), and sends it on its way. The receiver side waits until it gets a complete packet, strips it of its start and stop bits, puts it in an input buffer, and then tells the CPU to fetch that data. While the UART is busy, it must signal both its own CPU and the remote sender as to when it will be ready to receive more characters. Such status bits are defined in the interface as well, and make up what is called *handshaking.*

The port is passive. It can only send and receive packets and tell the CPU what it has found. Protocols define the meaning of the received codes, and define what actions are to be taken as responses if applicable.

Synchronous Communications

To be synchronized means to be "in time." In synchronous communication the sending and receiving sites run at the same clock, or are in synch during the entire data block transfer. The most difficult part of such a method is the framing, because the synchronization is critical in the decoding of the bits on the receiving end.

In synchronous protocols, there is a synchronization pattern, composed of either one or two characters, which signals that a frame is beginning, analogous to the way in which a start works in asynchronous systems (Fig. 3-10). In the EBCDIC system, the pattern is called SYN, and is binary 00110010. Because this is an eight-bit protocol, the frame is eight bits wide. The receiver now expects the next eight bits to be a second SYN, and if it is, it will expect the message itself to begin. Note that the odds of having 16 random bits forming two SYNs by accident is remote, and thus there are very few false starts. In the IPARS protocol, there are two different synch characters, SYN1 and SYN2, which must be received to establish the frame start.

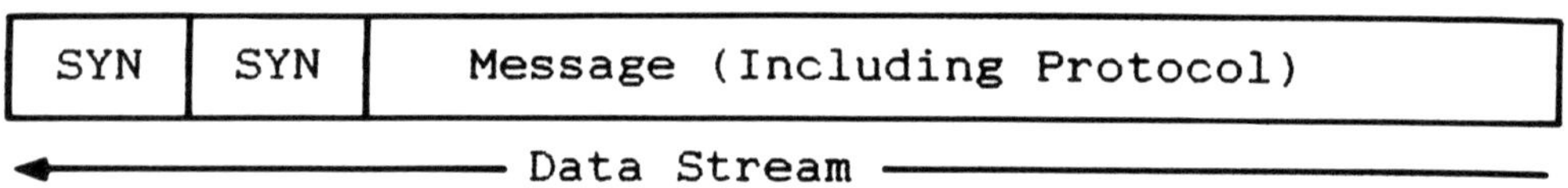

Fig. 3-10. Synchronous data packet format.

There is a lot more to a synchronous data packet. Often there are Start of Message, End of Message, and Cyclic Redundancy Check (CRC) patterns as well. These are all embedded in the protocol.

The clock is often in the modem itself, but both the host and remote modems must use the same clock. The synchronous port expects a character at a specific interval, determined by the baud rate. If, for any reason, a character fails to arrive, the packet *times out* and is discarded, using the protocol error handling to either request a packet retransmission or to cancel the session.

Synchronous communication is inherently less error prone than asynchronous and is the most widely used in the mainframe environments where large data packet volumes are common. These systems require more hardware, more expensive modems, and more protocol overhead, which is why they are less popular on the microcomputer scene.

Most mainframes use very high speed (2400-9600 baud) synchronous modems on leased data lines. Sometimes several data streams can be multiplexed and transmitted at higher baud rates, as described in the previous section.

In multi-drop, protocol intensive applications, a terminal control unit (or concentrator) must exist at the remote site. The TCU is actually a dedicated processor that manages the protocol overhead and data traffic, producing compact data packets to be delivered to the host when polled. Referencing IBM model numbers, these are the 3274 devices to which terminals (3278/9) and printers are connected (as in Fig. 3-11).

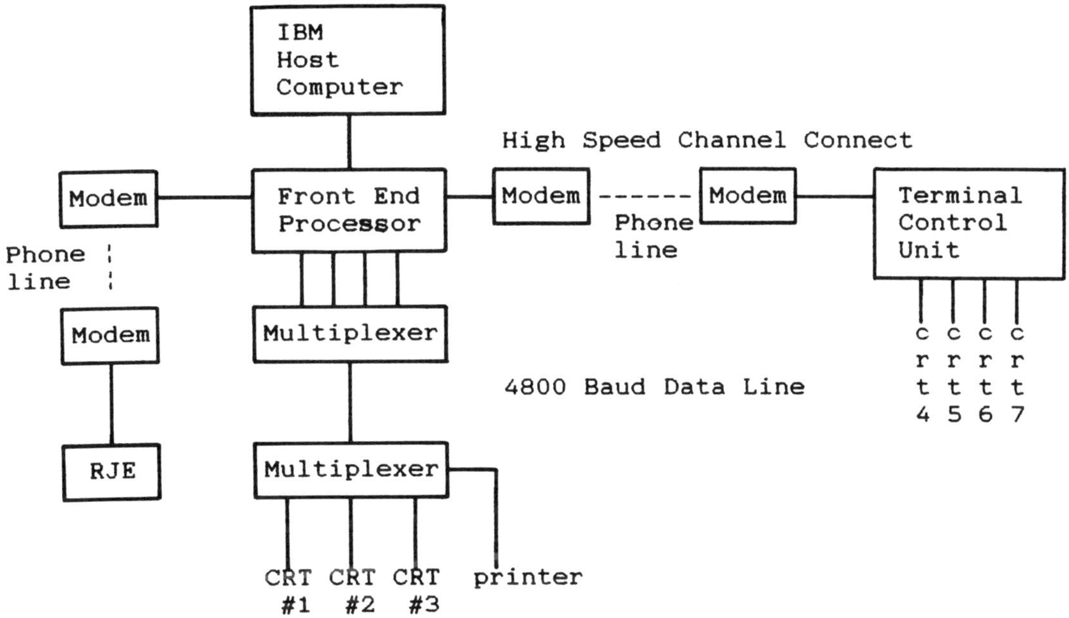

Fig. 3-11. Typical IBM (3270-type) data communication system.

Another type of device that can be linked via a modem to a host is a remote job entry station (RJE), which acts as a batch console device at a remote site (IBM 3780). The systems include a card reader, card punch, printer, and magnetic storage. They enable the remote sites to submit jobs to the host processor and have the output routed back to the remote site's output devices. Such devices are dwindling in numbers as more interactive computing is replacing batch processing as the major operational methodology. Many minicomputers and word processors, such as Prime and Wang, have 3780/RJE type ports for file transfer capabilities.

In the modern multi-protocol data communications universe, there are even intelligent devices that can be linked into the communications network to allow different species of computing machines to interact in a transparent fashion. These are called *protocol converters,* and often include the ability to allow for the use of asynchronous devices on synchronous systems. Protocol converters actually perform both hardware and software translations as required. It is thus possible to use inexpensive asynchronous terminals on 3270-type synchronous data communications systems, with the cost of the protocol converter being justified by the cost differential in the terminals and printers. Many information centers have microcomputers hooked up to mainframes using protocol converters and terminal emulation programs running on the PCs. This is an excellent integration path as far as the communications demands are concerned.

In an overview of data communications systems themselves, it is important to notice that these networks are, topologically, inverted trees. One CPU (or group of CPUs) can be connected to thousands of local and remote devices. Managing data flow is complex, critical, and strict. Large banks, airlines, government agencies and a myriad of other institutions have come to rely on the quality and correctness of this data traffic management. A major aspect of maintaining the data integrity is the data communication protocol and error handling scheme.

DATA REPRESENTATION CODES

Digital computers can only express themselves in binary bit oriented formats, so it is up to the ingenuity of man to come up with schemes that use bits to represent letters, numbers and graphics characters. An early code that shows this ingenuity is the Baudot code, a five-bit system invented by a French postal engineer in the 1870s. The Baudot code is shown in Fig. 3-12. It is still in use in many Telex installations throughout the world.

Because five bits can only have 32 different patterns, Baudot used two codes to extend the usability of the method. As can be seen in the figure, there is a letter shift code (31) which is 11111 in binary. Once the letter shift code is sent, all subsequent codes are to be deciphered using the letter character column of the chart. A figure shift (27, or 11011) tells the decoding device to use the figure column. Note that only uppercase letters and a minimal punctuation set are available, due to the lack of distinct bit representations in a five-bit code. The message "IT'S 3%" would look like the data stream shown in Fig. 3-13.

While this code seems unwieldy, it did work, and is still in use. The conversions and decoding were accomplished by mechanical, and later on, electronic, devices.

Another major code type is the Binary Coded Decimal (BCD), used by early IBM systems. It was an "enhanced" bit code, which corresponded to the standard card code used on the data punch cards of that era. BCD was the basic representation code of many of the major time-sharing systems of the sixties and early seventies, particularly the airline reservation systems, which are among the largest systems in the world. The basic protocol, called IPARS (International Protocol for Airline Reservation Systems) is still in use in American Airlines Sabre, TWA PARS, and United's Apollo today. The BCD chart is shown in Fig. 3-14.

Decimal	Binary	Octal	Hex	Letters	Figures
0	00000	0	0	blank	blank
1	00001	1	1	E	3
2	00010	2	2		LF
3	00011	3	3	A	-
4	00100	4	4	SP	Space
5	00101	5	5	S	'
6	00110	6	6	I	8
7	00111	7	7	U	7
8	01000	10	8	‹ Carriage Rtn	
9	01001	11	9	D	Who Are You?
10	01010	12	A	R	4
11	01011	13	B	J	BELL
12	01100	14	C	N	,
13	01101	15	D	F	%
14	01110	16	E	C	:
15	01111	17	F	K	(
16	10000	20	10	T	5
17	10001	21	11	Z	+
18	10010	22	12	L	)
19	10011	23	13	"	2
20	10100	24	14	H	British Pound
21	10101	25	15	Y	6
22	10110	26	16	P	0
23	10111	27	17	Q	1
24	11000	30	18	O	9
25	11001	31	19	B	?
26	11010	32	1A	G	$
27	11011	33	1B	Figure	Shift
28	11100	34	1C	M	.
29	11101	35	1D	X	/
30	11110	36	1E	V	=
31	11111	37	1F	Letter	Shift

Fig. 3-12. The Baudot code (5-bit).

Desired Code	Binary
Letter Shift	11111
I	00110
T	10000
Figure Shift	11011
'	00101
Letter Shift	11111
S	00101
SPACE	00100
Figure Shift	11011
3	00001
%	01101
Letter Shift	11111

Fig. 3-13. Baudot message ("IT'S 3%").

The next major code is perhaps the most popular, the ASCII (American Standard Code for Information Interchange). This is a seven-bit code that has 128 different representations, and can define uppercase and lowercase letters, numbers, punctuation, and a number of special control codes, as shown in Fig. 3-15.

As mentioned in Chapter 1, ASCII is the code used in most microcomputers and many minicomputers. Because it is used by such a wide class of computers, it allows for data to be interchanged without the need for code translations, as might be the case if the host uses some other standard.

In many communications protocols, a parity bit is added to the seven-bit ASCII to make it appear to be an eight-bit code. Parity is used to aid in error detection, and is discussed later.

On the high end, in the realm of mainframes and large minicomputers there is the eight-bit Extended Binary Coded Decimal Interchange Code (EBCDIC). Eight bits allow for 256 different codes. Such a large number of codes enable this system to use many codes for control and special functions, as can be seen by the code chart in Fig. 3-16.

Character	Standard BCD
0	100 1010
1	000 0001
2	000 0010
3	100 0011
4	000 0100
5	100 0101
6	100 0110
7	000 0111
8	000 1000
9	100 1001
A	011 0001
B	011 0010
C	111 0011
D	011 0100
E	111 0101
F	111 0110
G	011 0111
H	011 1000
I	111 1001
J	110 0001
K	110 0010
L	010 0011
M	110 0100
N	010 0101
O	010 0110
P	110 0111
Q	110 1000
R	010 1001
S	101 0010
T	001 0011
U	101 0100
V	101 0101
W	001 0110
X	101 0111
Y	101 1000
Z	001 1001

Fig. 3-14. Binary Coded Decimal.

Decimal	Binary	Octal	Hex	Character
0	0000000	000	00	NUL
1	0000001	001	01	SOH

Fig. 3-15. The ASCII code (7-bit, IBM). (Continued through page 32.)

2	0000010	002	02	STX
3	0000011	003	03	ETX
4	0000100	004	04	EOT
5	0000101	005	05	ENQ
6	0000110	006	06	ACK
7	0000111	007	07	BEL
8	0001000	010	08	BS
9	0001001	011	09	HT
10	0001010	012	0A	LF
11	0001011	013	0B	VT
12	0001100	014	0C	FF
13	0001101	015	0D	CR
14	0001110	016	0E	SO
15	0001111	017	0F	SI
16	0010000	020	10	DLE
17	0010001	021	11	DC1
18	0010010	022	12	DC2
19	0010011	023	13	DC3
20	0010100	024	14	DC4
21	0010101	025	15	NAK
22	0010110	026	16	SYN
23	0010111	027	17	ETB
24	0011000	030	18	CAN
25	0011001	031	19	EM
26	0011010	032	1A	SUB
27	0011011	033	1B	ESC
28	0011100	034	1C	FS
29	0011101	035	1D	GS
30	0011110	036	1E	RS
31	0011111	037	1F	US
32	0100000	040	20	SP
33	0100001	041	21	!
34	0100010	042	22	"
35	0100011	043	23	#
36	0100100	044	24	$
37	0100101	045	25	%
38	0100110	046	26	&
39	0100111	047	27	'
40	0101000	050	28	(
41	0101001	051	29	)
42	0101010	052	2A	*
43	0101011	053	2B	+
44	0101100	054	2C	,
45	0101101	055	2D	–
46	0101110	056	2E	.
47	0101111	057	2F	/
48	0110000	060	30	0
49	0110001	061	31	1
50	0110010	062	32	2
51	0110011	063	33	3

52	0110100	064	34	4
53	0110101	065	35	5
54	0110110	066	36	6
55	0110111	067	37	7
56	0111000	070	38	8
57	0111001	071	39	9
58	0111010	072	3A	:
59	0111011	073	3B	;
60	0111100	074	3C	<
61	0111101	075	3D	=
62	0111110	076	3E	>
63	0111111	077	3F	?
64	1000000	100	40	@
65	1000001	101	41	A
66	1000010	102	42	B
67	1000011	103	43	C
68	1000100	104	44	D
69	1000101	105	45	E
70	1000110	106	46	F
71	1000111	107	47	G
72	1001000	110	48	H
73	1001001	111	49	I
74	1001010	112	4A	J
75	1001011	113	4B	K
76	1001100	114	4C	L
77	1001101	115	4D	M
78	1001110	116	4E	N
79	1001111	117	4F	O
80	1010000	120	50	P
81	1010001	121	51	Q
82	1010010	122	52	R
83	1010011	123	53	S
84	1010100	124	54	T
85	1010101	125	55	U
86	1010110	126	56	V
87	1010111	127	57	W
88	1011000	130	58	X
89	1011001	131	59	Y
90	1011010	132	5A	Z
91	1011011	133	5B	[
92	1011100	134	5C	\
93	1011101	135	5D	]
94	1011110	136	5E	^
95	1011111	137	5F	_
96	1100000	140	60	`
97	1100001	141	61	a
98	1100010	142	62	b
99	1100011	143	63	c
100	1100100	144	64	d
101	1100101	145	65	e
102	1100110	146	66	f

103	1100111	147	67	g
104	1101000	150	68	h
105	1101001	151	69	i
106	1101010	152	6A	j
107	1101011	153	6B	k
108	1101100	154	6C	l
109	1101101	155	6D	m
110	1101110	156	6E	n
111	1101111	157	6F	o
112	1110000	160	70	p
113	1110001	161	71	q
114	1110010	162	72	r
115	1110011	163	73	s
116	1110100	164	74	t
117	1110101	165	75	u
118	1110110	166	76	v
119	1110111	167	77	w
120	1111000	170	78	x
121	1111001	171	79	y
122	1111010	172	7A	z
123	1111011	173	7B	{
124	1111100	174	7C	¦
125	1111101	175	7D	}
126	1111110	176	7E	~
127	1111111	177	7F	DEL

Decimal	Binary	Octal	Hex	Character
0	00000000	00	00	NUL
1	00000001	01	01	SOH
2	00000010	02	02	STX
3	00000011	03	03	ETX
4	00000100	04	04	SEL
5	00000101	05	05	HT
6	00000110	06	06	RNL
7	00000111	07	07	DEL
8	00001000	10	08	GE
9	00001001	11	09	SPS
10	00001010	12	0A	RPT
11	00001011	13	0B	VT
12	00001100	14	0C	FF
13	00001101	15	0D	CR
14	00001110	16	0E	SO
15	00001111	17	0F	SI
16	00010000	20	10	DLE
17	00010001	21	11	DC1
18	00010010	22	12	DC2
19	00010011	23	13	DC3

Fig. 3-16. The EBCDIC code (8-bit, IBM). (Continued through page 37.)

20	00010100	24	14	RES/ENP
21	00010101	25	15	NL
22	00010110	26	16	BS
23	00010111	27	17	POC
24	00011000	30	18	CAN
25	00011001	31	19	EM
26	00011010	32	1A	UBS
27	00011011	33	1B	CU1
28	00011100	34	1C	IFS
29	00011101	35	1D	IGS
30	00011110	36	1E	IRS
31	00011111	37	1F	ITB/IUS
32	00100000	40	20	DS
33	00100001	41	21	SOS
34	00100010	42	22	FS
35	00100011	43	23	WUS
36	00100100	44	24	BYP/IMP
37	00100101	45	25	LF
38	00100110	46	26	ETB
39	00100111	47	27	ESC
40	00101000	50	28	SA
41	00101001	51	29	SFE
42	00101010	52	2A	SM/SW
43	00101011	53	2B	CSP
44	00101100	54	2C	MFA
45	00101101	55	2D	ENQ
46	00101110	56	2E	ACK
47	00101111	57	2F	BEL
48	00110000	60	30	
49	00110001	61	31	
50	00110010	62	32	SYN
51	00110011	63	33	IR
52	00110100	64	34	PP
53	00110101	65	35	TRN
54	00110110	66	36	NBS
55	00110111	67	37	EOT
56	00111000	70	38	SBS
57	00111001	71	39	IT
58	00111010	72	3A	RFF
59	00111011	73	3B	CU3
60	00111100	74	3C	DC4
61	00111101	75	3D	NAK
62	00111110	76	3E	
63	00111111	77	3F	SUB
64	01000000	100	40	SP
65	01000001	101	41	
66	01000010	102	42	
67	01000011	103	43	
68	01000100	104	44	
69	01000101	105	45	
70	01000110	106	46	

71	01000111	107	47	
72	01001000	110	48	
73	01001001	111	49	
74	01001010	112	4A	CENTS
75	01001011	113	4B	.
76	01001100	114	4C	<
77	01001101	115	4D	(
78	01001110	116	4E	+
79	01001111	117	4F	¦
80	01010000	120	50	&
81	01010001	121	51	
82	01010010	122	52	
83	01010011	123	53	
84	01010100	124	54	
85	01010101	125	55	
86	01010110	126	56	
87	01010111	127	57	
88	01011000	130	58	
89	01011001	131	59	
90	01011010	132	5A	!
91	01011011	133	5B	$
92	01011100	134	5C	*
93	01011101	135	5D	)
94	01011110	136	5E	;
95	01011111	137	5F	¬
96	01100000	140	60	-
97	01100001	141	61	/
98	01100010	142	62	
99	01100011	143	63	
100	01100100	144	64	
101	01100101	145	65	
102	01100110	146	66	
103	01100111	147	67	
104	01101000	150	68	
105	01101001	151	69	
106	01101010	152	6A	¦
107	01101011	153	6B	,
108	01101100	154	6C	%
109	01101101	155	6D	_
110	01101110	156	6E	>
111	01101111	157	6F	?
112	01110000	160	70	
113	01110001	161	71	
114	01110010	162	72	
115	01110011	163	73	
116	01110100	164	74	
117	01110101	165	75	
118	01110110	166	76	
119	01110111	167	77	
120	01111000	170	78	
121	01111001	171	79	

122	01111010	172	7A	:
123	01111011	173	7B	#
124	01111100	174	7C	@
125	01111101	175	7D	'
126	01111110	176	7E	=
127	01111111	177	7F	"
128	10000000	200	80	
129	10000001	201	81	a
130	10000010	202	82	b
131	10000011	203	83	c
132	10000100	204	84	d
133	10000101	205	85	e
134	10000110	206	86	f
135	10000111	207	87	g
136	10001000	210	88	h
137	10001001	211	89	i
138	10001010	212	8A	
139	10001011	213	8B	
140	10001100	214	8C	
141	10001101	215	8D	
142	10001110	216	8E	
143	10001111	217	8F	
144	10010000	220	90	
145	10010001	221	91	j
146	10010010	222	92	k
147	10010011	223	93	l
148	10010100	224	94	m
149	10010101	225	95	n
150	10010110	226	96	o
151	10010111	227	97	p
152	10011000	230	98	q
153	10011001	231	99	r
154	10011010	232	9A	
155	10011011	233	9B	
156	10011100	234	9C	
157	10011101	235	9D	
158	10011110	236	9E	
159	10011111	237	9F	
160	10100000	240	A0	
161	10100001	241	A1	~
162	10100010	242	A2	s
163	10100011	243	A3	t
164	10100100	244	A4	u
165	10100101	245	A5	v
166	10100110	246	A6	w
167	10100111	247	A7	x
168	10101000	250	A8	y
169	10101001	251	A9	z
170	10101010	252	AA	
171	10101011	253	AB	
172	10101100	254	AC	

173	10101101	255	AD		
174	10101110	256	AE		
175	10101111	257	AF		
176	10110000	260	B0		
177	10110001	261	B1		
178	10110010	262	B2		
179	10110011	263	B3		
180	10110100	264	B4		
181	10110101	265	B5		
182	10110110	266	B6		
183	10110111	267	B7		
184	10111000	270	B8		
185	10111001	271	B9		
186	10111010	272	BA		
187	10111011	273	BB		
188	10111100	274	BC		
189	10111101	275	BD		
190	10111110	276	BE		
191	10111111	277	BF		
192	11000000	300	C0	{	
193	11000001	301	C1	A	
194	11000010	302	C2	B	
195	11000011	303	C3	C	
196	11000100	304	C4	D	
197	11000101	305	C5	E	
198	11000110	306	C6	F	
199	11000111	307	C7	G	
200	11001000	310	C8	H	
201	11001001	311	C9	I	
202	11001010	312	CA		
203	11001011	313	CB		
204	11001100	314	CC		
205	11001101	315	CD		
206	11001110	316	CE		
207	11001111	317	CF		
208	11010000	320	D0	}	
209	11010001	321	D1	J	
210	11010010	322	D2	K	
211	11010011	323	D3	L	
212	11010100	324	D4	M	
213	11010101	325	D5	N	
214	11010110	326	D6	O	
215	11010111	327	D7	P	
216	11011000	330	D8	Q	
217	11011001	331	D9	R	
218	11011010	332	DA		
219	11011011	333	DB		
220	11011100	334	DC		
221	11011101	335	DD		
222	11011110	336	DE		
223	11011111	337	DF		

224	11100000	340	E0	\
225	11100001	341	E1	
226	11100010	342	E2	S
227	11100011	343	E3	T
228	11100100	344	E4	U
229	11100101	345	E5	V
230	11100110	346	E6	W
231	11100111	347	E7	X
232	11101000	350	E8	Y
233	11101001	351	E9	Z
234	11101010	352	EA	
235	11101011	353	EB	
236	11101100	354	EC	
237	11101101	355	ED	
238	11101110	356	EE	
239	11101111	357	EF	
240	11110000	360	F0	0
241	11110001	361	F1	1
242	11110010	362	F2	2
243	11110011	363	F3	3
244	11110100	364	F4	4
245	11110101	365	F5	5
246	11110110	366	F6	6
247	11110111	367	F7	7
248	11111000	370	F8	8
249	11111001	371	F9	9
250	11111010	372	FA	
251	11111011	373	FB	
252	11111100	374	FC	
253	11111101	375	FD	
254	11111110	376	FE	
255	11111111	377	FF	

Code conversion between disparate systems seems straightforward until one tries to go from a high-bit code to a low-bit code. There will simply be some EBCDIC characters that have no meaning in ASCII. In some cases, such as going from ASCII to Baudot, lowercase can be converted to upper, but the translator module will also need to take care of letter/figure shifting.

A number of conversion algorithms exist, and are often packaged as part of communications products that are designed to interface such things as ASCII devices to EBCDIC hosts.

ERROR CHECKING

Beyond character translation, the data communications interface must also be able to handle error detection methodologies. Noise in a data line can corrupt a bit in a data stream and turn the message into useless information. Somehow the receiver must have a way of testing the integrity of the data set.

The most common method is the use of a parity bit. It is appended to a data packet using an even or odd calculation algorithm. *Odd parity* results by counting the one bits in the packet. If the result is odd, the parity bit is zero. If the count is even, the parity bit is one. This means that the total number of ones in an odd parity scheme is always odd. *Even parity* is just the reverse. Parity schemes are only successful in catching one-bit errors; a two-bit error can mask itself.

In cases where data integrity is more critical, an error detection method called the Cyclic Redundancy Check (CRC) is often used. This is a message- or block-oriented algorithm in which a very complicated calculation is done on each bit of the data stream and the result appended to the message. The receiver does the same calculation and accepts the message as good only if the calculated CRC matches the transmitted CRC. The probability of error detection in this method approaches 100%. In many systems, the CRC is calculated using dedicated hardware, and is done bit by bit as the data is sent or received.

Other error checking and error recovery techniques exist as part of specific protocols, and must be completely adhered to in the creation of a data communications link between any two systems.

THE OSI STANDARD

The International Standards Organization defined, in 1977, a layered architectural model for the interconnection of heterogeneous computing devices. The result is known as the Open Systems Interconnection (OSI) model, Fig. 3-17.

	ISO Definition
7	Application Layer
6	Presentation Layer
5	Session Layer
4	Transport Layer
3	Network Layer
2	Data Link Layer
1	Physical Layer

Fig. 3-17. Open Systems Interconnection model.

The philosophical basis of the model is that there is a hierarchical set of layers that define various communication functions. Each layer performs a related subset of the activities necessary to communicate with another "open" system, which is also using the OSI model. The layer relies on the next lower layer to perform "lower level functions" and to conceal the nature of those functions from the higher level. There is thus layer independence, because problems should be localized in the current level. The peer levels of communications are governed by a group of rules and conventions called *protocols.*

The lowest level of the OSI model is called the *physical layer.* This layer is concerned with the transmission of an unstructured data stream. It addresses issues of voltages, timing, and electromechanical linkages. The RS-232-C is a protocol at this layer.

The next higher level is known as the *data link layer.* This is the first level at which structure is imposed on the bit stream. It usually defines the framing methodology, error detection, checksums, and acknowledgment schemes. Protocols at this level include high-level data link control (HDLC), synchronous data link control (SDLC), and bisynchronous.

Level number three is called the *network layer,* and is responsible for the actual transmission of the data packets as defined in the data link layer. Packets can be independent (*datagrams*) or make use of a pre-established network connection (*virtual circuit*). This level is also responsible for all routing and congestion control. A widely used protocol at this layer is X.25, layer 3.

The *transport layer* is next in the hierarchy, and provides for the reliable, transparent transmission of data between end points. It also provides for end-to-end error recovery and flow control.

The fifth level is called the *session layer,* and provides the means to establish, manage, and terminate connections between processes.

Next is the *presentation layer,* at which generally useful transformations on data are performed to provide a standardized application interface and a common communications interface. Typical functions at this level include encryption, text compression, and reformatting.

The highest level in the model is the *application layer.* This is where the application interface exists. Services such as transaction service, file transfer protocols, and network management reside here. This layering as viewed from the data packet level is shown in Fig. 3-18.

The lower levels append headers and, where applicable, trailers to the data stream coming down from the upper layers. The packet is transmitted to another system where the headers and trailers are stripped away as the packet is passed up in level. In this way, only the actual data is transferred at the application layer. Neither system needs to be concerned with the envelopes imposed in the interim processes. Almost all of the communications protocols in existence today are structurally and philosophically similar to this very well-supported standard.

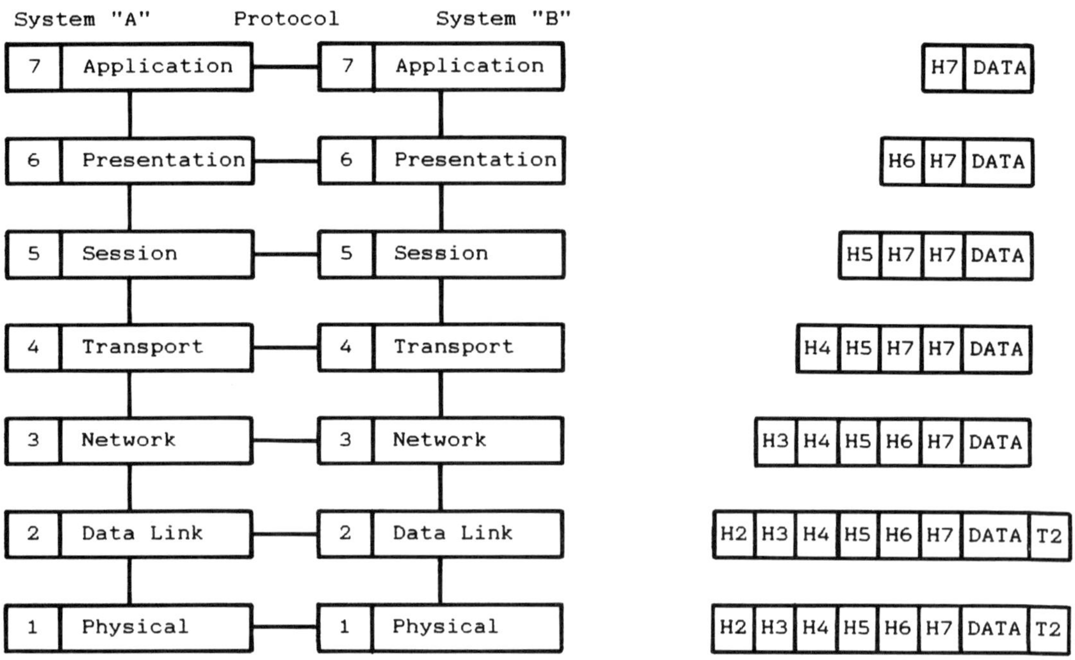

Fig. 3-18. OSI connections and packet structures (Hn are headers,Tn are trailers).

DISTRIBUTED PROCESSING NETWORKS

Up to this point, concentration has been upon system architectures that can be classed as time-sharing systems. A number of end-user devices share, through the data communications network, a central computer and its memory devices. The end-users have terminals and printers with little or no intelligence, and must rely completely on the main CPU for computational power. Response time is variable, and is based on data communication load factors as well as the load on the CPU.

Over the last few years, millions of microcomputers have found their way on to the end-user's desk. While these devices can be configured to appear as terminals to the host, they also have the ability to compute on their own. Thus a new architecture can be defined—distributed computing. A data communication system linking a number of intelligent microcomputer workstations in such a way so as to allow them to share data and resources is called a local area network.

LOCAL AREA NETWORKS

Local area networks (LANs) are a class of network systems that are geographically "local" (on the order of a few miles), usually in a single organization using a homogeneous system architecture (similar types of devices) and sharing whatever transmission medium under some access protocol.

LAN Transmission Schemes and Performance Issues

There are two basic transmission methods used in LANs today. One is called *baseband,* in which the transmission makes use of the entire cable band width. The other is called *broadband,* in which there are a number of transmission frequencies on a single cable. In a broadband network, the cable band width can be shared between voice, data, graphics and even television signals. Basebands are dedicated cable systems.

An excellent example of the use and utility of broadband is the linking of data communications equipment on the existing television cables, using unassigned channels for the data. The city government of Mountain View, California is using the town's broadband cable television network to perform data communications. They are using Net 20 radio frequency modems from Sytek to perform terminal-to-mainframe linkages, while the mainframe is a Hewlett-Packard 3000 located at the police and fire building. The terminal speed is 19.2K baud, and the communications occur on the same cable already in place to provide commercial television and premium channel service to the town's residents. Thus, no additional cable needed to be installed to link the 55 remote terminals to the mainframe. Many universities have "institutional" television cable systems in place already, and see the "piggy-backing" of LAN and terminal-to-mainframe data traffic onto the existing broadband systems as a very effective means of providing wide areas with network services. The use of existing broadband cable plants can thus justify, economically, the selection of broadband over baseband technologies. It is important to note that in the case of a new installation, baseband is less expensive to install and maintain than broadband.

LANs are very high-speed communication systems. They often offer peer-to-peer interaction. The speeds can approach those of the computer data bus itself. LANs exist on the market today with data speeds as high as ten megabits per second. Laboratory LANs currently under development are capable of speeds in the range of tens of gigabits. These speeds are several orders of magnitude higher than what is available under leased-line data communications in what can be called *wide area networks* (WAN), which is just a new term to describe standard data communication networks.

The first LAN technology was introduced by Datapoint in 1977. It was called ARCNet (Attached Resource Computer Network), and was a baseband, token-passing bus architecture. By 1985, there were over ten thousand ARC-Nets installed worldwide.

The major use for small LANs is as a methodology for sharing resources, such as printers and hard disk drives. As the complexities of applications grew, the single user microcomputers were "forced" into multiuser environments, typically using LAN software to alter the single-user DOS.

Other LAN vendors arose, such as Corvus, Nestar, Davong, Novell and 3COM, each coming up with a new way to patch into DOS. Not until DOS 3.1 has there been a standard LAN command structure. Now NETBIOS exists, and more and more of the modern LANs and multiuser applications are conforming to it. Standardization at the software/hardware interface will make LANs more viable in the future.

Another major standardization effort in the LAN area has been undertaken by the IEEE (Institute of Electrical and Electronic Engineers). It is called the IEEE 802 Standard, and governs all aspects of LAN communication protocols, including the token bus, token ring and CSMA/CD schemes. Most of the major manufacturers have agreed, or are in the process of agreeing, to support this standard.

Transmission Media

There are three types of cable in use in LAN technology today. First, there is *twisted pair.* This is simply copper wire, unshielded, cheap, and easy to install. It is also very susceptible to noise, and cannot run long distances. In very small, very local networks, its cost versus performance benefits give it an edge.

Another cable in wide use is the *coaxial* (RG-59 or RG-62) shielded type. This is more expensive, but has the benefit of higher resistance to noise. Because electromagnetic interference generates errors in high-speed networks, the cost of shielding is often justified when data integrity, throughput and reliability over longer transmission distances is required. This cable is exactly the same as that used in the cable television industry, so the cost of installation is often lower than that of more specialized cables because competition between a large number of competent installers tends to drive the price down. This competition works to lower the cost of cable and connectors as well.

The most expensive and exotic form of cable is *fiber optic.* This is actually a crystalline fiber that uses light rather than electricity to transmit signals. Being optical makes the signal impervious to electromagnetic interference. This is very important in manufacturing automation systems, where electromagnetic pulses from heavy machinery and welders can wreck havoc on other LAN cable signals. The military also has required fiber optics in all defense applications because it is impervious to the electromagnetic pulses created by the high-altitude detonation of a large thermonuclear device. There is a Tempest certification for computers and data communication systems that are impervious to disruption by such pulses.

Fiber optics is extremely difficult to install, because each splice must be optically perfect to within one quarter of a wavelength of the light in the cable. Thus, the cable, connectors, transceivers, and the labor required to put it all together cost much more than in any of the other cable technologies. Nevertheless, the issue of noise immunity will drive fiber to first place in total installed cable feet by the end of the century.

LAN Topologies

In the interconnection of any data communication devices, standard issues of topology must be addressed. LANs are not unlike standard communications networks in that one must design, from the outset, the way in which connections will be made at the physical level. Just as in the case of telephone systems, point-to-point connections become unworkable for more than two sites. There are three major topologies available in LANs. The workstations are called *nodes* and are connected by communication *links*.

The most simple topology is one in which the nodes are linked to a central node (file server or host) in a *star*, as shown in Fig. 3-19. Stars are useful in systems that rely on central control. Messages must be routed to the hub and then back out to other nodes. If most of the traffic is between the center and a node, such a design is efficient, giving high data rates. If, however, traffic goes from one node, to the hub, and then out to another node, the switching and traffic management overhead at the central node can seriously degrade the systems performance.

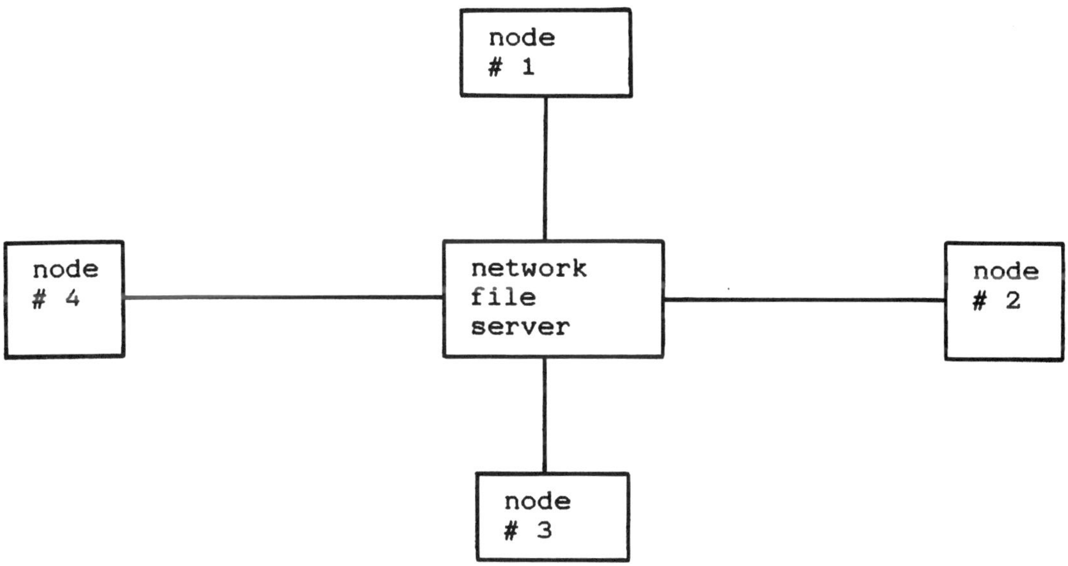

Fig. 3-19. LAN star topology.

The second type of topology is called a *ring*, as shown in Fig. 3-20. In a ring there is no central control. Each node must act as an active repeater. It must take data in, add or remove information from the data stream, and pass it on to the next node. The data goes round and round, and permission to add or remove data is granted by a special bit pattern, defined by the protocol, which is called the token.

A major fault in the ring architecture is that if one node fails, the ring fails. The data stream also stops if the cable is broken. The IBM Token Ring makes

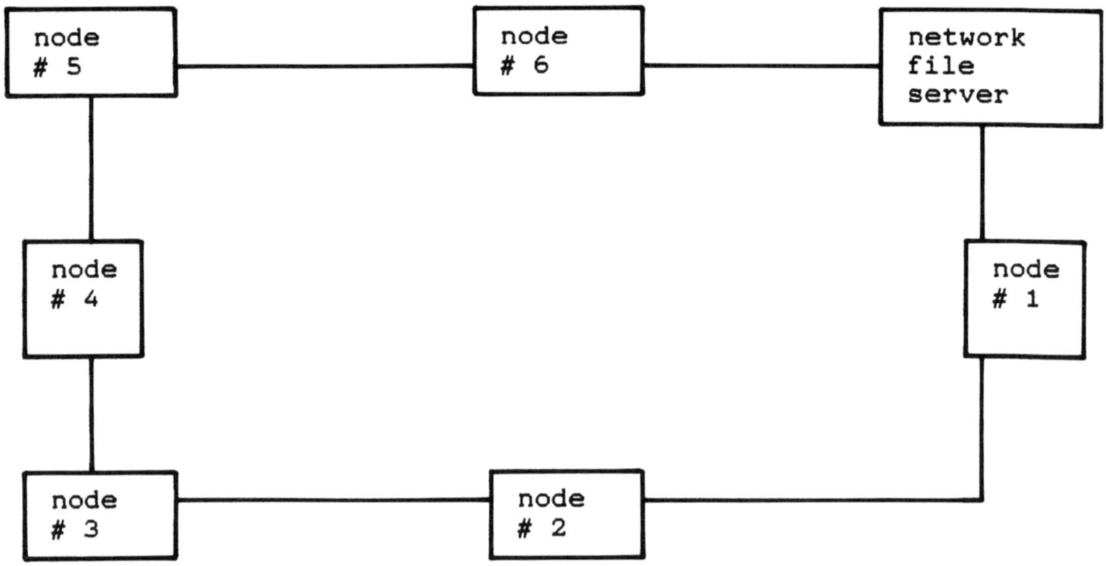

Fig. 3-20. LAN ring topology.

use of a variation of the ring topology, as shown in Fig. 3-21, in which the ring cable is brought into a "wiring cabinet."

If node 1 fails, the wiring cabinet reconfigures the path (after a protocol-defined time out) so that the ring now looks like Fig. 3-22.

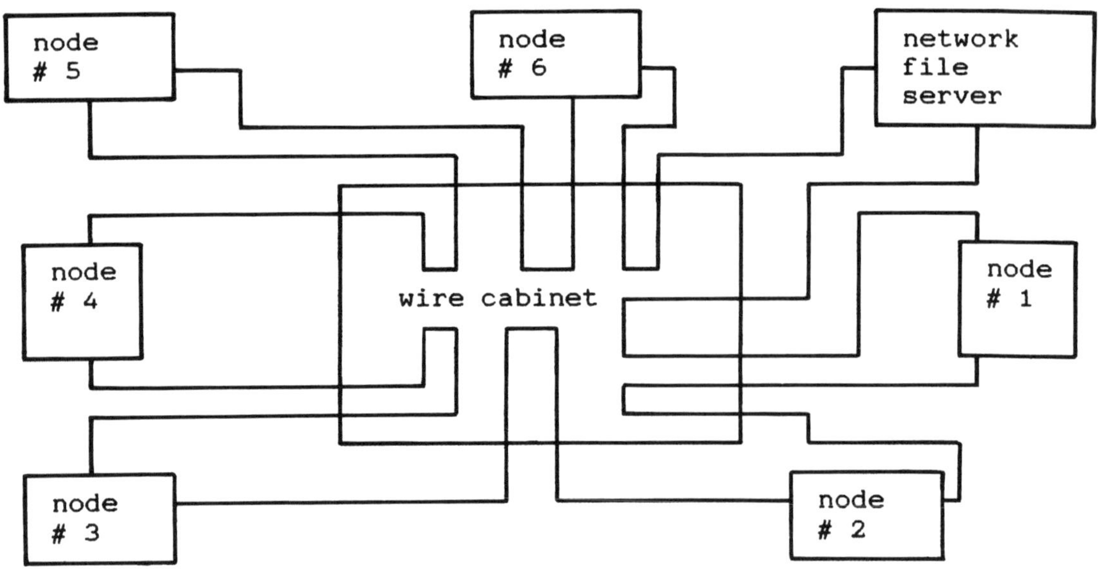

Fig. 3-21. IBM Token Ring (with wiring cabinet).

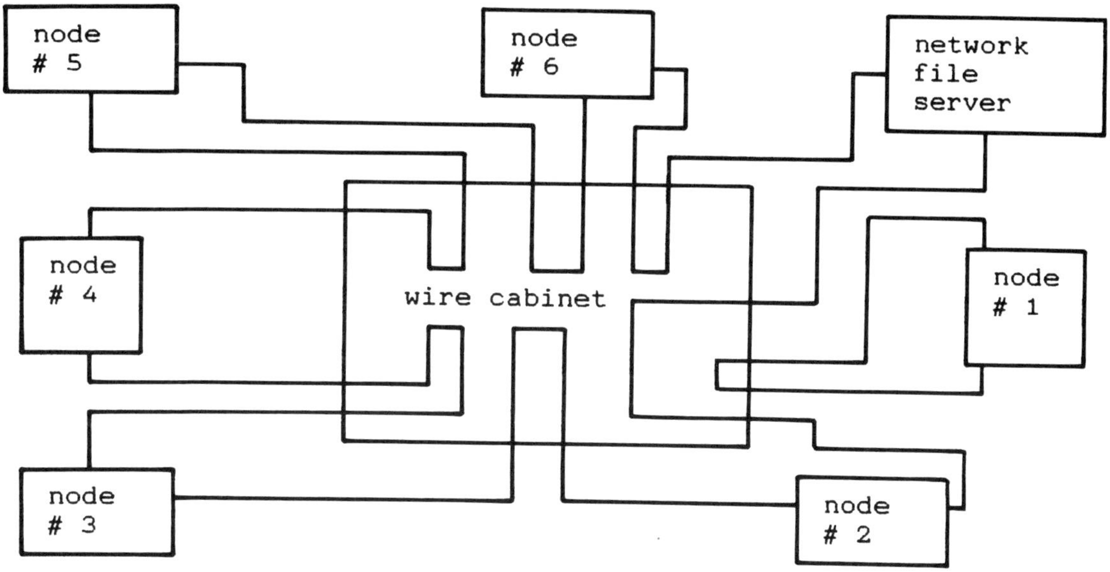

Fig. 3-22. IBM Token Ring (reconfigured after node 1 failure).

The IBM scheme reduces the major problem with the ring topology, but does tend to increase the cost of the cable plant considerably.

The IBM cable for the Token Ring is part of a long-range data communication philosophy on the part of IBM. They have introduced a cable that contains COAX, optical fiber and twisted pair in one physical housing. They recommend that the installation of such a cable guarantees that the cable plant will not become obsolete by new transmission media technology. Indeed, because all of the major elements exist in this one product, you can be sure that the cable will be useful for many years to come.

The third possible topology is the *bus*. In the bus, all devices share a single physical cable, as shown in Fig. 3-23. The bus is most like a multi-drop

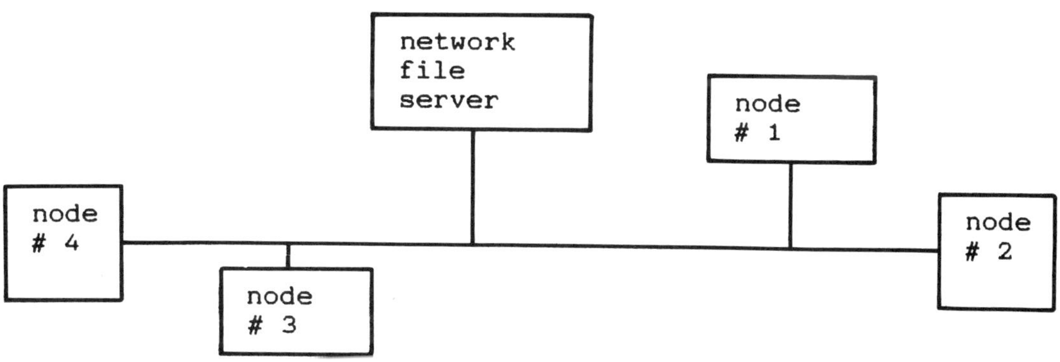

Fig. 3-23. LAN bus topology.

telephone line. Messages are broadcast to every node at the same time. A node must have hardware and software to recognize its own incoming messages, do the error checking, and either acknowledge or request retransmission. The failure of any node does not bring the network down. Physical connection to the cable can be as simple as a splitter or tap connector. Cable costs are lower than either a star or ring because there is just one path.

LAN Access Models

In any data communication system, there must be a well defined method by which users can have access to the system at both a logical and physical level. Many of these same data communication issues exist in LAN architectures. There are two major access methods on the market today. These access methods describe the way in which each device will be allowed to communicate over the network cable.

One method is a variation of the polling technique used in time sharing. In this method, each node or device is offered a chance to talk. The offer is called a token, which is a specific bit pattern on the cable. The node either takes the token and sends its message, or passes the token on to the next node. This is called *token passing.* The major types of token-passing LAN products on the market today are the ARCNET Token Bus, originally designed by Data Point, and the IBM Token Ring.

Token passing has the advantage of guaranteeing every user a worst-case access time. It is called a deterministic access method because it is possible to calculate this worst case, which is dependent on the LAN transmission speed, the token-passing scheme, the size of the packet, and the number of network nodes. The disadvantage in token-passing schemes is the overhead associated with the token-passing process itself. Even if only one node needs access, it must wait for the token to be passed to every other node each session cycle. Such networks are most efficient under a heavy load.

The second major access method in modern LAN technology is known as *carrier-sense multiple access/with collision detect* (CSMA/CD). In this scheme, any node that wishes to transmit checks to see if the line is free, then sends. If another node begins to transmit at the same time, a collision occurs. Both transmitters shut down. Each waits a random amount of time and then retries. The throughput is statistical. The busier the network gets, the lower the data rate. There is no overhead in this scheme, so the speed is higher in low-load situations. The major product of this type is Ethernet.

WIDE AREA NETWORKING

There are a number of networking schemes in use today that define the ways in which many mainframes and intelligent peripherals can communicate over long distances on telephone lines. Developments in this area include the creation of packet-switching network standards, and the subsequent introduction of third-party suppliers of companies providing data communication services. One of the most popular standards is the X.25 interface. Users can log onto huge international packet-switching data networks like Tymnet and TeleNet, and gain access to host computers and services throughout the world. A number of network architecture exist that ease the data communications tasks between the end-users and these multiple hosts.

SYSTEMS NETWORK ARCHITECTURE

IBM introduced its Systems Network Architecture (SNA) in 1974. It was the first design based on the distribution of functionality to the place in the data communications network where it could best be handled. It is considered to be a direct result of the impact of the use of Very Large Scale Integration (VLSI) chip technology on the system peripherals themselves. As the terminals and remote processors became smarter, it became more reasonable to "off-load" computational and overhead to remote units. This required the creation of a hardware/software entity that could handle such distribution at a systems level.

The first announcement included the release of several new products. The first was the Virtual Terminal Access Method (VTAM), which provided the telecommunications scheme for the host system, which was the IBM S/370, the state-of-the-art mainframe at that time. The second new product was the network control program (NCP), which was the software required to run the network controllers, the newly announced IBM 3705 front end processor. The 3705 was actually a dedicated processor, whose sole function was to take care of all of the overhead involved in network communications, and thus free the main processor to compute more efficiently. A very high speed link was defined for the 3705 to move its data back and forth to the host. The protocol used to packetize data down the tree from the 3705 became generically known as the 3270 protocol.

Subsequent SNA releases provided for the local attachment of cluster controllers (or terminal control units like the 3274), remote cluster controllers, intelligent terminal nodes, and the support of switched communication lines. With the third SNA release, it became possible to have multiple hosts in the network. SNA 4.2 introduced the SNA Path Control Layer, giving full networking capabilities to SNA, and defining the concept of virtual routing between network nodes.

SNA handles all communication between end-users via ports into the network, which are called *logical units* (LUs). Thus, the end-users themselves are not known to the network. The interface between the end-user and the logical unit is not defined in the SNA architecture and is, in fact, implementation specific. The LUs perform all (session-specific) communication functions between the users and the network. The logical units are then interconnected via a path control network that enacts all of the network functions needed to enable the transportation of messages from one LU to another.

The LU is only one of a class of communicating objects in the SNA scheme called network-addressable units. There is also a class called physical units, which addresses the interface control functions between the network and a given piece of communication equipment. The third group is known as system services control points, which are used for the management and control of the network.

Communication between network-addressable units (NAUs) takes place via messages which SNA calls request units. The responses to these messages are called response units. These messages can only be passed between two points if a session has been set up. Thus, SNA is a layered model closely following the OSI scheme. Figure 3-24 shows the comparison of the two structures.

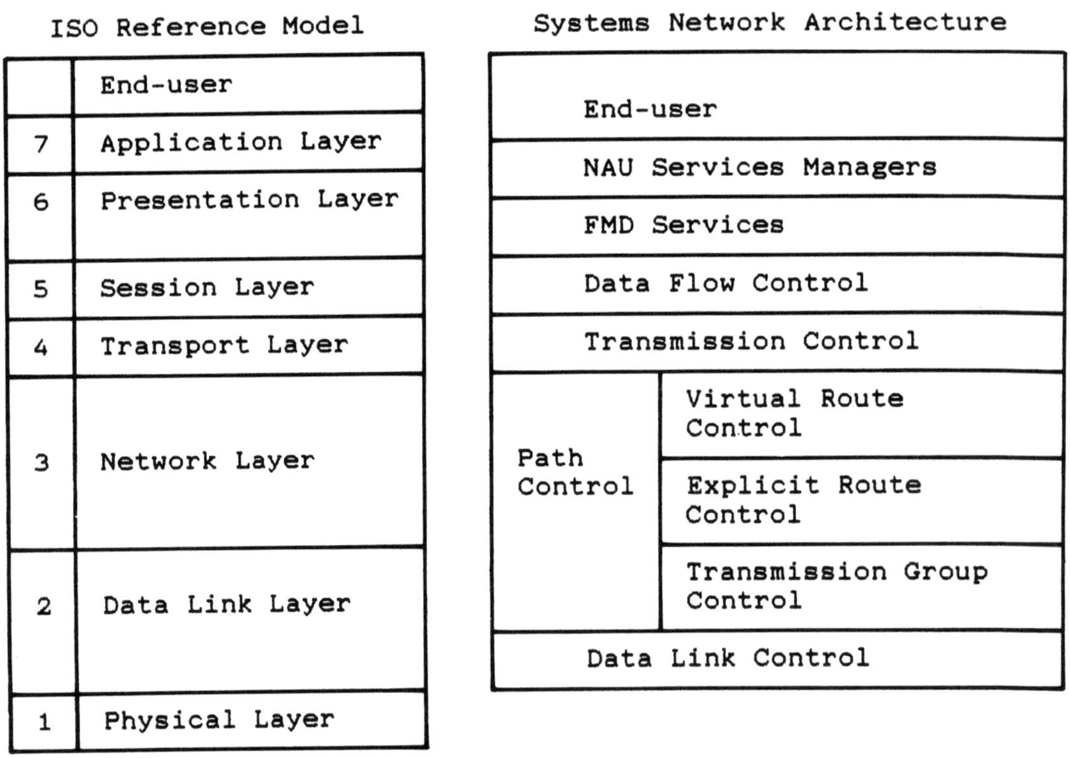

Fig. 3-24. Comparison of OSI and SNA layers.

For more detail as to the specific message traffic functions and formats for SNA, consult *Microcomputer LANs* by Michael Hordeski (book 2888, TAB BOOKS, Inc., 1987) or the book by Anton Meijer and Paul Peters called *Computer Network Architectures* (Computer Science Press, 1982).

FILE STRUCTURES

There are two major classes of data file structures. One is a file in which the data is stored on the disk exactly as if it was printed, character by character, on paper. This is called text format. If the file were to be displayed, the user would actually see data characters, and perhaps control and file data.

The second class is called binary format, in which a bit pattern is stored in the file. Displaying such a file would show "garbage," as can be seen by the DOS DEBUG utility display of a Lotus 1-2-3 spreadsheet shown in Fig. 3-25.

```
258C:0620  00 FF 02 00 01 00 22 41-63 63 6F 75 6E 74 00 0F   ......"Account..
258C:0630  00 0F 00 FF 03 00 01 00-22 49 6E 74 65 72 65 73   ........"Interes
258C:0640  74 00 0F 00 0B 00 FF 04-00 01 00 22 4C 6F 61 6E   t.........."Loan
258C:0650  00 0F 00 0D 00 FF 00 00-02 00 27 4E 75 6D 62 65   ..........'Numbe
258C:0660  72 00 0F 00 0E 00 FF 02-00 02 00 22 42 61 6C 61   r.........."Bala
258C:0670  6E 63 65 00 0F 00 0B 00-FF 03 00 02 00 22 52 61   nce.........."Ra
258C:0680  74 65 00 0F 00 0E 00 FF-04 00 02 00 22 42 61 6C   te.........."Bal
258C:0690  61 6E 63 65 00 0F 00 08-00 FF 00 00 03 00 5C 3D   ance..........\=
258C:06A0  00 0F 00 08 00 FF 01 00-03 00 5C 3D 00 0F 00 08   ..........\=....
258C:06B0  00 FF 02 00 03 00 5C 3D-00 0F 00 08 00 FF 03 00   ......\=........
258C:06C0  03 00 5C 3D 00 0F 00 08-00 FF 04 00 03 00 5C 3D   ..\=..........\=
258C:06D0  00 0F 00 0E 00 FF 00 00-04 00 27 30 30 30 35 30   ..........'00050
258C:06E0  30 30 00 0F 00 20 00 FF-01 00 04 00 27 41 20 26   00... ......'A &
258C:06F0  20 42 20 53 61 66 65 20-26 20 4C 6F 63 6B 20 53    B Safe & Lock S
258C:0700  65 72 76 69 63 65 00 0E-00 0D 00 A2 02 00 04 00   ervice..........
258C:0710  D7 A3 70 3D 0A C3 75 40-0E 00 0D 00 82 03 00 04   ..p=..u@........
258C:0720  00 00 00 00 00 00 00 25-40 0E 00 0D 00 A2 04 00   .......%@.......
258C:0730  04 00 0A D7 A3 70 3D 6A-41 40 0F 00 0E 00 FF 00   .....p=jA@......
258C:0740  00 05 00 27 30 31 30 36-30 30 30 00 0F 00 1F 00   ...'0106000.....
258C:0750  FF 01 00 05 00 27 41 4C-4F 4E 20 4D 6F 74 6F 72   .....'ALON Motor
258C:0760  20 43 6F 6D 70 61 6E 79-2C 20 49 6E 63 2E 00 0E    Company, Inc...
258C:0770  00 0D 00 A2 02 00 05 00-5C 8F C2 F5 28 9C 57 40   ........\...(.W@
258C:07A0  FF 00 00 06 00 27 30 30-30 32 30 30 30 00 0F 00   .....'0002000...
258C:07B0  25 00 FF 01 00 06 00 27-41 63 6D 65 20 42 72 61   %......'Acme Bra
258C:07C0  73 73 20 26 20 41 6C 75-6D 69 6E 75 6D 20 4D 66   ss & Aluminum Mf
258C:07D0  67 2C 49 6E 63 2E 00 0D-00 07 00 A2 02 00 06 00   g,Inc...........
258C:07E0  13 0B 0E 00 0D 00 82 03-00 06 00 00 00 00 00 00   ................
258C:07F0  00 25 40 0E 00 0D 00 A2-04 00 06 00 AE 47 E1 7A   .%@..........G.z
258C:0800  94 A3 B4 40 0F 00 0E 00-FF 00 00 07 00 27 30 30   ...@.........'00
258C:0810  39 36 30 30 31 00 0F 00-17 00 FF 01 00 07 00 27   96001..........'
258C:0820  41 6C 70 69 6E 65 20 4F-69 6C 20 43 6F 72 70 2E   Alpine Oil Corp.
258C:0830  00 0E 00 0D 00 A2 02 00-07 00 29 5C 8F C2 20 17   ..........)\.. .
258C:0840  28 41 0E 00 0D 00 82 03-00 07 00 00 00 00 00 00   (A..............
258C:0850  00 23 40 0E 00 0D 00 A2-04 00 07 00 B8 1E 85 6B   .#@............k
258C:0860  EE 0F 24 41 0F 00 0E 00-FF 00 00 08 00 27 32 30   ..$A.........'20
258C:0870  31 38 30 30 31 00 0F 00-1F 00 FF 01 00 08 00 27   18001..........'
```

Fig. 3-25. DOS DEBUG screen dump of LOAN.WKS file.

Each computer language has specific structures for its data fields, as do major application packages. Thus, files written in MicroSoft BASIC are completely different from those used by the Business Basic used by the Open Systems Accounting programs. Turbo Pascal data files cannot be used in C programs, unless file conversion routines are created. Such products do exist, as in the case of the Lattice dBASE-to-C package, which enables C programmers to read, write, and otherwise use dBASE file formats in their C programs.

Two fundamental file architectures exist as well. One is the *random access file.* It is a well-structured object, with a header, record lengths and pointers. Such a file can be written to or read from in any order. This is the usual structure for a database file or any file in which specific data elements are held.

The other file architecture is the *sequential access file,* in which the data must be read starting at the first byte until the desired data is found. New data can only be appended to such files; an internal rewrite is not possible. These files may be useful in text or graphics-oriented applications.

If the user knows the exact structure of any file, it becomes possible to write programs to extract data and/or convert such data into other data file formats. It is often necessary to examine such file structures using the DOS DEBUG utility or the Norton Utility programs. There are some very good reference books that provide readers with exact file structures for a wide variety of popular application programs. One such book is Jeff Walden's *File Formats for Popular PC Software* (Wiley Press, 1986), which includes information on Lotus1-2-3, Symphony, MultiMate, dBASE, SuperCalc, DIF, and more. In the absence of such reference material, the end-user faces hours of tedious detective work trying to decipher the complex structures of application program data files.

PROTOCOLS

The set of rules and conventions governing a data communication session is called a protocol. One of the major character-oriented standards is the Binary Synchronous Communication (BSC) Protocol widely used on IBM type mainframes. A chart of control codes for this protocol is given in Fig. 3-26.

Symbol	Definition	EBCDIC	ASCII	Function
WACK	WAIT BEFORE TRANSMIT POSITIVE ACKNOWLEDGEMENT	10h6Bh	10h3Bh	Same as ACK, but means that receiver is not yet ready to receive another block. Response is usually ENQ with WACK until receiver is ready, then ACK is sent.
NAK	NEGATIVE ACKNOWLEDGEMENT	3Dh	15h	Previous block was received in error.
DLE	DATA LINK ESCAPE	10h	10h	Used to create WACK, ACK0, ACK1, and RVI 2 character sequences. Controls transparent data transfers.

RVI	REVERSE INTERRUPT	10h7Ch	10h3Ch	Positive acknowledgement but requests sender to terminate transmission because of need to send high priority message.
TTD	TEMPORARY DELAY	03h2Dh	N/A	Used by transmitting station not ready to transmit but wishing to retain line.
SOH	START OF HEADER	01h	01h	Beginning of BSC header
STX	START OF TEXT	02h	02h	Start of Data Field
ETB	END OF TRANSMISSION BLOCK	26h	N/A	Indicates the end of block of characters which began with SOH or STX. BCC follows ETB. Requires a response: NAK, ACK0, ACK1, WACK, or RVI.
ITB	END OF INTERMEDIATE TRANSMISSION BLOCK	1Fh	N/A	Separates message into packets for error detection purposes.
ETX	END OF TEXT	03h	03h	Same as ETB, except that it means there are no more data blocks to be sent.
EOT	END OF TRANSMISSION	37h	04h	Indicates end of transmission, including text blocks and headings
ENQ	ENQUIRY	2Dh	05h	Used to bid for line in point-to-point communications. Also, used to request re-transmission of ACK/NAK response when either is garbled.
ACK0 ACK1	POSITIVE ACKNOWLEDGEMENT	10h70h 10h71h	10h00h 10h01h	Means previous block was accepted without error; Another block may be sent. ACK0 is used for even blocks, ACK1 for odd blocks in sequence.

Fig. 3-26. Binary synchronous communication control characters.

Binary Synchronous Protocol (Bisynch)

This protocol is EBCDIC based, and control codes are used to control session management, error detection, and data packet acknowledgments. There are two basic modes of packet structure, the nontransparent mode, in which the control codes are sent without data link escape (DLE) prefixes, and the transparent mode, (Fig. 3-27) in which the DLE is used to signal the presence of control codes unambiguously (Fig. 3-28). A time evolution diagram of a typical bisynch session is shown in Fig. 3-29.

SYN	SYN	SOH	Header	STX	Data	ETX	BCC

Fig. 3-27. BSC data message format (nontransparent mode).

SYN	SYN	DLE	SOH	Header	DLE	STX	Data	DLE	ETX	BCC

Fig. 3-28. BSC data message format (transparent mode) all control characters preceded by a DLE.

Transmitting Station Function		Flow	Receiving Station Function	
ENQ	Request to send	→		
		←	ACK0	Okay, go ahead
	Data message (Fig 3-28)	→		
		←	ACK1	Received without error
	Data message	→		
		←	ACK0	Received without error
	Data message	→		
		←	WACK	Recvd OK, but wait
ENQ	Okay to send yet?	→		
		←	WACK	Still busy, wait
ENQ	Okay to send yet?	→		
		←	ACK1	Okay to send
	Data message	→		
		←	ACK0	Received without error
EOT	End of transmission	→		

Fig. 3-29. Sample communication session in BSC protocol.

Transmitting Station Function		Flow	Receiving Station Function	
ENQ	Request to send	→		
		←	ACK0	Okay, go ahead
	Data message (Fig 3-28)	→		
		←	ACK1	Received without error
	Data message	→		
		←	ACK0	Received without error
	Data message	→		
		←	WACK	Recvd OK, but wait
ENQ	Okay to send yet?	→		
		←	WACK	Still busy, wait
ENQ	Okay to send yet?	→		
		←	ACK1	Okay to send
	Data message	→		
		←	ACK0	Received without error
EOT	End of transmission	→		

Notice that such a session is very conversational, closely paralleling human telephone communications. Concepts like "Are you there?," "Are you ready?," "Did you hear that correctly?," and "Hold on for a moment, I'm busy" are all mirrored in the session protocol. The most important thing to understand about all computer-to-computer data communications is that they must occur within a well-defined set of rules that enable the sender and receiver to "know" what is happening at any point in the process. The rules governing the timing, coding, and error recovery must be very well delineated on both ends for there to be any chance of having a successful session in which accurate information is exchanged.

Bit-Oriented Data Link Protocols (HDLC/SDLC)

The bisynchronous protocol discussed in the previous section is considered to be a character-oriented protocol. Another major class of protocols in wide use in a large number of systems today are bit-oriented. Examples of such bit-oriented protocols are IBM's Synchronous Data Link Control (SDLC) and the High Level Data Link Control (HDLC) protocol as defined by the International Standards Organization. SDLC is quite similar to HDLC, and in this overview will be considered generically. Bit-oriented protocols rely upon a unique bit pattern that performs the frame synchronization in a similar fashion to the SYN characters in bisynch. This special character pattern, called the FLAG, is used to delineate message frames in a type of short header. It is the FLAG that is used to control protocol functions.

SDLC is a serial, full-duplex bit transmission system under centralized control. The FLAG pattern is a zero, then six ones, followed by a zero. It is used to identify the beginning and end of each message packet. There is a very interesting mechanism that exists in this protocol to guarantee the uniqueness of the FLAG pattern. The hardware makes sure that a string of six one bits can only exist in characters intended to be FLAGs. For all other characters, the hardware inserts a zero bit if it detects a string of five one bits between two FLAGs. On the receiving end, the hardware removes any zeros that it finds following five one bits between FLAGs. The general message format for bit-oriented protocols is shown in Fig. 3-30.

FLAG	HEADER	TEXT	FRAME CHECK	FLAG

Fig. 3-30. General message format for bit-oriented protocols.

The FLAG pattern is framed by the hardware much in the same way that the SYN characters are framed in bisynch. In this type of protocol, only one FLAG is required to establish synchronization.

There are three types of SDLC messages: information transfer, supervisory, and nonsequenced. The specific format for SDLC messages is displayed in Fig. 3-31. The three specific SDLC control byte formats are shown in Fig. 3-32.

SDLC message traffic can become extremely complex, and is beyond the scope of this book. The reader is referred to the ISO standards for HDLC or IBM's technical reference notes for SDLC, if such detail is required.

The most popular modern synchronous protocols are the character oriented bisynchronous and the bit-oriented SDLC/HDLC schemes. The protocols are

FLAG = 01111110

FLAG	ADDRESS	CONTROL	INFORMATION	CRC	FLAG

{ Only used in Information, }
{Nonsequenced Information, }
{and Command Reject Messages}

Fig. 3-31. SDLC data message format.

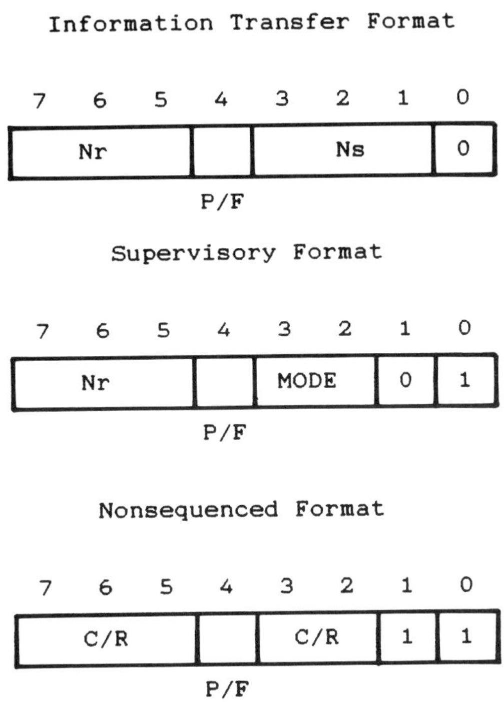

Nr = Sending Sequence Number (3 bits)
Ns = Receiving Sequence Number (3 bits)
P = Primary Station Poll, when set to 1 and sent from Primary Station
F = Secondary Station Final transmission when set to 1 and sent from Secondary Station (bit #4)

Fig. 3-32. Control byte formats for SDLC.

extremely structured and are implemented by a combination of both hardware and software on both the sending and receiving ends. In microcomputer-to-mainframe communication links, the actual details of the protocol overhead are often left to the interconnection devices themselves, much in the same way that character code representations are translated, without end-user intervention. Products that perform these transparent protocol translation functions are discussed in the next section.

PROTOCOL CONVERSION AND TERMINAL EMULATION PRODUCTS

The major method by which microcomputers are currently being linked into institutional data processing and information distribution networks is the use of hardware and software packages that perform terminal emulation processes. Figure 3-33 depicts such a process, in which there is a physical data path (keyboard to microcomputer to asynchronous port to modem to host, then

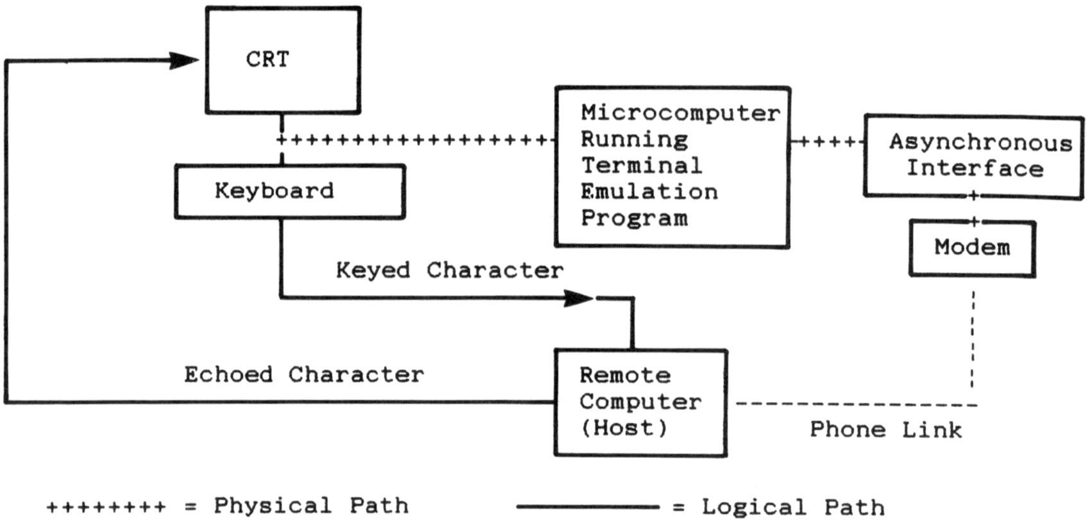

Fig. 3-33. Terminal emulation data paths.

back to modem, port, microcomputer, and finally to the CRT), as well as a "logical" data path, by which the user seems to be directly communicating with the host as if the user were sitting at a host specific terminal.

In some cases, the host is synchronous and requires a direct coaxial hook-up. These emulation packages include plug-in cards for the microcomputer that contain circuitry and firmware (software in ROMs) that perform the protocol conversions, the data representation code translations, and the communications overhead without the intervention of the end-user. Such products are available from Digital Communications (the IRMA line), AST Research, Techland Inc. (Blue Lynx products), and a variety of others. IBM also sells a 3270 card for the PC that performs all of these functions.

One of the most important functions of this class of products is that they enable the user to capture mainframe data to a local disk drive. This can either be done by designating the local disk as a printer (giving it a printer LU in 3270/SNA), or turning on a screen-capture mode that passes all data to a disk file as it scrolls on the screen. This data-capture capability enables end-users to acquire desired data sets for later processing on their microcomputer application packages, which forms the basis of the fundamental methods for data file interchange.

The microcomputer terminal applications programs also perform keyboard remapping, so that there can even be an emulation of a foreign keyboard. In some applications, users can purchase keyboards that contain the key maps required, such as 3270 terminal keyboards, and plug them into their microcomputers in place of the standard keyboard. Many corporate users have replaced 3270 terminals with IBM PC compatible machines that have been upgraded with 3270 type cards and keyboards. The result is that the users need very little retraining, because the emulation system is so close, in terms of its interface, to the original.

There are also devices known as protocol converters available that allow for the use of different types of data communications equipment with alien hosts. It is thus possible to link inexpensive, "dumb," ASCII asynchronous terminals to synchronous EBCDIC hosts using protocol converters. These products also tend to homogenize a typically heterogeneous environment, making end-user interfacing more uniform.

CONCLUSION

This chapter has been a fairly extensive journey through the field of data communications. The hardware, software, system architectures, philosophies and most of the terms used have been defined. Data communications is a large field, growing each day, and you are referred to the trade press and manufacturer's reference manuals for additional study.

Chapter 4

Current Methods of Data File Interchange

Information exists in many forms in many different places. University students are well versed in the philosophy that everything is in the library. Somewhere. The word "research" implies the finding of something again. Sometimes information exists in a number of printed documents, and a user needs to extract various pieces of this data and "compile" it into a new document. This is a fundamental process of information exchange throughout the world.

In the ever-expanding data processing environment, more and more data exists in various magnetic forms from a wide variety of computers. The need to find the data, extract needed information, and recompile this information into new reports is just as universal in the electronic age as it was in the paper age. Unfortunately, the means of data interchange are not as well-developed as they need to be.

To fill this gap, most users employ old tried and true skills, namely, the research method of manually extracting information, culling it for necessary subsets, and reforming it into a required end product.

MANUAL FILE MANIPULATION AND REKEYING OF DATA

As an example, suppose that an officer at a small branch bank wishes to do a financial analysis of the loans written to all of his oil clients. Bank headquarters runs on an IBM 3270 type mainframe, located in another city, and his branch bank has 3278 terminals and 3276 printers. His user interface on the terminal limits him to single customer account status queries, and the printed reports are merely listings of all current customer account activity. With his officer password, he can get loan information to the screen, but this is limited to one loan at a time.

This officer has an IBM PC/AT in his office, upon which he has loaded Lotus 1-2-3 and dBASE III PLUS. After taking a few one-day courses in each program at a local computer store, playing with the tutorials, buying a few how-to books, and "pounding" away for about six months, he feels confident that he can use 1-2-3 to do the analysis required by his loan committee.

The first problem that faces him is how to get the data. Because he has no programming or database interface to the host, he must rely on the existing end-user information dissemination methods, as sparse as they are.

He needs a list of all loans for all customers that can be classified as being in the oil sector. The customer account status report printed each day has over 800 pages of detailed transaction data for every customer in the bank, but only shows loan payments, if any were made. This report also does not identify customers by industry type.

The loan status inquiry screen will give him the information he needs on each loan, but it is a loan-by-loan, customer-by-customer screen-only report.

After careful deliberation, the officer develops a strategy. Taking one of the daily reports, which will give him a list of all account numbers and names, he will have to highlight the information for each oil industry client. With this list, a query from the loan status screen can be made, giving an up-to-date status of each loan. Only after writing down the data needed from each screen will he be ready to key in all of the combined information into a Lotus 1-2-3 spreadsheet.

While this might seem difficult, it is the only way a non-interfaced user with no way of initiating queries up to the host might accomplish such a task. The time consumed is astronomical, sometimes on the order of months. For an officer being paid as a financial professional, this can become extremely expensive for the bank, and a questionable use of the person's time.

If the final product is of some importance, so that other members of the firm might want to do additional work with this data, it might actually be necessary for them to rekey the desired data into other software packages such as word processors, other spreadsheets, and database management systems. The flow of information in such a system goes from machine to person to machine, and possibly to other person-machine cycles.

TEXT FILE CAPTURE, MANIPULATION, AND REKEYING

Assume that, somehow, this person becomes aware of the microcomputer's ability, with the addition of some hardware and software, to act like an IBM 3278 terminal. He goes to a user group meeting and gets the bank to purchase an IRMA-type board that allows for terminal emulation. He installs the board and its attendant software in the AT, removes the 3278 terminal from his office, and connects the coaxial cable to his microcomputer.

What has he gained? Well, perhaps not much. Now, thanks to the software that came with his card, he can capture data screens to an ASCII text file. He can thus construct a file of the oil company client's loan data for later printing. Such a file is not in a form for easy transmission to Lotus or any other application, being two-dimensional (screen-oriented) rather than the one-dimensional (line-oriented) columnar report that the spreadsheet would find most acceptable.

If the officer has some communication with the data center, he could request and be granted a logical unit (LU) code, giving his microcomputer a designation as a printer to the host. In such a case, he could request the daily customer status report to be printed to his printer LU, and he could capture the report to his disk as an ASCII file. This file would look exactly as if the report had been printed to the disk, carriage returns, line feeds, form feeds and all. Such a file, called BANK.TXT, is shown in Fig. 4-1.

A text editor could be used to delete all headers, footers, and any customers not in the oil industry, producing a list of the names, account numbers, and some financial data that the officer would need in the final report. Notice that in this scenario he was still required to manually select records that met his filter criterion.

This trimmed ASCII file could be imported into 1-2-3 as a basis for his template, but he will still have to manually select and enter the loan data from the data capture in the loan screen query mode. Because current versions of DOS are single-tasking, he will still have to print out the captured loan screen data, so that he can enter it into the Lotus template.

He has thus saved himself the keystrokes required to enter the desired clients into the spreadsheet, and has a hard copy of the captured screen data from which to extract the loan information. While a great deal of time has been saved by the additional hardware and software expense, this is still far from a "user friendly" interface.

COMPLETE DATA FILE MANIPULATION WITH TRANSFER TO APPLICATION

There is a way to avoid the time-consuming task of rekeying data. The following example shows the process from the point of the mainframe-printed report capture through to the Lotus 1-2-3 spreadsheet. Some text file manipulation is performed, using a generic type of screen-oriented text editor, such as Personal Editor 2, or even WordStar in the nondocument mode.

A disk-captured printout looks exactly like the paper version, so it is almost always necessary to strip out any headings and footings. This is accomplished by placing the cursor on the line in question and issuing a line delete command. After this process, the multipage report has been transformed into a file called BANK2.TXT that looks like Fig. 4-2, which is just a list of data records.

```
                         First National Interstate Bank & Trust

                              Houston-East Branch # 12
                            Customer Account Status Report
=============================================================================================
!Account!Customer Name                 !  Account!     M-T-D!  Interest!      Last! Number!      Loan!
!Number !                              !  Balance!  Activity!      Rate!  Payment!   Trans!   Balance!
=============================================================================================
!0164006!Houston Linen Service, Inc.   !  78120.28!   8835.00!     10.50!     30.38!     82!   5812.08!
!0170007!Howard Safe & Lock Co.        !   4588.60!    514.60!     10.50!     88.60!     58!   4458.85!
!0068006!Browning-Ferris Industries    !  21349.00!   3341.38!     10.50!    349.00!     34!   1134.93!
!2018001!Always & Forever Florist      !   2114.75!   5575.00!     10.50!    114.75!     51!   5211.45!
!0304000!Southline Equipment Company   !   1413.19!   2254.52!     10.50!     13.19!     21!   4141.32!
!0072007!Budget Paper Supply           !    715.15!   1105.00!     10.50!    185.80!     11!      0.00!
!0326002!Thompson Industries           !  12222.73!   9950.00!     10.50!   6693.95!     92!    222.39!
!0224002!Nationwide Papers             !    821.40!     27.24!     10.50!    813.19!      2!     82.30!
!0184008!G.M. Woods Company, Inc.      !  16236.90!   8892.30!     10.50!   3010.00!     83!   2623.08!
!0082008!Cargill                       !  31185.00!  14435.18!     10.50!   5197.50!     48!   5118.74!
!0074007!Bunge Edible Oil Corporation  !  36115.20!   8824.00!      8.50!  11918.02!     81!   4611.88!
!0156005!Holly Sugar Corporation       !  26690.28!   7799.22!     10.50!  13151.33!     79!   9669.17!
!0090009!Charter Oil -Houston          !   6039.35!   8840.25!      9.50!   5989.35!     83!    603.98!
!0234003!Northwest Electric Supply     !  17411.68!   4471.12!     10.50!    625.81!     41!   1741.54!
!2115001!Easter Plumbing Co.           !    227.50!   8817.40!     10.50!    227.50!     82!     22.78!
!0196009!Lockwood Manufacturing Inc.   !   4372.35!   4422.80!     10.50!   4372.35!     47!   2437.24!
!0290109!Exxon Exploration Services    ! 338732.17!  22835.00!      9.50!  18082.54!     83!   5873.28!
!0178007!International Coal & Energy   !  16436.25!   5214.60!      9.50!    168.00!     23!   4643.82!
!0005000!A & B Safe & Lock Service     !    348.19!   9341.38!     10.50!    348.19!     34!     34.83!
!0001000!A & E Messenger Service       !     92.75!    575.00!     10.50!     48.50!     59!      0.00!
!2038103!Automatic Data Processing     !     75.00!   2254.52!     10.50!     75.00!     27!      0.00!
!0002000!Acme Brass & Aluminum Mfg,Inc. !  2835.00!    835.00!     10.50!   2835.00!     83!   5283.58!
!0032003!AT&T                          !     14.60!     14.60!     10.50!     14.60!      1!      0.00!
!0100000!Con Agra,Inc.                 !   5341.38!    341.38!     10.50!   5341.38!     34!   1534.13!
!2104000!Winter Egg Products, Inc.     !  10575.00!    575.00!     10.50!  10575.00!     57!   5057.55!
!0108000!DCA Food Industries Inc       !  15254.52!  13254.52!     10.50!   1256.12!     25!   4525.62!
!0119001!Daniel Goodson                !    105.00!    105.00!     10.50!    105.00!     10!      0.00!
!0166006!Houston Pecan Company         !   1950.00!    950.00!     10.50!   1950.00!     95!    195.09!
!0168006!Terrance Tile Co.             !     27.24!     27.24!     10.50!     27.24!      2!      0.00!
!0190009!Koza's Custom Cresting        !   7892.30!    892.30!     10.50!   5127.50!     89!   2789.78!
!0200000!Astro Management, Inc.        !    435.18!    435.18!     10.50!    147.66!     43!      0.00!
!0214001!Metal Kitchen Fabricators, Inc !  4824.00!    824.00!     10.50!   4824.00!     82!   4482.48!
!0242004!Petaluma Pumps, Inc.          !   1799.22!    799.22!     10.50!    909.49!     79!      0.00!
!0284008!Schepps Packaging Inc         !  19840.25!   2840.25!     10.50!   7112.16!     84!    984.28!
!0312501!Allen Parkway Restaurant      !    471.12!    471.12!     10.50!    471.12!     47!      0.00!
!0324002!Alfred Winters Associates     !    817.40!    817.40!     10.50!    397.00!     81!      0.00!
!0346004!Young Pecan Shelling Co., Inc. ! 11422.80!    422.80!     10.50!   1012.80!     42!    142.24!
!0120002!Entex                         !    207.56!    207.56!      8.50!    207.56!     20!      0.00!
!0308000!Southwestern Bell             !    577.99!    577.99!     10.50!    449.20!     57!      0.00!
!0160006!Houston Lighting & Power      !    916.55!    916.55!     10.50!    916.55!     91!      0.00!
!0338003!A.F. Wilson, Inc.             !   1295.19!    211.59!     10.50!      0.00!      9!      0.00!
!0081008!U.T. Alumni Fund              !    236.71!    236.71!     10.50!    236.71!     23!      0.00!
!0076007!Benson & Benson               !   3558.25!   7478.12!     10.50!    231.25!     45!    355.14!
!0270007!SWT Products Corporation      !   9702.00!    110.19!     10.50!    604.98!     10!    970.41!
=============================================================================================
! This information is CONFIDENTIAL as is intended for the use of employees of the bank only
=============================================================================================
Page Number 1                                                                          03/21/87
```

Fig. 4-1. Page 1 of sample captured mainframe report (BANK.TXT).

```
!0164006!Houston Linen Service, Inc.   !  78120.28!   8835.00!     10.50!     30.38!    82!   5812.08!
!0170007!Howard Safe & Lock Co.        !   4588.60!    514.60!     10.50!     88.60!    58!   4458.85!
!0068006!Browning-Ferris Industries    !  21349.00!   3341.38!     10.50!    349.00!    34!   1134.93!
!2018001!Always & Forever Florist      !   2114.75!   5575.00!     10.50!    114.75!    51!   5211.45!
!0304000!Southline Equipment Company   !   1413.19!   2254.52!     10.50!     13.19!    21!   4141.32!
!0072007!Budget Paper Supply           !    715.15!   1105.00!     10.50!    185.80!    11!      0.00!
!0326002!Thompson Industries           !  12222.73!   9950.00!     10.50!   6693.95!    92!    222.39!
!0224002!Nationwide Papers             !    821.40!     27.24!     10.50!    813.19!     2!     82.30!
!0184008!G.M. Woods Company, Inc.      !  16236.90!   8892.30!     10.50!   3010.00!    83!   2623.08!
!0082008!Cargill                       !  31185.00!  14435.18!     10.50!   5197.50!    48!   5118.74!
!0074007!Bunge Edible Oil Corporation  !  36115.20!   8824.00!      8.50!  11918.02!    81!   4611.88!
!0156005!Holly Sugar Corporation       !  26690.28!   7799.22!     10.50!  13151.33!    79!   9669.17!
!0090009!Charter Oil -Houston          !   6039.35!   8840.25!      9.50!   5989.35!    83!    603.98!
!0234003!Northwest Electric Supply     !  17411.68!   4471.12!     10.50!    625.81!    41!   1741.54!
!2115001!Easter Plumbing Co.           !    227.50!   8817.40!     10.50!    227.50!    82!     22.78!
!0196009!Lockwood Manufacturing Inc.   !   4372.35!   4422.80!     10.50!   4372.35!    47!   2437.24!
!0290109!Exxon Exploration Services    ! 338732.17!  22835.00!      9.50!  18082.54!    83!   5873.28!
!0178007!International Coal & Energy   !  16436.25!   5214.60!      9.50!    168.00!    23!   4643.82!
!0005000!A & B Safe & Lock Service     !    348.19!   9341.38!     10.50!    348.19!    34!     34.83!
!0001000!A & E Messenger Service       !     92.75!    575.00!     10.50!     48.50!    59!      0.00!
!2038103!Automatic Data Processing     !     75.00!   2254.52!     10.50!     75.00!    27!      0.00!
!0002000!Acme Brass & Aluminum Mfg,Inc. !   2835.00!    835.00!     10.50!   2835.00!    83!   5283.58!
!0032003!AT&T                          !     14.60!     14.60!     10.50!     14.60!     1!      0.00!
!0100000!Con Agra,Inc.                 !   5341.38!    341.38!     10.50!   5341.38!    34!   1534.13!
!2104000!Winter Egg Products, Inc.     !  10575.00!    575.00!     10.50!  10575.00!    57!   5057.55!
!0108000!DCA Food Industries Inc       !  15254.52!  13254.52!     10.50!   1256.12!    25!   4525.62!
!0119001!Daniel Goodson                !    105.00!    105.00!     10.50!    105.00!    10!      0.00!
!0166006!Houston Pecan Company         !   1950.00!    950.00!     10.50!   1950.00!    95!    195.09!
!0168006!Terrance Tile Co.             !     27.24!     27.24!     10.50!     27.24!     2!      0.00!
!0190009!Koza's Custom Cresting        !   7892.30!    892.30!     10.50!   5127.50!    89!   2789.78!
!0200000!Astro Management, Inc.        !    435.18!    435.18!     10.50!    147.66!    43!      0.00!
!0214001!Metal Kitchen Fabricators, Inc !   4824.00!    824.00!     10.50!   4824.00!    82!   4482.48!
!0242004!Petaluma Pumps, Inc.          !   1799.22!    799.22!     10.50!    909.49!    79!      0.00!
!0284008!Schepps Packaging Inc         !  19840.25!   2840.25!     10.50!   7112.16!    84!    984.28!
!0312501!Allen Parkway Restaurant      !    471.12!    471.12!     10.50!    471.12!    47!      0.00!
!0324002!Alfred Winters Associates     !    817.40!    817.40!     10.50!    397.00!    81!      0.00!
!0346004!Young Pecan Shelling Co., Inc. !  11422.80!    422.80!     10.50!   1012.80!    42!    142.24!
!0120002!Entex                         !    207.56!    207.56!      8.50!    207.56!    20!      0.00!
!0308000!Southwestern Bell             !    577.99!    577.99!     10.50!    449.20!    57!      0.00!
!0160006!Houston Lighting & Power      !    916.55!    916.55!     10.50!    916.55!    91!      0.00!
!0338003!A.F. Wilson, Inc.             !   1295.19!    211.59!     10.50!      0.00!     9!      0.00!
!0081008!U.T. Alumni Fund              !    236.71!    236.71!     10.50!    236.71!    23!      0.00!
!0076007!Benson & Benson               !   3558.25!   7478.12!     10.50!    231.25!    45!    355.14!
!0270007!SWT Products Corporation      !   9702.00!    110.19!     10.50!    604.98!    10!    970.41!
!0128006!Filtration Sciences Corp.     !  21050.00!   1950.20!     10.50!    234.56!    21!   1055.00!
!0142007!Howard Jackson                !   3547.62!    390.20!     10.50!   3515.22!    11!   3544.00!
!0226006!Nationwide Papers             !  93207.50!   2139.20!     10.50!   3175.42!    92!   3200.00!
!0154001!Holly Sugar Corporation       !  13270.56!   2213.90!     10.50!  13005.15!     2!   3277.00!
!0236000!Woodlands Pipe Supply, Inc.   !   6210.72!   2721.40!     10.50!    210.72!    83!   2211.00!
!0216007!Meyer Rubber Stamp Company    !  21942.90!   9372.70!     10.50!    142.90!    48!   2244.00!
```

Fig. 4-2. Partially stripped sample captured mainframe report (BANK2.TXT).

In the example, the host program has separated data fields using the exclamation point character. Further "cleaning" requires the user to space over to these delineation character columns and either delete them or overwrite them with a space. What is left is the file shown in Fig. 4-3.

0164006Houston Linen Service, Inc.	78120.28	8835.00	10.50	30.38	82	5812.08
0170007Howard Safe & Lock Co.	4588.60	514.60	10.50	88.60	58	4458.85
0068006Browning-Ferris Industries	21349.00	3341.38	10.50	349.00	34	1134.93
2018001Always & Forever Florist	2114.75	5575.00	10.50	114.75	51	5211.45
0304000Southline Equipment Company	1413.19	2254.52	10.50	13.19	21	4141.32
0072007Budget Paper Supply	715.15	1105.00	10.50	185.80	11	0.00
0326002Thompson Industries	12222.73	9950.00	10.50	6693.95	92	222.39
0224002Nationwide Papers	821.40	27.24	10.50	813.19	2	82.30
0184008G.M. Woods Company, Inc.	16236.90	8892.30	10.50	3010.00	83	2623.08
0082008Cargill	31185.00	14435.18	10.50	5197.50	48	5118.74
0074007Bunge Edible Oil Corporation	36115.20	8824.00	8.50	11918.02	81	4611.88
0156005Holly Sugar Corporation	26690.28	7799.22	10.50	13151.33	79	9669.17
0090009Charter Oil -Houston	6039.35	8840.25	9.50	5989.35	83	603.98
0234003Northwest Electric Supply	17411.68	4471.12	10.50	625.81	41	1741.54
2115001Easter Plumbing Co.	227.50	8817.40	10.50	227.50	82	22.78
0196009Lockwood Manufacturing Inc.	4372.35	4422.80	10.50	4372.35	47	2437.24
0290109Exxon Exploration Services	338732.17	22835.00	9.50	18082.54	83	5873.28
0178007International Coal & Energy	16436.25	5214.60	9.50	168.00	23	4643.82
0005000A & B Safe & Lock Service	348.19	9341.38	10.50	348.19	34	34.83
0001000A & E Messenger Service	92.75	575.00	10.50	48.50	59	0.00
2038103Automatic Data Processing	75.00	2254.52	10.50	75.00	27	0.00
0002000Acme Brass & Aluminum Mfg,Inc.	2835.00	835.00	10.50	2835.00	83	5283.58
0032003AT&T	14.60	14.60	10.50	14.60	1	0.00
0100000Con Agra,Inc.	5341.38	341.38	10.50	5341.38	34	1534.13
2104000Winter Egg Products, Inc.	10575.00	575.00	10.50	10575.00	57	5057.55
0108000DCA Food Industries Inc	15254.52	13254.52	10.50	1256.12	25	4525.62
0119001Daniel Goodson	105.00	105.00	10.50	105.00	10	0.00
0166006Houston Pecan Company	1950.00	950.00	10.50	1950.00	95	195.09
0168006Terrance Tile Co.	27.24	27.24	10.50	27.24	2	0.00
0190009Koza's Custom Cresting	7892.30	892.30	10.50	5127.50	89	2789.78
0200000Astro Management, Inc.	435.18	435.18	10.50	147.66	43	0.00
0214001Metal Kitchen Fabricators, Inc	4824.00	824.00	10.50	4824.00	82	4482.48
0242004Petaluma Pumps, Inc.	1799.22	799.22	10.50	909.49	79	0.00
0284008Schepps Packaging Inc	19840.25	2840.25	10.50	7112.16	84	984.28
0312501Allen Parkway Restaurant	471.12	471.12	10.50	471.12	47	0.00
0324002Alfred Winters Associates	817.40	817.40	10.50	397.00	81	0.00
0346004Young Pecan Shelling Co., Inc.	11422.80	422.80	10.50	1012.80	42	142.24
0120002Entex	207.56	207.56	8.50	207.56	20	0.00
0308000Southwestern Bell	577.99	577.99	10.50	449.20	57	0.00
0160006Houston Lighting & Power	916.55	916.55	10.50	916.55	91	0.00
0338003A.F. Wilson, Inc.	1295.19	211.59	10.50	0.00	9	0.00
0081008U.T. Alumni Fund	236.71	236.71	10.50	236.71	23	0.00
0076007Benson & Benson	3558.25	7478.12	10.50	231.25	45	355.14
0270007SWT Products Corporation	9702.00	110.19	10.50	604.98	10	970.41
0128006Filtration Sciences Corp.	21050.00	1950.20	10.50	234.56	21	1055.00
0142007Howard Jackson	3547.62	390.20	10.50	3515.22	11	3544.00
0226006Nationwide Papers	93207.50	2139.20	10.50	3175.42	92	3200.00
0154001Holly Sugar Corporation	13270.56	2213.90	10.50	13005.15	2	3277.00
0236000Woodlands Pipe Supply, Inc.	6210.72	2721.40	10.50	210.72	83	2211.00
0216007Meyer Rubber Stamp Company	21942.90	9372.70	10.50	142.90	48	2244.00

Fig. 4-3. Sample captured mainframe report with all delimiters removed.

Data that is unwanted can now be deleted in the text editor or carried over to the new file format. Only pertinent information, such as account name, number, loan balance and account balance, will be sent to the spreadsheet in this example. The user notes in his preliminary perusal of the data that the oil clients appear to have the best interest rates, so he will send this data field to the spreadsheet as well. The final data file to be interchanged is shown in Fig. 4-4. It is trimmed of all extraneous information and is in a minimal form for data interchange to some other application program.

0164006Houston Linen Service, Inc.	78120.28	10.50	5812.08
0170007Howard Safe & Lock Co.	4588.60	10.50	4458.85
0068006Browning-Ferris Industries	21349.00	10.50	1134.93
2018001Always & Forever Florist	2114.75	10.50	5211.45
0304000Southline Equipment Company	1413.19	10.50	4141.32
0072007Budget Paper Supply	715.15	10.50	0.00
0326002Thompson Industries	12222.73	10.50	222.39
0224002Nationwide Papers	821.40	10.50	82.30
0184008G.M. Woods Company, Inc.	16236.90	10.50	2623.08
0082008Cargill	31185.00	10.50	5118.74
0074007Bunge Edible Oil Corporation	36115.20	8.50	4611.88
0156005Holly Sugar Corporation	26690.28	10.50	9669.17
0090009Charter Oil -Houston	6039.35	9.50	603.98
0234003Northwest Electric Supply	17411.68	10.50	1741.54
2115001Easter Plumbing Co.	227.50	10.50	22.78
0196009Lockwood Manufacturing Inc.	4372.35	10.50	2437.24
0290109Exxon Exploration Services	338732.17	9.50	5873.28
0178007International Coal & Energy	16436.25	9.50	4643.82
0005000A & B Safe & Lock Service	348.19	10.50	34.83
0001000A & E Messenger Service	92.75	10.50	0.00
2038103Automatic Data Processing	75.00	10.50	0.00
0002000Acme Brass & Aluminum Mfg,Inc.	2835.00	10.50	5283.58
0032003AT&T	14.60	10.50	0.00
0100000Con Agra,Inc.	5341.38	10.50	1534.13
2104000Winter Egg Products, Inc.	10575.00	10.50	5057.55
0108000DCA Food Industries Inc	15254.52	10.50	4525.62
0119001Daniel Goodson	105.00	10.50	0.00
0166006Houston Pecan Company	1950.00	10.50	195.09
0168006Terrance Tile Co.	27.24	10.50	0.00
0190009Koza's Custom Cresting	7892.30	10.50	2789.78
0200000Astro Management, Inc.	435.18	10.50	0.00
0214001Metal Kitchen Fabricators, Inc	4824.00	10.50	4482.48
0242004Petaluma Pumps, Inc.	1799.22	10.50	0.00
0284008Schepps Packaging Inc	19840.25	10.50	984.28
0312501Allen Parkway Restaurant	471.12	10.50	0.00
0324002Alfred Winters Associates	817.40	10.50	0.00
0346004Young Pecan Shelling Co., Inc.	11422.80	10.50	142.24
0120002Entex	207.56	8.50	0.00
0308000Southwestern Bell	577.99	10.50	0.00
0160006Houston Lighting & Power	916.55	10.50	0.00
0338003A.F. Wilson, Inc.	1295.19	10.50	0.00
0081008U.T. Alumni Fund	236.71	10.50	0.00
0076007Benson & Benson	3558.25	10.50	355.14
0270007SWT Products Corporation	9702.00	10.50	970.41
0128006Filtration Sciences Corp.	21050.00	10.50	1055.00
0142007Howard Jackson	3547.62	10.50	3544.00
0226006Nationwide Papers	93207.50	10.50	3200.00
0154001Holly Sugar Corporation	13270.56	10.50	3277.00
0236000Woodlands Pipe Supply, Inc.	6210.72	10.50	2211.00
0216007Meyer Rubber Stamp Company	21942.90	10.50	2244.00

Fig. 4-4. Sample file ready for import into dBASE III (BANK3.TXT).

Printout standards can vary, from 10, to 12, to even 16½ characters to the inch. Whatever the spacing, the user needs to know the width of each data field and whether it is a character or numeric field. The character counting method for the sample data file by which one determines the data structure is shown in Fig. 4-5.

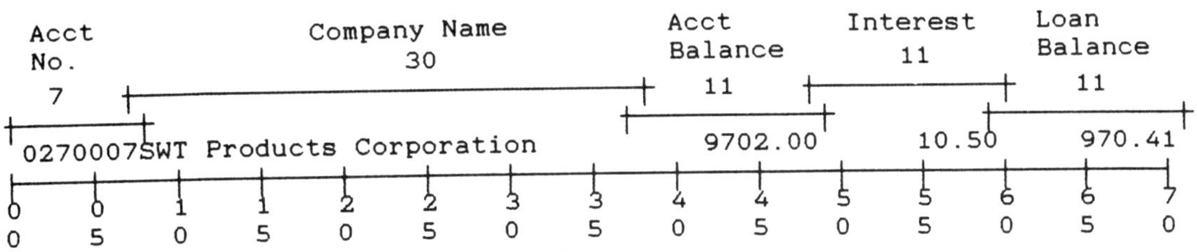

Fig. 4-5. Character counting to determine data structure.

Now there is an ASCII file, containing the desired data for all of the accounts in the branch, and a data structure that can be used in the interchange procedure. What follows is a scenario by which this data can be transferred to dBASE III PLUS, culled somewhat, and then sent to Lotus 1-2-3.

The first step is to load the dBASE III PLUS program. The CREATE command is then invoked, and the derived database structure is entered to tell dBASE how to construct the file that will hold the information to be imported. The data file will be called LOAN. To start this procedure the user types the following from the dBASE dot prompt:

.CREATE LOAN

Then the dBASE CREATE utility is used to define the five fields as shown in Fig. 4-6.

```
                                                  Bytes remaining:   3930

    Field Name  Type       Width  Dec         Field Name  Type      Width  Dec

1   ACCNUMBER   Character      7
2   ACCNAME     Character     30
3   ACCBAL      Numeric       11    2
4   INTEREST    Numeric       11    2
5   LOANBAL     Numeric       11    2

CREATE          |<C:>|LOAN                    |Field: 1/5        |     |
                            Enter the field name.
 Field names begin with a letter and may contain letters,digits and underscores
```

Fig. 4-6. dBASE III PLUS Create screen for LOAN.DBF.

Once the dBASE III database file, LOAN.DBF, is created, the trimmed ASCII file BANK3.TXT can be imported by typing the following from the dBASE dot prompt:

```
.APPEND FROM BANK3.TXT SDF
```

SDF is the dBASE III command telling it to take the data from a standard data file. The resulting DBF file is shown, using the BROWSE mode, in Fig. 4-7.

```
ACCNUMBER ACCNAME---------------------- ACCBAL----- INTEREST--- LOANBAL----
0170007   Howard Safe & Lock Co.            4588.60       10.50     4458.85
0068006   Browning-Ferris Industries       21349.00       10.50     1134.93
2018001   Always & Forever Florist          2114.75       10.50     5211.45
0304000   Southline Equipment Company       1413.19       10.50     4141.32
0072007   Budget Paper Supply                715.15       10.50        0.00
0326002   Thompson Industries              12222.73       10.50      222.39
0224002   Nationwide Papers                  821.40       10.50       82.30
0184008   G.M. Woods Company, Inc.         16236.90       10.50     2623.08
0082008   Cargill                          31185.00       10.50     5118.74
0074007   Bunge Edible Oil Corporation     36115.20        8.50     4611.88
0156005   Holly Sugar Corporation          26690.28       10.50     9669.17
0090009   Charter Oil -Houston              6039.35        9.50      603.98
0234003   Northwest Electric Supply        17411.68       10.50     1741.54
2115001   Easter Plumbing Co.                227.50       10.50       22.78
0196009   Lockwood Manufacturing Inc.       4372.35       10.50     2437.24
0290109   Exxon Exploration Services      338732.17        9.50     5873.28
0178007   International Coal & Energy      16436.25        9.50     4643.82

BROWSE          |<C:>|LOAN           |Rec: 2/71          |     |
                    View and edit fields.
```

Fig. 4-7. dBASE III PLUS Browse screen showing LOAN.DBF.

Now that the data is in a dBASE file format, the user can SORT, SUM, REPORT and LIST using filters. In fact, all of the power of a relational database comes into play. For example, a user who wanted the data set sorted by account name could type:

```
.SORT ON ACCNAME TO LOAN2
.USE LOAN2
```

The file now looks like Fig. 4-8.

ACCNUMBER	ACCNAME----------------------	ACCBAL-----	INTEREST---	LOANBAL----
0005000	A & B Safe & Lock Service	348.19	10.50	34.83
0001000	A & E Messenger Service	92.75	10.50	0.00
0338003	A.F. Wilson, Inc.	1295.19	10.50	0.00
0106000	ALON Motor Company, Inc.	94.44	10.50	99.00
0032003	AT&T	14.60	10.50	0.00
0002000	Acme Brass & Aluminum Mfg,Inc.	2835.00	10.50	5283.58
0016002	Albert Woodworks	9400.00	10.50	0.00
0324002	Alfred Winters Associates	817.40	10.50	0.00
0312501	Allen Parkway Restaurant	471.12	10.50	0.00
0096001	Alpine Oil Corp.	789392.38	9.50	657399.21
2018001	Always & Forever Florist	2114.75	10.50	5211.45
0022009	American Products Company	21165.72	11.50	23166.00
0200000	Astro Management, Inc.	435.18	10.50	0.00
0126000	Atlantic Richfield # 123	431096.97	10.50	211099.00
2038103	Automatic Data Processing	75.00	10.50	0.00
0040003	Aztec	345634.66	8.50	321133.00
0092008	Bayou Transportation Co.	5832.26	10.50	15833.00

BROWSE | <C:> | LOAN2 | Rec: 1/71 | | Caps

View and edit fields.

Fig. 4-8. LOAN2.DBF (LOAN.DBF sorted by ACCNAME).

As a first logical filter, all records that have no loan balance can be removed by typing:

```
.DELETE ALL FOR LOANBAL=0
.PACK
```

The database now contains a list of all loan customers sorted by name. The end-user only wants oil customers in the final file, so the other files should be marked, in some logical way, for deletion. One way might be to go into the BROWSE mode and set the INTEREST to zero for all those customers who are not oil clients, then type the following:

```
.DELETE ALL FOR INTEREST=0
.PACK
```

All of the data has now been extracted and is ready for Lotus analysis. To export the data to Lotus, simply type:

```
.COPY TO LOAN.PRN DELIMITED
```

The ASCII file LOAN.PRN produced is shown in Fig. 4-9. Notice that the character fields are enclosed in quotes, and numeric fields are not.

```
"0005000","A & B Safe & Lock Service",348.19,10.50,34.83
"0106000","ALON Motor Company, Inc.",94.44,10.50,99.00
"0002000","Acme Brass & Aluminum Mfg,Inc.",2835.00,10.50,5283.58
"0096001","Alpine Oil Corp.",789392.38,9.50,657399.21
"2018001","Always & Forever Florist",2114.75,10.50,5211.45
"0022009","American Products Company",21165.72,11.50,23166.00
"0126000","Atlantic Richfield # 123",431096.97,10.50,211099.00
"0040003","Aztec",345634.66,8.50,321133.00
"0092008","Bayou Transportation Co.",5832.26,10.50,15833.00
"0076007","Benson & Benson",3558.25,10.50,355.14
"0048007","Best Uniform Supply Co.",5660.96,11.50,66.00
"0068006","Browning-Ferris Industries",21349.00,10.50,1134.93
"0074007","Bunge Edible Oil Corporation",36115.20,8.50,4611.88
"0098000","Calvert Systems, Inc",2018.22,10.50,2011.00
"0348008","CanLab Corporation",3764.74,9.50,3766.00
"0082008","Cargill",31185.00,10.50,5118.74
"0090009","Charter Oil -Houston",6039.35,9.50,603.98
"0101000","Colorado County Fuel",21343.05,9.50,9344.00
"0100000","Con Agra,Inc.",5341.38,10.50,1534.13
"0150003","Conoco Research Center",312704.11,9.50,452700.00
"0108000","DCA Food Industries Inc",15254.52,10.50,4525.62
"0140009","Dale Gainers",350.00,12.51,355.00
"2115001","Easter Plumbing Co.",227.50,10.50,22.78
"0290109","Exxon Exploration Services",338732.17,9.50,5873.28
"0128006","Filtration Sciences Corp.",21050.00,10.50,1055.00
"0184008","G.M. Woods Company, Inc.",16236.90,10.50,2623.08
"0148003","Heights Pump Supply",21208.42,9.50,61200.00
"0154001","Holly Sugar Corporation",13270.56,10.50,3277.00
"0156005","Holly Sugar Corporation",26690.28,10.50,9669.17
"0164006","Houston Linen Service, Inc.",78120.28,10.50,5812.08
"0166006","Houston Pecan Company",1950.00,10.50,195.09
"0142007","Howard Jackson",3547.62,10.50,3544.00
"0170007","Howard Safe & Lock Co.",4588.60,10.50,4458.85
"0178007","International Coal & Energy",16436.25,9.50,4643.82
"0085000","John S. Smith",1819.97,10.50,1811.00
"0190009","Koza's Custom Cresting",7892.30,10.50,2789.78
"0196009","Lockwood Manufacturing Inc.",4372.35,10.50,2437.24
"0209005","McMillon Electric Co. Inc.",3856.90,10.50,855.00
"0214001","Metal Kitchen Fabricators, Inc",4824.00,10.50,4482.48
"0216007","Meyer Rubber Stamp Company",21942.90,10.50,2244.00
"0226006","Nationwide Papers",93207.50,10.50,3200.00
"0224002","Nationwide Papers",821.40,10.50,82.30
"0234003","Northwest Electric Supply",17411.68,10.50,1741.54
"0254000","Ranch Auto, Inc.",43.25,10.50,44.00
"0270007","SWT Products Corporation",9702.00,10.50,970.41
"0274009","Santa Anna Electric Co.",39123.34,10.50,21945.33
"0284008","Schepps Packaging Inc",19840.25,10.50,984.28
"0304000","Southline Equipment Company",1413.19,10.50,4141.32
"0326002","Thompson Industries",12222.73,10.50,222.39
"2104000","Winter Egg Products, Inc.",10575.00,10.50,5057.55
```

Fig. 4-9. Delimited file LOAN.PRN output from dBASE III PLUS.

The user copies the file onto the subdirectory where Lotus resides, enters Lotus, then uses the Lotus File-Import-Numbers menu options to load the LOAN.PRN file into the spreadsheet workspace. The result of this process is displayed in Fig. 4-10. Notice that the column widths are wrong, and that there is no formatting of the numbers. After some local column width changes, the creation of titles, and range formatting, the spreadsheet looks like the one shown in Fig. 4-11.

Now, at last, the user can enter the equations and additional data to do the analysis. While this seems like a very complex chain of operations, it can be made somewhat automatic by lumping the dBASE commands into a program file and setting up the Lotus spreadsheet as a template into which the data can be imported.

Still, this is what end-users must do as passive data-gatherers in mainframe to microcomputer data exchange. Notice that a number of intermediate steps were involved:

- ☐ Capture the print image.
- ☐ Strip off extraneous headers, footers, form feeds, etc.
- ☐ Remove delimiters.
- ☐ Delete columns of unwanted data.
- ☐ Go to dBASE.
- ☐ Create a data structure.

A1: '0005000 READY

	A	B	C	D	E	F	G	H
1	0005000	A & B Saf	348.19	10.5	34.83			
2	0106000	ALON Moto	94.44	10.5	99			
3	0002000	Acme Bras	2835	10.5	5283.58			
4	0096001	Alpine Oi	789392.3	9.5	657399.2			
5	2018001	Always &	2114.75	10.5	5211.45			
6	0022009	American	21165.72	11.5	23166			
7	0126000	Atlantic	431096.9	10.5	211099			
8	0040003	Aztec	345634.6	8.5	321133			
9	0092008	Bayou Tra	5832.26	10.5	15833			
10	0076007	Benson &	3558.25	10.5	355.14			
11	0048007	Best Unif	5660.96	11.5	66			
12	0068006	Browning-	21349	10.5	1134.93			
13	0074007	Bunge Edi	36115.2	8.5	4611.88			
14	0098000	Calvert S	2018.22	10.5	2011			
15	0348008	CanLab Co	3764.74	9.5	3766			
16	0082008	Cargill	31185	10.5	5118.74			
17	0090009	Charter O	6039.35	9.5	603.98			
18	0101000	Colorado	21343.05	9.5	9344			
19	0100000	Con Agra,	5341.38	10.5	1534.13			
20	0150003	Conoco Re	312704.1	9.5	452700			

Fig. 4-10. Delimited file LOAN.PRN imported into Lotus 1-2-3.

```
E3: "Balance                                                              READY

                  B                      C        D          E
1
2    Customer                         Account  Interest       Loan
3                                     Balance      Rate    Balance
4    ============================================================
5    A & B Safe & Lock Service        $348.19     10.50     $34.83
6    ALON Motor Company, Inc.          $94.44     10.50     $99.00
7    Acme Brass & Aluminum Mfg,Inc.  $2,835.00    10.50  $5,283.58
8    Alpine Oil Corp.              $789,392.38     9.50 $657,399.21
9    Always & Forever Florist        $2,114.75    10.50  $5,211.45
10   American Products Company      $21,165.72    11.50 $23,166.00
11   Atlantic Richfield # 123      $431,096.97    10.50 $211,099.00
12   Aztec                         $345,634.66     8.50 $321,133.00
13   Bayou Transportation Co.        $5,832.26    10.50 $15,833.00
14   Benson & Benson                 $3,558.25    10.50    $355.14
15   Best Uniform Supply Co.         $5,660.96    11.50     $66.00
16   Browning-Ferris Industries     $21,349.00    10.50  $1,134.93
17   Bunge Edible Oil Corporation   $36,115.20     8.50  $4,611.88
18   Calvert Systems, Inc            $2,018.22    10.50  $2,011.00
19   CanLab Corporation              $3,764.74     9.50  $3,766.00
20   Cargill                        $31,185.00    10.50  $5,118.74
```

Fig. 4-11. LOAN.WKS after cell and range processing.

- ☐ Append to the new data structure in standard data format.
- ☐ Sort, delete, or do whatever is necessary to make target file.
- ☐ Copy to a PRN file DELIMITED for Lotus input.
- ☐ Go to Lotus 1-2-3.
- ☐ Use File-Import-Numbers to get the PRN file into 1-2-3.
- ☐ Adjust the column width, and data formats.
- ☐ Setup headers, footers and spreadsheet equations.

Tedious. But still easier than typing in potentially thousands of characters of information.

This is by no means the only path from source to target file formats, even using dBASE III and Lotus 1-2-3. In dBASE, the user could have typed:

```
.USE LOAN2
.COPY TO LOAN2 DIF
```

In this case, the output file would be produced in data interchange format (DIF), and would look like Fig. 4-12. Lotus 1-2-3 has the ability to import DIF Files, a vestige of the old days when 1-2-3 sought to maintain compatibility to VisiCalc. The user thus could have achieved the same result via a different logical path. This is called a *multipath solution scheme.* Because such multiple possibilities exist, the solutions are not unique, and the potential for error in the process itself is enhanced.

Fig. 4-12. DIF file produced by dBASE III COPY TO LOAN2 DIF.

```
TABLE
0,1
""
TUPLES
0,72
""
VECTORS
0,5
""
DATA
0,0
""
-1,0
BOT
1,0
"ACCNUMBER"
1,0
"ACCNAME"
1,0
"ACCBAL"
1,0
"INTEREST"
1,0
"LOANBAL"
-1,0
BOT
1,0
"0164006"
1,0
"Houston Linen Service, Inc."
0,78120.28
V
0,10.50
V
0,5812.08
V
-1,0
BOT
1,0
"0170007"
1,0
"Howard Safe & Lock Co."
0,4588.60
V
0,10.50
V
0,4458.85
V
-1,0
```

STANDARD IMPORT/EXPORT UTILITIES IN POPULAR PACKAGES

Many programs also allow for the direct import of translation of files from other programs such as 1-2-3 Symphony, dBASE II, dBASE III, Multiplan, WordStar, and Multimate. This ability has become nearly a necessity for any product to compete in the microcomputer market place. In this section, a number of popular MS-DOS programs, along with the types of files with which they are conversant, are discussed.

There are a number of "semistandard" file formats that seem to be supported across many application packages. The previously mentioned standard data format file (SDF in dBASE), is merely a "flat" ASCII file containing no control codes or special characters. The other widely used ASCII file format is known as comma delimited format (delimited). A delimited file is one in which data is separated by commas or some other special character.

A major interapplication file format is known as *data interchange format* (DIF). It was invented by the VisiCalc people in the late seventies, and was a file structure that many other microcomputer applications have been "trained" to recognize either for direct importation or for translation. There are super sets of DIF formats, particularly those used by SuperCalc, that use the suffix SDI (SuperCalc Data Interchange) rather than the standard suffix of DIF.

SuperCalc 4

SuperCalc 4 is an integrated spreadsheet, database management system, and graphics package by Computer Associates that is designed to compete with 1-2-3. The user interface is very Lotus-like, and there is extensive online context specific help available. The menu dialogue in Fig. 4-13 shows the

```
Data   Export   Import   Macro
  3>//
MENU   Load foreign spreadsheet (1-2-3 XDIF DIF CSV Numbers Text VisiCalc)

1-2-3  XDIF  DIF  CSV  Numbers  Text  VisiCalc
 10>//Import,
MENU   DIF file format

Enter File Name
 18>//Import,DIF,loan
FILE   F1:Help F2:Edit F3:File-List  Ctrl-Break:Cancel

Colwise  Rowwise
 19>//Import,DIF,loan,
MENU   Import Vectors as Columns

All  Consolidate  Part
 27>//Import,DIF,loan,Colwise,
MENU   Import entire file
```

Fig. 4-13. SuperCalc 4 Import menu dialogue.

method and nature of the built-in import/export utilities available in the standard package. Note that 1-2-3, DIF, SDI, ASCII, and Commas Separated Variables and Numbers (CSVN) formats are directly available.

Figure 4-14 shows the result of a DIF import of the previously defined LOAN data. The 1-2-3 import of LOAN.WKS is shown in Fig. 4-15. Notice that the DIF import did not bring with it any column or numeric format information, while the 1-2-3 import did. The on-line help screen for the Import function is displayed in Fig. 4-16.

Paradox

Paradox, by ANSA, is an extremely powerful relational database management system that has a Lotus 1-2-3 user interface, an excellent programming language, called PAL (Paradox Application Language), graphics, and powerful report writing routines. The product has a unique "query-by-example" function, which makes complex, multifile queries (called tables in the Paradox jargon) extremely straightforward and easy to use. This is probably one of the reasons for its popularity.

The most current release of Paradox, Version 2.0, is a full-blown multiuser database system for use on microcomputer LANs. It is being jointly marketed by ANSA and 3Com, the company that produces the 3Plus Share operating system for their own 3Plus Network. The blending of an advanced multiuser database with a high-end CSMA/CD file-server-based LAN has created a very

```
   |   A    ||   B    ||   C    ||   D    ||   E    ||   F    ||   G    ||   H    |
1
2   Account  Customer Account  Interest Loan
3   Number            Balance  Rate      Balance
4   ========================================================================
5   0005000  A & B Saf   348.19       10.5     34.83
6   0106000  ALON Moto    94.44       10.5        99
7   0002000  Acme Bras     2835       10.5   5283.58
8   0096001  Alpine Oi 789392.4        9.5  657399.2
9   2018001  Always &   2114.75       10.5   5211.45
10  0022009  American  21165.72       11.5     23166
11  0126000  Atlantic  431097.0       10.5    211099
12  0040003  Aztec     345634.7        8.5    321133
13  0092008  Bayou Tra  5832.26       10.5     15833
14  0076007  Benson &   3558.25       10.5    355.14
15  0048007  Best Unif  5660.96       11.5        66
16  0068006  Browning-    21349       10.5   1134.93
17  0074007  Bunge Edi  36115.2        8.5   4611.88
18  0098000  Calvert S  2018.22       10.5      2011
19  0348008  CanLab Co  3764.74        9.5      3766
20  0082008  Cargill      31185       10.5   5118.74
 A1
Enter File Name and extension: .WK1 for 2.0 or .WKS for 1A (optional)
 29>//Import,1-2-3,\ws4\loan.wks
EDIT   F1:Help F3:File-List  Ctrl-Break:Cancel
```

Fig. 4-14. SuperCalc 4 imported LOAN.DIF file.

```
    |              B             ||      C      ||   D   ||       E      |
1
2   Customer                            Account Interest           Loan
3                                       Balance     Rate         Balance
4   ====================================================================
5   A & B Safe & Lock Service           $348.19     10.50          $34.83
6   ALON Motor Company, Inc.             $94.44     10.50          $99.00
7   Acme Brass & Aluminum Mfg,Inc.    $2,835.00     10.50       $5,283.58
8   Alpine Oil Corp.                $789,392.38      9.50     $657,399.21
9   Always & Forever Florist          $2,114.75     10.50       $5,211.45
10  American Products Company        $21,165.72     11.50      $23,166.00
11  Atlantic Richfield # 123        $431,096.97     10.50     $211,099.00
12  Aztec                           $345,634.66      8.50     $321,133.00
13  Bayou Transportation Co.          $5,832.26     10.50      $15,833.00
14  Benson & Benson                   $3,558.25     10.50         $355.14
15  Best Uniform Supply Co.           $5,660.96     11.50          $66.00
16  Browning-Ferris Industries       $21,349.00     10.50       $1,134.93
17  Bunge Edible Oil Corporation     $36,115.20      8.50       $4,611.88
18  Calvert Systems, Inc              $2,018.22     10.50       $2,011.00
19  CanLab Corporation                $3,764.74      9.50       $3,766.00
20  Cargill                          $31,185.00     10.50       $5,118.74
  E3     TR    P Text="Balance
Width: 14  Memory: 183  Last Col/Row:E65
  1>
READY F1:Help F3:Names  Ctrl-Break:Cancel
```

Fig. 4-15. SuperCalc 4 imported LOAN.WKS file.

Import SuperCalc4 AnswerScreen

Loads a foreign data file into the spreadsheet. The function converts as much data as possible into its SuperCalc4 counterparts.	
1-2-3	Loads a Lotus 1-2-3 spreadsheet-either release 1A (.WKS) or release 2 (.WK1).
XDIF	Loads the spreadsheet from the extended DIF format.
DIF	Loads the spreadsheet from the DIF file format. Colwise imports vectors as columns. Rowwise imports vectors as rows.
CSV	Loads the spreadsheet from the Comma Separated Values format.
Numbers	Loads numbers and text contained in double quotes from an ASCII file.
Text	Loads an ASCII file as text, one line per cell.
VisiCalc	Loads a spreadsheet produced by VisiCalc.

Fig. 4-16. SuperCalc 4 Import menu Help screen.

powerful information processing system for the corporate users that have "grown up" on the Lotus 1-2-3 type of interface.

With the multiuser locking and concurrency issues being handled closer to the operating system level, the system more closely emulates those features normally found in minicomputer and mainframe DBMS products. Paradox has the ability to directly import files from Lotus 1-2-3, Symphony, VisiCalc, DIF and ASCII formats. Direct importation denotes the fact that Paradox will automatically create the database structure in native format as a part of the import process itself.

R:base 5000

MicroRim's R:base product line is another major selling relational database system with the ability to import and export foreign data file formats. The utility that accomplishes this is called FileGateway, and has its main menu displayed in Fig. 4-17. The on-line help screen defining the various options is shown in Fig 4-18, and a sample import of a DIF format file is depicted in Fig. 4-19.

R:base is capable of reading data directly by automatically creating the R:base database from the source file without the need for predefinition. R:base recognizes source files from dBASE, Lotus 1-2-3, Symphony, PFS:File, VisiCalc, DIF, SYLK (MultiPlan), and ASCII formats.

Reflex

Borland International's Reflex package accomplishes the file translation function in a separate program. The program's graphic-oriented user interface allows for the translation of Lotus 1-2-3, dBASE, and DIF files into Reflex tables that can be manipulated using a number of different "views" in the main Reflex program. Figure 4-20 is a screen dump of the Reflex translate program screen, with the resulting "list view" of the imported dBASE file displayed in Fig. 4-21.

```
                     FileGateway
Copyright (c) 1984,1985 by Microrim, Inc. (Ver. 1.01 PC-DOS)

            Select an option - [F10] for help
    (1) DIF file (from VISICALC or other programs).
    (2) SYLK file (from MULTIPLAN or other programs).
    (3) ASCII file with data fields in fixed locations.
    (4) ASCII file with data fields separated by delimiters.
    (5) LOTUS 1-2-3 worksheet files.
    (6) dBASE II files.
    (7) PFS:FILE files.
    (8) Exit.
```

Fig. 4-17. R:base 5000 Import menu.

```
                        Input File Format
 * DIF files are special output files you can create from inside
   VisiCalc or other programs (DIF = Data Interchange Format)

 * SYLK files are special output files you can create from inside Multiplan
   or other programs (SYLK = Symbolic Link format)

 * ASCII files can be created in any editor or as output from other
   programs such as accounting packages.  ASCII data can be extracted from
   mainframe or minicomputer files and loaded into your personal computer
   via communications links, giving you CLOUT with corporate data.
   (ASCII = American Standard Code for Information Interchange.)
   Data in these files can be converted if the individual data fields are
   either in fixed locations (as if in tabular form), or if they are
   separated by some unique character (called a delimiter).
         Examples:    Fixed Location           Commas for Delimiter
                      ----------------         --------------------
                      123  red    789              123,red,789
                      23   blue   2234             23,blue,2234

 * LOTUS 1-2-3, PFS:FILE, and dBASE II files are the files created through
   regular use of those products.
```

Fig. 4-18. R:base 5000 Import menu Help screen.

```
                       File Conversion Editor
   The listing below shows the fields found in your input file along with
   the most likely type for that field, and a sample of the data found.
   To make changes in the name, type, and/or length of a field, move the
   cursor to that field and type in the new information.
     Up, Dn, Lt, Rt, PgUp, PgDn, Home, End . Moves the cursor between fields
     +  ................................... Gets next record of sample data
     F10  ................................. Help
     ESC  ................................. When changes are complete

Field Name   Type of Data    Maxlength       Sample values
----------   ------------    ---------    ------------------------------
 FLD00001       Text            10          05-726-692
 FLD00002       Text            15          Skill Saw
 FLD00003       Date                        07/15/84
 FLD00004       Time                        09:15:00
 FLD00005       Date                        07/15/84
 FLD00006       Time                        15:40:00
 FLD00007       Integer                     -0-
 FLD00008       Integer                              7
 FLD00009       Real                                          15.00

 Begin adding data to the database.
  Records loaded:
 Database :      5            Exception :      0

 Finished adding data to the database.
```

Fig. 4-19. R:base 5000 Import Function screen.

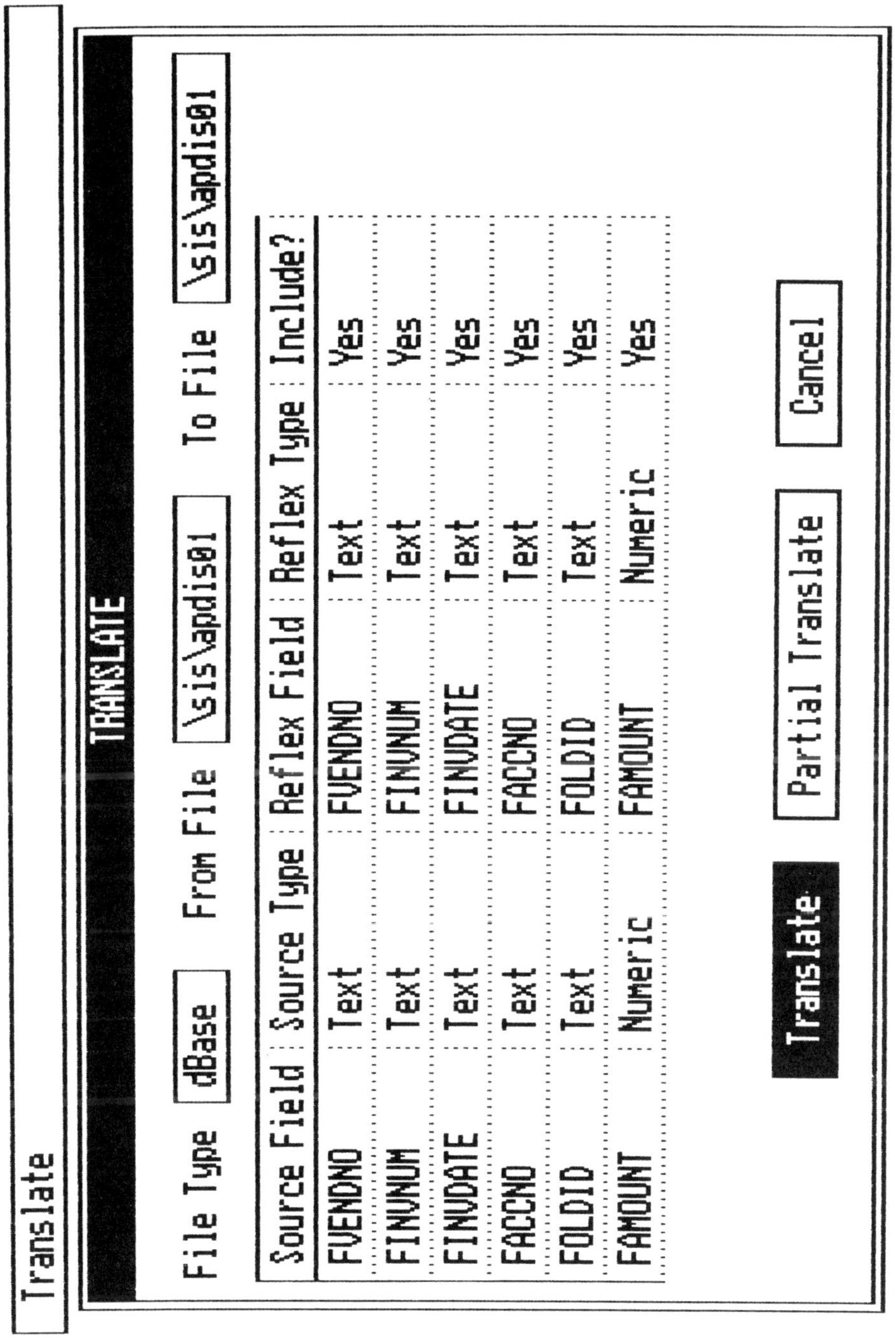

Fig. 4-20. Reflex Translate data screen.

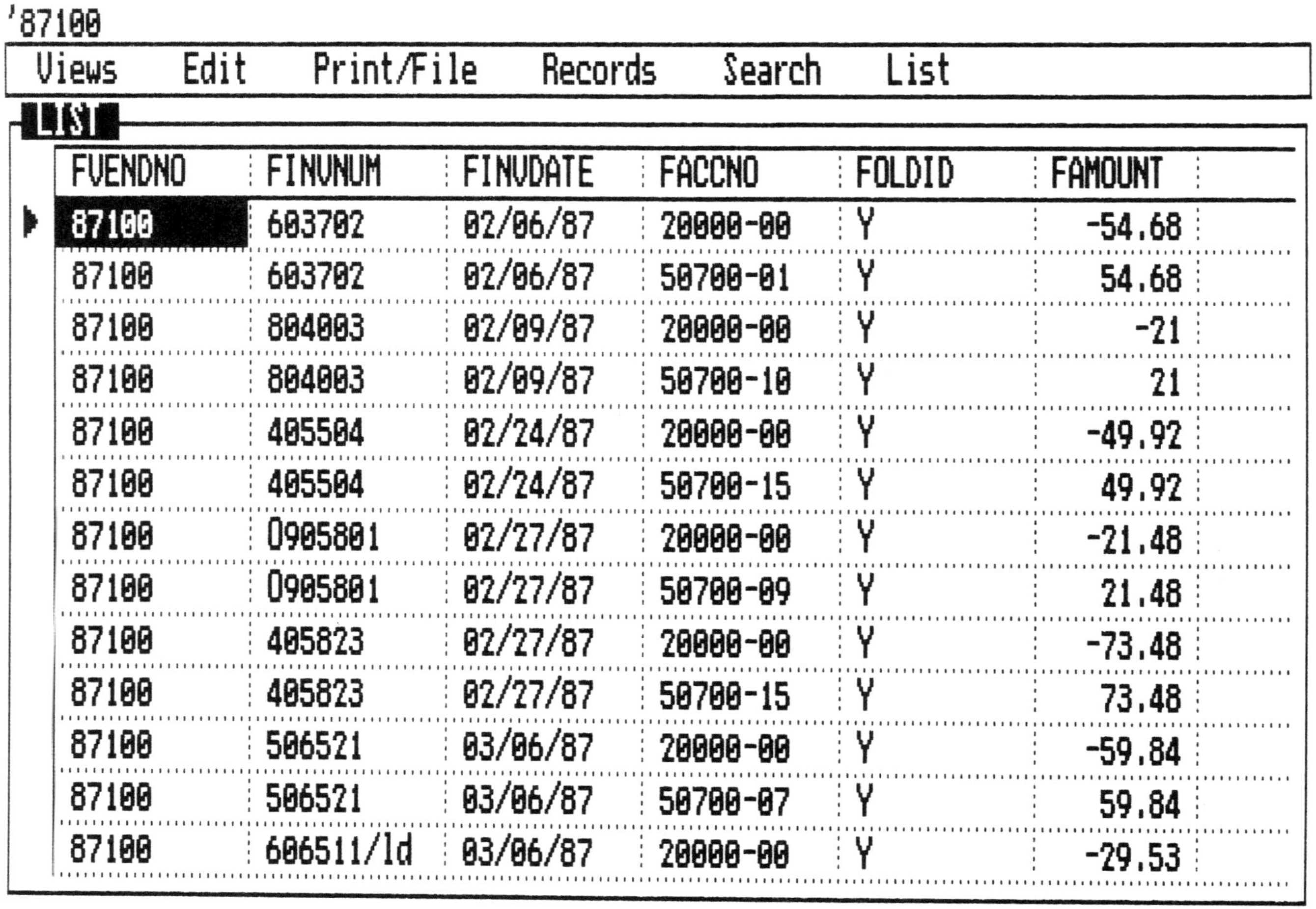
'87100

Views Edit Print/File Records Search List

LIST

FVENDNO	FINVNUM	FINVDATE	FACCNO	FOLDID	FAMOUNT
87100	603702	02/06/87	20000-00	Y	-54.68
87100	603702	02/06/87	50700-01	Y	54.68
87100	804003	02/09/87	20000-00	Y	-21
87100	804003	02/09/87	50700-10	Y	21
87100	405504	02/24/87	20000-00	Y	-49.92
87100	405504	02/24/87	50700-15	Y	49.92
87100	0905801	02/27/87	20000-00	Y	-21.48
87100	0905801	02/27/87	50700-09	Y	21.48
87100	405823	02/27/87	20000-00	Y	-73.48
87100	405823	02/27/87	50700-15	Y	73.48
87100	506521	03/06/87	20000-00	Y	-59.84
87100	506521	03/06/87	50700-07	Y	59.84
87100	606511/ld	03/06/87	20000-00	Y	-29.53

Fig. 4-21. Reflex list view of imported data.

A large number of users have chosen this product precisely for its ability to look at data from a number of different perspectives. The two-step translation process is fairly common across this product spectrum.

Lotus 1-2-3 Version 2.01

The latest release of the industry's most popular spreadsheet includes a full-blown translation utility as an external program called from the main Lotus access menu. Figure 4-22 displays the first of the series of screens in the file conversion process.

Note that files can be translated from both Lotus formats (the .WKS from Version 1A and the .WK1 use in Version 2.01), both dBASE II and dBASE III, DIF, VisiCalc, and the Lotus Symphony formats, into any one of the Lotus formats. There must be an internal translate for Lotus because the Version 2.01 files cannot be read by Version 1A programs. After selecting the file format to translate from, the user must choose a target file format, as shown in Fig. 4-23.

If a dBASE format is chosen as the source file, the translate utility displays a set of warnings as to its limitations in this conversion, as is seen in Fig. 4-24. As the translation occurs, the program displays the status screen in Fig. 4-25. The final imported data is displayed in Fig. 4-26.

Notice that the column widths are correct, as are the data types and range

```
                Lotus  1-2-3  Release 2.01 Translate Utility
   Copyright 1986 Lotus Development Corporation  All Rights Reserved

What do you want to translate FROM?

        1-2-3 release 1A
        1-2-3 rel 2 or 2.01
        dBase II
        dBase III
        DIF
        Jazz
        SYMPHONY 1.0
        SYMPHONY 1.1 or 1.2
        VISICALC



       Move the menu pointer to your selection and press [RETURN].
              Press [ESCAPE] to leave the Translate Utility.
                    Press [HELP] for more information.
```

Fig. 4-22. Lotus 1-2-3 v2.0 first Translate screen

```
                 Lotus  1-2-3  Release 2.01 Translate Utility
     Copyright 1986 Lotus Development Corporation  All Rights Reserved

 Translate FROM: dBase III            What do you want to translate TO?

                                            1-2-3 release 1A
                                            1-2-3 rel 2 or 2.01
                                            SYMPHONY 1.0
                                            SYMPHONY 1.1 or 1.2

         Move the menu pointer to your selection and press [RETURN].
            Press [ESCAPE] to return to the source selection menu.
                      Press [HELP] for more information.
```

Fig. 4-23. Lotus 1-2-3 v2.0 second Translate screen.

```
                 Lotus  1-2-3  Release 2.01 Translate Utility
     Copyright 1986 Lotus Development Corporation  All Rights Reserved

 Translate does not include deleted records from the dBASE-III
 source file or memos from a dBASE-III text file (.DBT) in the
 1-2-3 destination file.

 -Labels longer than 240 characters will be truncated.
 -Records after record number 8191 will not be translated.

 --------------------- Press [ESCAPE] to continue ---------------------
```

Fig. 4-24. Lotus 1-2-3 v2.0 third Translate screen.

```
          Lotus  1-2-3  Release 2.01 Translate Utility
    Copyright 1986 Lotus Development Corporation  All Rights Reserved

 Translate FROM: dBase III                 Translate TO: 1-2-3 2.01

 Source File: C:\WS4\LOAN.DBF

 Destination: D:\LOTUS\LOAN.WK1


                 Translation in progress... Please wait

                         Percent Translated
           0    10    20    30    40    50    60    70    80    90   100
```

Fig. 4-25. Lotus 1-2-3 v2.0 last Translate screen.

```
A1: [W7] 'ACCNUMBER                                              READY

        A                B                      C          D
1   ACCNUMBACCNAME                          ACCBAL     INTEREST
2   0164006Houston Linen Service, Inc.     78120.28       10.50
3   0170007Howard Safe & Lock Co.           4588.60       10.50
4   0068006Browning-Ferris Industries      21349.00       10.50
5   2018001Always & Forever Florist         2114.75       10.50
6   0304000Southline Equipment Company      1413.19       10.50
7   0072007Budget Paper Supply               715.15       10.50
8   0326002Thompson Industries             12222.73       10.50
9   0224002Nationwide Papers                 821.40       10.50
10  0184008G.M. Woods Company, Inc.        16236.90       10.50
11  0082008Cargill                         31185.00       10.50
12  0074007Bunge Edible Oil Corporation    36115.20        8.50
13  0156005Holly Sugar Corporation         26690.28       10.50
14  0090009Charter Oil -Houston             6039.35        9.50
15  0234003Northwest Electric Supply       17411.68       10.50
16  2115001Easter Plumbing Co.               227.50       10.50
17  0196009Lockwood Manufacturing Inc.      4372.35       10.50
18  0290109Exxon Exploration Services     338732.17        9.50
19  0178007International Coal & Energy     16436.25        9.50
20  0005000A & B Safe & Lock Service         348.19       10.50
19-Jun-87  03:14 PM
```

Fig. 4-26. Lotus 1-2-3 v2.0 directly imported dBASE III file.

formats. The columns are also labeled with the data field names that they had in their dBASE III file. This is very useful, relieving end-user of the need to do the column width and range format functions that are required in the DIF or .PRN import methodologies.

There are many other popular programs that contain these types of translation utilities. Often they are as simple as naming the file and its type. A number of inherent problems exist, however, in the translation scenarios. One is time. It can take a fair amount of time, not to mention disk space, to translate a large database file into another format. Most of these translation programs and procedures are "blind," which means that they take all of the source data and translate it into the target format. Typically, the user must then extract the data needed in the target application program. This might require more logic or programming skill than the nonsophisticated user is capable of. The rearranging, adding, and deleting of data fields is not as straightforward as you might think. The standard interapplication data file translators are simply not sophisticated enough to perform anything other than the direct conversion of the data files from one program's record format to another.

ISSUES AND LIMITATIONS

This scenario is a realistic picture of the type of methods of data file interchange currently occurring in business, a world in which the microcomputer has, until recently, been considered to be outside the data processing establishment. Thus, even in more progressive institutions, microcomputers are used as terminals to capture screen and printout data. These limitations belie the potential power of the microcomputer in this environment. To take the computational ability of an 80286- or an 80386-based computer and use it to run programs that enable it to emulate a dumb terminal or printer is less than efficient. Nevertheless, this is exactly what is being done.

Even in microcomputer-to-mainframe links that allow for file transfer, there are still considerable obstacles to overcome. Basically, it is highly unlikely that a mainframe file is of a form that can be easily utilized by a semi-sophisticated end-user. The mechanisms of the file transfer itself can be handled by hardware and software available off the shelf. Protocols like the 3780 RJE allow a remote site to request the transmission of a file (or list of files) down a communication line for storage on the remote site's hard disk. Such file transfer methodologies include excellent error checking, guaranteeing the integrity of the transmitted data. Even so, a number of disturbing questions need to be asked.

To illustrate the conceptual problems, consider a situation in which a large data file exists on a mainframe and a user needs to get the field, extract some data, and process it in some analysis to be defined by the user. The bank officer might think it would be a good idea to download the entire customer database from the host, then extract the necessary data.

The first problem comes from the mechanics of the download itself. The mainframe files are typically many megabytes in size. They are organized based on the software and operating system that was used to generate them. Suppose that the complete customer database on the mainframe contains all client data for all of the bank's branches, including historic information. It is not unreasonable to assume that such a file might be 10 megabytes in size. At 1200 baud, roughly 120 characters per second are transmitted, thus, the transfer of a 10-megabyte file will take roughly 83,333 seconds, or 23 hours.

Even if such transfer times were acceptable, the user would still have to analyze the file structure. If the file were binary, the situation would be nearly hopeless. If it were a text file, and the data interchange product had completed the EBCDIC to ASCII conversion, the user would still need to come up with a database management capable of processing his or her queries.

In the passive user interface mode, downloading mainframe files is futile, even if data communication enables such transfers. In the old days, when a file was sent to a 3780 RJE site, the remote had the same operating system and application software, so remote processing was reasonable. Sending an entire mainframe file to a microcomputer is just not philosophically sound. (Note that this argument needs to be adjusted in the case of systems in which the same or similar software products exist on both ends, as is the case for Focus and PC-Focus. These systems are discussed in Chapter 6.)

Because the definition of a passive user interface precludes the ability of the user to ask the host to "prepare" the downloaded file, this mode of operation will always contain these limitations.

Chapter 5

The Custom Programming Alternative

The solution to most communications problems is goal-oriented. Typically, a specific subset of information needs to be moved from one application to another in what is called a *production environment*. This is a euphemism for repetitive, day to day work.

For example, assume that there is some transaction data on a mainframe out of which some specific information needs to be extracted, sent to some other machine, reformatted, imported and processed for a report. Let's further insist that this process be completely transparent to the end-user, that he or she need not go through any of the complex machinations described in Chapter 4. A system needs to be set up by which this user can merely press a menu option key on a microcomputer to get the desired report. This scheme requires the intervention of a competent programmer to create the code on the various computers involved, in their native environments, so that the file interchange procedure can be less demanding on the end-user.

As already shown, this is far from trivial. The task itself must be divided into three specific components. First, a program must be written, on the host, to extract the desired data from the main data file and place it in a form that can be easily absorbed on the end-user side. These are still passive environments. For example, the user cannot go into dBASE and extract data from a mainframe database file. A user who had "interactive" status could make queries in terminal emulation mode, using a mainframe database management system, like System Query Language (SQL). In the passive mode, however, a user can only get what the mainframe has been set up to give. This new, specific, program will create a new data set for eventual downloading.

In a generic "structured" type of computer language, the host program could look like the one shown in Fig. 5-1. Such a routine would sequentially read through the main data file (MAIN.DAT) and print only those records where the variable E has the value "LOAN" to a text file called SEND.TXT.

This program could be queued to run once at the end of each day, so that the SEND.TXT file is the complete subset as of the end of the previous day's business. The use of a format statement in the mainframe program could "pre-process" the file so that only desired data is included in columnar fashion with no noncharacter codes. Even though this might be an EBCDIC file on the host, the downloading link, which is a combination of both hardware and software

```
        HEADER
/* Open a file (SEND.TXT) for output, call it file #1
                OPEN,"O","SEND.TXT",#1
/* Open a file (MAIN.DAT) for input, call it file #2
                OPEN,"I","MAIN.DAT",#2
/* Do the commands in theis loop until the end of file #2
                DO WHILE NOT EOF
/* Read from file #2 variable list A,B,C,D,E,F
                    INPUT #2,A,B,C,D,E,F
/* If variable E is the string "LOAN", print the data A,C,D,F to file # 1
                    IF E="LOAN"
/* Use the format described
                        PRINT #1,A,B,C,D,E,F  FORMAT###
/* End of If loop
                    ENDIF
/* End of DO loop
                ENDDO
/* Close all disk files
                CLOSE
/* End of program
```

Fig. 5-1. Generic program to extract data from host file.

on the microcomputer, typically does the EBCDIC to ASCII conversion "on the fly" (as the download occurs).

Thus, the file that arrives on the microcomputer's hard disk can be such that it is already a "flat" ASCII file ready for processing. A fragment of the

```
INV.OUT - Produced by Host Program

"10"00.000
"00070E4AA"00"CS070  2"        316"
""""0"0"0"
""""0.000"00
""""0.000"0
"10"00.000
"00070G4AA"00"CS070  3"        316"
""""0"0"0"
""""0.000"00
""""0.000"0
"10"00.000
"00070H4AA"00"CS070  4"        316"
""""0"0"0"
""""0.000"00
""""0.000"0
"10"00.000
"00070J4AA"00"CS070  6"        316"
""""0"0"0"
""""0.000"00
""""0.000"0
"10"00.000
"00080C4AA"00"CS080  1 1/2"  316"
""""0"0"0"
""""48.000"00
""""48.000"0
"10"00.000
"00080E4AA"00"CS080  2"        316"
""""0"0"0"
""""52.000"00
""""52.000"0
"10"00.000
"00080F4AA"00"CS080  2 1/2"  316"
""""0"0"0"
""""71.000"00
""""71.000"0
"10"00.000
"00080G4AA"00"CS080  3"        316"
""""0"0"0"
""""75.000"00
""""75.000"0
"10"00.000
"00080H4AA"00"CS080  4"        316"
""""0"0"0"
""""132.000"00
""""132.000"0

continued in right hand column....
```

```
INV.OUT - (Continued from left)

"10"00.000
"01502E1AA"00"1502  2"      X"
""""0"0"0"
""""87.780"00
""""87.780"0
"10"00.000
"01502G1AA"00"1502  3"      X"
""""0"0"0"
""""126.350"00
""""126.350"0
"10"00.000
"01502H1AA"00"1502  4"      X"
""""0"0"0"
""""146.300"00
""""146.300"0
"10"00.000
"01502J1AA"00"1502  6"      X"
""""0"0"0"
""""236.740"00
""""236.740"0
"10"00.000
"01502L1AA"00"1502  8"      X"
""""0"0"0"
""""372.400"00
""""372.400"0
"10"00.000
"01502M1AA"00"1502  10"     X"
""""0"0"0"
""""582.540"00
""""582.540"0
"10"00.000
"01502N1AA"00"1502  12"     X"
""""0"0"0"
""""775.390"00
""""775.390"0
"10"00.000
"01503G2DA"30"1503  3"      XU  S/40"
""""0"0"3"
""""139.650"00
""""139.650"0
"10"00.000
"01503H2DA"00"1503  4"      XU  S/40"
""""0"0"0"
""""162.260"00
""""162.260"0

end of data file fragment
```

Fig. 5-2. ASCII data file produced by host application program.

sample file, INV.OUT, is shown in Figure 5.2. This data is the ASCII file produced by some host computer inventory management system. There appears to be little sense to the pattern of information, and it should be obvious that an unsophisticated user would be unable to use the techniques discussed in Chapter 4 to reformat this file into anything that would be easy to import into dBASE or Lotus 1-2-3. The pattern appears to be cyclic, with five line clusters. Some of the variables are enclosed in quotes, while others appear to be numeric with decimal places. On the second line of each cluster, there is what might be an inventory identification number enclosed in quotes, followed by two zeros, and then what could be an item description field.

This example is made exceptionally difficult because the description includes the symbol for inches, which is the same quote character used to delineate character fields in most languages. The programmer would need to meet with the end-user to identify the field names, data types, and widths, so that code could be designed to process this complex array into meaningful data.

At this point, programs can be written in dBase, BASIC or whatever to perform all of the steps necessary to ingest the data into some final applications program. It is obvious that the custom programming alternative requires careful consideration as to design and implementation. A number of extremely useful development tools exist on the microcomputer side that could ease this process. These include programming languages, like Microsoft's QuickBASIC, as well as a wide variety of application packages that include file import and export functionality.

A seemingly complex source data file can be processed by a "hardcoded" BASIC program. This program was developed to process the sample file INV.OUT was written in QuickBASIC 2.0 by Microsoft. This environment is typical of the new user-friendly development systems available in the MS-DOS world. It is window-oriented, mouse driven (optional), and has the editor, debugger and compiler closely integrated to form a good user interface.

The programmer must examine the source file closely, in order to determine structural parameters, identify data fields, and develop a strategy for conversion. The BASIC program listed in Fig. 5-3 should be studied to understand how the data from the download file was read, processed, and reformatted.

```
10 REM ***************************************************************
*************
20 REM *
     *
30 REM *  OPEN SYSTEMS INVENTORY DATA TO DBASE III SDF FILE  02/0
2/86          *
40 REM *
     *
50 REM *  COPYRIGHT 1986, BODNER, HUTCHINS & ASSOCIATES, INC. HOU
STON, TX      *
```

Fig. 5-3. BASIC program to convert INV.OUT to INV.APP. (Continued through page 89.)

```
60 REM *
    *
70 REM ***********************************************************
*************
80 REM
90 COLOR 10,1:COUNT=0
100 LOCATE 11,14:PRINT"Converting Open System INVENTORY to dBase
III format"
110 LOCATE 17,16:PRINT"Copyright 1986, Bodner, Hutchins & Assoc.,
 Inc. "
120 LOCATE 13,12:PRINT"┌─────────────────────────────────────────
─────────────────┐"
130 LOCATE 14,12:PRINT"│ Figure #                    Inventory #
       Qty       │"
140 LOCATE 15,12:PRINT"└─────────────────────────────────────────
─────────────────┘"
150 WIDTH "LPT1:",132
160 OPEN "O",#2,"INV.APP"
170 DIM A$(13),B$(13),C$(14)
180 OPEN "I",#1,"INV.OUT"
190 IF EOF(1) THEN CLOSE #1:CLOSE #2:END
200 FOR I=1 TO 5
210 LINE INPUT #1,A$(I)
220 NEXT
230 B$(1)=MID$(A$(1),2,2)
240 B$(2)=RIGHT$(A$(1),LEN(A$(1))-4)
250 B$(4)=MID$(A$(2),2,9)
260 N=12:IF MID$(A$(2),12,1)=CHR$(34) THEN N=13:B$(4)=MID$(A$(2),
2,10)
270 FOR I=N+1 TO LEN(A$(2))
280 IF MID$(A$(2),I,1)=CHR$(34) THEN N=I:GOTO 300
290 NEXT:N=I
300 B$(5)=MID$(A$(2),12,N-13)
310 FOR I=LEN(A$(2)) TO N STEP-1
320 IF MID$(A$(2),I,1)=CHR$(34) THEN M=I:GOTO 340
330 NEXT
340 B$(6)=MID$(A$(2),N+1,M-N-1)
350 FOR I=4 TO LEN(A$(3))
360 IF MID$(A$(3),I,1)=CHR$(34) THEN N=I:GOTO 380
370 NEXT:N=I
380 B$(7)=MID$(A$(3),4,N-4)
390 IF LEFT$(B$(7),1)=CHR$(34) THEN B$(7)=RIGHT$(B$(7),LEN(B$(7))
-1)
400 FOR I=N+1 TO LEN(A$(3))
410 IF MID$(A$(3),I,1)=CHR$(34) THEN M=I:GOTO 430
420 NEXT:M=I
430 B$(8)=RIGHT$(A$(3),LEN(A$(3))-M)
440 B$(8)=LEFT$(B$(8),LEN(B$(8))-1)
450 IF RIGHT$(B$(8),1)="-" THEN B$(8)="-"+LEFT$(B$(8),LEN(B$(8))-
1)
460 FOR I=4 TO LEN(A$(4))
470 IF MID$(A$(4),I,1)=CHR$(34) THEN N=I:GOTO 490
480 NEXT:N=I
490 B$(9)=MID$(A$(4),4,N-4)
500 B$(10)=RIGHT$(A$(4),LEN(A$(4))-N-1)
510 FOR I=4 TO LEN(A$(5))
```

```
520 IF MID$(A$(5),I,1)=CHR$(34) THEN N=I:GOTO 540
530 NEXT:N=I
540 B$(11)=MID$(A$(5),4,N-4)
550 B2=VAL(B$(10))+VAL(B$(8))-VAL(B$(5))
560 B$(3)=STR$(B2):B$(3)=RIGHT$(B$(3),LEN(B$(3))-1)
570 B$(2)=RIGHT$(B$(2),LEN(B$(2))-LEN(B$(3)))
580 C$(1) =LEFT$(B$(1)+"                    ",2)
590 C$(12)=LEFT$(B$(2)+"                    ",11)
600 C$(6) =LEFT$(B$(3)+"                    ",4)
610 C$(2) =LEFT$(B$(4)+"                    ",12)
620 C$(7) =LEFT$(B$(5)+"                    ",4)
630 C$(3) =LEFT$(B$(6)+"                                                  ",25)
640 C$(8) =LEFT$(B$(7)+"                    ",4)
650 C$(4) =LEFT$(B$(8)+"                    ",4)
660 C$(9) =LEFT$(B$(9)+"                    ",11)
670 C$(5) =LEFT$(B$(10)+"                    ",4)
680 C$(10)=LEFT$(B$(11)+"                    ",11)
690 C$(11)="          "
700 C$(13)="            "
710 C$(14)="            "
720 IF LEFT$(C$(7),1)=CHR$(34) THEN C$(7)=RIGHT$(C$(7),LEN(C$(7))
-1)+" "
730 LN$=C$(1)+C$(2)+C$(3)+C$(4)+C$(5)+C$(6)+C$(7)+C$(8)+C$(9)+C$(
10)
740 LN$=LN$+C$(11)+C$(12)+C$(13)+C$(14)
750 LOCATE 14,24:PRINT LEFT$(C$(3),12):LOCATE 14,49:PRINT C$(2):L
OCATE 14,65:PRINT C$(8)
760 LOCATE 19,39:COUNT=COUNT+1:PRINT COUNT
770 PRINT #2,LN$
780 GOTO 190
```

This program uses pure IBM BASICA syntax, and was compiled using the MicroSoft QuickBASIC Compiler. Look at the data file INV.OUT. It is delimited with variable length fields containing numbers and characters. The records are multiline. A strategic design needs to be developed that makes sense out of the data file pattern to identify data fields, field widths, and data types. In BASIC, a programmer needs to set up dimension statements, open the fields in various formats for reading and writing, and do the character manipulations. The output of this program, a data file called INV.APP, is shown in Fig. 5-4. Notice that the data is now in a flat ASCII format and is row-oriented, much as the file BANK3.TXT used in Chapter 4.

The final step in the process is the APPENDing in SDF format into dBASE. The program listing INV.PRG (Fig. 5-5) shows a menu-driven user interface for accomplishing this final function in a transparent manner. The imported data file is displayed under the BROWSE command in Fig. 5-6 and the EDIT feature in Fig. 5-7, and has its structure displayed in Fig. 5-8.

The output file INV.APP can be processed in several ways because other microcomputer products with file import and translation utilities are available. The problems involved in the gross translation process can, of course, be overcome in the custom programming approach.

```
1000070E4AA  CS070  2"      316       0   0   0   0   0   0.000     0.000     0.000
1000070G4AA  CS070  3"      316       0   0   0   0   0   0.000     0.000     0.000
1000070H4AA  CS070  4"      316       0   0   0   0   0   0.000     0.000     0.000
1000070J4AA  CS070  6"      316       0   0   0   0   0   0.000     0.000     0.000
1000080C4AA  CS080  1 1/2"  316       0   0   0   0   0   48.000    48.000    0.000
1000080E4AA  CS080  2"      316       0   0   0   0   0   52.000    52.000    0.000
1000080F4AA  CS080  2 1/2"  316       0   0   0   0   0   71.000    71.000    0.000
1000080G4AA  CS080  3"      316       0   0   0   0   0   75.000    75.000    0.000
1000080H4AA  CS080  4"      316       0   0   0   0   0   132.000   132.000   0.000
1001502E1AA  1502  2"      X          0   0   0   0   0   87.780    87.780    0.000
1001502G1AA  1502  3"      X          0   0   0   0   0   126.350   126.350   0.000
1001502H1AA  1502  4"      X          0   0   0   0   0   146.300   146.300   0.000
1001502J1AA  1502  6"      X          0   0   0   0   0   236.740   236.740   0.000
1001502L1AA  1502  8"      X          0   0   0   0   0   372.400   372.400   0.000
1001502M1AA  1502  10"     X          0   0   0   0   0   582.540   582.540   0.000
1001502N1AA  1502  12"     X          0   0   0   0   0   775.390   775.390   0.000
1001503G2DA  1503  3"      XU  S/40   3   0   0   3   0   139.650   139.650   0.000
1001503H2DA  1503  4"      XU  S/40   0   0   0   0   0   162.260   162.260   0.000
1001503J2DA  1503  6"      XU  S/40   0   0   0   0   0   263.340   263.340   0.000
1001512E1AA  1512  2"      X          57  80  12  125 150 88.570    87.851    0.000
1001512E2AA  1512  2"      XU         49  0   0   49  0   97.430    97.430    0.000
1001512E4AA  1512  2"      L          7   0   0   7   6   105.860   8.822     667.000
1001512F1AA  1512  2 1/2"  X          15  12  2   25  25  127.140   127.031   646.000
1001512G1AA  1512  3"      X          131 71  13  189 230 127.130   71.412    646.000
1001512G2AA  1512  3"      XU         3   0   0   3   0   140.250   140.250   0.000
1001512G4AA  1512  3"      L          2   11  0   13  17  151.620   151.669   934.000
1001512H1AA  1512  4"      X          78  109 30  157 150 147.030   147.030   754.000
1001512H2AA  1512  4"      XU         9   0   0   9   0   162.390   162.390   0.000
1001512H4AA  1512  4"      L          0   15  0   15  15  176.290   176.290   1102.00
1001512I1AA  1512  5"      X          0   11  4   7   7   236.740   236.829   1219.00
1001512J1AA  1512  6"      X          31  118 47  102 100 236.740   236.740   1219.00
1001512J2AA  1512  6"      XU         0   5   5   0   0   0.000     0.000     0.000
1001512J4AA  1512  6"      L          6   2   0   8   10  284.620   0.000     1762.00
1001512J5AA  1512  6"      B          0   20  20  0   0   237.590   237.590   0.000
1001512L1AA  1512  8"      X          50  12  29  33  60  372.710   301.556   1910.00
1001512L2AA  1512  8"      XU         0   2   2   0   0   0.000     0.000     0.000
1001512L4AA  1512  8"      L          0   8   2   6   6   447.190   447.190   2761.00
1001512L5AA  1512  8"      B          0   15  15  0   0   372.710   372.710   0.000
```

Fig. 5-4. ASCII data file produced by INV.BAS.

```
* ------------------------------------------------------------------
-------------
*
* Program:              INV.PRG
* System:               Sample Inventory Database
* Programmer:           Michael Simon Bodner
* Written:              01/20/86
* Revised By:           Michael Simon Bodner
* Revision Date:        01/25/86
*
* ------------------------------------------------------------------
-------------
*
* Comments:             This is the main program for the INV system
*
* ------------------------------------------------------------------
-------------
*
* Calls:                INVGO,INVADD,INVGET,INVIO,INVRPT
*
* ------------------------------------------------------------------
-------------
IF ISCOLOR()
 SET COLOR to W/ , /W
 CLEAR
 SET COLOR to GR+/B,R+/
ELSE
 CLEAR
ENDIF
IF CLIPPER
 STORE SPACE(4096) TO SCREEN1
ENDIF
SELECT 1
USE INVENTORY INDEX INV,CA
STORE .T. TO MMOR
CALL_PRG='INV'
DO WHILE MMOR
   STORE ' ' TO MCMD
   IF HLPFLG=0
   @ 4,12 SAY DATE()
   @ 4,63 SAY MREV
   @ 2,26 SAY '    Inventory Database System    '
   @ 3,26 SAY '███████████████████████████████████'
    @ 5,12 GET ML1
    @ 6,12 GET ML2
    @ 7,12 GET ML3
    @ 8,12 SAY '|
         |'
```

Fig. 5-5. dBASE III program to import INV.APP to INVENTORY.DBF. (Continued through page 94.)

```
  @ 9,12 SAY '|                (A)dd new item into Inventory Databas
e           |'
 @ 10,12 SAY '|
            |'
 @ 11,12 SAY '|                (G)et/Edit existing Inventory Data
            |'
 @ 12,12 SAY '|
            |'
 @ 13,12 SAY '|                (R)un Reports
            |'
 @ 14,12 SAY '|
            |'
 @ 15,12 SAY '|                (I)mport Open Systems Inventory File
            |'
 @ 16,12 SAY '|
            |'
 @ 17,12 SAY '|                (E)xit to Main System Menu
            |'
 @ 18,12 SAY '|
            |'
 @ 19,12 GET ML4
 @ 20,12 GET ML5
 @ 21,12 GET ML6
 CLEAR GETS
 ELSE
  HLPFLG=0
 ENDIF
 @ 20,63 GET MCMD
 @ 22,62 SAY TIME()
 @ 22,12 SAY MDAYNAME
 READ
 IF CLIPPER
    CALL _scrsave WITH SCREEN1
    SAVE SCREEN
 ENDIF
 DO CASE
    CASE UPPER(MCMD)='I'
    SELECT INVENTORY
    IL1='┌──────────────────────────────────────────────────
──┐'
    IL2='|  Are you really sure that you want to do this (Y/N)?
 |'
    IL3='└──────────────────────────────────────────────────
──┘'
    @ 12,12 GET IL1
    @ 13,12 GET IL2
    @ 14,12 GET IL3
    CLEAR GETS
    MANS=' '
    DO WHILE MANS<>'Y' .AND. MANS<>'N'
```

```
      @ 13,67 GET MANS
      READ
      MANS=UPPER(MANS)
      ENDDO MANS
      IF MANS='Y'
         IL2='|  Now importing Inventory files - DO NOT DISTURB !
!!!   |'
         @ 12,12 GET IL1
         @ 13,12 GET IL2
         @ 14,12 GET IL3
         CLEAR GETS
         IF CLIPPER
            SAVE SCREEN
         ENDIF
         ! INV
         IF CLIPPER
            RESTORE SCREEN
         ENDIF
         SELECT INVENTORY
         ZAP
         IL2='|  Now restructuring Inventory   - DO NOT DISTURB !
!!!   |'
         @ 12,12 GET IL1
         @ 13,12 GET IL2
         @ 14,12 GET IL3
         CLEAR GETS
         APPEND FROM INV.APP SDF
         IL2='|  Now REINDEXING Inventory files - DO NOT DISTURB
!!!!  |'
         @ 13,12 GET IL2
         CLEAR GETS
         SELECT INVENTORY
         INDEX ON INVENUMBER TO INV
         INDEX ON CATEGORY TO CA
         SELECT 1
         USE INVENTORY INDEX INV,CA
       ENDIF MANS
         IF CLIPPER
            CALL _scrrest WITH SCREEN1
         ELSE
            CLEAR
         ENDIF
         RELEASE IL1,IL2,IL3,MANS
         LOOP
      CASE UPPER(MCMD)='A'
         CALL_PRG='NUL'
         DO INVADD
         IF CLIPPER
            CALL _scrrest WITH SCREEN1
         ELSE
```

```
            CLEAR
         ENDIF
         LOOP
      CASE UPPER(MCMD)='G'
         CALL_PRG='GET'
         DO INVGET
         HELPFLG=0
         CALL_PRG='INV'
         IF CLIPPER
            CALL _scrrest WITH SCREEN1
         ELSE
            CLEAR
         ENDIF
         LOOP
      CASE UPPER(MCMD)='R'
         CALL_PRG='RPT'
         HELPFLG=1
         DO INVRPT
         IF CLIPPER
            CALL _scrrest WITH SCREEN1
         ELSE
            CLEAR
         ENDIF
         CALL_PRG='INV'
         LOOP
      CASE UPPER(MCMD)='H'
         DO HELP
         LOOP
      CASE UPPER(MCMD)='E'
         CLEAR
         RETURN
   ENDCASE
ENDDO
```

APPLICATION DISTRIBUTION

Another alternative to the multistep manual translation or data interchange process is the distribution of the application process itself. A process can be created in which a set of dBASE or Lotus 1-2-3 programs are written to allow unsophisticated end-users (not versed in either dBASE or Lotus) to run the applications. The high level programmer writes a process that takes the data from source to a target format using only custom code. This code performs all translation and conversion functions, and yields a direct logical path from host process to final result.

Such things can be accomplished in the dBASE world via the use of compilers, such as Nantucket's Clipper or WordTech's QuickSilver. Compilers take the source code that would normally run under the interpreted dBASE III PLUS package, and turn it into executable programs that do not require dBASE. These programs can be user-friendly, and force the end-user into a limited set

```
CATEGORY INVENUMBER-- FIGURENUMB--------------- QTYONHAND QTYONORDER QTYSOLD
10       01502H1AA    1502  4"        X                 0          0       0
10       01502J1AA    1502  6"        X                 0          0       0
10       01502L1AA    1502  8"        X                 0          0       0
10       01502M1AA    1502  10"       X                 0          0       0
10       01502N1AA    1502  12"       X                 0          0       0
10       01503G2DA    1503  3"        XU  S/40          3          0       0
10       01503H2DA    1503  4"        XU  S/40          0          0       0
10       01503J2DA    1503  6"        XU  S/40          0          0       0
10       01512E1AA    1512  2"        X                57         80      12
10       01512E2AA    1512  2"        XU               49          0       0
10       01512E4AA    1512  2"        L                 7          0       0
10       01512F1AA    1512  2 1/2"    X                15         12       2
10       01512G1AA    1512  3"        X               131         71      13
10       01512G2AA    1512  3"        XU                3          0       0
10       01512G4AA    1512  3"        L                 2         11       0
10       01512H1AA    1512  4"        X                78        109      30
10       01512H2AA    1512  4"        XU                9          0       0

BROWSE        |<D:>|INVENTOR           |Rec: 12/673        |      |
                          View and edit fields.
```

Fig. 5-6. dBASE III Browse screen for INVENTORY.DBF after import.

```
CATEGORY    10
INVENUMBER  01502H1AA
FIGURENUMB  1502  4"        X
QTYONHAND      0
QTYONORDER     0
QTYSOLD        0
AVAILTOSEL     0
TARGET         0
LASTCOST          146.30
AVGCOST           146.30
DISCOUNT    0.0000
LISTPRICE           0.00
ITEMWEIGHT     0.00
CUBICFEET      0.00

EDIT          |<D:>|INVENTOR           |Rec: 12/673        |      |
```

Fig. 5-7. dBASE III Edit screen for INVENTORY.DBF after import.

```
Structure for database: D:INVENTOR.dbf
Number of data records:      673
Date of last update   : 03/03/86
Field  Field Name  Type       Width    Dec
    1  CATEGORY    Character      2
    2  INVENUMBER  Character     12
    3  FIGURENUMB  Character     25
    4  QTYONHAND   Numeric        4
    5  QTYONORDER  Numeric        4
    6  QTYSOLD     Numeric        4
    7  AVAILTOSEL  Numeric        4
    8  TARGET      Numeric        4
    9  LASTCOST    Numeric       11      2
   10  AVGCOST     Numeric       11      2
   11  DISCOUNT    Numeric        6      4
   12  LISTPRICE   Numeric       11      2
   13  ITEMWEIGHT  Numeric        7      2
   14  CUBICFEET   Numeric        7      2
** Total **                     113

Command Line     |<D:>|INVENTOR                 |Rec: 12/673      |      |
                   Enter a dBASE III PLUS command.
```

Fig. 5-8. dBASE III Display Structure screen for INVENTORY.DBF.

of actions. They can be menu-driven, error trapping, data validation programs, producing only the desired output.

There is even a product known as a "menu-driven program converter" that converts Lotus 1-2-3 worksheet files into BASIC source code programs. This remarkable program is called The Baler, and is sold by Brubaker Software. When the BASIC source program is compiled, it can precisely emulate the functions of the Lotus 1-2-3 template that was used to create it. Thus, end-users do not need to run a copy of 1-2-3 in order to run the application, and also need not know any Lotus commands. Corporate users can therefore legally run multiple copies of Lotus 1-2-3 applications without the need for multiple copies of the spreadsheet itself.

It is even possible for the programmers to "tweak," or optimize, the BASIC code to enhance its performance or add features not normally found in Lotus 1-2-3. The extension of capabilities is one of the main reasons that so many programmers use the dBASE compilers. Those products allow for the use of C and Assembler modules in the compiled dBASE applications code, thus adding functionality to that environment as well. The compiled dBASE and "Baled" Lotus applications also run faster, because they are executable files rather than interpreted commands running under another program.

DIRECT CREATION OF TARGET FILES

In one extremely powerful custom programming scheme, programmers write code in their own programs that actually build the output files in the native format of the target applications. This is possible if the programmers have access to the exact file structures required. It will be easier to follow this discussion with an example. Figure 5-9 is a capture screen showing a fragment of a Paradox file called APDIS01.DB. As has already been discussed, Paradox can import and export data files to and from foreign formats.

In this case, Paradox will be considered the source process, and an Export to a DIF format will be chosen. A detailed analysis of the resulting DIF file is given in Fig. 5-10. This table gives the structure and explanation of each of the elements in the DIF file, as well as the DIF "standard" definitions. Notice that the DIF structure is cyclic in triads. The meaning of the data in each sequential triad is governed by the standard.

The next table, Fig. 5-11, shows a detailed structure listing for the dBASE

Paradox Data Table used to produce sample DIF, DBF, PFS, ASCII, and WKS Files

Viewing Apdis01 table: Record 1 of 1180 Main

APDIS01	Fvendno	Finvnum	Finvdate	Faccno	Foldid	Famount
1	87100	603702	02/06/87	20000-00	Y	(54.68)
2	87100	603702	02/06/87	50700-01	Y	54.68
3	87100	804003	02/09/87	20000-00	Y	(21.00)
4	87100	804003	02/09/87	50700-10	Y	21.00
5	87100	405504	02/24/87	20000-00	Y	(49.92)
6	87100	405504	02/24/87	50700-15	Y	49.92
7	87100	0905801	02/27/87	20000-00	Y	(21.48)
8	87100	0905801	02/27/87	50700-09	Y	21.48
9	87100	405823	02/27/87	20000-00	Y	(73.48)
10	87100	405823	02/27/87	50700-15	Y	73.48
11	87100	506521	03/06/87	20000-00	Y	(59.84)
12	87100	506521	03/06/87	50700-07	Y	59.84
13	87100	606511/ld	03/06/87	20000-00	Y	(29.53)
14	87100	606511/ld	03/06/87	50700-20	Y	.73
15	87100	606511/ld	03/06/87	50000-20	Y	28.80
16	87100	307516	03/12/87	20000-00	Y	(70.28)
17	87100	307516	03/12/87	50700-05	Y	70.28
18	87100	P907501	03/16/87	20000-00	Y	(30.52)
19	87100	P907501	03/16/87	50700-09	Y	30.52
20	87100	5408305	03/24/87	20000-00	Y	(80.44)
21	87100	5408305	03/24/87	50700-15	Y	80.44
22	87100	33087	03/30/87	20000-00	1180 records converted	

Fig. 5-9. Paradox screen showing table APDIS01.DB.

DIF File	Explanation of data in DIF File	DIF Standard
TABLE 0,1 "APDIS01"	First entry in DIF Header {Vector}=0 [entire file], {Version}=1 Title of File	TABLE 0,{Version#} "<title>"
VECTORS 0,6 ""	Vector Count There are 6 vectors (Columns) in file	VECTORS 0,{Count} ""
TUPLES 0,1180 ""	Tupple Count There are 1180 Tupples (Rows/Records)	TUPLES 0,{Count} ""
LABEL 1,0 "Fvendno"	The label of the first vector = Fvendno	LABEL Vector#,Line# "<Label>"
LABEL 2,0 "Finvnum"	The label of the second vector = Finvnum	LABEL Vector#,Line# "<Label>"
LABEL 3,0 "Finvdate"	The label of the third vector = Finvdate	LABEL Vector#,Line# "<Label>"
LABEL 4,0 "Faccno"	The label of the fourth vector = Faccno	LABEL Vector#,Line# "<Label>"
LABEL 5,0 "Foldid"	The label of the fifth vector = Foldid	LABEL Vector#,Line# "<Label>"
LABEL 6,0 "Famount"	The label of the sixth vector = Famount	LABEL Vector#,Line# "<Label>"
DATA 0,0 ""	Marks begining of DIF Data section	DATA 0,0 ""
-1,0 BOT 1,0 "87100" 1,0 "603702" 1,0 "02/06/87" 1,0 "20000-00" 1,0 "Y" 0,-54.68 V	{Special Data Value}=-1, BOT or EOD Beginning of Tupple {SDV}=1, String value="87100" {SDV}=0,"V" implies value=-54.68	type indicator,val string Type=-1 BOT = 0 Number = 1 String

-1,0 BOT 1,0 "87100" 1,0 "603702" 1,0 "02/06/87" 1,0 "50700-01" 1,0 "Y" 0,54.68 V	Beginning of next Tupple	

Fig. 5-10. Data interchange format for file APDIS01.DIF.

<table>
<tr><th colspan="4">dBase III Plus Data File Structure</th></tr>
<tr><td>Byte</td><td>Information</td><td colspan="2">Comments</td></tr>
<tr><td>0</td><td>Version Number</td><td colspan="2">03h --> no .DBT (memo) file associated
83h --> a memo file exists</td></tr>
<tr><td>1-3</td><td>Last Update</td><td colspan="2">Date of last file update (YYMMDD)</td></tr>
<tr><td>4-7</td><td>Number of Records</td><td colspan="2">32-bit number</td></tr>
<tr><td>8-9</td><td>Header Length</td><td colspan="2">2-byte integer (length of header structure)</td></tr>
<tr><td>10-11</td><td>Record Length</td><td colspan="2">2-byte integer (length of each data record)</td></tr>
<tr><td>12-31</td><td>RESERVED</td><td colspan="2">Reserved by Ashton-Tate for future use</td></tr>
<tr><td rowspan="8">32-n</td><td rowspan="8">Field Descriptors</td><td colspan="2">Array of 32-byte descriptors, one for each data field that makes up the record. Each record may have as many as 128 fields. The Field Descriptor structure is:</td></tr>
<tr><td>Byte</td><td></td></tr>
<tr><td>0-10</td><td>Field Name (ASCII), or NULLS (00h)</td></tr>
<tr><td>11</td><td>Field Type (Char,Num,Logic,Memo,Date)</td></tr>
<tr><td>12-15</td><td>Field Data Address (32-bit mem. addr)</td></tr>
<tr><td>16</td><td>Field Length</td></tr>
<tr><td>17</td><td>Field Decimal Count, if Numeric Type</td></tr>
<tr><td>18-21</td><td>RESERVED</td></tr>
<tr><td>n + 1</td><td>Carriage Return</td><td colspan="2">0Dh --> Field Terminator</td></tr>
</table>

Fig. 5-11. dBASE III detailed file structure.

III database files. With such a listing, a programmer could construct the file in an external language like C or QuickBASIC. The resulting file would look to the application program exactly like one produced within its own environment. It would thus be possible to sidestep the translate or import step. The custom program could, on its own, create a DIF, dBASE III, Lotus, or any target file if the programmer has adhered to the structure for that file format. To further illustrate this concept, a code fragment written in BASIC is provided in Fig. 5-12.

```
2430 REM *******************************************************
************
2440 REM * CREATE DBASE DBF HEADER  FILE WITH NF AND SNF FIELDNAM
ES          *
2450 REM *
            *
2460 REM *******************************************************
************
2470 FOR I= 1 TO 64:DTLN$(I)="00":DTND$(I)="00":NEXT
2480 DB$(1)="03"
2490 DB$(2)=RIGHT$(DATE$,2)
2500 DB$(3)=LEFT$(DATE$,2)
2510 DB$(4)=MID$(DATE$,4,2)
2520 FOR I=5 TO 8:DB$(I)="00":NEXT
2530 FD$=LEFT$(FL$+"        ",8)+".DBF"
2540 FOR I= 1 TO NF STEP 3
2550 IF I=1 THEN KI=1:GOTO 2630
2560 IF I=4 THEN KI=2:GOTO 2630
2570 IF I=7 THEN KI=3:GOTO 2630
2580 IF I=10 THEN KI=4:GOTO 2630
2590 IF I=13 THEN KI=5:GOTO 2630
2600 IF I=16 THEN KI=6:GOTO 2630
2610 IF I=19 THEN KI=7:GOTO 2630
2620 IF I=22 THEN KI=8
2630 DTAF$(I)=F1$(1,KI):DTAF$(I+1)=F1$(2,KI):DTAF$(I+2)=F1$(3,KI)
2640 DTTP$(I)=TP1$(1,KI):DTTP$(I+1)=TP1$(2,KI):DTTP$(I+2)=TP1$(3,
KI)
2650 DTLN$(I)=STR$(WDT(1,KI)):DTLN$(I+1)=STR$(WDT(2,KI)):DTLN$(I+
2)=STR$(WDT(3,KI))
2660 IF DTTP$(I)="F" OR DTTP$(I)="I" THEN DTND$(I)=STR$(DP1(1,KI)
)
2670 IF DTTP$(I+1)="F" OR DTTP$(I+1)="I" THEN DTND$(I+1)=STR$(DP1
(2,KI))
2680 IF DTTP$(I+2)="F" OR DTTP$(I+2)="I" THEN DTND$(I+2)=STR$(DP1
(3,KI))
2690 NEXT I
2700 FOR I= 1 TO NF:IF DTTP$(I)="I" OR DTTP$(I)="F" THEN DTTP$(I)
="N"
2710 IF DTTP$(I)="D" THEN DTTP$(I)="C":DTLN$(I)="8"
```

Fig. 5-12. BASIC code to create dBASE III file header structure. (Continued through page 102.)

```
2720 NEXT:M=I-1
2730 FOR I= 1 TO SNF STEP 3
2740 IF I=1 THEN KI=9:GOTO 2780
2750 IF I=4 THEN KI=10:GOTO 2780
2760 IF I=7 THEN KI=11:GOTO 2780
2770 IF I=10 THEN KI=12
2780 DTAF$(I+M)=F1$(1,KI):DTAF$(I+M+1)=F1$(2,KI):DTAF$(I+M+2)=F1$
(3,KI)
2790 DTTP$(I+M)=TP1$(1,KI):DTTP$(I+M+1)=TP1$(2,KI):DTTP$(I+M+2)=T
P1$(3,KI)
2800 DTLN$(I+M)=STR$(WDT(1,KI)):DTLN$(I+M+1)=STR$(WDT(2,KI)):DTLN
$(I+M+2)=STR$(WDT(3,KI))
2810 IF DTTP$(I+M)="F" OR DTTP$(I+M)="I" THEN DTND$(I+M)=STR$(DP1
(1,KI))
2820 IF DTTP$(I+M+1)="F" OR DTTP$(I+M+1)="I" THEN DTND$(I+M+1)=ST
R$(DP1(2,KI))
2830 IF DTTP$(I+M+2)="F" OR DTTP$(I+M+2)="I" THEN DTND$(I+M+2)=ST
R$(DP1(3,KI))
2840 NEXT I
2850 FOR I= 1 TO SNF:IF DTTP$(I+M)="I" OR DTTP$(I+M)="F" THEN DTT
P$(I+M)="N"
2860 IF DTTP$(I+M)="D" THEN DTTP$(I+M)="C":DTLN$(I+M)="8"
2870 NEXT
2880 LH=2+(32*(NF+NF+1)):LHH=INT(LH/256):LHL=LH-LHH*256
2890 DB$(9)=STR$(LHL)
2900 DB$(10)=STR$(LHH)
2910 FOR I=1 TO NF+SNF:NDATA=NDATA+VAL(DTLN$(I)):NEXT:NDATA=NDATA
+1
2920 NDH=INT(NDATA/256):NDL=NDATA-NDH*256
2930 DB$(11)=STR$(NDL):DB$(12)=STR$(NDH)
2940 FOR I=13 TO 32:DB$(I)="00":NEXT
2950 OPEN FD$ FOR OUTPUT AS #2
2960 FOR I=1 TO 32:PRINT #2,CHR$(VAL(DB$(I)));:NEXT
2970 FOR F=1 TO NF+SNF
2980 FOR L=1 TO 11:IF MID$(DTAF$(F),L,1)=" " THEN LK=L:GOTO 3000
2990 NEXT:LK=11
3000 FOR I=1 TO LK-1:DB$(I)=STR$(ASC(MID$(DTAF$(F),I,1))):NEXT
3010 FOR I=LK TO 11:DB$(I)="00":NEXT
3020 DB$(12)=STR$(ASC(DTTP$(F))):REM ASC OF TYPE
3030 DB$(13)=STR$(15+VAL(DTLN$(F-1)))
3040 DB$(14)="00"
3050 DB$(15)="00"
3060 DB$(16)="00"
3070 DB$(17)=DTLN$(F):REM ASC OF LENGTH
3080 DB$(18)="00":REM:IF DB$(12)<>"78" THEN 2610
3090 DB$(18)=DTND$(F):REM ASC OF NUMBER DEC
3100 FOR I=19 TO 32:DB$(I)="00":NEXT
3110 FOR I=1 TO 32:PRINT #2,CHR$(VAL(DB$(I)));:DB$(I)="00":NEXT
3120 NEXT F
```

```
3130 DB$(((SNF+NF+1)*32)+1)="13":DB$(((SNF+NF+1)*32)+2)="00"
3140 FOR I=((NF+SNF+1)*32)+1 TO ((SNF+NF+1)*32)+2:PRINT #2,CHR$(V
AL(DB$(I)));:NEXT
3150 CLOSE #2:RETURN
3160 OPEN FD$ FOR INPUT AS #2
3170 IF EOF(2) THEN 3220
3180 A=A+1
3190 DB$=INPUT$(1,#2)
3200 DB$(A)=RIGHT$("00"+HEX$(ASC(DB$)),2):IF ASC(DB$)=13 THEN 322
0
3210 GOTO 3170
3220  CLOSE #2:FOR I=1 TO A:PRINT DB$(I);" ";:IF INT(I/16)=I/16 T
HEN PRINT
3230  NEXT:PRINT
3240 RETURN
```

The BASIC language has the ability to write text files using the following syntax:

```
OPEN "O", #1, "TEST.TXT"
```

This command OPENs the file TEST.TXT for output and gives it the file designation number 1. As long as this file is open, any ASCII character code can be "printed" to the file in a sequential manner via the following command syntax:

```
PRINT #1, A$;
```

A$ is a string variable containing the data to be printed to the file, and the semicolon tells BASIC not to issue a carriage return/line feed. Using this syntax in BASIC, it is possible to create any possible file structure.

The above program fragment creates the header for a dBASE III file exactly as required by the dBASE III data file format. The program must decide what the values for the bytes in the header are to be. If no memo fields are to be used, the first byte written to the disk file will be a 03 hexadecimal. Then the current date must be recoded so that it goes from the form 06/12/87 to a sequence of six bytes containing the hexadecimal values for 8,7,0,6,1, and 2. The number of records can be set to zero, because none exist yet. Information as to record length, header length, field description names, types, and widths, must all be calculated, converted to hexadecimal, and "printed" to the disk file. This is by no means the only way in which this dBASE header can be constructed, but the fundamental principles are requisite in any program in any language.

The process for any custom programming solution is structured as follows:

- ☐ On the host, create programs, queries, or procedures to produce a "usable" output file.
- ☐ Analyze this file, identifying field locations, types, and widths as data.
- ☐ Write a program (or programs) to decipher source file, select desired data for target files, and create the output files in the format that is most efficient for your target application program.

The power of these customized programs are obvious. They can make the interapplication data file interchange automatic in the case where neither the source data files nor the needs of the target applications remain unchanged. If, for any reason, the host application rearranges its output file, or the end-user wants different data extracted, the customized interchange programs must be rewritten, retested, and reinstalled. This is far from acceptable in an ever-changing world.

Each logical interapplication data file interchange pair requires a unique custom program. Thus, if there is one host data file, out of which several different departments in a company require different data subsets for various target applications, the programming support required could rapidly get out of hand. There needs to be some way to easily allow even passive users to extract the data they need and to format it to the target applications of their choice with a minimum of data processing department programming. Such a method will be discussed in Chapter 8.

Chapter 6

Products That Span the Gap

Imagine, if you would, a perfect world. One in which everyone spoke the same language, used the same money, drove on the same side of the road, and shared the same philosophy. Wouldn't it be nice if such a thing came to pass! In the world of information interchange, the Tower of Babel effect has been shown to be an incredible hindrance to the efficient exchange of data. The converse of the Tower of Babel, an egalitarian, unified, method of information exchange, would be an excellent model to strive for.

In some respects the computer world is stratified by processor size. Microcomputer users develop programs in completely different languages and operating systems than do the users of minicomputers and mainframes. On the mainframe, the operating systems and database management systems were designed from the outset to be multiuser architectures with error recovery integrated into the foundation of the system. Thus, mainframe systems can protect files better than microcomputers can, and in the event of file corruption, can automatically reconstruct data files.

Mainframe database management systems (DBMS) exist, such as DB2, Focus, and Oracle, that contain much richer query and reporting capabilities than their microcomputer market competitors, like dBASE III. In recent years, some of these mainframe products have been "brought down" to microcomputers. This development provides a unique opportunity for a system to be constructed in which a single operating environment can exist across computer boundaries. A microcomputer user can access the mainframe data files interactively, using the same language and syntax as a mainframe user on a terminal.

In such cases, a broad range of previously insurmountable issues merely disappear. File compatibility replaces the need for file conversion and data translation. Data integrity and file recoverability can be maintained exactly in the same way as it is in the mainframe environment. Data can move bidirectionally (being both uploaded and downloaded), letting the DBMS manage concurrency and update issues. All data can be up-to-the-minute, correct, and useful.

The philosophical difference between microcomputer and mini/mainframe database management systems is vast. In the latter, the DBMS does all of the concurrency and file recovery in a manner that is almost transparent to the programmer. Microcomputer products provide all of the tools, such as record locking commands, but require each application developer to write new code each time to use these commands. Therefore, most microcomputer applications developers do not write concurrency and error-recovery control systems. It is worthwhile, therefore, to consider some of the "down-ported" DBMSs in the microcomputer environment.

A partial list of such products include Oracle, Focus and Informix. Other system query language (SQL) products are also beginning to arrive. System query language is about to become the cross-generational standard DBMS language; it is already widespread in the mainframe world. Microcomputer products like dBSQL and SQLBase are merely the first of the entries in this area. Future versions of dBASE are promised to include SQL support. With a standardized query language, users can extract information from a variety of systems in a comfortable and generic manner.

CONCURRENCY

When evaluating concurrency, it is necessary to understand the kinds of things that can happen in multiuser systems. At any time, any number of users can get various levels of access to different records in the data files. In such systems, two users might try to update the same record at the same time. As a result, the second user to write to the file will overwrite the first user's data. To prevent this, a good DBMS automatically issues locks. But what kind? What about database indexes? Automatic locking must be synchronized to all index files and related database files (and all of their index files) as well. The problem gets exponentially complex. Should the second user to be granted access have read-only rights, or simply be told that the record is in use?

File Locking

As an example, assume that a multiuser inventory control system is running on a LAN. Two salespeople wish to sell a product at the same time. Before the first salesperson, Sam, pulls up the record, there are five units in inventory, and five units listed in the record. Sam tells his customer that he can ship the four units that he needs at once. During that phone conversation, a second salesperson, Sue, pulls up the same record. Because no transaction has occurred, she also thinks that five units are available for sale. She quickly takes three units for her customer, leaving only two available for Sam. Depending on the sophistication of the software, Sam's screen might beep to show the update by the other user, but that is unlikely, because the DBMS tools on the microcomputer level are not that good. Sue gets her three units, and Sam might still try to pull his four, leaving the final update with one remaining. The integrity of the record is now at question, because seven units have been sold, out of only five on hand, and the computer still thinks that there is one unit available to sell. The well-known "computer messed up" telephone call will have to be made, as well as inventory adjustment entries.

To avoid this, the second user should not have been allowed any access, or all five units should have been "reserved" for Sam while he held the record. This is hard to do in dBASE code, but transparent in mainframe DBMSs. Products like IBM's DB2 have three types of locks:

- ☐ Exclusive
- ☐ Intent to update
- ☐ Nonexclusive

If Sam had issued an intent-to-update lock, Sue would have had to wait until the lock had cleared. She would have found only one unit left available to sell, shipped it, and created a backorder for the other two that her customer needed. All would be well. If the DBMS is smart enough, it can take care of all of these issues automatically. There is almost no way that single-user microcomputer DBMSs with record-locking tools can be programmed to be as easy to use as their "big brothers."

Deadly Embraces

Another issue of concurrency control is the need to prevent "deadly embraces." This is when two tasks, T1 and T2, lock out records R1 and R2 respectively. T1 then requests R2, which is locked by T2. T2 at the same time requests R1, which is held by T1. Each task will wait until the locked record is cleared, which will never happen because both parties are involved in this embrace, so the process is locked forever. A DBMS with concurrency control handles this by terminating one of the tasks and clearing its lock after a sufficient amount of time has passed to indicate the existence of a deadly embrace. It then requests the terminated task and processing continues.

In most microcomputer-based LANs, concurrency control is made considerably more difficult because there is no central control entity that can decide concurrency logic. Most LANs are "file server" architectures in which each node must maintain its own concurrency control logic without any communication to other DBMSs on the LAN.

The new IBM OS/2 SQL DBMS uses what is called a database server, which controls all locking and recovery control itself while the applications run at the nodes. Because there is only one copy of the DBMS, and it is in complete control of all transactions, there is higher data integrity and less architectural ambiguity as to control.

The Transaction Set

Another area that needs to be controlled is the transaction set. A single transaction might affect any given number of database files and indexes. None of the updates should actually occur until all of the transaction steps are complete. There is a beginning step, interim steps, and an ending step to every complex transaction. In mainframe DBMSs, there is a concept called a *logical unit of work* (LUW). In SQL, the LUW idea is enacted using COMMIT and ROLLBACK commands. COMMIT tells the DBMS to make the updates, ROLLBACK tells it to "back them out." This requires the DBMS to keep a "before" copy of the records in memory (or on file) until the system is sure that no ROLLBACK will be issued.

Thus, if a user is six steps through a 10-step LUW, and decides to terminate the transaction, the ROLLBACK goes to the system, which then restores the records from its "before" images, leaving all data as it was before the transaction. This is incredibly complex to do in dBASE or any of the other microcomputer DBMSs.

There is also the issue of catastrophic termination (also known as "the system crashed"). In a system that is taking care of keeping transaction logs for ROLLBACK possibility, the "before" images can be used to restore the data files to the state that they were in before the crash. Multiuser systems are particularly vulnerable to abnormal termination because transactions are often kept in buffers in memory, and there is no way to know whether or not these buffers were "flushed" (written to disk) before the system went down. Thus, the writing back to the master files of all COMMITted "before" files that have not been marked as completed is an excellent power-up procedure.

This discussion should make you aware of the shortcomings of the current microcomputer based DBMS products, and at the same time act as a justification to move up to one of the mainframe products that run on microcomputers.

FOCUS AND PC/FOCUS

One of the most popular DBMSs that exists in microcomputer, minicomputer and mainframe versions is the Focus product from Information Builders Inc. IBI, in its own documentation, defines Focus as a complete "Information Control System." Like many microcomputer DBMSs, it has a structural design that allows it to be used by novice end-users, as well as an advanced command interface that allows application developers to create fairly complex systems.

Focus is also a nonprocedural language, which can be operated using Focus executable procedures, which are made up of files of request elements. Such an .FEX might look like the following:

```
TABLE FILE filename
PRINT SALARY COLUMN_TOTAL
BY DEPARTMENT
END
```

This is analogous to .PRG files in dBASE, which are text files containing sequences of dBASE commands. PC/Focus has been "down-sized" from its big

Item	PC/FOCUS	FOCUS
Maximum number of active fields in a Master Description	250 fields	no limit
Maximum sum of the lengths of all data fields in a record	4096 bytes	12288 bytes
Maximum number of Dialogue Manager variables	128 variables	256 variables
HOLD Files	External format for numerical data	Internal format for numerical data
Session Monitor	Not Available	Standard
FOCSAM	Not Available	Standard
Date Functions (DTYMD, etc.)	Works on integer dates only	Works on both integer and alpha dates
Sort Sequence	ASCII A-Z, 0-9	EBCDIC 0-9, A-Z
JOIN	FOCUS files only	Standard

Fig. 6-1. Comparison of PC/Focus to Focus.

brothers to fit on the microcomputers. Figure 6-1 shows the various size and data limitations imposed by this down sizing.

PC/Focus is a fourth generation language with built-in database management functions. Included in the package are excellent report writing tools, graphics tools, and a PC/Export interface. This utility allows for the easy interchange with DIF, Lotus 1-2-3, and word processing type files. The latest release, Version 3.0, will add a window interface, pull-down menus, and the ability to use standard dBASE files as if they were Focus files, without the need to reformat, import or export. There is also a spreadsheet product, Foccalc, available that uses the Focus data files and reporting schemes. Other standard utilities include a graph package that allows for the creation of connected point plots, histograms, bar charts, pie charts, and scatter diagrams.

The new 3.0 release adds three-dimensional graphics, exploding pie charts, and a new scripting language that automates the log-on procedures to mainframes and VAX minicomputer systems.

The real value of PC/Focus comes from its communication capability. To the seasoned microcomputer user, its "mainframe" feel makes it seem clumsy and hard to use. It is this issue that the new version will try to address, but even so, PC/Focus would still be an expensive solution to a stand-alone microcomputer user's database needs.

In a corporation that runs Focus on its mainframe or VAX, however, the benefits far outweigh the higher costs. In such companies, where large Focus databases and application programs already exist, the downward mobility of the data and code is outstanding. The standard database administration (DBA) security, file integrity, and data recovery functions of mainframe Focus are mirrored in PC/Focus. A standard component of both packages is the LINK utility. This program is all that the user needs to link the microcomputer and mainframe and give both access to Focus files in real time. The LINK screen from PC/Focus is shown in Fig. 6-2.

```
                      PC/FOCUS Link Options

 Link via:                 Async Connection Options:

   3278 COAX....           System:  CMS (CMS,TSO)
   Async Dial...   X       Baud:   1200 (300,1200,2400,4800,9600)
   VT 102/220...           Duplex: FULL (Half,Full)
                           Parity: NONE (Odd,Even,None,Mark,Zero)
                           Stop Bits: 1 (1,2)
                           Data Bits: 8 (7,8)
                           Port     : 1 (1,2)

 PROTOCOL CONVERTER (VT only): 0  (1 = SIM3278, 2 = DATALYNX, 3 = 7171)

   Enter => Enter Link Mode                          F3 = Quit
```

Fig. 6-2. PC/Focus Link setup screen.

Notice that all you need to get going is to fill in the boxes as to the type of interface and communications parameters, then log on. Simultaneous access to both mainframe (or VAX Focus) and PC/Focus is maintained by a "hot-key" toggle (F2). The help screen for PC/Focus LINK is shown in Fig. 6-3.

Once the link is made, either by leased line, coax cable or dial-up asynchronous hookup, a number of very powerful features become available. The first is the easy way in which the microcomputer user can transfer Focus data from the mainframe. The user goes through the link and logs onto Focus in the host system. A request for the desired information is made, using standard Focus requests and a TABLE command. Instead of using the HOLD file designation, the user asks for the sorted data to be placed in a PCHOLD file. The syntax is:

ON TABLE PCHOLD AS C:*filename*

This command on the mainframe Focus extracts the desired data and transfers it to the user's local disk (Drive C:) as DOS PC/Focus usable files. If an extract in DIF format is desired, the syntax would be:

ON TABLE PCHOLD AS C:*Filename* FORMAT DIF

The DIF file transferred is now immediately usable by any microcomputer application that can import DIF files. Note that the transfer occurs without user intervention. The end-user in the scenario is not viewed by the host as a passive entity. A request for a specific data subset from the host has been made, and now only that subset is sent, ready to use by PC/Focus or any other microcomputer application. This is truly a most desirable situation, and can only be accomplished by products that have such "gap spanning" data communication built in. There is no concern for file structure, code representation or data communication at all.

The situation in which the microcomputer user wishes to get so-called "general" mainframe files (sequential or character data) is not much more complex than the transfer of a Focus file described above. Such a scheme could be used to download Focus master file descriptions, FOCEXEC procedures, or any other text file. The user once again uses LINK to sign on to mainframe FOCUS, then types:

XFER *Mfilename* FROM/TO *filename*

The mainframe filename (Mfilename) can be up to eight characters long. It must be described in a CMS FILEDEF or TSO ALLOCATE. If the file is new, the DCB values must be supplied.

If the user wishes to send a file up to the mainframe he or she must first enter the following, if in TSO (time-sharing option):

LINK Command

The LINK command is used to connect your personal computer to a mainframe computer. This can be done in two basic ways.

1-Asynchronously , via a telephone line and a modem, or direct.
2-Bisynchronously , via an IRMA board (manufactured by TAC) .

When you type LINK , or depress the F2 key (which upon entry to PC/FOCUS is set to mean LINK) a menu will appear. On the left is the asynchonous/ bisynchronous choice. If you place an X in the bisynchronous box your IRMA board is automatically activated. If you just depress the ENTER key the default are the options on the right of the menu. You can use the TAB key to select any of these options and change them before you depress the ENTER key.

In both modes of communication mainframe FOCUS and PC/FOCUS can use the facilities of :

1- ON TABLE PCHOLD [as name] [FORMAT DIF]

This transfers data from a mainframe FOCUS request directly to your PC disk. If the FORMAT DIF option is selected the data is written in the Data Interchange Format used by common spread sheet programs.

2- XFER ddname FROM/TO pcname

This is a general utility to transfer files from or to your PC.

3- FILEDEF pcname [IRMA/DIAL] LRECL nnn

This allows invisible dialogues to be conducted between mainframe and PC/FOCUS.

Repetetive operation

You can place the LINK command in a FOCEXEC file and execute it without bringing up the menu. Follow the command with the option name and value separated by a space. i.e.

```
LINK SYSTEM CMS  BAUD 1200
     or
LINK IRMA
```

Returning from mainframe to PC operation

In asynchronous mode use the F2 key to 'toggle' back and forth between mainframe and PC/FOCUS.

In IRMA mode depress both the shift keys at the same time. This is the standard IRMA method.

DIAL Command

The PC/FOCUS command DIAL is now the same as LINK, except in the FILEDEF option where it means asynchronous operation.

Fig. 6-3. PC/Focus Link help screen.

```
ATTRIB XYZ LRECL(80) BLKSIZE(800) RECFM(FB)
ALLOC F(NEWSTUF) DA(NEWSTUF,DATA) USING(XYZ)NEW
```

or, if in CMS:

```
FILEDEF NEWSTUF DISK NEWSTUF DATA A
(LRECL 80 BLKSIZE 1200 RECFM FB)
```

Then the following transfer command is typed:

```
XFER NEWSTUF FROM A:NEW.TMP
```

where A:NEW.TMP is a microcomputer data file on drive A.

It is also possible to have data from PC/Focus written directly to a file on the mainframe, and vice versa. This is done by setting up a FILEDEF on the microcomputer under PC/Focus by typing:

FILEDEF *mfilename* DIAL

This command routes the output to DIAL, which in turn is used by mainframe Focus. Both machines must have the same master file description (MFD). The dialogue between the host and the microcomputer is "invisible." Once the link is made, any procedure on the microcomputer will act as if the mainframe file was on its disk drive. What is in fact occurring is that there are two procedures running, one on each machine, and the procedures are communicating in the background.

The implied power of such interaction is great, and is indeed an excellent example of the type of system integration that can be achieved between microcomputers and mainframes.

ORACLE

Oracle was the first commercially available systems query language (SQL) relational database management system. It was released on mainframe and minicomputers in 1979. In subsequent years, Oracle Corporation ported Oracle onto a number of various computers and operating systems, including IBM/VM/CMS, IBM MS/SP, VAX/VMS, and DG/AOS/VS. This support of IBM mainframes, DEC, Data General, HP, Prime, AT&T and many other minicomputers, as well as a PC DOS version, gives Oracle the broadest existing user spectrum.

There are a number of integrated components to the Oracle system. An array of fourth-generation tools are packaged with each version of Oracle. They include SQL*Plus, which is the user query interface to the Oracle databases. This interface allows for complex queries, updates and general database functions. Oracle is fully compatible with both ANSI standard and IBM standard

SQL, so that applications developed on a microcomputer under Oracle can be directly ported to a large mainframe running either Oracle or IBM's DB2. A second basic Oracle tool is SQL*Report. This is a very elegant multi-database report generator, capable of extracting data from any number of Oracle databases to use in custom-designed reports.

A third, and very useful, component of the Oracle package is called SQL*Forms. This is a forms-based application generator. The user simply paints "forms" on the screen, defining queries and relationships along the way, and then has the program generate the end-user applications.

Finally, there is SQL*Calc, a 1-2-3-like spreadsheet that adds the power of a direct link into Oracle databases to all of the useful electronic spreadsheet functions. Using SQL*Calc also adds the query capabilities of SQL to the conditional logic of the spreadsheet.

The microcomputer version of ORACLE comes in three "flavors." The first is called the Professional Oracle. Recently announced, this version is said to be the first microcomputer DBMS to make use of the more advanced features of the Intel 80286 and 80386 processors, as well as unleashing the functionality of the new generation of IBM Personal System/2. The much-regretted 640K memory barrier of PC DOS is overcome in a very interesting way. Something called the Oracle kernel, which is the DBMS "engine" itself, is designed so that it executes in protected mode in the advanced chips, thus running above the 640K memory limit, in extended memory. Figure 6-4 shows a comparison of an Oracle memory map with one in which some other microcomputer DBMS resides, such as dBASE III PLUS.

Notice that in the Oracle model unmodified DOS, the application and the

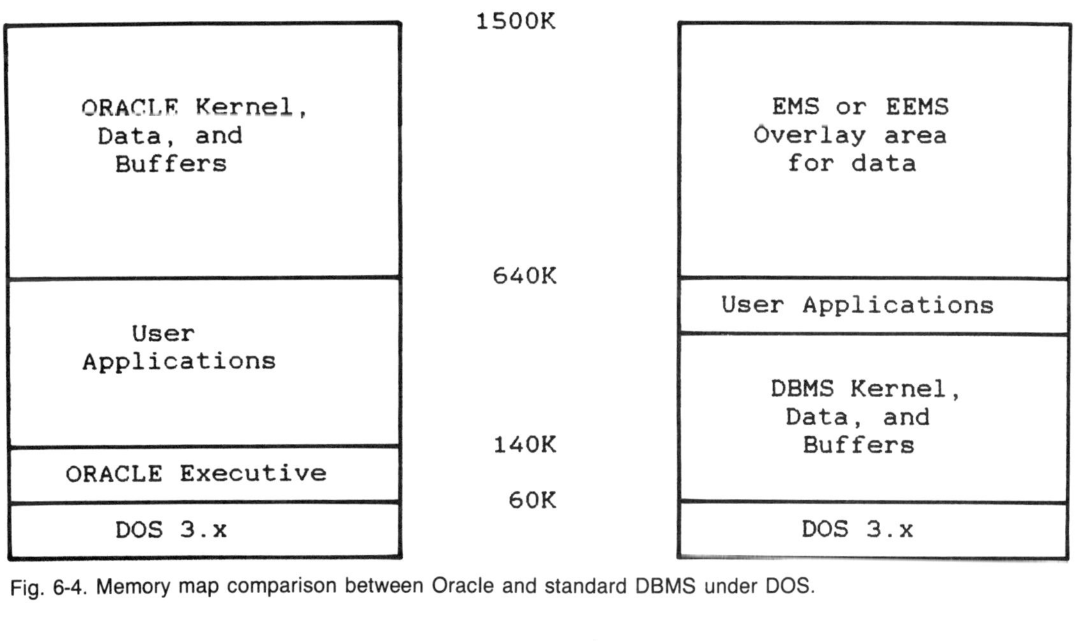

Fig. 6-4. Memory map comparison between Oracle and standard DBMS under DOS.

Oracle tools run in real mode below 640K. This allows for the construction of very large applications and the enhanced speed of working in the real mode without the need for the extra overhead involved in the overlay processes required when using the EMS (expanded memory specification) or EEMS (enhanced expanded memory specification) memory schemes. Another benefit is that memory resident utilities like SideKick and SuperKey can coexist with a large application.

A second version of Oracle on the microcomputer is called Networkstation Oracle. This version turns the desktop workstation into a member of a distributed application processing system. In this architecture, a user can dynamically access and update a remote database (either Oracle or IBM DB2) as if it existed on the microcomputer's hard disk. A special architecture, called SQL*Star, allows for the access and updating of local and remote databases simultaneously. These different databases can even be joined into a single view without any regard to their actual location. This is what is known as *seamless integration.* The user, without any extra manipulations, is able to simultaneously access and perform real time updates to any database on any machine under any operating system, as if it were his or her own.

Mainframe data security and data integrity schemes are still operational because these linkages are process-to-process schemes. It is thus required that Oracle system components are operating on each network component. The query system used to access distributed databases under Oracle is contained in SQL*Plus Version 2.0. A distributed query is one in which some or all of the tables queried reside in a database other than the main one to which the user is connected. Additional SQL syntax is required to create links to remote databases. Figure 6-5 shows a sample of this process in which a PUBLIC database link is created. Once this link is established a user can make a query in which a local table (DEPT) is joined with the table EMP in the Houston database, as shown in Fig. 6-6.

```
CREATE PUBLIC DATABASE LINK BANGOR
CONNECT TO NETWORK
IDENTIFIED BY NETPASS
USING 'D:HOUSTON-TEST'
```

☞ These commands allow table owners in the BANGOR database to decide which tables will be accessible to remote users; any tables for which permissions are not granted to NETWORK will not be accessible.

Fig. 6-5. SQL*Plus syntax to create link with remote database.

```
SELECT ENAME, DNAME
FROM EMP @ HOUSTON, DEPT
WHERE EMP.DEPTNO = DEPT.DEPTNO
```

☞ This SQL command set shows a query that joins a local table (DEPT) with the table EMP in the HOUSTON database.

Fig. 6-6. SQL*Plus query under distributed Oracle.

The link procedure simplifies user access to remote databases, making them as easy to use as those residing on the user's own system. The database administrator can set up passwords and access rights to limit user query capabilities if so desired.

Networkstation Oracle runs Ethernet on DEC NET, 3270 Coax using LU2 data streams, and RS-232 asynchronous dial-up protocols. Oracle Corporation plans the release of TCP/IP and APPC LU6.2 versions in the near future. The environments currently supported by the SQL*Net product are shown in Fig. 6-7.

The final Oracle version to be discussed is the LAN server. This program turns an IBM PC/AT or 80386 machine into a multiuser database server, and allows it to be connected over a LAN to PCs running Networkstation Oracle. The backend database server is architecturally superior to a standard LAN file server. In most file-server based LANs, the file server must act to manage network traffic, do record locking and file security, as well as try to prevent data corruption. The database server performs all functions related to data

Client	Server	Protocol
PC/MSDOS	VAX/VMS	Asynchronous
PC/MSDOS	DG/AOS/VS	Asynchronous
PC/MSDOS	Various UNIX	Asynchronous
PC/MSDOS	IBM/VM/CMS	Asynchronous, 3270
PC/MSDOS	IBM MVS/SP	Asynchronous, 3270
Various UNIX	Various UNIX	TCP/IP
VAX/VMS	VAX/VMS	DECNet

Fig. 6-7. Oracle SQL*Net-supported environments (version 1.0).

file integrity, access management for multiple users, and concurrency control.

To put it another way, in a typical LAN, each PC runs the DBMS, and thus different kernels are attempting to access a single database. There is no centralized control or responsibility for issues like integrity and security. Locking mechanisms in third-generation systems allow one user to lock out other users, but without centralized management, the issues of deadly embraces and failures in concurrency arise. In fourth-generation database servers, a single kernel executing on that server manages all locks and keeps control of a single transaction journal.

This allows for many users to simultaneously access database records in much the same way as in traditional mainframe DBMS architectures. This transaction journal maintains both a before and after image of database status during updating accesses. Such images in the journal can "rollback" interrupted transactions or restore the database in the case of a catastrophic system failure. Again, this is a standard mainframe DBMS feature previously unavailable on LANs. Conceptually, database servers are bound to be the future of LAN architectures. Coupled with other Oracle features, the distributions of functionality achieved is extremely high.

Thus, the Oracle system allows all IBM PCs and compatible microcomputers to act as application processors in conjunction with DBMSs running on other microcomputers, minicomputers or mainframes. The communication between an application and its required distributed databases can be asynchronous (RS-232) leased or dial-up lines, 3270 coaxial cable, Ethernet or Token Ring LANs. The wide variety of machines, operating systems, and communications seamlessly woven into the Oracle architecture make it an excellent model for the future of information interchange systems.

DATAFLEX

DataFlex, a DBMS/Application Development package from Data Access Corporation, runs on a wide variety of computers under several operating systems, and thus qualifies as a product that "spans the gap" between microcomputers, minicomputers, and mainframes. There are versions of DataFlex that run under PC/MS-DOS, UNIX, Xenix, CP/M-86, MP/M-86, Concurrent CP/M-86, and VMS. The DataFlex environment is complete and self-contained, so that applications developed on a microcomputer under PC DOS can be directly ported to a VAX under VMS. In operating system environments where multiuser access is available, DataFlex supports locking, file concurrency, and data integrity directly. The procedural language is the same across environments. To port an application, the user takes the source code, which is a flat ASCII test file, and compiles it with an environment-specific DataFlex compiler. The new "native" application code is customized to the new environment by the DataFlex package supplied for that system.

This portability of the application code is useful in a system in which both microcomputers and the terminals on the host data processing system need to run the same application, but there is no utility to directly link remote database files in real time as in Focus and Oracle. DataFlex users must perform distinct operations to move data between disparate systems.

There are methods by which data files from other languages can be brought into DataFlex. A BASIC data file must be output, under BASIC, to a sequential file. Then, using the DataFlex Read utility, the data is converted into a DataFlex file. It is also possible to transport data between two computers that are data-compatible only at the ASCII flat file level. This is the case when moving data files between MS-DOS and UNIX, because the native file formats in each operating system are so system-specific. Even if both operating environments can run the same DataFlex application program, the data must be translated. The actual transfer process involves using the DataFlex Query in the source (MS-DOS) environment to produce a "DataFlex readable" data file, transferring that data file by some standard data communications path, and then using the DataFlex Read utility to import that data into a previously created DataFlex file. The Query utility produces an ASCII line-delimited file. The Read utility can import either line-delimited or comma-delimited files.

This multi-step file interchange scheme is much more complicated than the remote link facility provided in the previously discussed Focus and Oracle environments. DataFlex will need to make this data file interchange process as easy to use as those of its competitors in order to challenge them in the marketplace. The only advantage to the DataFlex product is that its applications are identical at every level, and that its multiuser syntax is system specific.

CONCLUSION

In this chapter, several broad-spectrum products have been discussed. The first two, Focus and Oracle, exist on all three levels of computers and across a wide variety of operating systems. The third product, DataFlex, allows for developed applications to be easily ported to a wide variety of machines and operating systems, but still requires some import and export, via ASCII files, for data to make the migration. This product is thus seen as a partial solution to the multilevel data interchange problem.

What makes Focus and Oracle especially worthy of consideration is the seamless way in which intercomputer communications exist, enabling a user to access remote databases almost as easily as if they resided on his or her own system. Other products of this type exist as well, such as INFORMIX, and it is safe to say that intense competition will arise in this market over the next few years. Microcomputer DBMS vendors, such as Ashton-Tate, will bring dBASE up to minicomputers and mainframes, using SQL as a common query language. Users at all levels will thus be able to learn a single database query scheme, and have simultaneous access, in real time, to data without regard to its location.

There will thus be a convergence, from above and below, of the DBMS user interface. It will be with such products that the promises of distributed database systems are finally fulfilled.

Chapter 7

Data Security and Integrity

The interchange of electronic information between multiple sites and applications opens up a set of problems concerning the maintenance of data integrity and security. In the classical "data center" topology, there has always been a "master-slave" relationship between the host and the end-users. The mainframe contained all programs and data, and managed its distribution to "dumb" terminals and printers. Database integrity was maintained by the data processing staff. System maintenance, backup procedures, monthly closes and such were all under the control of a central group.

In such systems, users enter data into databases through extremely well-defined channels; programs and input screens have extensive error checking and data validation techniques. Audit trails are easy to maintain and the reconstruction of data files after catastrophic failures is, although tedious, just a matter of following well-laidout routines.

The data processing manager and staff of operators and programmers have all of the responsibility for system integrity, and the control necessary to operate the system. An end-user who needs some new report or analysis must submit a request to the data processing department. Impact studies and resource management analysis are then embarked upon, and, if all goes well, within a few months the user will get what is needed.

Enter the microcomputer. The end-users now have machines on their desks that are capable of a great deal of number-crunching. As they become more proficient in spreadsheets and database management programming, they become more hungry for corporate mainframe data. The users are now demanding connectivity, and access to the host data files.

Before the entrance of the microcomputer, the data processing group had both the control and responsibility for the management of the information flow. They now find themselves losing control. The first reaction is to grant only "passive" access to this new class of users. The microcomputers are granted minimal rights under terminal emulation and file downloading. This traffic is in one direction only—downstream. Data may still be entered into the mainframe data files, but only when the microcomputer is emulating a terminal running one of the standard, tried-and-true mainframe programs. The end-user has not gained any additional access rights or privileges by going to a microcomputer workstation.

The data processing group can still maintain, through the use of passwords and dedicated "console" ports, a strong measure of control over the environment. It is usually impossible, for example, for an end-user to get to the access level required to write programs on the host. Although a user might have the knowledge, permission is still needed to get into the mainframe editor and compiler to change any host program code. This is as it should be. Often, large application systems on corporate mainframes are fragile. Changes to code must be well thought-out, evaluated, and tested before they are allowed onto a production system. Even new programs, designed perhaps to extract data subsets, cannot be allowed access in an uncontrolled manner. Tinkering, or hacking, can unintentionally bring a system to its knees.

The only defense that the data processing departments have is to unilaterally forbid interactive entry. They have come to view the microcomputer-based end-user community as a potential threat to data and system integrity. This is a realistic position unless each user that has high-level clearance agrees to follow the same controls and standards that the data processing staff use. Still, the logistics of maintaining control over an ever-growing number of users precludes any secure belief that such control can be maintained.

Please note that the situation in which a "gap-spanning" product, such as Oracle or Focus, is running on all machines in the system is quite different. The data processing center manager can exert the same level of control over a microcomputer-based end-user as over terminal-based users. This level of interactive query is controlled by the Oracle or Focus environment itself, freeing the support staff of any additional considerations. Issues such as data validation, error recovery and concurrency are handled in exactly the same way on the microcomputer workstations as they are on the "standard" data entry terminals directly connected to the host. Once again, this adds to the argument in favor of this class of products.

PASSWORD SECURITY

Passwords are a standard security methodology for the mainframe world. They are composed of a sequence of characters of various lengths that are required for access rights to be granted. The security imposed by passwords is minimal at best. In the popular film *War Games*, a teenager was able to write a simple program that dialed each number on a given area code. Each time a modem answered (a well-defined situation), the program copied that number to a file. The movie's young hero then called each number in the file and looked to see what type of log-on came up. When he found an interesting one, he wrote a program to begin to test its password scheme. In theory, any password scheme passed on a simple sequence of characters can be broken by trying each possible sequence until the right one is found. At the end of *War Games*, the runaway computer tries to decode the Launch Control password using such a method.

Some host systems even help the hacking intruder by using underlines or Xs to indicate the width of the password field. If five underlines appear, the code breaker knows that the combination will be five or fewer characters. There are 26 letters, 10 numbers, and as many as 22 punctuation marks that might be allowed, so there are 585 possible codes for a five-letter password. A simple program could be written to try each one, and, although tedious even for a computer, the right code would be found. Most systems do not allow punctuation, and thus the task would be easier (only 365 possible combinations).

Because simple password systems are breakable by mere repetition, computer systems that require high levels of security do not use them. The Department of Defense, as a group, has very strict security requirements, and has a security system that is supposedly unbreakable, called the National Bureau of Standards Data Encryption Scheme. Its complexity is such that it supposedly would take a very fast supercomputer centuries to crack its cypher. This is quite a bold statement, perhaps more than one would tend to accept, but suffice it to say that this scheme is hard to break. Because it is being used to protect our most precious secrets, it needs to be very difficult to decipher.

Because of the expense in hardware, time and system overhead, there is no other password system that is advertised as infallible. There are, however, a number of very clever schemes that make unauthorized entry less of a problem.

The Call Back Method

One simple method is the "call back" scheme, in which the host maintains a file of passwords and telephone numbers. An end-user who calls in must supply a secret password as in the standard system. The host validates the password, then hangs up, and calls the user back. Thus, a hacker who is successful in finding the right code would only succeed in having the host call the end-user that owned that code. The only way to break into such a system would be to either put a new (different) telephone number in the file, or play call-forwarding games in the telephone system.

The Multiple Password Method

Another useful scheme that does not require hardware is the multiple password, or lock-and-key, method. In this approach, one password is the key to an algorithm that derives a second password. The algorithm is as complex and random as it can be, making the possibility of deriving the second password from the key nearly zero. Such a scheme is shown in the dBASE III program (SSM.PRG) listed in Fig. 7.1.

```
* ------------------------------------------------------------
-------------
*
* Program:                 SSM.PRG
* Programmer:              Michael Simon Bodner
* Written:                 12/19/85
* Revised By:              Michael Simon Bodner
* Revision Date:           01/12/85
*
* ------------------------------------------------------------
-------------
*
* Comments:                This is the PASSWORD CREATE PROGRAM
*
* ------------------------------------------------------------
-------------
PUBLIC CLIPPER
MLEVEL='00'
SET ESCAPE OFF
SET COLOR to 6/1,4/
SL1='┌────────────────────────────────────────────────────┐'
SL2='│                                                    │'
SL3='├────────────────────────────────────────────────────┤'
SL4='│                                                    │'
SL5='└────────────────────────────────────────────────────┘'
PH1='Password Creation Program'
MREV='rev 3.0'
USE SECPARM
COMP=SYSNAME
TP=TPMN
MFS=FS
USE
IF TP='C'
  SET COLOR to 6/1,4/
ELSE
  SET COLOR to 7/0,0/7
ENDIF
PTR=0
MQ=' '
LP=.T.
```

Fig. 7-1. dBASE III security system master program. (Continued through page 130.)

```
DO WHILE LP
MQ=' '
CLEAR
@1,1 SAY '                                                    - Password C
reation Program '+mrev
@2,1 SAY '_____________________________________________________________
_______________________'
@ 1,46 GET PH1
@ 1,1  SAY COMP
CLEAR GETS
@22,1 SAY '____________________________________________________________
_______________________'
@23,1 SAY '  (c) Copyright 1986 by Bodner, Hutchins & Associates,
 Inc., Houston, Texas'
*******************************************************************
*************
*
      *
*  MANAGMENT MENU
      *
*
      *
*******************************************************************
*************
@ 7,10 GET SL1
@ 8,10 GET SL2
@ 9,10 GET SL3
@10,10 GET SL4
@11,10 GET SL4
@12,10 GET SL4
@13,10 GET SL5
@ 8,18 SAY 'System Manager Main Security System Menu'
@10,12 SAY '    [A]ssign user password     [I]ndex databases
 '
@11,12 SAY '    [D]elete current user      [L]ist valid users
 '
@12,12 SAY '    [P]rint system log         [Q]uit
 '
CLEAR GETS
DO WHILE MQ=' '
  @ 15,24 SAY 'Please enter option code : ' GET MQ
  READ
  MQ=UPPER(MQ)
  IF MQ <> 'A' .AND. MQ <>'I' .AND. MQ<>'D' .AND. MQ<>'L' .AND. M
Q<>'P'.AND. MQ<>'Q'
   MQ=' '
  ENDIF
ENDDO
DO CASE
```

```
  CASE MQ='I'
    USE SECNUM
    INDEX ON NUM TO SECNUM
    USE SEC
    INDEX ON NAME TO SEC
    USE
  CASE MQ='A'
      @ 7,10 SAY SPACE(60)
      @ 8,10 SAY SPACE(60)
      @ 9,10 SAY SPACE(60)
      @10,10 SAY SPACE(60)
      @11,10 SAY SPACE(60)
      @12,10 SAY SPACE(60)
      @13,10 SAY SPACE(60)
      @15,10 SAY SPACE(60)
      STORE 5000 TO SEED
      NS=0
      DO WHILE NS=0
       @10,10 SAY 'Please enter a number from 1 to 9999 : ' GET SE
ED picture '9999'
       READ
        USE SECNUM INDEX SECNUM
        GOTO TOP
        SD=STR(SEED,4,0)
        FIND &SD
         IF EOF()
          APPEND BLANK
          REPLACE NUM WITH SD
          NS=1
         ENDIF
        PTR=RECNO()
        ENDDO
      KN=' Your Key Number for system entry is :  [     ]'
      @ 10,1 SAY SPACE(78)
      @ 9,10 SAY SL1
      @10,10 SAY SL2
      @11,10 SAY SL3
      @12,10 SAY SL4
      @13,10 SAY SL5
      @ 10,16 GET KN
      @ 10,57 SAY STR(SEED,4,0)
      CLEAR GETS
      SEED =SEED/10000
      @ 12,16 say 'Working .....'
      CHARNO =1
      CODESTRG=CHR(0)
      DO WHILE CHARNO < 7
        ?? '.'
        SEED=6307*SEED+.444801-(INT(6307*SEED+.444801))
```

```
    ?? '.'
    CHAR=CHR(SEED*57+65)
    IF ASC(CHAR) >= 91 .AND. ASC(CHAR) <=96
      CHAR=CHR(ASC(CHAR)+9)
    ENDIF
    ?? '.'
    CODESTRG=CODESTRG+CHAR
    ?? '.'
    CHARNO=CHARNO+1
    ?? '.'
  ENDDO
  ?
  CODESTRG=SUBSTR(CODESTRG,2,LEN(CODESTRG))
  PS=' Your PASSWORD for system entry is    : [      ]'
  @ 12,16 GET PS
  @ 12,56 SAY CODESTRG
  NT='[ The password must be entered exactly as shown for entr
y to be permitted !! ]'
  @ 14,1 get NT
  CLEAR GETS
  @18,10 SAY SL1
  @19,10 SAY SL4
  @20,10 SAY SL5
  UNAME='                              '
  MLEVEL='00'
  UDEPT='     '
  NMDP=1
  MDEP1='     '
  MDEP2='     '
  MDEP3='     '
  MDEP4='     '
  MDEP5='     '
  MDEP6='     '
  MDEP7='     '
  MDEP8='     '
  MDEP9='     '
  MDEP10='     '
  DO WHILE SUBSTR(UNAME,1,1) = ' '
    @17,17 SAY '                              '
    @19,10 SAY SL4
    @19,16 SAY 'Name' GET UNAME
    @19,52 SAY 'Level' GET MLEVEL PICTURE '99'
    READ
    UNAME=UPPER(UNAME)
    USE PERSONEL INDEX NAMES
    FIND &UNAME
      IF .NOT. EOF()
       MDEP1=DEPT
      ENDIF
```

```
 USE
 @17,17 SAY 'Department access allowed for '+UNAME
 @19,10 SAY SL4
 @19,12 SAY '#' GET NMDP PICTURE '99'
 @19,18 GET MDEP1 PICTURE '9999'
 READ
 IF NMDP>=2
 @19,23 GET MDEP2 PICTURE '9999'
 READ
 ENDIF
 IF NMDP>=3
 @19,28 GET MDEP3 PICTURE '9999'
 READ
 ENDIF
 IF NMDP>=4
 @19,33 GET MDEP4 PICTURE '9999'
 READ
 ENDIF
 IF NMDP>=5
 @19,38 GET MDEP5 PICTURE '9999'
 READ
 ENDIF
 IF NMDP>=6
 @19,43 GET MDEP6 PICTURE '9999'
 READ
 ENDIF
 IF NMDP>=7
 @19,48 GET MDEP7 PICTURE '9999'
 READ
 ENDIF
 IF NMDP>=8
 @19,53 GET MDEP8 PICTURE '9999'
 READ
 ENDIF
 IF NMDP>=9
 @19,58 GET MDEP9 PICTURE '9999'
 READ
 ENDIF
 IF NMDP=10
 @19,63 GET MDEP10 PICTURE '9999'
 READ
 ENDIF
ENDDO
N=1
SN=0
DO WHILE N<= LEN(CODESTRG)
  SN=SN+ASC(SUBSTR(CODESTRG,N,1))
  N=N+1
ENDDO
```

```
SNO=SN
SN=SN+PTR
USE SEC INDEX SEC
  FIND &UNAME
  IF .NOT. EOF()
    REPLACE CRC WITH SN
    REPLACE LASTACCESS WITH DATE()
    REPLACE LEVEL WITH MLEVEL
    IF NMDP >10
     NMDP=10
    ENDIF
    REPLACE NUMOFDEPTS WITH NMDP
    REPLACE DEPT1 WITH MDEP1
    REPLACE DEPT2 WITH MDEP2
    REPLACE DEPT3 WITH MDEP3
    REPLACE DEPT4 WITH MDEP4
    REPLACE DEPT5 WITH MDEP5
    REPLACE DEPT6 WITH MDEP6
    REPLACE DEPT7 WITH MDEP7
    REPLACE DEPT8 WITH MDEP8
    REPLACE DEPT9 WITH MDEP9
    REPLACE DEPT10 WITH MDEP10
  ELSE
    APPEND BLANK
    REPLACE CREATED WITH DATE()
    REPLACE NAME WITH UNAME
    REPLACE CRC WITH SN
    REPLACE LASTACCESS WITH CTOD('01/01/00')
    REPLACE LEVEL WITH MLEVEL
    IF NMDP >10
     NMDP=10
    ENDIF
    REPLACE NUMOFDEPTS WITH NMDP
    REPLACE DEPT1 WITH MDEP1
    REPLACE DEPT2 WITH MDEP2
    REPLACE DEPT3 WITH MDEP3
    REPLACE DEPT4 WITH MDEP4
    REPLACE DEPT5 WITH MDEP5
    REPLACE DEPT6 WITH MDEP6
    REPLACE DEPT7 WITH MDEP7
    REPLACE DEPT8 WITH MDEP8
    REPLACE DEPT9 WITH MDEP9
    REPLACE DEPT10 WITH MDEP10
  ENDIF
  SET PRINT ON
  ?
  ?
  ?
  ?'           '+COMP
```

```
        ?
 ? TIME()+'                    Password Document                    '+dto
c(date())
        ?'-----------------------------------------------------------------
----------'
        ? UNAME+' Key Number ['+SD+'] Password ['+CODESTRG+']'
        ?'-----------------------------------------------------------------
----------'
        ?'                  User Copy- CONFIDENTIAL !!'
        ?
        ?
        ? '         PLEASE NOTE :   These codes are assigned to you f
or secure'
        ? ' access to the system. Please keep this document in a s
afe place'
        ? ' and take measures to protect your passwords. If at any
 time you'
        ? ' feel that the  confidentiality of  these codes  might
have been'
        ? ' compromised, please contact the system manager to rece
ive a new'
        ? ' set of codes.'
        ? CHR(12)
        ?
        ?
        ?'            '+COMP
        ?
 ? TIME()+'                    Password Document                    '+dto
c(date())
        ?'-----------------------------------------------------------------
----------'
        ? UNAME+' Key Number ['+SD+'] Password ['+CODESTRG+']'
        ?'-----------------------------------------------------------------
----------'
        ? MLEVEL+' '+MDEP1+' '+MDEP2+' '+MDEP3+' '+MDEP4+' '+MDEP5
+' '+MDEP6+' '+MDEP7+' '+MDEP8+' '+MDEP9+' '+MDEP10
        ?'-----------------------------------------------------------------
----------'
        ?'         System Manager Copy - For File - CONFIDENTIAL !!
'
        ?
        ? CHR(12)
        SET PRINT OFF
      USE
   CASE MQ='L'
      CLEAR
      N=0
      USE SEC INDEX SEC
        DO WHILE .NOT. EOF()
```

```
  ? NAME+' '+LEVEL
  N=N+1
  IF N=20
    N=0
    WAIT
    CLEAR
  ENDIF
 SKIP
ENDDO
?
WAIT
CASE MQ='D'
  @ 7,10 SAY SPACE(60)
  @ 8,10 SAY SPACE(60)
  @ 9,10 SAY SPACE(60)
  @10,10 SAY SPACE(60)
  @11,10 SAY SPACE(60)
  @12,10 SAY SPACE(60)
  @13,10 SAY SPACE(60)
  @15,10 SAY SPACE(60)
   @10,10 GET SL1
   @11,10 GET SL4
   @12,10 GET SL5
   CLEAR GETS
   @ 9,22 SAY 'Enter user information for deletion'
   UNAME='                              '
   KEY='0000'
   DO WHILE SUBSTR(UNAME,1,1) = ' '
     @ 11,12 SAY 'User Name' GET UNAME
     @ 11,54 SAY 'Key#' GET KEY PICTURE '9999'
     READ
     UNAME=UPPER(UNAME)
   ENDDO
   FLAG=0
   USE SEC INDEX SEC
     FIND &UNAME
     IF .NOT. EOF()
       DELETE
     ELSE
       ? CHR(7)
       @ 14,25 SAY 'This User is not assigned !'
       FLAG=1
     ENDIF
   USE SECNUM INDEX SECNUM
     FIND &KEY
     IF EOF()
       ? CHR(7)
       @ 16,25 SAY 'This Key Number is not assigned !'
       FLAG=1
```

```
  ENDIF
  IF FLAG=0
     USE SECNUM INDEX SECNUM
     FIND &KEY
     REPLACE NUM WITH 'DELE'
     USE SEC INDEX SEC
     PACK
     FLAG=0
  ELSE
              USE SEC INDEX SEC
              RECALL ALL
              FLAG=0
            ENDIF
            USE
  CASE MQ='Q'
    LP=.F.
  CASE MQ='P'
    MLINE=4
    IF CLIPPER
      SAVE SCREEN
    ENDIF
    SET PRINT ON
    ?'      '+COMP
    ?
    ? TIME()+'     System Security Access Log        '+dtoc(date(
))
    ?'-------------------------------------------------------'
    USE SECLOG
    DO WHILE .NOT. EOF()
      ? MSG
      MLINE=MLINE+1
      IF MLINE>=50
        ?'-----------------------------------------------------
'
        ? CHR(12)
        ? '      '+COMP
        ?
        ? TIME()+'     System Security Access Log        '+dtoc(d
ate())
        ?'-----------------------------------------------------
'
      ENDIF
    SKIP
    ENDDO
    ?'-------------------------------------------------------'
    ? CHR(12)
    SET PRINT OFF
    MANS=' '
    CLEAR
```

```
      DO WHILE MANS <>'Y' .AND. MANS<>'N'
        @ 10,10 SAY 'Do you wish to clear System Log ? ' GET MANS
        READ
        MANS=UPPER(MANS)
      ENDDO
      IF MANS='Y'
         USE SECLOG
         ZAP
         USE
      ELSE
         USE
      ENDIF
      IF CLIPPER
        RESTORE SCREEN
      ENDIF
ENDCASE
ENDDO LP
SET ESCAPE ON
RETURN
```

The *seeding algorithm* is defined at the time of coding, so the programmer can change it at will, recompile the program, and issue new unlocking codes. In a high-security system, passwords should be changed regularly (weekly or monthly) and such a scheme further discourages unauthorized entry by the changing of the encryption algorithm itself. A dBASE III program (PSEC.PRG) that tests the encrypted passwords is listed in Fig. 7.2.

```
* ------------------------------------------------------------------
-------------
*
* Program:             PSEC.PRG
* Programmer:          Michael Simon Bodner
* Written:             12/19/85
* Revised By:          Michael Simon Bodner
* Revision Date:       01/10/85
*
* ------------------------------------------------------------------
-------------
*
* Comments:            This is the PASSWORD TESTING PROGRAM
*
* ------------------------------------------------------------------
-------------
MLEV='00'
IF CLIPPER
  SAVE SCREEN
```

Fig. 7-2. dBASE III password validation program. (Continued through page 134.)

```
ENDIF
SET ESCAPE OFF
SL1='┌────────────────────────────────────────────────────────┐'
SL2='│                                                        │'
SL3='├────────────────────────────────────────────────────────┤'
SL4='│                                                        │'
SL5='└────────────────────────────────────────────────────────┘'
PH1='Password Clearance'
PTR=0
@ 2,29 GET PH1
CLEAR GETS
@ 9,10 SAY SL1
@10,10 SAY SL2
@11,10 SAY SL3
@12,10 SAY SL4
@13,10 SAY SL5
STORE 1000 TO SEED
@10,15 SAY 'Please enter your Key Entry Number      : ' GET SEED
picture '9999'
READ
KN=' Your Key Number for system entry is     :   ' +STR(SEED,4,0)
@ 10,1 SAY SPACE(78)
@ 9,10 SAY SL1
@10,10 SAY SL2
@11,10 SAY SL3
@12,10 SAY SL4
@13,10 SAY SL5
@ 10,15 GET KN
CLEAR GETS
SELE SECNUM
GOTO TOP
SD=STR(SEED,4,0)
FIND &SD
IF .NOT. EOF()
  PTR=RECNO()
ELSE
  PTR=0
ENDIF
SEED =SEED/10000
@ 12,16 say 'Working .....'
CHARNO =1
CODESTRG=CHR(0)
DO WHILE CHARNO < 7
  ?? '.'
  SEED=6307*SEED+.444801-(INT(6307*SEED+.444801))
  ?? '.'
  CHAR=CHR(SEED*57+65)
  IF ASC(CHAR) >= 91 .AND. ASC(CHAR) <=96
    CHAR=CHR(ASC(CHAR)+9)
```

```
  ENDIF
  ?? '.'
  CODESTRG=CODESTRG+CHAR
  ?? '.'
  CHARNO=CHARNO+1
  ?? '.'
ENDDO
?
CODESTRG=SUBSTR(CODESTRG,2,LEN(CODESTRG))
NT='[ Your password must be entered exactly as given for entry to
 be permitted ! ]'
@ 16,1 get NT
CLEAR GETS
PSW='      '
@ 12,10 say Sl4
@ 12,15 SAY 'Please enter your System Entry Password :'GET PSW
READ
IF PSW <> CODESTRG
  CLEAR
  QUIT
ENDIF
SET ESCAPE ON
@ 9,1 SAY SPACE(78)
@10,1 SAY SPACE(78)
@11,1 SAY SPACE(78)
@12,1 SAY SPACE(78)
@13,1 SAY SPACE(78)
@14,1 SAY SPACE(78)
@15,1 SAY SPACE(78)
@16,1 SAY SPACE(78)
N=1
SN=0
DO WHILE N<= LEN(CODESTRG)
  SN=SN+ASC(SUBSTR(CODESTRG,N,1))
  N=N+1
ENDDO
SNO=SN
SN=SN+PTR
@12,10 SAY SL1
@13,10 SAY SL4
@14,10 SAY SL5
UNAME='                              '
DO WHILE SUBSTR(UNAME,1,1) = ' '
  @13,12 SAY 'Please enter your name' GET UNAME
  READ
ENDDO
SELE SEC
  FIND &UNAME
  IF .NOT. EOF()
```

```
IF CRC<>SN
  CLEAR
  ? CHR(7)
  ? CHR(7)
  ? 'Access denied. Now returning to menu system.......'
  QUIT
ENDIF
MLEV=LEVEL
MNDP=NUMOFDEPTS
IF SUBSTR(MLEV,1,1) <'6' .OR. SUBSTR(MLEV,2,1) <'6'
 DEPMAC='(DEPT= '+"'"+DEPT1+"'"
 IF MNDP>=2
   DEPMAC=DEPMAC+' .OR. DEPT = '+"'"+DEPT2+"'"
 ENDIF
 IF MNDP>=3
   DEPMAC=DEPMAC+' .OR. DEPT = '+"'"+DEPT3+"'"
 ENDIF
 IF MNDP>=4
   DEPMAC=DEPMAC+' .OR. DEPT = '+"'"+DEPT4+"'"
 ENDIF
 IF MNDP>=5
   DEPMAC=DEPMAC+' .OR. DEPT = '+"'"+DEPT5+"'"
 ENDIF
 IF MNDP>=6
   DEPMAC=DEPMAC+' .OR. DEPT = '+"'"+DEPT6+"'"
 ENDIF
 IF MNDP>=7
   DEPMAC=DEPMAC+' .OR. DEPT = '+"'"+DEPT7+"'"
 ENDIF
 IF MNDP>=8
   DEPMAC=DEPMAC+' .OR. DEPT = '+"'"+DEPT8+"'"
 ENDIF
 IF MNDP>=9
   DEPMAC=DEPMAC+' .OR. DEPT = '+"'"+DEPT9+"'"
 ENDIF
 IF MNDP=10
   DEPMAC=DEPMAC+' .OR. DEPT = '+"'"+DEPT10+"'"
 ENDIF
 DEPMAC=DEPMAC+')'
 DEPMAC2='(DPT= '+"'"+DEPT1+"'"
 IF MNDP>=2
   DEPMAC2=DEPMAC2+' .OR. DPT = '+"'"+DEPT2+"'"
 ENDIF
 IF MNDP>=3
   DEPMAC2=DEPMAC2+' .OR. DPT = '+"'"+DEPT3+"'"
 ENDIF
 IF MNDP>=4
   DEPMAC2=DEPMAC2+' .OR. DPT = '+"'"+DEPT4+"'"
 ENDIF
```

```
      IF MNDP>=5
        DEPMAC2=DEPMAC2+' .OR. DPT = '+"'"+DEPT5+"'"
      ENDIF
      IF MNDP>=6
        DEPMAC2=DEPMAC2+' .OR. DPT = '+"'"+DEPT6+"'"
      ENDIF
      IF MNDP>=7
        DEPMAC2=DEPMAC2+' .OR. DPT = '+"'"+DEPT7+"'"
      ENDIF
      IF MNDP>=8
        DEPMAC2=DEPMAC2+' .OR. DPT = '+"'"+DEPT8+"'"
      ENDIF
      IF MNDP>=9
        DEPMAC2=DEPMAC2+' .OR. DPT = '+"'"+DEPT9+"'"
      ENDIF
      IF MNDP=10
        DEPMAC2=DEPMAC2+' .OR. DPT = '+"'"+DEPT10+"'"
      ENDIF
      DEPMAC2=DEPMAC2+')'
    ENDIF
    REPLACE LASTACCESS WITH DATE()
    REPLACE LASTTIME WITH TIME()
  ELSE
    CLEAR
    ? CHR(7)
    ? CHR(7)
    ? 'Access denied. Now returning to menu system.......'
    QUIT
  ENDIF
AG='Access granted. Now loading system...................'
? CHR(7)
@ 16,12 GET AG
CLEAR GETS
SELECT 1
USE SECLOG
MMSG='User '+SUBSTR(UNAME,1,15)+' logged on at '+TIME()+' on '+DT
OC(DATE())
APPEND BLANK
REPLACE MSG WITH MMSG
IF CLIPPER
  RESTORE SCREEN
ENDIF
SET ESCAPE ON
RETURN
```

The seeding algorithm in both the password creation and this password testing programs must be the same, and care must be taken to make sure that both programs are recoded in the same way each time the seeding algorithm is altered. The dBASE database structure for the files necessary to run

SSM.PRG and PSEC.PRG are listed in Fig. 7.3. Both programs are compilable and, in fact, must be compiled in order to be even remotely useful.

ACCESS RIGHTS

Beyond the passwords issue is the question of access rights. Depending on the way users are set up, they can be limited to "passive" rights, in which a given menu of program options limits them to specific functionality and data,or they can be given higher access. Higher levels include the right to download files from one or many disk directories, the ability to write programs, and even to change existing programs. Such high-level rights involve extremely critical responsibilities. It is rare that any user be given the right to change system programs. Such work needs to be controlled at the data processing center, and this is rarely even at question. What does come up more and more these days is whether users on microcomputers should have the right to directly update the mainframe data files without the data verification, error checking and validation algorithms built into the mainframe programs. For example, should a Lotus user be able to "upload" the results of his calculations into the host data file?

This is an extremely critical issue. The best way to focus on this point is by an example. Suppose that a mainframe accounts receivable program is indexed by client code, a six-character field. A downstream data user pulls all transactions for a subset of customers, i.e., all clients in New York state. He downloads the data, manipulates it into a dBASE file, calculates some results, and constructs an uploadable data set. Although this data might be in the form required by the host program, there is no way to be sure that no erroneous results (such as bad arithmetic or mistyped codes) have been introduced.

The data processing center manager must not allow the direct uploading of "foreign" data. The uploaded data sets could be edited, using a mainframe text editor, effectively "hand validating" the data. This can be quite tedious, but is necessary to ensure the host data file's integrity. Another standard approach is to print out the data set and have a mainframe data-entry person key it into the host application. This is the most conservative approach, and is really only reasonable for small data files. Because the data is going in through the standard user interface, it will be exactly as valid as any other data entered.

The final, and most dangerous scheme, is the writing of custom programs on the mainframe that directly insert the uploaded data into the on-line data files. This should only be attempted after sufficient testing has been undertaken to guarantee that the new program and data will in no way corrupt the existing data. Even so, it is hard to recommend this approach in a system of any size, because the potential for large scale catastrophe exists in this scenario.

```
Structure for database: a:sec.dbf
Number of data records:       6
Date of last update   : 01/14/86
Field  Field Name  Type       Width    Dec
    1  NAME        Character     30
    2  CRC         Numeric        4
    3  CREATED     Date           8
    4  LASTACCESS  Date           8
    5  LASTTIME    Character      8
    6  LEVEL       Character      2
    7  NUMOFDEPTS  Numeric        2
    8  DEPT1       Character      4
    9  DEPT2       Character      4
   10  DEPT3       Character      4
   11  DEPT4       Character      4
   12  DEPT5       Character      4
   13  DEPT6       Character      4
   14  DEPT7       Character      4
   15  DEPT8       Character      4
   16  DEPT9       Character      4
   17  DEPT10      Character      4
** Total **                     103

Structure for database: a:secnum.dbf
Number of data records:      10
Date of last update   : 01/14/86
Field  Field Name  Type       Width    Dec
    1  NUM         Character      4
** Total **                       5

Structure for database: a:seclev.dbf
Number of data records:       1
Date of last update   : 12/24/85
Field  Field Name  Type       Width    Dec
    1  LEVEL       Character      2
** Total **                       3

Structure for database: a:secparm.dbf
Number of data records:       1
Date of last update   : 12/22/85
Field  Field Name  Type       Width    Dec
    1  SYSNAME     Character     44
    2  FN1         Numeric        5
    3  FN2         Numeric        8
    4  TPMN        Character      1
    5  FN3         Numeric        8
    6  RECD        Numeric        5
    7  FS          Character      1
** Total **                      73

Structure for database: a:seclog.dbf
Number of data records:      28
Date of last update   : 01/14/86
Field  Field Name  Type       Width    Dec
    1  MSG         Character     70
** Total **                      71

Command Line    |<C:>|SECLOG                   |Rec: 1/28       |      |

                    Enter a dBASE III PLUS command.
```

Fig. 7-3. Database file structures for SSM.PRG and PSEC.PRG.

MULTIPLE DATA FILE MANAGEMENT

The attraction of distributed computing is that a large number of end-users can have an incredible amount of computational power on their desktops, with which to perform almost any task that might come to mind. This is the driving force behind the infiltration of the microcomputer into the workings of corporate America. There is an interesting commercial from Apple Computer, Inc. in which two executives are marveling over the high quality of a recently produced report. One of the men assumes that it came from the huge mainframe group, seeking a justification for the millions spent. The other corrects him and tells him that it was done on a Macintosh and took only a week. This mythology of giving everyone in a company a microcomputer and watching productivity skyrocket is flawed at best.

Most end-users are not programmers. Most are not even mathematically oriented. In fact, simple logic might be beyond a large number of users. Note that at one time Apple was touting the Macintosh as "the computer for the rest of us." Apple was savvy enough to realize that the "rest of us" was a larger group than the "techies."

Nevertheless, IBM PCs and their clones are out there by the millions. There is no way to estimate the percentage of microcomputers involved in connectivity issues, but suffice it to say that there are a significant number involved in LANs, microcomputer to mainframe links, or remote modem communication.

The management of multiple versions of data files is a nightmare. On a central processing "data center" architecture, there is only one version of a database in existence, on-line, at a time. All users must "line up," get access, and update the records according to strict data validation and error checking rules imposed by the common user interface. The previous chapter discussed this issue of data integrity involving one file, but what of the case in which multiple files are involved?

For example, suppose an insurance company in Hartford, Connecticut has a large IBM 3270-type mainframe that supports branch offices throughout the United States. Each day the larger branches, due to their high volume, are allowed to download data files to the file server of a LAN in their own offices. The file transfer occurs overnight, so that at the opening of business the host and remote data files are identical. That is the last time that the two files contain the same data. During the day, transactions can be made at the branch and at the host. By the end of the day, each file might be considerably altered and have no nontrivial way to be mutually updated. This is true even if extensive software validation techniques exist on both the host and remote LAN.

A number of methods exist to overcome this diverging file information problem. One is for each site to maintain a transaction file, consisting of the information for each data set that was added, altered, or deleted during the day, as well as its time stamp. If a dozen branches are involved, there would be 13 transaction files, because the host (master data file) must have one as well.

At the end of the business day, each remote site uploads the transaction file only, leaving its locally updated "master" database as is. The host computer would then sort the transaction files by time stamp and batch process them in sequence, exactly as if they had been entered by operators at the source. The program that would do this could be set up to do all of the data validation and error checking required to guarantee the data integrity of the master data file. Many mainframe and minicomputer DBMS systems maintain this transaction log as a part of their own operating environment, freeing the user or the application itself from keeping track of such issues.

The transaction log performs the ultimate batch entry and finally updates the master data file. Once updated, this file can then be downloaded to the remote sites in time for the next day's work. This procedure will work for any combination of single or multiuser microcomputers at the remote sites.

The multi-file access problem for local area networks is in itself an issue of some complexity. Microcomputer operating systems such as MS-DOS are, by design, single-user, single-tasking architectures. Thus, most applications designed to run in this environment are also single-user, single-task programs. Applications like word processing, desktop publishing, spreadsheets, and graphics will probably always remain single-user programs. A large class of applications do, however, ultimately require multiuser access. Accounting, inventory control and database management systems are inherently more useful as multiuser programs.

As has been the case with the microcomputer industry in general, deficiencies in the machines and operating systems have been compensated for by third party vendors. Nowhere is this as strongly demonstrated as in the case of filling the requirements of multiuser access into DOS so that LANs can operate.

LAN/DOS MULTIUSER ISSUES

The first LANs were available when the IBM PC was introduced. Companies like Corvus and Nestar had board-level product that patched into DOS 1.1, then 2.0, and finally 2.1. The user needed to boot from a floppy disk that contained software patches to DOS to enable the LAN "virtual disk" to be accessed. They also needed locking procedures that were meaningless in a single-user environment. It was not until the release of DOS versions 3.0 and 3.1 that the LAN/DOS interface was actually defined as a standard. Figure 7-4 shows the DOS Version 3.x CALLs that pertain to LAN multiuser concerns. These CALLs are invoked by an interrupt 21H at the machine-code level.

Using this standardized CALL table, applications can query the environment as to the state of locks, virtual disk drives, and redirected logical devices. A relationship matrix showing all of the possible responses for multiple users demanding various access rights on the LAN is depicted in Fig. 7-5. You might find the matrix useful in learning the complexity of the responses to the vari-

Function of the DOS CALL		Reg. AH	Reg. AL
Open File (with sharing)		3D	
IOCTL	Is device redirected?	44	09
	Is Handler local or remote?		0A
	Change sharing retry count		0B
Get Extended Error		59	
Create Unique File		5A	
Create New File		5B	
Lock Byte Range		5C	00
Unlock Byte Range			01
Get Machine Name		5E	00
Set Printer Setup			02
Get Printer Setup			03
Get Redirection List Entry		5F	02
Redirect Device			03
Cancel Redirection			04
Set Handle Count		67	
Commit File		68	

Fig. 7-4. LAN-oriented DOS CALLs (using interrupt 21H).

ous ways that access rights can be demanded in a microcomputer LAN. As can be seen from the matrix, the application programmer has a great deal of planning to do to guarantee that all of the multiuser locking possibilities are covered in the code.

For example, suppose three microcomputers are linked in a LAN and are sharing a large database file in an accounting application. Microcomputer 1

SECOND AND SUBSEQUENT FILE OPEN ATTEMPTS

FIRST FILE OPEN MODE (Sharing ↓)	ACCESS	DENY READ/WRITE			DENY WRITE			DENY READ			DENY NONE			COMPAT-IBILITY		
		R	R/W	W	R	R/W	W	R	R/W	W	R	R/W	W	R	R/W	W
DENY READ/WRITE	R	2	2	2	2	2	2	2	2	2	2	2	2	3	3	3
	R/W	2	2	2	2	2	2	2	2	2	2	2	2	3	3	3
	W	2	2	2	2	2	2	2	2	2	2	2	2	3	3	3
DENY WRITE	R	2	2	2	1	2	2	2	2	2	1	2	2	5	3	3
	R/W	2	2	2	2	2	2	2	2	2	1	2	2	3	3	3
	W	2	2	2	2	2	2	1	2	2	1	2	2	3	3	3
DENY READ	R	2	2	2	2	2	1	2	2	2	2	2	1	3	3	3
	R/W	2	2	2	2	2	2	2	2	2	2	2	1	3	3	3
	W	2	2	2	2	2	2	2	2	1	2	2	1	3	3	3
DENY NONE	R	2	2	2	1	1	1	2	2	2	1	1	1	5	3	3
	R/W	2	2	2	2	2	2	2	2	2	1	1	1	3	3	3
	W	2	2	2	2	2	2	1	1	1	1	1	1	3	3	3
COMPAT-IBILITY	R	2	2	2	4	2	2	2	2	2	4	2	2	1	1	1
	R/W	2	2	2	2	2	2	2	2	2	2	2	2	1	1	1
	W	2	2	2	2	2	2	2	2	2	2	2	2	1	1	1

1 = Open succeeds
2 = Open fails with DOS error code 5 (access denied)
3 = Open fails, interrupt 24H is generated
4 = Open succeeds if file is read only; else fails with error code
5 = Open succeeds if file is read only; else inerrupt 24H is generated
R = Read   R/W = Read/Write   W = Write

Fig. 7-5. LAN file-sharing logic relationship matrix.

opens a file under DOS. This does several things; it moves some track and sector information into memory, "reserves" some blocks of the disk for writing, and alters the file allocation table (FAT). DOS assumes a single user and waits patiently for this user to finish file access, flush his memory buffers, write to the disk, and update the FAT. In a LAN, however, it is possible for microcomputer 2 or 3 to try to access the same file at the same time. This microcomputer opens the file, making erroneous assumptions about where to write new data and how to update the FAT. Such a situation is usually catastrophic because if the FAT is corrupted, all of the data on that disk drive might be destroyed.

Automatic Drive-Level Locking

To avoid this, even the most simple LANs invoke automatic drive-level locking. The moment that one user takes action to open the first file on a drive, the patched DOS would deny write access to any other user. In the case of a small LAN in which everyone is sharing one drive, this can become clumsy.

File Locking

A better, although inefficient, locking method is called file locking. Here, the patched DOS gives write access only to the user who first invokes the file lock. This means that several users can sort on the same disk at the same time so long as they each work on different files.

Record Locking

The most valuable, and most mainframe-like, multiuser access method is record locking. In such a scheme, the user invokes a lock only on the record that is needed. Other users can access different records in the same data file at the same time. This possibility exists only if the application program itself is issuing the proper DOS CALLs, as mentioned earlier, and responding in a logical manner to the various system responses to those CALLs. Current versions of dBASE III PLUS and its compilers (Clipper and Quicksilver) support this scheme. Although it is tedious, this code is sufficiently structured and straightforward to allow it to be generated automatically into running single-user applications. In fact, a product exists that does just that. It is called dAnalyst by TransSec Systems.

The code fragment in Fig. 7-6 shows the steps involved in multiuser locking access methods. Note that the user must first test the record to see if it is locked. If it is not locked, the locking command must be sent. Upon verification of the lock, the user is free to edit the record. Once the edit is complete (hopefully with data validation), the user issues the record unlock command.

Although record locking can be straightforward, there is often some complexity involved in keeping track of summary and transaction files. In an accounts receivable system, for example, credit limits are often assigned to customers. When the company is about to ship an order, the system might need to check to see if the client's credit limit would be exceeded by this order. In a multiuser system, the computer would read the limit, calculate the order amount, process the order on a locked transaction record, and then lock and update the customer master file.

For instance, if the customer credit limit is $5000 and he owes $3500, the logic would allow the system to ship a $1000 order. In a multiuser system,

```
* SAMPLE1.PRG - TO SHOW OFF MULTI USER RECORD LOCKING
USE MHMAST INDEX MHMAST
SET INDEX TO
SET INDEX TO NAME
PACK
REINDEX
ZAP
APPEND BLANK
REPLACE ADDRESS WITH STREET
CLOSE INDEX
CLOSE DATA
CLOSE ALL
USE
```

Above single user program converted to multi-user by dANALYST

```
dANALYST Ver. 7.0  Copyright 1985,1986,1987 BUZZWORDS Intl.
INPUT FILE:  SAMPLE1.PRG
      *  FILE NAME: SAMPLE1.PRG
      *  BY:
      *  DATE: June 28, 1987
      *  DESC:
      *  CALLED BY:
      *  DATA FILES:
      *  MULTI-USER RECORD/FILE LOCKING  +(M1)  dBASE III PLUS

      * TO SHOW OFF MULTI USER RECORD LOCKING
      DO dNET_USE WITH "MHMAST INDEX MHMAST", .F.
      SET INDEX TO
      SET INDEX TO NAME
      DO NET_EXCL WITH 'P'
      DO NET_EXCL WITH 'R'
      DO NET_EXCL WITH 'Z'
      YN = "Y"
 .--IF .NOT. FLOCK()
 !      DO FILELOCK WITH YN
 '--ENDIF
 .--IF UPPER(YN) = 'Y'
 !      APPEND BLANK
 '--ENDIF
      UNLOCK
      RELEASE YN
      YN = "Y"
 .--IF .NOT. RLOCK()
 !      DO RECLOCK WITH YN
 '--ENDIF
 .--IF UPPER(YN) = 'Y'
 !      REPLACE ADDRESS WITH STREET
 '--ENDIF
      UNLOCK
      RELEASE YN
      CLOSE INDEX
      CLOSE DATA
      CLOSE ALL
      USE
      *Formatted by: dANALYST Ver. 7.0  on June 28, 1987.
```

Fig. 7-6. Automatic conversion of single to multiuser dBASE III code.

it is possible that another user might read the data and conclude that the outstanding balance is $3500 before the first user can update the file to show the just-shipped $1000 transaction. The program would thus allow the second user to ship the $1000 second order, so that (even with correct record-locking allowing the writes), at the end of both transactions, the balance due would be $5500, which is greater than the credit limit.

Such interweaving of events makes multiuser applications significantly more complex than single-user applications. Great care must be taken to design the logic flow of code for such applications, particularly in the upgrading from single to multiuser environments.

ISSUES AND CONSIDERATIONS

Mainframe and minicomputer applications have been written and designed within multiuser environments, so that such problems are not an issue at that level. The microcomputer-LAN-to-mainframe boundary is further complicated by these problems on the LAN side.

Future versions of DOS will finally eliminate the burdens of the single-user design of the current versions. The new operating systems, such as OS/2, will, from the outset, control multiuser access to records and files in a manner similar to its mainframe and minicomputer counterparts. Taking full advantage of the 80286 and 80386 capabilities, these operating systems will make it easier for multiuser applications to exist on the LANs and communicate with their host databases.

The only alternative to the complexity involved in trying to distribute the data files and keep track of the currency of the updates is to limit the remote microcomputers to real-time transactions in a terminal emulation mode. Such a method tends to make little use of the power of the microcomputer itself, but does totally side-step all of the negative aspects of multiuser multi-file data management. Such an approach is widely used in corporations and institutions today, and is in fact the most prudent method until the multiuser operating systems are debugged and operational in the microcomputer environment.

Chapter 8

Automated Procedures for File Interchange

It is hard to argue with the statement that standards are useful. As more desktop microcomputer workstations are installed and become components of institutional data information exchange systems, an ever-increasing number of unsophisticated computer end-users are making demands. Thus far, a number of data interchange methodologies have been explored. The most ideal situation, and the most rare, is one in which all users run the same software on all machine levels, as is the case with products like Oracle and Focus. A more common situation is one in which the microcomputers have been systematically added to the institutional data processing network, where mainframes and minicomputers hold the master data files, and the microcomputers act as terminals, or at best, file capture systems. Often the architecture is one in which there is a host level, then some gateway, and an end-user level, possibly on a LAN, as displayed in Fig. 8-1.

The architectural and philosophical dichotomy that exists between the two levels creates a number of problems for data interchange. There are solutions to these problems. First, there is the method of printing data at either computational layer, then rekeying it into the other. In fact, this is probably still the most prevalent data interchange scheme in use today.

In the second alternative, "tweaking," an experienced programmer uses editors, translators, programming languages, and various development tools on the data to customize a source data file into a desired target format. This can be just as difficult as rekeying. Such custom design is only valuable if the task is going to be repetitious, as a part of a production system. Once the cus-

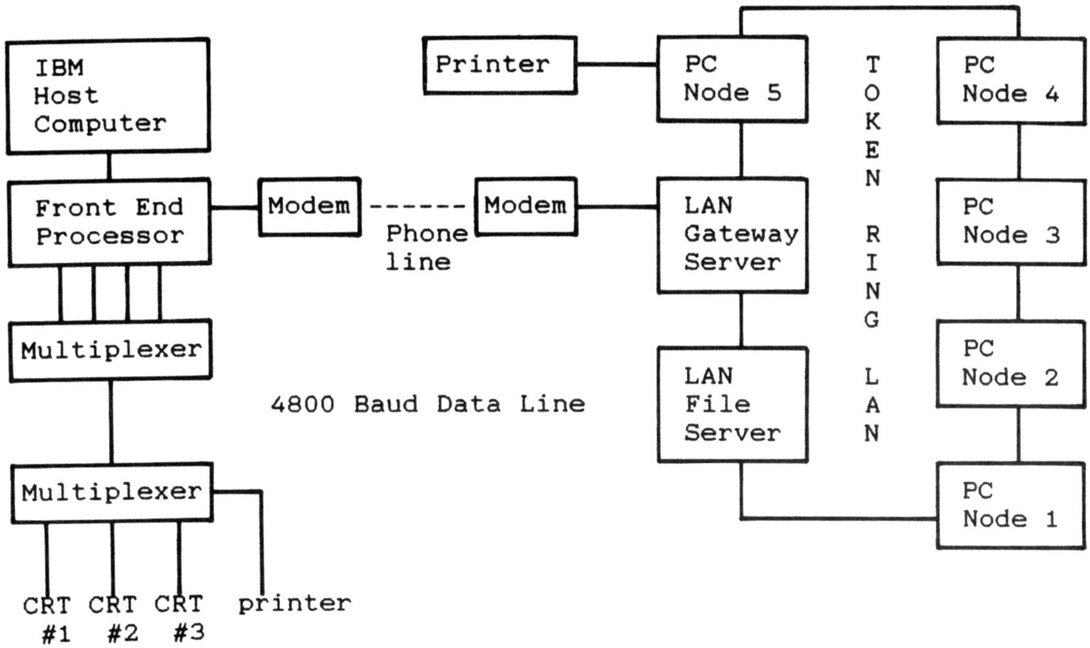

Fig. 8-1. Data communication system with LAN gateway.

tom code is written to take captured host data file A and convert it into a dBASE III PLUS DBF file B, and the process is debugged and validated, the program can become transparent. The coding might require a high level of technical expertise, while the resulting procedure could be simple enough to be run by a complete novice. This method is also widely in use today. The major problem with this approach is that the process is "hard coded." If either host or target file structures are ever altered in any way, the code must be changed, debugged and revalidated.

The third major approach is one in which the microcomputer user is sophisticated enough to use the file import and export capabilities of off-the-shelf applications programs, such as exporting dBASE data to Lotus 1-2-3. This method is a multipath topology, in that it is sometimes necessary to go through a number of intermediate steps to achieve the desired result, going from accounting, to dBASE, and then to Lotus, to get the data in the right shape. This scheme is very dependent on the expertise of the end-user, as well as the choice of translation products. It is thus hard to maintain quality control and data integrity in such a process. This method can create the confusion of final reports that do not agree with each other.

The major problem in the total integration of all computing resources into a transparently functioning data interchange system is that all users must have simple and accurate methods for acquiring "real" data, in real time, into whatever application they wish on whatever level of computer that they choose to work on. In short, it would be advantageous to undo the "Tower of Babel" effect.

THE DATA INTERCHANGE PROGRAM

To this end, an automated procedure for file interchange has been developed and included as a part of this book. The scheme is based on the fact that many of the so-called "custom" code methods are structurally similar. Over the course of several years, and dozens of projects, our firm has developed certain step-by-step methods for the conversion of one file into a form required by another application.

Given that standards make things easier, it was proposed that some standard would need to be defined that would enable the computer to automatically find key pieces of information about the structure of the source file. These key pieces would be exactly the kinds of things that the "sophisticated" file interchanger might need to find out in order to write custom translation code.

The complexity is vast. There are wide varieties of possible structures for the source data. Every host program puts out reports, charts, and tables of potentially any size and shape. There are no standard output structures. The standard could not be forced onto the host, i.e., it would not be possible (or economically reasonable) to require the host program to put out its data in a new (standardized) way. The standard had to be "passive," somehow being created after the fact.

To this end, an idea was borrowed from theoretical physics. In Nature, there are extremely complex systems, such as gasses, that cannot be studied component by component. The randomness of the motion of particles in a gas makes it impossible to describe the behavior of the system at the particle level. What can be done, however, is to develop a description of the system, and create artificial constructs, such as temperature and pressure. These description constructs themselves can be manipulated by equations, enabling the system to be studied.

The TDF Standard

In terms of data interchange, it was proposed that a Text Description File standard (TDF) could be constructed that would contain all (or enough) of the information necessary to describe the file structure to the computer. If the description was sufficiently complete, programs could be written to use the information in the description file to do the mechanical steps required to create target files for any application program.

The TDF standard is displayed in Fig. 8-2. A detailed structural and functional description of the data fields is provided in Appendix A as a part of the user's manual. The description process is straightforward and requires many of the same skills as are required in the custom code process. Indeed, a program-

Code	Bytes	Definition
FILENAME	08	FILENAME
LW	03	LINE WIDTH (1-255)
C	01	IS THERE A CARRIAGE RETURN (Y/N)
L	01	IS THERE A LINE FEED (Y/N)
F	01	IS THERE A FORM FEED (Y/N)
LP	03	NUMBER LINES/PAGE
SL	03	STARTING DATA LINE
EL	03	ENDING DATA LINE #
D DC1 DC2 DC3	01 03 03 03	IS THE FILE DELIMITED (Y/N) Delimiting code #1 Delimiting code #2 Delimiting code #3
ILC	08	IGNORE LINE CODE:
NF	02	NUMBER OF DATA FIELDS (1-24)
SDLC	08	SPECIAL DATA LINE CODE
O	01	SPECIAL DATA LINE OFFSET
SCS	03	START COLUMN SPECIAL CODE(1-255)
SN	02	NUMBER SPECIAL FIELDS(1-12)
NM1	10	NAME OF DATA FIELD 1
FS1	03	STARTING COLUMN OF FIELD 1
FS2	03	ENDING COLUMN OF FIELD 1
V	01	TYPE OF VARIABLE (FIDLC)
DP	02	NUMBER OF DECIMALS
sequence repeated for NF data fields (up to 24)		
SNM1	10	NAME OF DATA FIELD
FS1	03	STARTING COLUMN OF FIELD 1
FS2	03	ENDING COLUMN OF FIELD 1
V	01	TYPE OF VARIABLE (FIDLC)
DP	02	NUMBER OF DECIMALS
sequence repeated for SNF data fields (up to 12)		

Fig. 8-2. Text descriptor file standard structure.

mer could simply "drop into" a text editor and construct a TDF for any given file.

One of the goals of this development effort was to eliminate the need to have a programmer in the process, so a number of tools were developed to enable the unsophisticated end-user to create, edit, and use the TDF standard. These tools are in the form of a set of programs written in BASIC and the dBASE III command language, and are included in Appendix B. The user manual is reproduced in Appendix A.

The Programs

The first program is called TDF. It is used to generate a Text Description File for a given source data file. Refer to Appendix A to follow the step-by-step procedure involved in using the system. Essentially the end-user is guided through the process by answering a number of questions. To answer these questions, a printout of part of the source data file and a ruler that can count characters are required. The TDF program asks about numbers of lines per page, widths of data fields, data field types, and the like. After all of the questions are answered, a TDF file is constructed. This file is a complete description of the source file. A class of programs called Description File Processors (DFPs) have been created that use the information contained in the TDF to process the data contained in the source file, producing a target file of a desired type. There is also a program, TDFED, that allows the user to edit the structure of the TDF file.

Included in Appendix B are DFPs for the following environments:

- ☐ Lotus 1-2-3
- ☐ dBASE III PLUS
- ☐ MultiMate
- ☐ WordStar/Mailmerge
- ☐ Standard Data Format
- ☐ Delimited Format

These programs are written in BASIC, with the exception of DFPDBF2, which is a dBASE III program and should be compiled with products such as MicroSoft's QuickBASIC Compiler for the BASIC (.BAS) programs, and Nantucket's Clipper (Autumn 86) for the dBASE code (.PRG).

A number of supplementary files are also included in Appendix A, which are used with the various DFPs. Make use of these programs. They are provided as is, and can be entered as listed using any text editor or the BASICA interpreter that is distributed with most microcomputers. The only requirement is that the copyright notice remain in the code listing. Once entered, compiled, and linked, the programs will conform to those described in the user manual in Appendix A.

SAMPLE PROCESS

As a complete procedural example, the file BANK.TXT, which was defined in Chapter 4, is taken, step by step, through this automated data file interchange scheme. It is assumed that the file has been captured as a print image on the LAN file server or stand-alone workstation hard disk drive.

The first step is to create a complete description of the file, conforming to the Text Description File format. The user must perform the character counting procedure defined earlier, telling the TDF where each data field begins and ends. The user must also identify the data types, and which data fields should be transferred to the target files. It is possible to construct a TDF file using a text editor, but most users would prefer a more "user-friendly" approach. Such an interface exists, and is provided in the form of the program TDF.BAS. To execute the compiled version of this program, type the following from the DOS prompt:

TDF <return>

The log-on screen (Fig. 8-3) asks the user to supply the name of the text file for which a description is to be built.

There can be any number of TDF files created for a single ASCII text file. Thus, the host can download one file to the LAN, and a library of TDFs can be created for that file. Each TDF yields a unique output structure, so that multiple users can extract different data by using different TDFs on the same source file.

```
          Bodner-Hutchins Text Descriptor File System
--------------------------------------------------------------------
 This program will enable the user to create a standard Text Descriptor
 File (TDF) which can later be processed by Descriptor File Processors.

              Text Descriptor File Generator
              26 Jun 1987                  10:22:47
                       Version 1.80

              Enter TDF name :  [BANK_    ]

         Please enter the name of TDF file or Q to quit
--------------------------------------------------------------------
     Copyright (c) 1986, Bodner-Hutchins Inc., Houston, Texas
```

Fig. 8-3. Log-on screen for TDF.EXE.

Creating a TDF

The process of creating a new TDF is as simple as answering a sequence of questions about the source file. As can be seen in Fig. 8-4, the TDF itself is constructed as the user fills in responses, such as the name of the fourth data field, what column it begins in, where it ends, what type of variable it is, and so on.

The user does not need to name all of the variables in the source file. Only variables in which he or she has an interest need to be defined in any order that is desired. The sample file had several columns that needed to be manually deleted in the other methods of interchange. Using TDFs precludes the need for any manual operation of this kind. Figure 8-5 shows the completed TDF for the source file BANK.TXT. The data fields ACCNUMBER, ACCNAME, ACCBAL, INTEREST, and LOANBAL have been defined.

The description also shows that the data begins on line 9 and extends to line 52 of each page of the report, that there are carriage returns, line feeds, and form feeds in the data, and that the lines starting with "= = = = = = =" should be ignored. That is really all there is to the process.

Running a DFP

Once this definition has been constructed, the data file interchange is accomplished merely by running a Descriptor File Processor (DFP) program. The DFPs are target-format specific. Thus, to extract and convert the desired

```
Bod                                          rator (Rev 1.80) - Normal Data
     Name of data field 04:[_          ]
FIL                                          DC3 ILC...... NF SDLC... O SCS SN
BANK     120 Y Y Y 066 009 052 N 000 000 000 ========= 05 .     0 000 00
NM1        FS1 FS2 V DP NM2        FS1 FS2 V DP NM3        FS1 FS2 V DP TC
ACCNUMBER  009 015 C    ACCNAME    017 047 C    ACCBAL     049 058 F 02 *1
NM4        FS1 FS2 V DP NM5        FS1 FS2 V DP NM6        FS1 FS2 V DP TC
                                                                        *2
NM7        FS1 FS2 V DP NM8        FS1 FS2 V DP NM9        FS1 FS2 V DP TC
                                                                        *3
NM10       FS1 FS2 V DP NM11       FS1 FS2 V DP NM12       FS1 FS2 V DP TC
                                                                        *4
ENTER 1-10 ALPHANUMERIC CHARACTERS,NO SPACES ALLOWED,USE UNDERLINE FOR SPACE
                                                       Press Esc to Abort
```

Fig. 8-4. Data entry screen for TDF.EXE.

```
         Bodner-Hutchins Text Descriptor File Generator  (Rev 1.80)

BANK       120 Y Y Y 066 009 052 N 000 000 000 ========= 05 .       0 000 00
ACCNUMBER  009 015 C NA ACCNAME     017 047 C NA ACCBAL      049 058 F 02 *1
INTEREST   072 082 F 02 LOANBAL     105 115 F 02                          *2
                                                                          *3
                                                                          *4
                                                                          *5
                                                                          *6
                                                                          *7
                                                                          *8
                                                                          *9
                                                                          *A
                                                                          *B
                                                                          FF

        Data is being written to Text Descriptor File [BANK.TDF]

   This TDF, when used with its associated data file, can be processed by
 any Descriptor File Processor (DFPxxx.EXE) to create native file formats.
```

Fig. 8-5. Status report screen for TDF.EXE after processing BANK.TXT.

data from the file BANK.TXT into dBASE III format, the user needs to type the following from the DOS prompt:

DFPDBF <return>

The screen then displays the log-on screen shown in Fig. 8-6. The available

```
              Bodner-Hutchins Text Descriptor File System
--------------------------------------------------------------------------
                                                      TDF Files
                                                      ---------
                                                      CHAMBER
                                                      TESTFILE
               dBASE III (DBF) File Format            BANK
               ---------------------------
                Descriptor File Processor
                      Version 1.80

               06-26-1987              10:26:26


               Enter file name : [BANK_    ]

                 Enter Q to quit and return to DOS

      dBASE III & dBASE III Plus are trademarks of Ashton-Tate, Inc.
--------------------------------------------------------------------------
         Copyright (c) 1986, Bodner-Hutchins Inc., Houston, Texas
```

Fig. 8-6. Log-on screen for DFPDBF.EXE.

```
        Bodner-Hutchins Text Descriptor File Processor  (Rev 1.80)

BANK       120 Y Y Y 066 009 052 N 000 000 000 ========= 05 .        0 000 00
ACCNUMBER  009 015 C NA ACCNAME    017 047 C NA ACCBAL      049 058 F 02 *1
INTEREST   072 082 F 02 LOANBAL    105 115 F 02                          *2
                                                                         *3
                                                                         *4
                                                                         *5
                                                                         *6
                                                                         *7
                                                                         *8
                                                                         *9
                                                                         *A
                                                                         *B
                                                                         FF
     Data is being processed from Text Descriptor File [BANK.TXT]

   This TDF is being used by this DFP to convert the associated ASCII
  text file into a format directly useable by dBASE III & dBASE III Plus

              Now creating DBF header ..........

     Copyright (c) 1986, Bodner-Hutchins Inc., Houston, Texas
```

Fig. 8-7. DFPDBF creating DBF header for BANK.DBF.

TDF files on the directory are shown in the window in the upper right-hand quadrant. The user selects the needed TDF, and the program does the rest. Figure 8-7 shows the program in progress, with the final status reporting screen shown in Fig. 8-8.

Bodner-Hutchins Text Descriptor File Processor (Rev 1.80)

Field Name	Start	End	Type	Decimals	Width
ACCNUMBER	9	15	C	0	7
ACCNAME	17	47	C	0	31
ACCBAL	49	58	F	2	10
INTEREST	72	82	F	2	11
LOANBAL	105	115	F	2	11

File structure as determined from the Text Descriptor File

```
      This DFP has converted    71 data records from file     BANK.TXT
  and has created a DBF file with    5 data fields in file     BANK.DBF

     Copyright (c) 1986, Bodner-Hutchins Inc., Houston, Texas
```

Fig. 8-8. Status report screen for DFPDBF.EXE.

```
. USE BANK
. DISP STRU
Structure for database: C:BANK.dbf
Number of data records:        71
Date of last update   : 06/26/87
Field  Field Name  Type       Width    Dec
    1  ACCNUMBER   Character      7
    2  ACCNAME     Character     31
    3  ACCBAL      Numeric       10      2
    4  INTEREST    Numeric       11      2
    5  LOANBAL     Numeric       11      2
** Total **                      71

Command Line    |<C:>|BANK              |Rec: 1/71        |     | Caps
                    Enter a dBASE III PLUS command.
```

Fig. 8-9. dBASE Display Structure for BANK.DBF.

The DFP has actually created the file BANK.DBF and filled it with all of the required data from the source file. When the user goes to dBASE, or runs an application program in dBASE, the data is already there. Figure 8-9 shows the structure of the externally created file BANK.DBF, with the imported data shown in the BROWSE screen of Fig. 8-10.

The data has been converted and imported automatically by the DFP. The user did not need to CREATE and APPEND, as in the manual transport schemes. The nonsophisticated end-user does not need to invoke any dBASE commands at all. This is the essence of automated data file interchange. Using

```
ACCNUMBER ACCNAME------------------------ ACCBAL---- INTEREST--- LOANBAL---- -
0128006   Filtration Sciences Corp.        21050.00       10.50     1055.00
0142007   Howard Jackson                    3547.62       10.50     3544.00
0226006   Nationwide Papers                93207.50       10.50     3200.00
0154001   Holly Sugar Corporation          13270.56       10.50     3277.00
0236000   Woodlands Pipe Supply, Inc.       6210.72       10.50     2211.00
0216007   Meyer Rubber Stamp Company       21942.90       10.50     2244.00
0016002   Albert Woodworks                  9400.00       10.50        0.00
0088002   Central Freight Lines Inc.       26789.14       10.50        0.00
0348008   CanLab Corporation                3764.74        9.50     3766.00
0092008   Bayou Transportation Co.          5832.26       10.50    15833.00
0048007   Best Uniform Supply Co.           5660.96       11.50       66.00
0209005   McMillon Electric Co. Inc.        3856.90       10.50      855.00
0022009   American Products Company        21165.72       11.50    23166.00
0040003   Aztec                           345634.66        8.50   321133.00
0096001   Alpine Oil Corp.                789392.38        9.50   657399.21
0274009   Santa Anna Electric Co.          39123.34       10.50    21945.33
0140009   Dale Gainers                       350.00       12.51      355.00

BROWSE          |<C:>|BANK              |Rec: 45/71       |     |Caps
                          View and edit fields.
```

Fig. 8-10. dBASE Browse for externally created BANK.DBF.

the command line option of the DFP program, the user input could be as simple as the following:

DFPLTS BANK <return>

This would invoke the DFP program to create a Lotus .PRN file from the description contained in the file BANK.TDF. The status screen for this DFP is displayed in Fig. 8-11, and a fragment of the file BANK.PRN is listed in Fig. 8-12. The process of creating an SDF file is just as simple. Running DFPSDF yields the file shown in Fig. 8-13.

Extremely efficient data file interchanges are possible using this approach. The command-line option can be invoked from DOS batch files in such a way as to string a series of programs and procedures together. A single menu item could thus drive a multistep process involving several logical operations. The batch file TEST.BAT contains the following commands:

```
DFPDBF BANK
DBASE MAKEDIF
PARADOX GETDIF
```

while the dBASE program (MAKEDIF.PRG) contains these commands:

Bodner-Hutchins Text Descriptor File Processor (Rev 1.80)

Field Name	Start	End	Type	Decimals	Width
ACCNUMBER	9	15	C	0	7
ACCNAME	17	47	C	0	31
ACCBAL	49	58	F	2	10
INTEREST	72	82	F	2	11
LOANBAL	105	115	F	2	11

File structure as determined from the Text Descriptor File

```
This DFP has converted    71 data records and has created
a 1-2-3 file with     5 data fields in file BANK.PRN
```

Copyright (c) 1986, Bodner-Hutchins Inc., Houston, Texas

‹C:\TDF›

Fig. 8-11. Status report screen for DFPLTS.EXE.

```
" "
"-----------------------------------------------"
"  This data has been processed by DFPLTS.EXE"
"using a BODNER-HUTCHINS Text Descriptor File"
"-----------------------------------------------"
"  This conversion was done at 10:33:36"
"on 06-26-1987 from file BANK     .TXT"
"-----------------------------------------------"
" "
"=========================================================="
"ACCNUMBER","ACCNAME","ACCBAL","INTEREST","LOANBAL"
"=========================================================="
"0164006","Houston Linen Service, Inc.        ",78120.28,10.5,5812.08
"0170007","Howard Safe & Lock Co.             ",4588.6,10.5,4458.85
"0068006","Browning-Ferris Industries         ",21349,10.5,1134.93
"2018001","Always & Forever Florist           ",2114.75,10.5,5211.45
"0304000","Southline Equipment Company        ",1413.19,10.5,4141.32
"0072007","Budget Paper Supply                ",715.15,10.5,0
"0326002","Thompson Industries                ",12222.73,10.5,222.39
"0224002","Nationwide Papers                  ",821.4,10.5,82.3
"0184008","G.M. Woods Company, Inc.           ",16236.9,10.5,2623.08
"0082008","Cargill                            ",31185,10.5,5118.74
"0074007","Bunge Edible Oil Corporation       ",36115.2,8.5,4611.88
"0156005","Holly Sugar Corporation            ",26690.28,10.5,9669.17
"0090009","Charter Oil -Houston               ",6039.35,9.5,603.98
"0234003","Northwest Electric Supply          ",17411.68,10.5,1741.54
"2115001","Easter Plumbing Co.                ",227.5,10.5,22.78
"0196009","Lockwood Manufacturing Inc.        ",4372.35,10.5,2437.24
"0290109","Exxon Exploration Services         ",338732.17,9.5,5873.28
"0178007","International Coal & Energy        ",16436.25,9.5,4643.82
```

Fig. 8-12. BANK.PRN created by DFPLTS.EXE.

```
0164006Houston Linen Service, Inc.     78120.28     10.50    5812.08
0170007Howard Safe & Lock Co.           4588.60     10.50    4458.85
0068006Browning-Ferris Industries      21349.00     10.50    1134.93
2018001Always & Forever Florist         2114.75     10.50    5211.45
0304000Southline Equipment Company      1413.19     10.50    4141.32
0072007Budget Paper Supply               715.15     10.50       0.00
0326002Thompson Industries             12222.73     10.50     222.39
0224002Nationwide Papers                 821.40     10.50      82.30
0184008G.M. Woods Company, Inc.        16236.90     10.50    2623.08
0082008Cargill                         31185.00     10.50    5118.74
0074007Bunge Edible Oil Corporation    36115.20      8.50    4611.88
0156005Holly Sugar Corporation         26690.28     10.50    9669.17
0090009Charter Oil -Houston             6039.35      9.50     603.98
0234003Northwest Electric Supply       17411.68     10.50    1741.54
2115001Easter Plumbing Co.               227.50     10.50      22.78
0196009Lockwood Manufacturing Inc.      4372.35     10.50    2437.24
0290109Exxon Exploration Services     338732.17      9.50    5873.28
0178007International Coal & Energy     16436.25      9.50    4643.82
0005000A & B Safe & Lock Service         348.19     10.50      34.83
0001000A & E Messenger Service            92.75     10.50       0.00
2038103Automatic Data Processing          75.00     10.50       0.00
```

Fig. 8-13. SDF file created by DFPSDF.EXE.

```
USE BANK
COPY TO BANK DIF
QUIT
```

This program creates a DIF file from the data in BANK.DBF (Fig. 8-14).

```
TABLE
0,1
""

TUPLES
0,72
""

VECTORS
0,6
""

DATA
0,0
""

-1,0
BOT
1,0
"ACCNUMBER"
1,0
"ACCNAME"
1,0
"ACCBAL"
1,0
"INTEREST"
1,0
"LOANBAL"
1,0
""
```

```
-1,0
BOT
1,0
"0164006"
1,0
"Houston Linen Service"
0,78120.28
V
0,10.50
V
0,5812.08
V
0,
V

BOT
1,0
"0170007"
1,0
"Howard Safe & Lock Co."
0,4588.60
V
0,10.50
V
0,4458.85
V
0,
V
```

Fig. 8-14. DIF file fragment (BANK.DIF).

Control is then passed to the Paradox program, which runs a script that imports the DIF file and prints out a special preprogrammed report. Then the batch file ends, and control is returned to the end-user. All with a single command. Such is the power of this methodology. The end-user need not even be aware of the path taken to get the report. It might be amusing to watch the screens fly by, but intervention is not required. A fully automated process is thus executed, using the TDFs, DFPs, and other software tools in concert.

DISCUSSION

As has been shown, this procedure has a number of distinct advantages over the custom programming method. First, and most obvious, is that it is much less complex. The only work that needs to be done is to make sure that the TDF is correct. This work would need to be done anyway. Once the TDF exists, the conversion to a target file of any type is accomplished merely by running the DFP for that file type. The end-user needs only to know the name of the file and the name of the DFP program.

If, for any reason, the host file structure changes, all that would be required would be to edit the TDF to reflect the new source data file structure. No additional programming is needed. Different TDFs can be constructed to extract different data fields in various orders as required by a wide class of users.

In a LAN/Gateway system, the host data file is downloaded and can be simultaneously processed into multiple target file structures, because the source file is read-only. The DFP looks at the TDF, which tells it what to do to create the target. No multiuser locks or access issues arise. This means that one user could get data into dBASE in one form, while a second user, at the same time, uses another TDF to extract different data from the same file into Lotus 1-2-3.

In Focus/PC Focus type systems, interactive queries can be constructed to extract data from the host data files and print reports that have the formats of predefined TDFs, thus creating direct paths into other microcomputer applications on the LAN.

An additional level of power is introduced if the host processor is programmed to create TDFs for the reports and files that it outputs into the integrated information stream. Automatically generated TDFs are well within the realm of possibility for modern computers, and will be enhanced as artificial intelligence takes hold in the industry in the future.

The standard proposed here should be considered a first draft, and is intended purely to illustrate the types of things that can be accomplished with a file description standard. In coming years, the information processing industry will no doubt develop families of such standards that will advance the primary function of the industry itself: the efficient, transparent interchange of data between different applications on different generational levels of computers. The Tower of Babel undone. This is a goal worth striving for, and one whose resolution will benefit all computer users everywhere.

Chapter 9

Summary and Conclusion

To close a book of such broad scope is a relatively simple task. The main theme has been to tie the complex areas of data communications and data file interchange into a single, unified framework. You have been guided through a series of ever more complex layers of information in an attempt to define, explain, and organize these concepts into a useful set of ideas.

Data communications is, by its very nature, complex. This book provides an overview of most of the terms and structural elements of the data communications systems most widely used today. A number of useful tables and definitions have been provided for the reader to use as reference material as required. The products reviewed will, no doubt, exist in much improved versions and have considerable competition by the time this work is published. You are counseled to consult current trade literature as to the state of these products. Product reviews in a book of this type are provided more for illustrative purposes than to be used as the basis for purchasing decisions. Periodicals like *Datamation, ComputerWorld, Infoworld* and *Data Communications* are useful for current information in this field.

Microcomputers are part of an extremely volatile segment of the computer industry. While I feel comfortable taking the position that machines built on the Intel 80386 chip under true 32-bit, multiuser, multitasking operating systems will form the basis of the next few years of computing at this level, I might be wrong. Again, the reader must consult current literature to keep track of new releases of chips and operating systems. By the end of this decade, the

80486 and 80586 will be out, and the dream of having a mainframe on a desktop will be achieved.

The major message is one of *integration*, both at the hardware and the software level. Increasing the utility of the computers and the information that they process requires that the systems themselves begin to conform to standard user interfaces. The SQL family of DBMS products, coupled with intelligent communication subsystems, will certainly go a long way toward fulfilling these goals.

Appendix A

User Manual for TDF/DFP System

This Appendix is a reproduction of the preliminary user documentation provided with the Beta Test version of the Text Descriptor File/Descriptor File Processor system developed by Bodner-Hutchins, Inc. The programs and materials contained in these appendices are submitted to the reader for personal use, so long as the original copyrights are preserved. The programs are offered as is, and are included for illustrative use only.

OVERVIEW

With the proliferation of IBM PC compatible computers and applications packages, the problems of data interchange have reached major proportions. It is now estimated that nearly five million PCs exist, and more are being placed each day. Users have acquired many of these devices through noncentralized, nonstandard methods, often bypassing the traditional data processing center purchasing channels. Thus, it is not unusual to find, in any given site, a number of PCs running a variety of software packages, from word processors to database managers to spreadsheets.

As attempts are made to link the individual workstations into an integrated information processing environment, either by the use of LANs (local area networks) or the incorporation of the PCs into the mainframe or minicomputer systems as intelligent terminals, the "Tower of Babel" effect becomes more pronounced. Each user might have data that is needed by a variable subset of other users, but this data might not be directly compatible with all other packages.

A number of methods exist for data interchange, typically based on the use of "flat" ASCII text or delimited files. These methods require some sophistication on the part of the user to actually accomplish the data interchange, and often the task falls to a programmer in the MIS area. This problem is not difficult, but is also nontrivial. It is a task that is taking more and more time in corporate and institutional data processing areas. It is even more of an issue when a mainframe downloads data into the PC environment and some users want to use the data in dBASE, others in 1-2-3, others in Multimate, and so on. Because the conversion is mechanistic, it should be possible to automate the process.

At first, it might seem that the problems inherent in the automation of such a process are countless due to the number of different file structures that can exist. While it is true that the complexity of the file structures may be high, it is possible to construct a data structure that can offer a fairly complete description of a text or delimited file. This object, which can be called a Text Descriptor File (TDF), can be designed to contain enough information so that programs can be created to process the data in a text file by looking at its TDF. These programs, called Descriptor File Processors (DFP) can thus be used to perform the automated data interchange.

Users can create the TDF by studying the file to be described, using a hard copy or screen display, and extracting the parameters required by the TDF. Descriptor File Processors can be written for any application once the TDF is assumed to be a standard description of the text file. Using the description of the file, the program could know how to set up data fields, extract data, and format it directly into native file formats for the target programs.

Assuming that you have a library of DFPs, and a TDF exists for a given source file, you can process the data into your required target format knowing only the name of the file.

Floppy Disk Installation

If you have a two-drive floppy disk system, place a DOS diskette with the program DISKCOPY on it in drive A: and a blank diskette in drive B:. Close both doors. From the DOS A> prompt, type:

```
DISKCOPY A: B: <return>
```

You will then be prompted to place the source disk in drive A:. Remove DOS, insert the TDF system disk in drive A:, close the door, and press RETURN. At the end of this process, mark the disk in drive B: with a label as TDF Backup. Use this diskette as your working copy. You will be asked if you wish to make any more copies. If you have DFPs, say Y and repeat the process for each DFP you have purchased.

To configure the working copies, place each of them in drive A:. If you are using a monochrome display, please type the following from the DOS A> prompt:

MONO

If you have a color graphics system type this from the DOS A> prompt:

COLOR

Place the master diskettes in a safe place and proceed to the section on file creation.

Hard Disk Installation

If you are going to run the system on a hard disk, from the C> prompt please type the following to create a subdirectory:

MD\TDF

Then type this to go to that directory:

CD\TDF

Then place the TDF system diskette in drive A: and type:

COPY A:*.* C:\TDF

When this process ends, you can copy all of the DFPs on to this directory by placing each DFP disk in drive A: and typing the same command:

COPY A:*.* C:\TDF

If you will be using a monochrome display please type the following from the DOS C> prompt:

MONO

If you have a color graphics system type this from the DOS C> prompt:

COLOR

When done, please place all master diskettes in a safe place and continue.

FILE CREATION

Before you can begin creating a TDF, you must have the source file available so that you can answer the appropriate questions needed to fill in your TDF. For the purposes of this introduction, a sample file called TESTFILE.TXT is included in Fig. A-1. This example file will be used to direct you with the data entry questions.

```
Page No.      1
03/04/86
                         SAMPLE DATABASE REPORT

LAST NAME                       FIRST NAME            SALARY

BANKS                           DAVE                 1000.00
GODOT                           ROBERT              -2000.00
EDWARDS                         KAREN                3000.00
PESTO                           ADOLPH               4000.00
PEOLE                           WILLIAM              5000.00
VALLERIANA                      EVITA                6000.00
ECON                            TOM                  7000.00
ENG                             JOHN                 8000.00
ESTRADA                         CORINA               9000.00
BUCKHOLTZ                       WALTER              10000.00
FIELDS                          KAREN               11000.00
HALEY                           ALBERT              12000.00
JACKSON                         ANDREW              13000.00
YANG                            CHARLES             14000.00
ROSS                            DIANA               15000.00
WILLIAMS                        JOHN                16000.00
FRANKS                          HOWARD              17000.00
LOPEZ                           RICARDO             18000.00
CORPEZZIO                       ALBERTO             19000.00
WALDEN                          RALPH               20000.00
AQUILA                          MARCY               21000.00
ECHIVA                          WANDA               22000.00
JALESTA                         DEREK               23000.00
CHUNG                           CONNIE              24000.00
CLARK                           KENT                25000.00
DACKS                           RODNEY              26000.00
QUINN                           ANTHONY             27000.00
BENNETT                         WILLIAM             28000.00
FRAMIL                          IRENE               29000.00
MEADE                           JOHN                30000.00
YIP                             SINDNEY             31000.00
PHRESTER                        YEHUDA              32000.00
URATEN                          ERICA               33000.00
NORDICA                         RICHARD             34000.00
HERRERA                         ENRICO              35000.00
PRAFAL                          NATRAJ              36000.00
FORMIGGIA                       TONY                37000.00
```

Fig. A-1. Flat ASCII captured data file, TESTFILE.TXT, used for examples. (Continued through page 164.)

Page No. 2
03/04/86

SAMPLE DATABASE REPORT

LAST NAME	FIRST NAME	SALARY
GRANT	LOU	38000.00
RODRIGUEZ	ROSA	39000.00
VASQUEZ	ERICA	40000.00
DUNN	TONY	41000.00
HERALD	RICHARD	42000.00
CORRLEONE	VITO	43000.00
BELL	ALEXANDER	44000.00
NESTAR	RICKY	45000.00
GARCON	IGOR	46000.00
FLOUNDER	STUFFED	47000.00
GONZALEZ	PEDRO	48000.00
LEE	BRUCE	49000.00
MARCIANO	ROCKY	50000.00
PEDRONA	PHILLIP	51000.00
VALLE	RUDY	52000.00
YOUNG	MIGHTY JOE	53000.00
IULGENCIO	JULIO	54000.00
GRECO	JOSE	55000.00
MIRAMAR	ALBERT	56000.00
PHILLIPA	RICHARD	57000.00
SMELLING	ALFRED	58000.00
ZARDOZ	SEAN	59000.00
ANORICO	AUGUSTO	60000.00
BAUMEL	ABE	61000.00
BORLAND	PHILLIPE	62000.00
BOYERS	ROBERTA	63000.00
BROWN	RICHARD	64000.00
CASTRO	FIDEL	65000.00
CHIN	WILLIAM	66000.00
ESPERANZA	JOSE	67000.00
FORMERO	ALBERTO	68000.00
MARRAGIO	ALPHONSO	69000.00
MC LAIR	JOHN	70000.00
POPPOV	IVAN	71000.00
RICHARDSON	RALPH	72000.00
SANMARTINO	BRUNO	73000.00
TAGGERT	DAGNEY	74000.00
THREATEN	OMAR	75000.00
TRAVIS	JIM	76000.00
TULSA	JAMES	77000.00
HERNANDEZ	TITO	78000.00
MC GLAUGHLIN	RICHARD	79000.00
SCHAEFFER	RICHARD	80000.00
*** Total ***		
		3240000.00

There are on-line help messages displayed with each data entry prompt. These are designed to guide you along once you are familiar with the program. This manual will supply you with more detailed information for the novice. Creating TDFs are not difficult once the source document is "lined" out. Figure A-2 contains a segment of the sample file with line and column numbers overlaid so that you can follow the reasoning of the data entry procedure.

```
                                               42
                                               v
        09              25 27          40 43      50   54          65  69      76
        v               v  v           v  v       v    v           v   v       v
--------+---------------+-+-----------+-++-------+----+-----------+---+-------+

1       Page No.        1
2       03/04/86
3                                   SAMPLE DATABASE REPORT
4
5       LAST NAME               FIRST NAME      AGE     UNION          SALARY    HIRE
6                                                                                DATE
7
8       BANKS                   DAVE             21       Y           1000.00   02/12/78
9       GODOT                   ROBERT           19       Y           2000.00   12/13/82
.
.
.
33      HERNANDEZ               TITO             34       Y          78000.00   01/16/53
34      MC GLAUGHLIN            RICHARD          45       Y          79000.00   06/30/77
35      SCHAEFFER               RICHARD          26       Y          80000.00   01/29/81
36      *** Total ***
37                                                             3240000.00
-------+---------------------------------------------+---------+--------------
       ^                                             ^         ^
       08                                            54        65
```

Fig. A-2. Sample file fragment with ruler lines.

Entry for Nondelimited Text/Files

There are two basic classes of files handled by the TDF System, ASCII text (nondelimited) files and delimited files. For ASCII data entry, continue with this section. To see how delimited files are handled, turn to the section titled "Entry for Delimited Text/Files."

To begin the Text Descriptor File Generator simply type TDF from the DOS prompt. The Text Descriptor File Generator main menu (Fig. A-3) will be displayed and will be ready to accept the name of your new TDF. The TDF name may be different than the name of your source file, so that you can create many different TDFs for each source file, if you wish. If you just press return, the default name of TDF_051 (where the last four characters are the date) will be supplied. The finished TDF will always have .TDF as its suffix. The source file for this example is labeled TESTFILE.TXT and the TDF will be called TESTFILE.TDF.

Type TESTFILE and press RETURN. The Text Descriptor File

```
              Bodner-Hutchins Text Descriptor File System
_____________________________________________________________________

 ________________________________________________________________
|  This program will enable the user to create a standard Text Descriptor  |
|  File (TDF) which can later be processed by Descriptor File Processors.  |
|__________________________________________________________________________|

                 _________________________________
                |  Text Descriptor File Generator |
                |_________________________________|
                | 13 May 1986            02:07:05 |
                |                                 |
                |           Version 1.74          |
                |_________________________________|

                 _________________________________
                |  Enter TDF name :  [_        ]  |
                |_________________________________|

            Please enter the name of TDF file or Q to quit
_____________________________________________________________________
         Copyright (c) 1986, Bodner-Hutchins Inc., Houston, Texas
```

Fig. A-3. Front TDF screen.

Generator displays a data entry screen as shown in Fig. A-4. You are prompted at the bottom of the screen for the information needed for each entry. If you make a mistake while still in a field, simply use the BACKSPACE key to go back and correct your error. Press the RETURN key to enter the information.

```
SOURCE DOCUMENT FILE NAME - ANY VALID DOS FILE NAME (RETURN FOR TDF NAME)
 ______________________________________________________________________________
|FILENAME|LW.|C|L|F|LP.|SL.|EL.|D|DC1|DC2|DC3|ILC......|NF|SDLC...|O|SCS|SN|
|        |   | | | |   |   |   | |   |   |   |         |  |       | |   |  |
|______________________________________________________________________________|
|                                                                              |
|______________________________________________________________________________|
|NM1         |FS1|FS2|V|DP|NM2         |FS1|FS2|V|DP|NM3         |FS1|FS2|V|DP|TC|
|            |   |   | |  |            |   |   | |  |            |   |   | |  |  |
|______________________________________________________________________________|
|                                                                            *1|
|______________________________________________________________________________|
|NM4         |FS1|FS2|V|DP|NM5         |FS1|FS2|V|DP|NM6         |FS1|FS2|V|DP|TC|
|            |   |   | |  |            |   |   | |  |            |   |   | |  |  |
|______________________________________________________________________________|
|                                                                            *2|
|______________________________________________________________________________|
|NM7         |FS1|FS2|V|DP|NM8         |FS1|FS2|V|DP|NM9         |FS1|FS2|V|DP|TC|
|            |   |   | |  |            |   |   | |  |            |   |   | |  |  |
|______________________________________________________________________________|
|                                                                            *3|
|______________________________________________________________________________|
|NM10        |FS1|FS2|V|DP|NM11        |FS1|FS2|V|DP|NM12        |FS1|FS2|V|DP|TC|
|            |   |   | |  |            |   |   | |  |            |   |   | |  |  |
|______________________________________________________________________________|
|                                                                            *4|
|______________________________________________________________________________|
    | Filename : [_          ]           |
    |____________________________________|              Press Esc to Abort
```

Fig. A-4. Data entry screen.

If you make mistakes and you have passed the field, you can bring up TESTFILE.TDF with TDFED and make any corrections.

Field: FILENAME

FILENAME

For the filename, type TESTFILE and press RETURN.

The filename must be the name of the source file. If you do not know the name of your source file, you can press RETURN and accept the default of TDF__051, which would be your system date. Once you have the source name, you can bring up your TDF in TDFED and change this filename to your source name. TDFs and DFPs will not be able to process any data unless this field matches your source file.

Field: LW

LINE WIDTH (1-255)

The data line width of the example is 76, so type 76 and press RETURN.

TDF will accept a range from 1 to 255 characters. Using a computer ruler, measure the number of characters on a data line in your source file.

ERROR TRAP: This entry must be greater than zero and less than 256.

Field: C

IS THERE A CARRIAGE RETURN (Y/N)

Type Y and press RETURN.

This is determined by looking at the source file to see if it wraps around on the end of the line, as shown in Fig. A-5. If no wrap occurs, the response would be Y.

ERROR TRAP: This field will not accept any response except Y or N.

```
           BANKS               DAVE              21        Y          1000.00    02/12/78
       GODOT              ROBERT          19        Y          2000.00    12/13/82
EDWARDS             KAREN           34        N          3000.00    10/15/79          P
O               ADOLPH          45        N          4000.00    11/29/83          PEOLE
             WILLIAM          26        N          5000.00    04/04/48          VALLERIAN
         EVITA              31        Y          6000.00    01/16/53
```

Fig. A-5. Sample of file with no carriage return.

Field: L

IS THERE A LINE FEED (Y/N)

Type Y and press RETURN.

In most modern-day systems, a carriage return and line feed are issued together. If you answered Y to field C usually you would respond Y in this field.

ERROR TRAP: This field will not accept any response except Y or N.

Field: F

IS THERE A FORM FEED (Y/N)

The example breaks, so type Y and press RETURN.

Is your source file continuous or does it break at the end of the page? If it breaks, skips a few lines and begins at the top of the next page, answer Y.

ERROR TRAP: This field will not accept any response except Y or N.

Field: LP

NUMBER LINES/PAGE

Type 66 and press RETURN.

The standard for an 11-inch page is 66 lines. For unusual formats, multiply the page length in inches by six.

ERROR TRAP: This field entry must be greater than zero.

Field: SL

STARTING DATA LINE

The example has data starting on line 8, so type 8 and press RETURN.

This should be the starting line of data that you wish to be processed. This is usually the first line after any header or label information.

ERROR TRAP: This field entry must be greater than zero.

Field: EL

ENDING DATA LINE #

Type 59, and press RETURN.

This is the last line of data on the page that is to be processed. This is not the end of file, but merely the bottom of the page whose length was defined by variable LP above. Do not include footer information. Totals and "special data" lines must be included in this number.

ERROR TRAP: This field entry must be less than or equal to the number of lines per page and greater than zero.

Field: D

IS THE FILE DELIMITED (Y/N)

Enter N and press RETURN.

Field: DC1
Field: DC2
Field: DC

These pertain to delimited files, and are automatically bypassed when N is entered for the previous question. See "Entry for Delimited Text/Files."

Field: ILC

IGNORE LINE CODE

The example does not have any lines that need to be ignored. You will therefore keep the default of a period (.) by pressing the RETURN key.

Enter the sequence of characters that mark a line to be ignored in processing. This could be a line with = = = = or - - - -.

TIP: The default of a period (.) prevents a data line beginning with 10 blanks from being ignored.

NOTE: The DFP programs already ignore totally blank lines.

Field: NF

NUMBER OF DATA FIELDS (1-24)

You are going to process all six fields in the example: LASTNAME, FIRSTNAME, SALARY, UNION, HIREDATE, and AGE. Type 6 and press RETURN.

TDFs can be set up to process only the data fields that you want processed, and appear in any order in the target file.

TIP: The data fields do not have to be in the same order as in the source file, or contain all of the data that your file contains. The TDF system will allow for a total of 24 data fields to be defined. An additional data field definition screen will be displayed if one or more fields are to be defined.

ERROR TRAP: This field entry must be greater than zero and less than or equal to 24.

Field: SDLC

SPECIAL DATA LINE CODE

Type (***) TOT and press RETURN.

You must tell your TDF and subsequent DFP to process this as special data information instead of normal data information. The example shows *** Total ***, which is considered a special data line. As you probably noticed, the special data line code was too large for the field. Do not be alarmed; this is enough information for the TDF and DFP to process the information correctly. This is the code that identifies a line containing special data such as subtotals, totals or averages.

Field: O

SPECIAL DATA LINE OFFSET

Figure A-6 shows *** Total *** on one line, yet the actual amount (5482000.00) is one line lower. Therefore, type 1, and press RETURN.

This field holds the number of lines that the special data is offset from the special character code line.

Field: SCS

START COLUMN SPECIAL CODE (1-255)

*** Total *** starts in column 8. Type 8 and press RETURN.

```
                                                   42
                                                   v
         09                25 27            40   43       50   54            65   69       76
         v                 v  v             v    v        v    v             v    v        v
--------+----------------+-+-------------+-++-------+---+-----------+---+-------+-
33       HERNANDEZ          TITO                34       Y          78000.00    01/16/53
34       MC GLAUGHLIN       RICHARD             45       Y          79000.00    06/30/77
35       SCHAEFFER          RICHARD             26       Y          80000.00    01/29/81
36      *** Total ***
37                                                                5482000.00
-------+----------------------------------------------+----------+-----------
       ^                                              ^          ^
       08                                             54         65
```

Fig. A-6. Offset display.

The starting column of the special data line code in your text/file goes here. The range allowed is from 1 to 255. This tells the DFP where to look for the special data code.

Field: SN

NUMBER SPECIAL FIELDS (1-12)
The example has only one special field (5482000.00), which you will later below. Type 1 and press RETURN.

Enter the number of special data fields desired to be processed in the target file. The system allows up to 12 special data fields.

NOTE: The data entry prompts are now being displayed in the upper part of the screen.

The Target File. Now is the time to select field placement for your target file. Although the example file is structured LASTNAME, FIRSTNAME, AGE, UNION, SALARY, and HIREDATE, TDFs can be set up in any order (Fig. A-7). For this example, you will have your target file setup as FIRSTNAME, LASTNAME, SALARY, UNION, HIREDATE and AGE.

TIP: With the TDF system you do not have to take all of the fields from your text/file. You only need to designate the fields that you want processed.

Field: NM1

NAME OF DATA FIELD 1
Type FIRSTNAME and press RETURN.

This entry can contain 1 to 10 alphanumeric characters, but no spaces are allowed. You can use the underline (_) key as a hard space if desired. Thus, FIRST_NAME is a valid data field name. If you press RETURN, the default of FIELD_01 will be selected.

Field: FS1

STARTING COLUMN OF FIELD 1
FIRSTNAME field starts at column 27. Therefore, type 27 and press RETURN.

```
Bod                                    rator (Rev 1.74) - Normal Data
   | Name of data field 01:[_          ] |
|FIL|                                    |DC3|ILC......|NF|SDLC...|O|SCS|SN|
|                                                                           |
|TESTFILE 076 Y Y Y 066 008 059 N 000 000 000 .         06 *** TOT 1 008 01|
|                                                                           |
|NM1       |FS1|FS2|V|DP|NM2       |FS1|FS2|V|DP|NM3       |FS1|FS2|V|DP|TC|
|                                                                           |
|                                                                        *1|
|                                                                           |
|NM4       |FS1|FS2|V|DP|NM5       |FS1|FS2|V|DP|NM6       |FS1|FS2|V|DP|TC|
|                                                                           |
|                                                                        *2|
|                                                                           |
|NM7       |FS1|FS2|V|DP|NM8       |FS1|FS2|V|DP|NM9       |FS1|FS2|V|DP|TC|
|                                                                           |
|                                                                        *3|
|                                                                           |
|NM10      |FS1|FS2|V|DP|NM11      |FS1|FS2|V|DP|NM12      |FS1|FS2|V|DP|TC|
|                                                                           |
|                                                                        *4|
|                                                                           |
ENTER 1-10 ALPHANUMERIC CHARACTERS,NO SPACES ALLOWED,USE UNDERLINE FOR SPACE
                                                         Press Esc to Abort
```

Fig. A-7. Data field definition screen.

Enter the starting column from your source file which is to be the first field for the target file.

ERROR TRAP: This field entry must be greater than zero.

Field: FS2

ENDING COLUMN OF FIELD 1

You want FIRSTNAME to be 14 characters wide. Type 40 and press RETURN.

This determines the width of the field FIRSTNAME in your target file. You are not restricted to the width in your source file. TDFs and DFPs will make your target file to your specifications.

ERROR TRAP: This field entry must be greater than zero.

Field: V

TYPE OF VARIABLE (FIDLC)

FIRSTNAME is a character field, so type C and press RETURN.

The TDF system will accept all of the types listed below:

Floating point decimal	(currency/numeric with decimal)
Integer	(whole number)
Date	(date)
Logical	(true/false)
Character	(alphanumeric)

ERROR TRAP: This field entry must be F, I, D, L or C.

Field: DP

NUMBER OF DECIMALS

This field has been skipped because you answered C for the type of variable.

This prompt will only appear if you have entered F (floating point decimal), and would then require you to enter the number of digits to the right of the decimal point.

Field: NM2

NAME OF DATA FIELD 2

Type LASTNAME and press RETURN.

This entry can contain 1 to 10 alphanumeric characters, but no spaces are allowed. You can use the underline (_) key as a hard space if you wish. Thus, LAST_NAME is a valid data field name. If you press RETURN, the default of FIELD_02 will be selected.

Field: FS1

STARTING COLUMN OF FIELD 2

LASTNAME field starts at column 9. Therefore, type 9 and press return.

Enter the starting column from your source file which is to be the second field for the target file.

ERROR TRAP: This field entry must be greater than zero.

Field: FS2

ENDING COLUMN OF FIELD 2

You want LASTNAME to be 17 characters wide. Type 25 and press RETURN.

This determines the width of the field LASTNAME in your target file. You are not restricted to the width in your text/file. TDFs and DFPs will make your target file to your specifications.

ERROR TRAP: This field entry must be greater than zero.

Field: V

TYPE OF VARIABLE (FIDLC)

LASTNAME is a character field, so type C and press RETURN.

The TDF system will accept all of the types listed below:

Floating point decimal	(currency/numeric with decimal)
Integer	(whole number)
Date	(date)
Logical	(true/false)
Character	(alphanumeric)

ERROR TRAP: This field entry must be F, I, D, L or C.

Field: DP

NUMBER OF DECIMALS

This field has been skipped because you answered C for the type of variable.

This prompt will only appear if you have entered F (floating point decimal), and would then require you to enter the number of digits to the right of the decimal point.

Field: NM

NAME OF DATA FIELD

Type SALARY and press RETURN.

This entry can contain 1 to 10 alphanumeric characters, but no spaces are allowed. You can use the underline (_) key as a hard space. Thus, SALARY is a valid data field name. If you press RETURN, the default of FIELD_0 will be selected.

Field: FS1

STARTING COLUMN OF FIELD

SALARY field starts at column 54. Therefore type 54 and press return.

Enter the starting column from your source file which is to be the third field for the target file.

ERROR TRAP: This field entry must be greater than zero.

Field: FS2

ENDING COLUMN OF FIELD

You want SALARY to be 12 characters wide. Type 65 and press RETURN.

This determines the width of the field SALARY in your target file. You are not restricted to the width in your source file. TDFs and DFPs will make your target file to your specifications.

ERROR TRAP: This field entry must be greater than zero.

Field: V

TYPE OF VARIABLE (FIDLC)

SALARY is a floating point decimal field so type F and press RETURN.

The TDF system will accept all of the types listed below.

Floating point decimal	(currency/numeric with decimal)
Integer	(whole number)
Date	(date)
Logical	(true/false)
Character	(alphanumeric)

ERROR TRAP: This field entry must be F, I, D, L or C.

Field: DP

NUMBER OF DECIMALS

SALARY has two decimal placements. Type 2 and press RETURN.

The number of digits desired to the right of the decimal point.

ERROR TRAP: This number cannot be more than the length of the number minus one.

Field: NM4

NAME OF DATA FIELD 4

Type UNION and press RETURN.

This entry can contain 1 to 10 alphanumeric characters, but no spaces are allowed. You can use the underline (_) key as a hard space if you wish. If you press RETURN, the default of FIELD_04 will be selected.

Field: FS1

STARTING COLUMN OF FIELD 4

UNION is a logical field, making it one character wide. The field starts at column 50, so type 50 and press RETURN.

Enter the starting column from your source file which is to be the fourth field for the target file.

NOTE: Logical fields should only be one character wide. Therefore, the starting and ending column must always be the same number.

ERROR TRAP: This field entry must be greater than zero.

Field: FS2

ENDING COLUMN OF FIELD 4

UNION is a logical field one character wide. Type 50 and press RETURN.

This determines the width of the field UNION in your target file. Because this is a logical field, you are restricted to a one character field length.

Field: V

TYPE OF VARIABLE (FIDLC)

UNION is a logical field, so type L and press RETURN.

The TDF system will accept all of the types listed below:

Floating point decimal	(currency/numeric with decimal)
Integer	(whole number)
Date	(date)
Logical	(true/false)
Character	(alphanumeric)

ERROR TRAP: This field entry must be F, I, D, L or C.

Field: DP

NUMBER OF DECIMALS

This field has been skipped because you answered L for the type of variable.

This prompt will only appear if you have entered F (floating point decimal), and would then require you to enter the number of digits to the right of the decimal point.

Field: NM5

NAME OF DATA FIELD 5

Type HIRE_DATE and press RETURN.

This entry can contain 1 to 10 alphanumeric characters, but no spaces are allowed. You can use the underline (_) key as a hard space. Thus, HIRE_DATE is a valid data field name. If you press RETURN, the default of FIELD_05 will be selected.

Field: FS1

STARTING COLUMN OF FIELD 5

HIREDATE field starts at column 69. Therefore, type 69 and press RETURN.

Enter the starting column from the source file which is to be the fifth field for the target file.

Field: FS2

ENDING COLUMN OF FIELD 5

You want HIRE_DATE to be 8 characters wide. Type 76 and press RETURN.

This determines the width of the field HIRE_DATE in your target file. You are not restricted to the width in your source file. TDFs and DFPs will make your target file to your specifications.

Field: V

TYPE OF VARIABLE (FIDLC)

HIRE_DATE is a date field so type D and press RETURN.

The TDF system will accept all of the types listed below.

Floating point decimal	(currency/numeric with decimal)
Integer	(whole number)
Date	(date)
Logical	(true/false)
Character	(alphanumeric)

ERROR TRAP: This field entry must be F, I, D, L or C.

Field: DP

NUMBER OF DECIMALS

This field has been skipped because you answered D for the type of variable.

This prompt will only appear if you have entered F (floating point decimal), and would then require you to enter the number of digits to the right of the decimal point.

Field: NM6

NAME OF DATA FIELD 6

Type AGE and press RETURN.

This entry can contain 1 to 10 alphanumeric characters but no spaces are allowed. You can use the underline (_) key as a hard space if desired. If you press RETURN, the default of FIELD_06 will be selected.

Field: FS1

STARTING COLUMN OF FIELD 6

AGE field starts at column 42. Therefore, type 42 and press RETURN.

Enter the starting column from your source file, which is to be the sixth field for the target file.

Field: FS2

ENDING COLUMN OF FIELD 6

You want AGE to be 2 characters wide. Type 4 and press RETURN.

This determines the width of the field AGE in your target file. You are not restricted to the width in your source file. TDFs and DFPs will make your target file to your specifications.

Field: V

TYPE OF VARIABLE (FIDLC)

AGE is an Integer field so type I and press RETURN.

The TDF system will accept all of the types listed below.

Floating point decimal	(currency/numeric with decimal)
Integer	(whole number)
Date	(date)
Logical	(true/false)
Character	(alphanumeric)

ERROR TRAP: This field entry must be F, I, D, L or C.

Field: DP

NUMBER OF DECIMALS

This field has been skipped because you answered I for the type of variable (Fig. A-8).

This prompt will only appear if you have entered F (floating point decimal), and would then require you to enter the number of digits to the right of the decimal point.

```
Bod ___________________________________ rator (Rev 1.74) - Normal Data
___| Type of variable (FIDLC)       [I] |________________________________
|FIL|___________________________________|DC3|ILC......|NF|SDLC...|O|SCS|SN|
|                                                                          |
|TESTFILE 076 Y Y Y 066 008 059 N 000 000 000 .         06 *** TOT 1 008 01|
|                                                                          |
|NM1        |FS1|FS2|V|DP|NM2        |FS1|FS2|V|DP|NM3        |FS1|FS2|V|DP|TC|
|                                                                          |
|FIRSTNAME   027 040 C    LASTNAME    009 025 C    SALARY      054 065 F 02 *1|
|                                                                          |
|NM4        |FS1|FS2|V|DP|NM5        |FS1|FS2|V|DP|NM6        |FS1|FS2|V|DP|TC|
|                                                                          |
|UNION       050 050 L    HIRE_DATE   069 076 D    AGE         042 043 I    *2|
|                                                                          |
|NM7        |FS1|FS2|V|DP|NM8        |FS1|FS2|V|DP|NM9        |FS1|FS2|V|DP|TC|
|                                                                          |
|                                                                        *3|
|                                                                          |
|NM10       |FS1|FS2|V|DP|NM11       |FS1|FS2|V|DP|NM12       |FS1|FS2|V|DP|TC|
|                                                                          |
|                                                                        *4|
|                                                                          |
FLOATING POINT DECIMAL, INTEGER, DATE, LOGICAL, OR CHARACTER
                                                        Press Esc to Abort
```

Fig. A-8. Completed data entry screen.

Special Data Fields. Now is the time to define any special data fields. Shown below is a blank special data screen. You are once again prompted to enter all pertinent information (Fig. A-9). Please note that the data structure is identical to that of normal data lines.

```
 _____________________________________
| Name of data field 01:[_          ] |
|_____________________________________|

 Bodner-Hutchins Text Descriptor File Generator (Rev 1.74) - Special Data

|SNM1       |FS1|FS2|V|DP|SNM2       |FS1|FS2|V|DP|SNM3       |FS1|FS2|V|DP|TC|
|                                                                          |
|                                                                        *9|
|                                                                          |
|SNM4       |FS1|FS2|V|DP|SNM5       |FS1|FS2|V|DP|SNM6       |FS1|FS2|V|DP|TC|
|                                                                          |
|                                                                        *A|
|                                                                          |
|SNM7       |FS1|FS2|V|DP|SNM8       |FS1|FS2|V|DP|SNM9       |FS1|FS2|V|DP|TC|
|                                                                          |
|                                                                        *B|
|                                                                          |
|SNM10      |FS1|FS2|V|DP|SNM11      |FS1|FS2|V|DP|SNM12      |FS1|FS2|V|DP|EF|
|                                                                          |
|                                                                        FF|
|                                                                          |
ENTER 1-10 ALPHANUMERIC CHARACTERS,NO SPACES ALLOWED,USE UNDERLINE FOR SPACE
                                                        Press Esc to Abort
```

Fig. A-9. Blank special data entry screen.

Field: SNM1

NAME OF DATA FIELD 1

Type TOTSALARY and press RETURN.

Previously you built the TDF to process *** as the special data line code identifier, and gave an offset value of 1, indicating that the actual data was on the next line. Now you can label this data field in your target file. The name of any special data fields requested earlier will have a default of SPECL__01 if you do not enter any other name and press RETURN.

Field: FS1

STARTING COLUMN OF FIELD 1

In the example, 5482000.00 starts at line 54. Type 54 and press RETURN.

Enter the starting column of a special data field from your source text/file.

Field: FS2

ENDING COLUMN OF FIELD 1

You want the total amount to be 13 spaces wide. Type 66 and press RETURN.

This determines the width of the special data field.

Field: V

TYPE OF VARIABLE (FIDLC)

This is an amount field (54820000.00), so type F and press RETURN.

The TDF system will accept all of the types listed below:

Floating point decimal	(currency/numeric with decimal)
Integer	(whole number)
Date	(date)
Logical	(true/false)
Character	(alphanumeric)

Field: DP

NUMBER OF DECIMALS

54820000.00 requires a two decimal placement. Type 2 and press RETURN.

The number of digits desired to the right of the decimal point is held here.

ERROR TRAP: This number cannot be more than the length of the number minus one.

You are now finished configuring your TDF and will have a finished file called TESTFILE.TDF. The screen in Fig. A-10 displays the data you entered in its completed format. If you have made any mistakes, simply edit the file with TDFED. Figures A-11 and A-12 show the results of this example.

```
| Number of decimals : [2_ ]                       |
|__________________________________________________|

Bodner-Hutchins Text Descriptor File Generator (Rev 1.74) - Special Data
 ______________________________________________________________________________________________
|SNM1          |FS1|FS2|V|DP|SNM2          |FS1|FS2|V|DP|SNM3          |FS1|FS2|V|DP|TC|
|              |   |   | |  |              |   |   | |  |              |   |   | |  |__|
|TOTSALARY   054 065 F 02                                                               *9|
|______________________________________________________________________________________________|
|SNM4          |FS1|FS2|V|DP|SNM5          |FS1|FS2|V|DP|SNM6          |FS1|FS2|V|DP|TC|
|              |   |   | |  |              |   |   | |  |              |   |   | |  |__|
|                                                                                       *A|
|______________________________________________________________________________________________|
|SNM7          |FS1|FS2|V|DP|SNM8          |FS1|FS2|V|DP|SNM9          |FS1|FS2|V|DP|TC|
|              |   |   | |  |              |   |   | |  |              |   |   | |  |__|
|                                                                                       *B|
|______________________________________________________________________________________________|
|SNM10         |FS1|FS2|V|DP|SNM11         |FS1|FS2|V|DP|SNM12         |FS1|FS2|V|DP|EF|
|              |   |   | |  |              |   |   | |  |              |   |   | |  |__|
|                                                                                       FF|
|______________________________________________________________________________________________|
NUMBER OF DIGITS DESIRED TO THE RIGHT OF THE DECIMAL POINT
                                                                          Press Esc to Abort
```

Fig. A-10. Completed special data entry screen.

Entry for Delimited Text/Files

Before you can begin creating a TDF, you must have the source file available so that you can answer the appropriate questions needed to fill in your TDF. For the purposes of this introduction, a sample file called

```
          Bodner-Hutchins Text Descriptor File Generator  (Rev 1.74)
 ______________________________________________________________________________
|TESTFILE 076 Y Y Y 066 008 059 N 000 000 000 .          06 *** TOT 1 008 01|
|FIRSTNAME   027 040 C NA LASTNAME    009 025 C NA SALARY      054 065 F 02 *1|
|UNION       050 050 L NA HIRE_DATE   069 076 D NA AGE         042 043 I NA *2|
|                                                                          *3|
|                                                                          *4|
|                                                                          *5|
|                                                                          *6|
|                                                                          *7|
|                                                                          *8|
|TOTSALARY   054 065 F 02                                                  *9|
|                                                                          *A|
|                                                                          *B|
|                                                                          FF|
|______________________________________________________________________________|

          Data is being written to Text Descriptor File [TESTFILE.TDF]

 ______________________________________________________________________________
|   This TDF, when used with its associated data file, can be processed by    |
| any Descriptor File Processor (DFPxxx.EXE) to create native file formats.   |
|______________________________________________________________________________|
```

Fig. A-11. TDF processing screen.

```
           Bodner-Hutchins Text Descriptor File System
________________________________________________________________



        Program terminated normally. TDF generated.

                  13 May 1986          02:26:11



________________________________________________________________
   Copyright (c) 1986, Bodner-Hutchins Inc., Houston, Texas
```

Fig. A-12. Final TDF screen.

CHAMBER.TXT is included in Fig. A-13. This example file will be used to direct you with the data entry questions.

There are on-line help messages displayed with each data entry prompt. These are designed to guide you along once you are familiar with the program. This manual will supply you with more detailed information for the novice.

Delimited files are handled differently than the ASCII files discussed in the previous section. Rather than counting columns, you will merely need to identify field names and widths desired in the target file. Figure A-14 contains a segment of the sample file showing the data fields of various lengths separated by the delimiter characters quote, comma, quote.

To begin the Text Descriptor File Generator, simply type TDF from the DOS prompt. The Text Descriptor File Generator main menu will be displayed (Fig. A-15) and will be ready to accept the name of your new TDF. This name may be different than the name of your source file, so that you can create many different TDFs for each source file if you wish.

If you just press return, the default name of TDF__051 (where the last four characters are the date) will be supplied. The finished TDF will always have .TDF as its suffix. In this example, the source file is labeled CHAMBER.TXT and the TDF will be called CHAMBER.TDF. Type CHAMBER and press RETURN.

The Text Descriptor File Generator displays a data entry screen as shown in Fig. A-16. You are prompted at the bottom of the screen for the information needed for each entry. If you make a mistake while still in a field, simply use the BACKSPACE key to go back and correct your error. Press the return key to enter the information. If mistakes are made and you have passed the field, you can bring up CHAMBER.TDF with TDFED and make any corrections.

```
Delimited File CHAMBER.TXT used for examples in User Manual

"Austin Chamber of Commerce","901 W. Riverside Drive","Austin","TX","78704"
"Albuquerque Chamber of Commerce","401 Second Street, N.W.","Albuquerque","NM","87102"
"Atlanta Chamber of Commerce","1300 N. Omni International","Atlanta","GA","30303"
"Boston Chamber of Commerce","125 High Street","Houston","TX","02110"
"Cincinnati Chamber of Commerce","120 W. Fifth Street","Cincinnati","OH","45202"
"Columbus Area Chamber of Commerce","P.O. Box 1527","Columbus","OH","43216"
"Dallas Chamber of Commerce","1507 Pacific","Dallas","TX","75201"
"Greater Detroit Chamber of Commerce","150 Michigan Avenue","Detroit","MI","48226"
"Fort Worth Chamber of Commerce","700 Throckmorton","Fort Worth","TX","76102"
"Chamber of Commerce of Greater Kansas City","920 Main Street","Kansas City","MO","64105"
"Los Angeles Chamber of Commerce","404 S. Bixel Street","Los Angeles","CA","90017"
"Memphis Area Chamber of Commerce","P.O. Box 224","Memphis","TN","38103"
"Greater Minneapolis Chamber of Commerce","15 South Fifth Street",
   "Minneapolis","MN","55402"
"Nashville Area Chamber of Commerce","161 Fourth Avenue North","Nashville","TN","37219"
"New Orleans and the River Region Chamber of Commerce","301 Camp Street",
   "New Orleans","LA","70130"
"Omaha Chamber of Commerce","1620 Dodge Street","Omaha","NE","68102"
"Greater Philadelphia Chamber of Commerce","1617 John F. Kennedy Boulevard",
   "Philadelphia","PA","19103"
"Phoenix Chamber of Commerce","805 North Second Street","Phoenix","AZ","85004"
"San Diego Chamber of Commerce","110 West C Street, Suite 1600","San Diego","CA","92101"
"Greater San Antonio Chamber of Commerce","P.O. Box 1628, 602 E. Commerce",
   "San Antonio","TX","78296"
"Greater San Francisco Chamber of Commerce","465 California Street",
   "San Francisco","CA","94104"
"St. Louis Regional Commerce & Growth Association","10 Broadway","St. Louis","MO","63102"
"Seattle Chamber of Commerce","215 Columbia","Seattle","WA","98104"
"Tucson Chamber of Commerce","P.O. Box 991","Tucson","AZ","85702"
"Metropolitan Tulsa Chamber of Commerce","616 S. Boston","Tulsa","OK","74119"
"D. C. Chamber of Commerce","1319 F Street, N.W.","Washington","DC","20004"
```

Fig. A-13. Delimited file, CHAMBER.TXT, used for examples.

Field: FILENAME

FILENAME

For the filename, type CHAMBER and press RETURN.

This must be the name of the source file. If you do not know the name of your source file, you can press RETURN and accept the default of TDF__051, which would be your system date. Once you have the source name,

```
"Austin Chamber of Commerce","901 W. Riverside Drive","Austin","TX","78704"
"Boston Chamber of Commerce","125 High Street","Houston","TX","02110"
"Columbus Area Chamber of Commerce","P.O. Box 1527","Columbus","OH","43216"
"Dallas Chamber of Commerce","1507 Pacific","Dallas","TX","75201"
"Memphis Area Chamber of Commerce","P.O. Box 224","Memphis","TN","38103"
"Omaha Chamber of Commerce","1620 Dodge Street","Omaha","NE","68102"
```

Fig. A-14. Sample fragment of delimited file.

```
 This program will enable the user to create a standard Text Descriptor
 File (TDF) which can later be processed by Descriptor File Processors.

            Text Descriptor File Generator

            13 May 1986                 02:07:05

                      Version 1.74

            Enter TDF name :  [_        ]

        Please enter the name of TDF file or Q to quit

        Copyright (c) 1986, Bodner-Hutchins Inc., Houston, Texas
```

Fig. A-15. Front screen.

you can bring up your TDF in TDFED and change this filename to your source name. TDFs and DFPs will not be able to process any data unless this field matches your source file.

```
SOURCE DOCUMENT FILE NAME - ANY VALID DOS FILE NAME (RETURN FOR TDF NAME)

|FILENAME|LW.|C|L|F|LP.|SL.|EL.|D|DC1|DC2|DC3|ILC......|NF|SDLC...|O|SCS|SN|

|NM1      |FS1|FS2|V|DP|NM2      |FS1|FS2|V|DP|NM3      |FS1|FS2|V|DP|TC|
                                                                      *1
|NM4      |FS1|FS2|V|DP|NM5      |FS1|FS2|V|DP|NM6      |FS1|FS2|V|DP|TC|
                                                                      *2
|NM7      |FS1|FS2|V|DP|NM8      |FS1|FS2|V|DP|NM9      |FS1|FS2|V|DP|TC|
                                                                      *3
|NM10     |FS1|FS2|V|DP|NM11     |FS1|FS2|V|DP|NM12     |FS1|FS2|V|DP|TC|
                                                                      *4
   Filename : [_        ]
                                                     Press Esc to Abort
```

Fig. A-16. Data entry screen.

Field: LW

LINE WIDTH (1-255)

In the case of delimited files, enter a D press RETURN.

D in this field sets the delimited file flag and skips over those data entry fields which do not pertain to delimited files.

TIP: This entry must be D for delimited files.

Field: C
Field: L
Field: F
Field: LP
Field: SL
Field: EL

These pertain to ASCII files and are automatically bypassed when D is entered for the previous question.

Field: D

IS THE FILE DELIMITED (Y/N)

This has already been set to Y when you entered D in the line width prompt.

Field: DC1

DELIMITER CHARACTER #1

The first delimiter character in the example is a quotation mark. Type it and press RETURN.

This will display the ASCII value of the character typed (in this case 034).

Field: DC2

DELIMITER CHARACTER #2

The second delimiter character in the example is a comma. Type it and press RETURN.

This will display the ASCII value of the character typed (in this case 044).

Field: DC

DELIMITER CHARACTER #3

The third delimiter character in the example is a quotation mark. Type it and press RETURN.

This will display the ASCII value of the character typed (in this case 034).

Field: ILC

This field is bypassed in delimited mode.

Field: NF

NUMBER OF DATA FIELDS (1-24)

You are going to process all five fields in the example: NAME, ADDRESS, CITY, STATE, and ZIPCODE. Type 5 and press RETURN.

In a delimited file you must process all fields.

ERROR TRAP: This field entry must be greater than zero and less than or equal to 24.

Field: SDLC
Field: O
Field: SCS
Field: SN

These pertain to ASCII files and are automatically bypassed when in the delimited mode.

The Data Fields. Now you will begin to enter the information defining the data fields for the target file. Data entry prompts are displayed in the upper part of the screen as shown in Fig. A-17.

```
Bod _________________________________________ rator (Rev 1.74) - Normal Data
___| Name of data field 01:[_          ] |______________________________________
|FIL|________________________________________|DC3|ILC......|NF|SDLC...|O|SCS|SN|
|_____|____|__|__|__|____|____|____|__|_|____|___|_________|__|________|_|___|__|
|CHAMBER   000 N  N  N 066  001  066  Y 034  044  034 .          05 .        0 000 00|
|___________________________________________________________________________________|
|NM1         |FS1|FS2|V|DP|NM2          |FS1|FS2|V|DP|NM3          |FS1|FS2|V|DP|TC|
|____________|___|___|_|__|_____________|___|___|_|__|_____________|___|___|_|__|__|
|                                                                              #1|
|________________________________________________________________________________|
|NM4         |FS1|FS2|V|DP|NM5          |FS1|FS2|V|DP|NM6          |FS1|FS2|V|DP|TC|
|____________|___|___|_|__|_____________|___|___|_|__|_____________|___|___|_|__|__|
|                                                                              #2|
|________________________________________________________________________________|
|NM7         |FS1|FS2|V|DP|NM8          |FS1|FS2|V|DP|NM9          |FS1|FS2|V|DP|TC|
|____________|___|___|_|__|_____________|___|___|_|__|_____________|___|___|_|__|__|
|                                                                              #3|
|________________________________________________________________________________|
|NM10        |FS1|FS2|V|DP|NM11         |FS1|FS2|V|DP|NM12         |FS1|FS2|V|DP|TC|
|____________|___|___|_|__|_____________|___|___|_|__|_____________|___|___|_|__|__|
|                                                                              #4|
|________________________________________________________________________________|
ENTER 1-10 ALPHANUMERIC CHARACTERS,NO SPACES ALLOWED,USE UNDERLINE FOR SPACE
                                                              Press Esc to Abort
```

Fig. A-17. Data field definition screen.

Field: NM1

NAME OF DATA FIELD 1

Type CHAMBNAME and press RETURN.

This entry can contain 1 to 10 alphanumeric characters but no spaces are allowed. You can use the underline (_) key as a hard space if you wish. Thus, CHAMB_NAME is a valid data field name. If you press RETURN the default of FIELD_01 will be selected.

Field: FS1

The starting column is bypassed and set equal to 001 for delimited files.

Field: FS2

ENDING COLUMN OF FIELD 1

You want CHAMBNAME to be 50 characters wide. Type 50 and press RETURN.

This determines the width of the field CHAMBNAME in your target file. You are not restricted to the width in your source file. TDFs and DFPs will make your target file to your specifications.

ERROR TRAP: This field entry must be greater than zero.

Field: V

TYPE OF VARIABLE (FIDLC)

CHAMBNAME is a character field, so type C and press RETURN.

The TDF system will accept all of the types listed below:

Floating point decimal	(currency/numeric with decimal)
Integer	(whole number)
Date	(date)
Logical	(true/false)
Character	(alphanumeric)

ERROR TRAP: This field entry must be F, I, D, L or C.

Field: DP

NUMBER OF DECIMALS

This field has been skipped because you answered C for the type of variable.

This prompt will only appear if you have entered F (floating point decimal), and would then require you to enter the number of digits to the right of the decimal point.

Field: NM2

NAME OF DATA FIELD 2

Type ADDRESS and press RETURN.

This entry can contain 1 to 10 alphanumeric characters, but no spaces are allowed. You can use the underline (_) key as a hard space. If you press RETURN the default of FIELD_02 will be selected.

Field: FS1

The starting column is bypassed and set equal to 001 for delimited files.

Field: FS2

ENDING COLUMN OF FIELD 2

You want ADDRESS to be five characters wide. Type 5 and press RETURN.

This determines the width of the field ADDRESS in your target file. You are not restricted to the width in your text/file. TDFs and DFPs will make your target file to your specifications.

ERROR TRAP: This field entry must be greater than zero.

Field: V

TYPE OF VARIABLE (FIDLC)

ADDRESS is a character field, so type C and press RETURN.

The TDF system will accept all of the types listed below:

Floating point decimal	(currency/numeric with decimal)
Integer	(whole number)
Date	(date)
Logical	(true/false)
Character	(alphanumeric)

ERROR TRAP: This field entry must be F, I, D, L or C.

Field: DP

NUMBER OF DECIMALS

This field has been skipped because you answered C for the type of variable.

This prompt will only appear if you have entered F (floating point decimal), and would then require you to enter the number of digits to the right of the decimal point.

Field: NM

NAME OF DATA FIELD

Type CITY and press RETURN.

This entry can contain 1 to 10 alphanumeric characters, but no spaces are allowed. You can use the underline (_) key as a hard space if desired. If you press RETURN, the default of FIELD_0 will be selected.

Field: FS1

The starting column is bypassed and set equal to 001 for delimited files.

Field: FS2

ENDING COLUMN OF FIELD

You want CITY to be 25 characters wide. Type 25 and press RETURN.

This determines the width of the field CITY in your target file. You are not restricted to the width in your source file. TDFs and DFPs will make your target file to your specifications.

ERROR TRAP: This field entry must be greater than zero.

Field: V

TYPE OF VARIABLE (FIDLC)

CITY is a character field so type C and press RETURN.

The TDF system will accept all of the types listed below:

Floating point decimal	(currency/numeric with decimal)
Integer	(whole number)
Date	(date)
Logical	(true/false)
Character	(alphanumeric)

ERROR TRAP: This field entry must be F, I, D, L or C.

Field: DP

NUMBER OF DECIMALS

This field has been skipped because you answered C for the type of variable.

This prompt will only appear if you have entered F (floating point decimal), and would then require you to enter the number of digits to the right of the decimal point.

Field: NM4

NAME OF DATA FIELD 4

Type STATE and press RETURN.

This entry can contain 1 to 10 alphanumeric characters but no spaces are allowed. You can use the underline (_) key as a hard space if you wish. If you press RETURN, the default of FIELD_04 will be selected.

Field: FS1

The starting column is bypassed and set equal to 001 for delimited files.

Field: FS2

ENDING COLUMN OF FIELD 4

You want STATE to be two characters wide. Type 2 and press RETURN.

This determines the width of the field STATE in your target file.

Field: V

TYPE OF VARIABLE (FIDLC)

STATE is a character field, so type C and press RETURN.

The TDF system will accept all of the types listed below:

Floating point decimal	(currency/numeric with decimal)
Integer	(whole number)
Date	(date)
Logical	(true/false)
Character	(alphanumeric)

ERROR TRAP: This field entry must be F, I, D, L or C.

Field: DP

Number Of Decimals

This field has been skipped because you answered C for the type of variable.

This prompt will only appear if you have entered F (floating point decimal), and would then require you to enter the number of digits to the right of the decimal point.

Field: NM5

Name Of Data Field 5

Type ZIPCODE and press RETURN.

This entry can contain 1 to 10 alphanumeric characters, but no spaces are allowed. You can use the underline (_) key as a hard space. Thus, ZIP_CODE is a valid data field name. If you press RETURN, the default of FIELD_05 will be selected.

Field: FS1

The starting column is bypassed and set equal to 001 for delimited files.

Field: FS2

Ending Column Of Field 5

You want ZIPCODE to be five characters wide. Type 5 and press RETURN.

This determines the width of the field ZIPCODE in your target file. You are not restricted to the width in your source file. TDFs and DFPs will make your target file to your specifications.

Field: V

Type Of Variable (FIDLC)

ZIPCODE is a character field so type C and press RETURN.

The TDF system will accept all of the types listed below:

Floating point decimal	(currency/numeric with decimal)
Integer	(whole number)
Date	(date)
Logical	(true/false)
Character	(alphanumeric)

ERROR TRAP: This field entry must be F, I, D, L, or C.

Field: DP

Number Of Decimals

This field has been skipped because you answered C for the type of variable.

This prompt will only appear if you have entered F (floating point decimal), and would then require you to enter the number of digits to the right of the decimal point.

You are now finished configuring your TDF and will have a finished file called CHAMBER.TDF. The screen in Fig. A-18 displays the data you entered in its completed format. If you have made a mistake, simply edit the file with TDFED. The finished file produces the results shown in Figs. A-19 and A-20.

```
Bod                                                rator (Rev 1.74) - Normal Data
   | Type of variable (FIDLC)           [C] |
|FIL|                                        |DC3|ILC......|NF|SDLC...|O|SCS|SN|
|
|CHAMBER   080 N N N 066 001 066 Y 034 044 034 .          05 .         0 000 00|
|
|NM1          |FS1|FS2|V|DP|NM2          |FS1|FS2|V|DP|NM3          |FS1|FS2|V|DP|TC|
|
|CHAMBNAME    001 050 C     ADDRESS      001 035 C     CITY         001 025 C     *1|
|
|NM4          |FS1|FS2|V|DP|NM5          |FS1|FS2|V|DP|NM6          |FS1|FS2|V|DP|TC|
|
|STATE        001 002 C     ZIPCODE      001 005 C                                *2|
|
|NM7          |FS1|FS2|V|DP|NM8          |FS1|FS2|V|DP|NM9          |FS1|FS2|V|DP|TC|
|
|                                                                               *3|
|
|NM10         |FS1|FS2|V|DP|NM11         |FS1|FS2|V|DP|NM12         |FS1|FS2|V|DP|TC|
|
|                                                                               *4|
|
FLOATING POINT DECIMAL, INTEGER, DATE, LOGICAL, OR CHARACTER
                                                              Press Esc to Abort
```

Fig. A-18. Completed data entry screen.

```
        Bodner-Hutchins Text Descriptor File Generator  (Rev 1.74)

|CHAMBER   080 N N N 066 001 066 Y 034 044 034 .        05            0 000 00|
|CHAMBNAME    001 050 C NA ADDRESS     001 035 C NA CITY        001 025 C NA *1|
|STATE        001 002 C NA ZIPCODE     001 005 C NA                          *2|
|                                                                            *3|
|                                                                            *4|
|                                                                            *5|
|                                                                            *6|
|                                                                            *7|
|                                                                            *8|
|                                                                            *9|
|                                                                            *A|
|                                                                            *B|
|                                                                            FF|

        Data is being written to Text Descriptor File [CHAMBER.TDF]

|  This TDF, when used with its associated data file, can be processed by   |
| any Descriptor File Processor (DFPxxx.EXE) to create native file formats. |
|
```

Fig. A-19. TDF processing screen.

```
Program terminated normally. TDF generated.

           13 May 1986          02:26:11

Copyright (c) 1986, Bodner-Hutchins Inc., Houston, Texas
```

Fig. A-20. Final TDF screen.

FILE MAINTENANCE: THE TDFED

In order to make any changes in a TDF, you need to run the program called TDFED. This program uses a simple screen-oriented editing function with keyed help, and overlays to designate the data fields. TDFED can also be run using command-line prompts, as discussed in the upcoming section named Command Line Options.

When you type TDFED from the DOS prompt, the screen shown in Fig. A-21 will be displayed. At this point, you must enter the name of the TDF file that you wish to edit. If you do not remember the filename, just press RETURN and a window displaying the available TDFs will appear. You must choose a valid TDF name or press Q and RETURN to quit. The window appears as shown in Fig. A-22.

Once you have entered a valid TDF name, in this case TESTFILE, the main TDFED screen will appear (Fig. A-23). You are prompted in the highlighted box near the bottom of the screen to enter the line number corresponding to the data that you wish to change. Type the number 1 and RETURN. The program will overlay a grid designating the data fields on the line and place the cursor at the first position. On-line help is displayed in the prompt box corresponding to the field in which the cursor is resting.

To make any changes in the data, use the right or left arrow keys to move to the data you wish to edit, type in the new data and press RETURN. The screen with its overlay is shown in Fig. A-24.

If you type 2 at the line number prompt, the overlay for the normal data fields will appear and you will again use the right and left arrows to move to

```
Text Descriptor File Data Editor

13 May 1986                    08:17:45

          Version 1.72


Enter file name : [_          ]

Enter Q to quit and return to DOS

Copyright (c) 1986, Bodner-Hutchins Inc., Houston, Texas
```

Fig. A-21. Front entry screen for TDFED.

```
                                         TDF Files

                                         TESTFILE
                                         CHAMBER

Text Descriptor File Data Editor

13 May 1986                    08:17:24

          Version 1.72


Enter file name : [_          ]

Enter Q to quit and return to DOS

Copyright (c) 1986, Bodner-Hutchins Inc., Houston, Texas
```

Fig. A-22. TDFED display window screen.

```
          Bodner-Hutchins Text Descriptor File Data Editor   (Rev 1.72)
 _____________________________________________________________________________
|  1|TESTFILE 076 Y Y Y 066 008 059 N 000 000 000 .         06 *** TOT 1 008 0|
|  2|FIRSTNAME   027 040 C NA LASTNAME    009 025 C NA SALARY      054 065 F 02 *|
|  3|UNION       050 050 L NA HIRE_DATE   069 076 D NA AGE         042 043 I NA *|
|  4|                                                                        *|
|  5|                                                                        *|
|  6|                                                                        *|
|  7|                                                                        *|
|  8|                                                                        *|
|  9|                                                                        *|
|10|TOTSALARY   054 065 F 02                                                  *|
|11|                                                                         *|
|12|                                                                         *|
|13|                                                                         F|
|__|__________________________________________________________________________|
05/13/86  This is the data contained in Descriptor File [TESTFILE.TDF] 08:18:4

 | This program allows you to directly change the information in the       |
 | Text Descriptor File selected. A non-valid line number (0) ends Edit.   |
 |_________________________________________________________________________|
 | Please enter line number you wish to change (1-13)  [  ]                |
 |_________________________________________________________________________|
          Copyright (c) 1986, Bodner-Hutchins Inc., Houston, Texas
```

Fig. A-23. Main TDFED entry screen.

the data location that you wish to edit. Make the changes, then press RETURN to go back to the line number prompt. This overlay is shown in Fig. A-25. The special data lines begin at line 10. An entry of 10 at the line prompt would

```
 __|FILENAME|LW.|C|L|F|LP.|SL.|EL.|D|DC1|DC2|DC3|ILC......|NF|SDLC...|O|SCS|S|
|  1|TESTFILE 076 Y Y Y 066 008 059 N 000 000 000 .         06 *** TOT 1 008 0|
|  2|_______________________________________________________________________|
|  3|UNION       050 050 L NA HIRE_DATE   069 076 D NA AGE         042 043 I NA *|
|  4|                                                                        *|
|  5|                                                                        *|
|  6|                                                                        *|
|  7|                                                                        *|
|  8|                                                                        *|
|  9|                                                                        *|
|10|TOTSALARY   054 065 F 02                                                  *|
|11|                                                                         *|
|12|                                                                         *|
|13|                                                                         F|
|__|__________________________________________________________________________|
05/13/86  This is the data contained in Descriptor File [TESTFILE.TDF] 08:18:1

 | This program allows you to directly change the information in the       |
 | Text Descriptor File selected. A non-valid line number (0) ends Edit.   |
 |_________________________________________________________________________|
 |SOURCE DOCUMENT FILE NAME - ANY VALID DOS FILE NAME                       |
 |_________________________________________________________________________|
          Copyright (c) 1986, Bodner-Hutchins Inc., Houston, Texas
```

Fig. A-24. Editing overlay for line 1.

```
          Bodner-Hutchins Text Descriptor File Data Editor   (Rev 1.72)
 ____________________________________________________________________________
| 1 ______________________________________________________________________   |
| 2|NM1        |FS1|FS2|V|DP|NM2        |FS1|FS2|V|DP|NM3        |FS1|FS2|V|DP|T|
| 3|UNION       050 050 L NA HIRE_DATE   069 076 D NA AGE          042 043 I NA *|
| 4|______________________________________________________________________     |
| 5|                                                                        * |
| 6|                                                                        * |
| 7|                                                                        * |
| 8|                                                                        * |
| 9|                                                                        * |
|10|TOTSALARY  054 065 F 02                                                 * |
|11|                                                                        * |
|12|                                                                        F |
|13|                                                                          |
|__|__________________________________________________________________________|
05/13/86  This is the data contained in Descriptor File [TESTFILE.TDF] 08:19:2
   ______________________________________________________________________
  |  This program allows you to directly change the information in the   |
  | Text Descriptor File selected. A non-valid line number (0) ends Edit. |
  |______________________________________________________________________|
  |ENTER 1-10 ALPHANUMERIC CHARACTERS,NO SPACES ALLOWED,USE UNDERLINE     |
  |______________________________________________________________________|
         Copyright (c) 1986, Bodner-Hutchins Inc., Houston, Texas
```

Fig. A-25. Edit overlay for normal data lines.

result in the overlay screen shown in Fig. A-26.

When you are finished editing, press RETURN and you will be asked whether or not you wish to save the changes made. At this point the screen

```
          Bodner-Hutchins Text Descriptor File Data Editor   (Rev 1.72)
 ____________________________________________________________________________
| 1|TESTFILE 076 Y Y Y 066 008 059 N 000 000 000 .        06 *** TOT 1 008 0|
| 2|FIRSTNAME   027 040 C NA LASTNAME    009 025 C NA SALARY      054 065 F 02 *|
| 3|UNION       050 050 L NA HIRE_DATE   069 076 D NA AGE         042 043 I NA *|
| 4|                                                                        * |
| 5|                                                                        * |
| 6|                                                                        * |
| 7|                                                                        * |
| 8|______________________________________________________________________    |
| 9|NM1        |FS1|FS2|V|DP|NM2        |FS1|FS2|V|DP|NM3        |FS1|FS2|V|DP|T|
|10|TOTSALARY   054 065 F 02                                                * |
|11|______________________________________________________________________    |
|12|                                                                        * |
|13|                                                                        F |
|__|__________________________________________________________________________|
05/13/86  This is the data contained in Descriptor File [TESTFILE.TDF] 08:20:7
   ______________________________________________________________________
  |  This program allows you to directly change the information in the   |
  | Text Descriptor File selected. A non-valid line number (0) ends Edit. |
  |______________________________________________________________________|
  |ENTER 1-10 ALPHANUMERIC CHARACTERS,NO SPACES ALLOWED,USE UNDERLINE     |
  |______________________________________________________________________|
         Copyright (c) 1986, Bodner-Hutchins Inc., Houston, Texas
```

Fig. A-26. Edit overlay for special data fields.

```
         Bodner-Hutchins Text Descriptor File Data Editor   (Rev 1.72)
 ___________________________________________________________________________
| 1|TESTFILE 076 Y Y Y 066 008 059 N 000 000 000 .        06 *** TOT 1 008 0|
| 2|FIRSTNAME   027 040 C NA LASTNAME    009 025 C NA SALARY  054 065 F 02 *|
| 3|UNION       050 050 L NA HIRE_DATE   069 076 D NA AGE     042 043 I NA *|
| 4|                                                                       *|
| 5|                                                                       *|
| 6|                                                                       *|
| 7|                                                                       *|
| 8|                                                                       *|
| 9|                                                                       *|
|10|TOTSALARY   054 065 F 02                                               *|
|11|                                                                       *|
|12|                                                                       *|
|13|                                                                       *|
|__|                                                                       F|
05/13/86  This is the data contained in Descriptor File [TESTFILE.TDF] 08:20:9
  ________________________________________________________________________
 |  This program allows you to directly change the information in the     |
 | Text Descriptor File selected. A non-valid line number (0) ends Edit.  |
 |________________________________________________________________________|
 |  Are you sure that you wish to save the changes (Y/N) [ ]              |
 |________________________________________________________________________|
            Copyright (c) 1986, Bodner-Hutchins Inc., Houston, Texas
```

Fig. A-27. Save option screen.

appears as shown in Fig. A-27. You must enter a Y or N to continue. Press Y and RETURN. The TDFED program final screen will be displayed (Fig. A-28), announcing the completion of the editing process.

```
          Bodner-Hutchins Text Descriptor File System
________________________________________________________________



        Program terminated normally. Edit completed.

              05/13/86              08:21:01



________________________________________________________________
   Copyright (c) 1986, Bodner-Hutchins Inc., Houston, Texas
```

Fig. A-28. Final TDFED screen.

ADVANCED FEATURES

The Descriptor File Processor programs will usually reside on their own subdirectory, while the target files need to be in the subdirectories used by dBASE, Lotus, etc. Thus, you have the option in each DFP to designate the output path for the target. For example, if WordStar is in a subdirectory \WS, and the DFP is to process TESTFILE, you would enter WS in the box querying the target path.

If you wish to send the output to drive A:, you enter A: at the prompt. This output designation feature sends the appropriate files to the target directory and erases the working files from the default directory path. If no destination is given, the files are created on the default directory.

Command Line Options

In some cases, you might wish to execute DFPs from the DOS command line. This would enable them to be completely executed from batch files or in a menu system. The syntax is:

DFP*xxx Filename Destination*

If either the Filename or the Destination path do not exist, you will be dropped into the query screen of the DFP. For example, if the dBASE output for TESTFILE is desired, and needs to be sent to the subdirectory called \DBASE, the command line option would be invoked by typing:

```
DFPDBF TESTFILE DBASE
```

In a batch file you may invoke the command line parameters using %n syntax:

```
DFP1.BAT

    COPY C:\COMM\%1.TXT
    DFPDBF %1 %2
    CD\%2
    DBASE
```

This batch file could then be invoked by typing the following:

```
DFP1 TESTFILE DBASE
```

This would cause TESTFILE.TXT to be copied from the directory C:\COMM, then have the file processed by DFPDBF, then have the result sent to the path C:\DBASE, then go to that path and run dBASE.

This method can help integrate the file interchange process for the novice user, or just make it a transparent part of a production system.

Identifying Normal Data Lines

On some columnar reports, there are page totals and report totals on each page. Because the system can designate only one "special" data line type, this might be a problem. A good work around this is to designate one total line, perhaps the page total, as a normal data line, because the columns usually line up and thus the data would line up correctly in the target file. In such a case, the text field might contain the word "page total" in the last name field, but this could be processed in the target system.

USING DESCRIPTOR FILE PROCESSORS

Once a TDF has been created using TDF.EXE, you are ready to run any one of the Descriptor File Processors in your library. The current DFP list is shown below:

- ☐ DFPDBF—Convert to dBASE III PLUS DBF files.
- ☐ DFPLTS—Convert to Lotus PRN files.

```
           Bodner-Hutchins Text Descriptor File System
______________________________________________________________

                                                 | TDF Files |
                                                 |___________|
                                                 | CHAMBER   |
                                                 | TESTFILE  |
           | dBASE III (DBF) File Format      |  |___________|
           |__________________________________|
           |   Descriptor File Processor      |
           |         Version 1.7X             |
           |                                  |
           | 04-24-1986             07:36:13  |
           |__________________________________|


           | Target Path [DBASE          ]    |
           |__________________________________|

dBASE III & dBASE III PLUS are trademarks of Ashton-Tate, Inc.
______________________________________________________________
  Copyright (c) 1986, Bodner-Hutchins Inc., Houston, Texas
```

Fig. A-29. Screen produced by DFPDBF at the DOS prompt.

- ☐ DFPWSM—Convert to WordStar/Mailmerge files.
- ☐ DFPMMT—Convert to Multimate/Print Merge files.
- ☐ DFPSDF—Convert to standard data format files.
- ☐ DFPDLM—Convert to delimited files.

To execute a DFP, just type its name at the DOS prompt. For example, if you were to type DFPDBF and press return, you would see the screen shown in Fig. A-29.

You are prompted to enter a file name. If you do not remember the filename, just press RETURN and a window will open showing you the available TDFs on your subdirectory. If your file is not there, press Q and RETURN to quit, and go back to TDF to create a TDF for your file.

You will also be prompted to enter a target path. If your version of dBASE resides on a subdirectory called \DBASE, just enter DBASE at the prompt. The program will take care of the back slash. If the path is on another drive, enter the drive designator (A:) or the drive and path (D:\DBASE). If you do not enter a target path, the system will produce an output file on the default directory. You would then need to copy the files to the directory on which you want them. Using the target path option makes these operations unnecessary. The target path query screen is shown in Fig. A-30.

```
            Bodner-Hutchins Text Descriptor File System
_______________________________________________________________________


              ____________________________________
             |    dBASE III (DBF) File Format     |
             |____________________________________|
             |     Descriptor File Processor      |
             |            Version 1.7X            |
             |                                    |
             |  04-24-1986              07:35:37  |
             |____________________________________|


              ____________________________________
             |   Enter file name : [          ]   |
             |____________________________________|
                        Press Q to Quit

   dBASE III & dBASE III PLUS are trademarks of Ashton-Tate, Inc.
_______________________________________________________________________
     Copyright (c) 1986, Bodner-Hutchins Inc., Houston, Texas
```

Fig. A-30. Target path query screen.

FINAL NOTES

In Lotus, you can load a WKS or WK1 file DFP which will automatically load your PRN file by pressing ALT-A.

You may use any program that can read target files produced by the DFPs. Because Paradox, R:base 5000, VP-Planner, and many other programs can use DBF files, you may use DFPDBF to process data for use in these programs.

Appendix B

Program Listings

```
10 REM **********************************************************
**********
20 REM *
         *
30 REM *      DESCRIPTOR FILE GENERATOR PROGRAM
         *
40 REM **********************************************************
**********
50 REM * COPYRIGHT 1986 BODNER-HUTCHINS INC. REV 05/09/86
         *
60 REM *
         *
70 REM **********************************************************
**********
80 DIM A$(13),B$(13),F$(20),H$(30)
90 H$(1)="SOURCE DOCUMENT FILE NAME - ANY VALID DOS FILE NAME (RE
TURN FOR TDF NAME)   "
100 H$(2)="THE WIDTH OF THE LONGEST DATA LINE IN THE SOURCE FILE
-ENTER D FOR DELIMITED"
110 H$(3)="IF THE SOURCE FILE WRAPS AT END OF LINE THEN ANSWER N,
 IF NOT, ENTER Y       "
120 H$(4)="NORMALLY Y IF THERE IS A CARRIAGE RETURN
                        "
130 H$(5)="IS THE SOURCE CONTINUOUS OR DOES IT BREAK AT END OF PA
GE (SKIP OVER PERF)   "
140 H$(6)="STANDARD 11 INCH PAGE IS 66 LINES. FOR OTHERS MULTIPLY
 PAGE LENGTH BY SIX   "
150 H$(7)="THE STARTING LINE OF DATA THAT IS TO BE PROCESSED IN T
HE SOURCE FILE        "
160 H$(8)="THE LAST LINE OF DATA THAT IS TO BE PROCESSED IN THE S
OURCE FILE            "
170 H$(9)="IS THE SOURCE FILE VARIABLE LENGTH SEPARATED BY DELIME
TERS? IF SO, ENTER Y  "
180 H$(10)="TYPE THE FIRST DELIMETER CHARACTER (FOR EXAMPLE "+CHR
$(34)+" )                            "
190 H$(11)="TYPE THE SECOND DELIMETER CHARACTER (FOR EXAMPLE "+CH
R$(44)+" )                           "
200 H$(12)="TYPE THE THIRD DELIMETER CHARACTER (FOR EXAMPLE "+CHR
$(34)+" )                            "
210 H$(13)="THE SEQUENCE OF CHARACTERS THAT MARK A LINE TO BE IGN
ORED DURING PROCESSING "
220 H$(14)="FIELDS DESIRED TO BE PROCESSED FROM SOURCE TO TARGET
FILE                    "
230 H$(15)="THE SEQUENCE OF CHARACTERS IDENTIFYING A LINE FOR SPE
CIAL PROCESSING         "
240 H$(16)="THE NUMBER OF LINES THAT THE SPECIAL DATA IS OFFSET F
ROM THE CODE LINE       "
250 H$(17)="THE STARTING COLUMN OF THE SPECIAL DATA LINE CODE IN
THE SOURCE FILE(1-255) "
260 H$(18)="NUMBER OF SPECIAL DATA FIELDS DESIRED TO BE PROCESSED
 TO THE TARGET FILE     "
270 H$(19)="ENTER 1-10 ALPHANUMERIC CHARACTERS,NO SPACES ALLOWED,
USE UNDERLINE FOR SPACE"
280 H$(20)="ENTER THE STARTING COLUMN OF THE NAMED DATA FIELD
                        "
```

```
290 H$(21)="ENTER THE DESIRED END OF THE NAMED DATA FIELD.DEFINES
 WIDTH FOR TARGET FILE "
300 H$(22)="FLOATING POINT DECIMAL, INTEGER, DATE, LOGICAL, OR CH
ARACTER                 "
310 H$(23)="NUMBER OF DIGITS DESIRED TO THE RIGHT OF THE DECIMAL
POINT                   "
320 MN$="JanFebMarAprMayJunJulAugSepOctNovDec"
330 NN=VAL(LEFT$(DATE$,2))
340 DTE$=MID$(DATE$,4,2)+" "+MID$(MN$,((NN-1)*3)+1,3)+" "+RIGHT$(
DATE$,4)
350 FOR I= 1 TO 13:A$(I)="
                                      ":NEXT
360 A$(1)=A$(1)+"  "
370 C$=A$(1)
380 OPEN "I",#1,"CONFIG.TD"
390 INPUT #1,FFG
400 INPUT #1,FFB
410 INPUT #1,FFC
420 CLOSE #1
430 MREV$="1.80"
440 BX1$="┌────────────────────────────────────┐"
450 BX2$="│                                    │"
460 BX3$="└────────────────────────────────────┘"
470 FOR I=2 TO 10:B$(I)="*"+RIGHT$(STR$(I-1),1):NEXT
480 COLOR 15,0:CLS:PRINT "                    Bodner-Hutchins Text D
escriptor File System                  "
490 PRINT"───────────────────────────────────────────────────────────
────────────────────"
500 PRINT"┌──────────────────────────────────────────────────────────
───────────────────┐"
510 PRINT"│  This program will enable the user to create a standa
rd Text Descriptor     │"
520 PRINT"│  File (TDF) which can later be processed by Descripto
r File Processors.   │"
530 PRINT"└──────────────────────────────────────────────────────────
───────────────────┘":COLOR FFG,FFB
540 LOCATE  8,20:PRINT BX1$
550 LOCATE  9,20:PRINT "│   Text Descriptor File Generator    │"
560 LOCATE 10,20.PRINT "├────────────────────────────────────┤"
570 LOCATE 11,20:PRINT "│  "+DTE$+"              "+TIME$+"  │"
580 LOCATE 12,20:PRINT "│                                    │"
590 LOCATE 13,20:PRINT "│          Version "+MREV$+"
 │"
600 LOCATE 14,20:PRINT BX2$
610 LOCATE 15,20:PRINT BX3$:COLOR 15,0:LOCATE 21,1
620 PRINT "                ";:COLOR FFC,0:PRINT"Please enter the n
ame of TDF file or Q to quit";:COLOR 15,0
630 LOCATE 22,1:PRINT"───────────────────────────────────────────
──────────────────────────────────"
640 LOCATE 23,2:PRINT "         Copyright (c) 1986, Bodner-Hutchi
ns Inc., Houston, Texas      "
650 COLOR FFB,0:FLAG=0:FLAG2=0
660 LOCATE 17,20:PRINT BX1$
670 LOCATE 18,20:PRINT BX2$
680 LOCATE 19,20:PRINT BX3$;
```

```
690 LOCATE 18,24:PRINT "Enter TDF name :  [          ]"
700 Y$=""
710 FOR I= 1 TO 8
720 LOCATE 18,42+I:COLOR 28,0:PRINT "_";:COLOR 12,0:F$(I)=INKEY$
730 LOCATE 11,20:COLOR FFG,FFB:PRINT "|   "+DTE$+"                "+T
IME$+"   |":COLOR FFB,0
740 IF F$(I)="" THEN 720
745 IF LEN(F$(I))=2 THEN 720
750 IF ASC(F$(I))=8 AND I=1 THEN PRINT CHR$(7);:F$(I)="":I=1:GOTO
 720
760 IF ASC(F$(I))=8 THEN LOCATE 18,42+I:PRINT " ";:I=I-1:Y$=LEFT$
(Y$,LEN(Y$)-1):GOTO 720
770 IF ASC(F$(I))=13 THEN 830
780 LOCATE 18,42+I:PRINT F$(I);:Y$=Y$+F$(I)
790 NEXT
800 IF LEN(Y$)<8 THEN 830
810 YY$=INKEY$:IF YY$=""  THEN 810
820 IF ASC(YY$)<>13 THEN PRINT CHR$(7);:GOTO 810
830 IF Y$="Q" OR Y$="q" THEN CLOSE:GOTO 3290
840 IF Y$="" THEN Y$="TDF_"+LEFT$(DATE$,2)+MID$(DATE$,4,2)
850 B$(11)="*A"
860 B$(12)="*B"
870 B$(13)="FF"
880 FOR I=2 TO 13:A$(I)=A$(I)+B$(I):NEXT
890 COLOR 15,0:CLS:PRINT " Bodner-Hutchins Text Descriptor File G
enerator (Rev "+MREV$+") -Normal Data":COLOR 0,FFC
900 PRINT"┌────────┬───┬─┬─┬─┬───┬───┬───┬─┬───┬───┬───────────
┬──┬───────┬─┬───┬──┐"
910 PRINT"|FILENAME|LW.|C|L|F|LP.|SL.|EL.|D|DC1|DC2|DC3|ILC......
|NF|SDLC...|O|SCS|SN|"
920 PRINT"├────────┴───┴─┴─┴─┴───┴───┴───┴─┴───┴───┴───┴───────────
┴──┴───────┴─┴───┴──┤"
930 PRINT"|
                                 |"
940 PRINT"├────────────┬───┬───┬─┬──┬────────────┬───┬───┬─┬──┬────
────┬───┬───┬─┬──┬──┤"
950 PRINT"|NM1         |FS1|FS2|V|DP|NM2         |FS1|FS2|V|DP|NM3
    |FS1|FS2|V|DP|TC|"
960 PRINT"├────────────┴───┴───┴─┴──┴────────────┴───┴───┴─┴──┴────
────┴───┴───┴─┴──┴──┤"
970 PRINT"|
                                 |"
980 PRINT"├────────────┬───┬───┬─┬──┬────────────┬───┬───┬─┬──┬────
────┬───┬───┬─┬──┬──┤"
990 PRINT"|NM4         |FS1|FS2|V|DP|NM5         |FS1|FS2|V|DP|NM6
    |FS1|FS2|V|DP|TC|"
1000 PRINT"├────────────┴───┴───┴─┴──┴────────────┴───┴───┴─┴──┴────
────┴───┴───┴─┴──┴──┤"
1010 PRINT"|
                              *2|"
1020 PRINT"├────────────┬───┬───┬─┬──┬────────────┬───┬───┬─┬──┬────
────┬───┬───┬─┬──┬──┤"
1030 PRINT"|NM7         |FS1|FS2|V|DP|NM8         |FS1|FS2|V|DP|NM9
    |FS1|FS2|V|DP|TC|"
1040 PRINT"├────────────┴───┴───┴─┴──┴────────────┴───┴───┴─┴──┴────
```

```
────┴────┴────┴──┴────┴────┤"
1050 PRINT"│
                    *3│"
1060 PRINT"├──────────────────┼────┬────┬──┬──┬──────────┬────┬──┬──┬────
────┬────┬────┬──┬────┬────┤"
1070 PRINT"│NM10          │FS1│FS2│V│DP│NM11          │FS1│FS2│V│DP│NM12
     │FS1│FS2│V│DP│TC│"
1080 PRINT"├──────────────────┴────┴────┴──┴──┴──────────┴────┴──┴──┴────
────┴────┴────┴──┴────┴────┤"
1090 PRINT"│
                    *4│"
1100 PRINT"└──────────────────────────────────────────────────────────────
─────────────────────────┘"
1110 COLOR 15,0
1120 LOCATE 5,2:PRINT A$(1)
1130 LOCATE 9,2:PRINT A$(2)
1140 LOCATE 13,2:PRINT A$(3)
1150 LOCATE 17,2:PRINT A$(4)
1160 LOCATE 21,2:PRINT A$(5):COLOR 12,0
1170 LOCATE 22,5:PRINT BX1$
1180 LOCATE 23,5:PRINT BX2$
1190 LOCATE 24,5:PRINT BX3$;:COLOR 15,0
1200 H=1:GOSUB 4080:LOCATE 23,7:PRINT "Filename : [         ]"
1210 LOCATE 23,19:LBL=23:LEB=18:LY=8:GOSUB 4200:IF YZ$="" THEN YZ
$=Y$
1220 F1$=LEFT$(YZ$+"          ",8):T$=F1$:GOSUB 4130:F1$=T$:LOCAT
E 5,2:PRINT F1$;
1230 H=2:GOSUB 4080:LOCATE 23,7:PRINT "Line width (1-255) : [    ]
"
1240 LOCATE 23,29:LBL=23:LEB=28:LY=3:GOSUB 4200:F2$=RIGHT$("000"+
YZ$,3):LOCATE 5,11:PRINT F2$;
1241 IF F2$<>"00D" AND F2$<>"00d" THEN 1250
1242 F2$="000":LOCATE 5,11:PRINT F2$;:F3$="N":LOCATE 5,15:PRINT F
3$;:F4$="N":LOCATE 5,17:PRINT F4$;:FF$="N":LOCATE 5,19:PRINT FF$;
1243 F5$="066":LOCATE 5,21:PRINT F5$;:F6$="001":LOCATE 5,25:PRINT
 F6$;:F7$="066":LOCATE 5,29:PRINT F7$;:F8$="Y":GOTO 1710
1250 IF VAL(F2$)=0 THEN 1230
1260 IF VAL(F2$)<0 OR VAL(F2$)>255 THEN PRINT CHR$(7);:GOTO 1230
1270 H=3:GOSUB 4080:LOCATE 23,7:PRINT "Is there a carriage return
(Y/N)[ ]"
1280 LOCATE 23,39:COLOR 28,0:PRINT "_";:COLOR 12,0:F3$=INKEY$:IF
F3$="" THEN 1280
1290 IF ASC(F3$)=27 THEN Y$="Q":GOTO 3290
1300 IF F3$<>"Y" AND F3$<>"N" AND F3$<>"y" AND F3$<>"n" THEN 1270
1310 IF F3$="y" THEN F3$="Y"
1320 IF F3$="n" THEN F3$="N"
1330 LOCATE 23,39:PRINT F3$;:LOCATE 23,39:YY$=INKEY$:IF YY$="" TH
EN 1330
1331 IF (ASC(YY$)=8 OR ASC(RIGHT$(YY$,1))=75) THEN F3$="":GOTO 12
70
1340 IF ASC(YY$)<>13 THEN 1330
1350 LOCATE 5,15:PRINT F3$;
1360 H=4:GOSUB 4080:LOCATE 23,7:PRINT "Is there a line feed      (
Y/N) [ ]"
1370 LOCATE 23,39:COLOR 28,0:PRINT "_";:COLOR 12,0:F4$=INKEY$:IF
```

```
F4$="" THEN 1370
1380 IF ASC(F4$)=27 THEN Y$="Q":GOTO 3290
1390 IF F4$<>"Y" AND F4$<>"N" AND F4$<>"y" AND F4$<>"n" THEN 1360
1400 IF F4$="y" THEN F4$="Y"
1410 IF F4$="n" THEN F4$="N"
1420 LOCATE 23,39:PRINT F4$;:LOCATE 23,39:YY$=INKEY$:IF YY$="" TH
EN 1420
1421 IF (ASC(YY$)=8 OR ASC(RIGHT$(YY$,1))=75) THEN F4$="":GOTO 13
60
1430 IF ASC(YY$)<>13 THEN 1420
1440 LOCATE 5,17:PRINT F4$;
1450 H=5:GOSUB 4080:LOCATE 23,7:PRINT "Is there a form feed     (
Y/N) [ ]"
1460 LOCATE 23,39:COLOR 28,0:PRINT "_";:COLOR 12,0:FF$=INKEY$:IF
FF$="" THEN 1460
1470 IF ASC(FF$)=27 THEN Y$="Q":GOTO 3290
1480 IF FF$<>"Y" AND FF$<>"N" AND FF$<>"y" AND FF$<>"n" THEN 1450
1490 IF FF$="y" THEN FF$="Y"
1500 IF FF$="n" THEN FF$="N"
1510 LOCATE 23,39:PRINT FF$;:LOCATE 23,39:YY$=INKEY$:IF YY$="" TH
EN 1510
1511 IF (ASC(YY$)=8 OR ASC(RIGHT$(YY$,1))=75) THEN FF$="":GOTO 14
50
1520 IF ASC(YY$)<>13 THEN 1510
1530 LOCATE 5,19:PRINT FF$
1540 H=6:GOSUB 4080:LOCATE 23,7:PRINT "Number lines/page   : [   ]
     "
1550 LOCATE 23,29:LBL=23:LEB=28:LY=3:GOSUB 4200:F5$=RIGHT$("000"+
YZ$,3):LOCATE 5,21:PRINT F5$;
1560 IF VAL(F5$)=0 THEN 1540
1570 H=7:GOSUB 4080:LOCATE 23,7:PRINT "Starting data line : [   ]
     "
1580 LOCATE 23,29:LBL=23:LEB=28:LY=3:GOSUB 4200:F6$=RIGHT$("000"+
YZ$,3):LOCATE 5,25:PRINT F6$;
1590 IF VAL(F6$)=0 THEN 1570
1600 H=8:GOSUB 4080:LOCATE 23,7:PRINT "Ending data line # : [   ]
     "
1610 LOCATE 23,29:LBL=23:LEB=28:LY=3:GOSUB 4200:F7$=RIGHT$("000"+
YZ$,3):LOCATE 5,29:PRINT F7$;
1620 IF VAL(F7$)=0 OR (VAL(F7$)<=VAL(F6$)) OR (VAL(F7$)>VAL(F5$))
 THEN 1600
1630 H=9:GOSUB 4080: LOCATE 23,7:PRINT "Is the file delimited
(Y/N) [ ]"
1640 LOCATE 23,39:COLOR 28,0:PRINT "_";:COLOR 12,0:F8$=INKEY$:IF
F8$="" THEN 1640
1650 IF ASC(F8$)=27 THEN Y$="Q":GOTO 3290
1660 IF F8$<>"Y" AND F8$<>"N" AND F8$<>"y" AND F8$<>"n" THEN 1630
1670 IF F8$="y" THEN F8$="Y"
1680 IF F8$="n" THEN F8$="N"
1690 LOCATE 23,39:PRINT F8$;:LOCATE 23,39:YY$=INKEY$:IF YY$="" TH
EN 1690
1691 IF (ASC(YY$)=8 OR ASC(RIGHT$(YY$,1))=75) THEN F8$="":GOTO 16
30
1700 IF ASC(YY$)<>13 THEN 1690
1710 LOCATE 5,33:PRINT F8$;
```

```
1720 IF F8$="N" THEN 1950
1721 FLAG=1
1730 H=10:GOSUB 4080:LOCATE 23,7:PRINT "Delimeter character numbe
r 1 [    ]"
1740 LOCATE 23,37:F9$=INKEY$:IF F9$="" THEN 1740
1750 F9$=RIGHT$(STR$(ASC(F9$)),2):F9$=RIGHT$("000"+F9$,3):
1760 LOCATE 23,37:PRINT F9$;:LOCATE 23,39:YY$=INKEY$:IF YY$="" TH
EN 1760
1770 IF ASC(YY$)<>13 THEN 1760
1780 LOCATE 5,35:PRINT F9$;
1790 IF VAL(F9$)=0 AND F9$<>"000" THEN 1730
1800 H=11:GOSUB 4080:LOCATE 23,7:PRINT "Delimeter character numbe
r 2 [    ]"
1810 LOCATE 23,37:F10$=INKEY$:IF F10$="" THEN 1810
1820 F10$=RIGHT$(STR$(ASC(F10$)),2):F10$=RIGHT$("000"+F10$,3)
1830 LOCATE 23,37:PRINT F10$;:LOCATE 23,39:YY$=INKEY$:IF YY$="" T
HEN 1830
1840 IF ASC(YY$)<>13 THEN 1830
1850 LOCATE 5,39:PRINT F10$;
1860 IF VAL(F10$)=0 AND F10$<>"000" THEN 1810
1870 H=12:GOSUB 4080:LOCATE 23,7:PRINT "Delimeter character numbe
r 3 [    ]"
1880 LOCATE 23,37:F11$=INKEY$:IF F11$="" THEN 1880
1890 F11$=RIGHT$(STR$(ASC(F11$)),2):F11$=RIGHT$("000"+F11$,3)
1900 LOCATE 23,37:PRINT F11$;:LOCATE 23,39:YY$=INKEY$:IF YY$="" T
HEN 1900
1910 IF ASC(YY$)<>13 THEN 1900
1920 LOCATE 5,43:PRINT F11$;
1930 IF VAL(F11$)=0 AND F11$<>"000" THEN 1880
1940 F12$=".        ":GOTO 1990
1950 F9$="000":F10$=F9$:F11$=F9$:LOCATE 5,35:PRINT F9$;:LOCATE 5,
39:PRINT F10$;:LOCATE 5,43:PRINT F11$;
1960 H=13:GOSUB 4080:LOCATE 23,7:PRINT "Ignore line code    : [.
        ] "
1970 LOCATE 23,30:LBL=23:LEB=29:LY=9:GOSUB 4200:F12$=YZ$:IF F12$=
"" THEN F12$="."
1980 F12$=LEFT$(F12$+"         ",9):LOCATE 5,47:PRINT F12$;
1990 H=14:GOSUB 4080:LOCATE 23,7:PRINT "Number of data fields (1-
24) [  ] "
2000 LOCATE 23,37:LBL=23:LEB=36:LY=2:GOSUB 4200:F13$=RIGHT$("00"+
YZ$,2):LOCATE 5,57:PRINT F13$;
2010 IF VAL(F13$)=0 THEN 1990
2020 IF VAL(F13$)>24 THEN PRINT CHR$(7);:GOTO 1990
2030 IF F8$="Y" THEN F14$=".      ":FF14$="0":F15$="000":F16$="00
":LOCATE 5,60:PRINT F14$;:LOCATE 5,68:PRINT FF14$;:LOCATE 5,70:PR
INT F15$;:LOCATE 5,74:PRINT F16$;:GOTO 2150
2040 H=15:GOSUB 4080:LOCATE 23,7:PRINT "Special data line code :
[       ] "
2050 LOCATE 23,33:LBL=23:LEB=32:LY=7:GOSUB 4200:F14$=YZ$:IF F14$=
"" THEN F14$="."
2055 F14$=LEFT$(F14$+"       ",7):LOCATE 5,60:PRINT F14$;
2060 H=16:GOSUB 4080:LOCATE 23,7:PRINT "Special data line offset
:      [ ] "
2070 LOCATE 23,39:LBL=23:LEB=38:LY=1:GOSUB 4200:FF14$=RIGHT$("0"+
YZ$,1):LOCATE 5,68:PRINT FF14$;
```

```
2080 H=17:GOSUB 4080:LOCATE 23,7:PRINT "Starting column special c
ode:[    ]"
2090 LOCATE 23,37:LBL=23:LEB=36:LY=3:GOSUB 4200:F15$=RIGHT$("000"
+YZ$,3):LOCATE 5,70:PRINT F15$;
2100 IF VAL(F15$)=0 AND F15$<>"000" THEN 2090
2110 H=18:GOSUB 4080:LOCATE 23,7:PRINT "Number special fields (1-
12) [   ] "
2120 LOCATE 23,37:LBL=23:LEB=36:LY=2:GOSUB 4200:F16$=RIGHT$("00"+
YZ$,2):LOCATE 5,74:PRINT F16$;
2130 IF VAL(F16$)>12 THEN PRINT CHR$(7);:GOTO 2110
2140 IF VAL(F16$)=0 AND F16$<>"00" THEN 2110
2150 NF=VAL(F13$):SNF=VAL(F16$)
2160 A$(1)=F1$+" "+F2$+" "+F3$+" "+F4$+" "
2170 A$(1)=A$(1)+FF$+" "+F5$+" "+F6$+" "+F7$+" "+F8$
2180 A$(1)=A$(1)+" "+F9$+" "+F10$+" "+F11$+" "+F12$
2190 A$(1)=A$(1)+" "+F13$+" "+F14$+" "+FF14$+" "+F15$+" "+F16$
2200 COLOR 15,0:LOCATE 1,1:PRINT " Bodner-Hutchins Text Descripto
r File Generator (Rev "+MREV$+") - Normal Data":COLOR 0,FFC
2210 COLOR 0,FFC
2220 LOCATE 21,1:PRINT"│
                                  *4│"
2230 PRINT"└──────────────────────────────────────────────────────
──────────────────────┘"
2240 COLOR 15,0
2250 LOCATE 21,2:PRINT A$(5)
2260 LOCATE 23,2:PRINT "        Copyright (c) 1986, Bodner-Hutch
ins Inc., Houston, Texas       "
2270 LOCATE 24,5:PRINT "                                         ";
2280 F1$="":F2$="":F3$="":F4$="":F5$="":F6$="":F7$="":F8$="":F9$=
"":F10$="":F11$="":F12$="":F13$="":F14$="":F15$="":FF$="":F16$=""
2290 COLOR 12,0
2300 LOCATE 1,5:PRINT BX1$
2310 LOCATE 2,5:PRINT BX2$
2320 LOCATE 3,5:PRINT BX3$;:COLOR 15,0
2330 LN=9:K=2:J=1:GOSUB 3370
2340 IF NF<4 THEN 2770
2350 LN=13:K=3:J=4:GOSUB 3370
2360 IF NF<7 THEN 2770
2370 LN=17:K=4:J=7:GOSUB 3370
2380 IF NF<10 THEN 2770
2390 LN=21:K=5:J=10:GOSUB 3370
2400 COLOR 15,0:IF NF<13 THEN 2770
2410 CLS:LOCATE 5,1:PRINT "  Bodner-Hutchins Text Descriptor File
 Generator (Rev "+MREV$+") - Normal Data2":COLOR 0,FFC
2420 PRINT"┌──────────┬───┬───┬─┬──┬──────────┬───┬───┬─┬──┬───────
──┬───┬───┬─┬──┬──┐"
2430 PRINT"│NM13      │FS1│FS2│V│DP│NM14      │FS1│FS2│V│DP│NM15
  │FS1│FS2│V│DP│TC│"
2440 PRINT"├──────────┴───┴───┴─┴──┴──────────┴───┴───┴─┴──┴───────
──┴───┴───┴─┴──┴──┤"
2450 PRINT"│
                        *5│"
2460 PRINT"├──────────┬───┬───┬─┬──┬──────────┬───┬───┬─┬──┬───────
──┬───┬───┬─┬──┬──┤"
2470 PRINT"│NM16      │FS1│FS2│V│DP│NM17      │FS1│FS2│V│DP│NM18
```

```
     │FS1│FS2│V│DP│TC│"
2480 PRINT"├──────────────────┴──────┴──────┴───┴─────┴──────────────────┴──────┴──────┴───┴─────────
──────┴──────┴─────┴───┴──────┴──────┤"
2490 PRINT"│
                    *6│"
2500 PRINT"├──────────────────┬──────┬──────┬───┬─────┬──────────────────┬──────┬──────┬───┬─────────
──────┬──────┬─────┬───┬──────┬──────┤"
2510 PRINT"│NM19              │FS1│FS2│V│DP│NM20              │FS1│FS2│V│DP│NM21
     │FS1│FS2│V│DP│TC│"
2520 PRINT"├──────────────────┴──────┴──────┴───┴─────┴──────────────────┴──────┴──────┴───┴─────────
──────┴──────┴─────┴───┴──────┴──────┤"
2530 PRINT"│
                    *7│"
2540 PRINT"├──────────────────┬──────┬──────┬───┬─────┬──────────────────┬──────┬──────┬───┬─────────
──────┬──────┬─────┬───┬──────┬──────┤"
2550 PRINT"│NM22              │FS1│FS2│V│DP│NM23              │FS1│FS2│V│DP│NM24
     │FS1│FS2│V│DP│TC│"
2560 PRINT"├──────────────────┴──────┴──────┴───┴─────┴──────────────────┴──────┴──────┴───┴─────────
──────┴──────┴─────┴───┴──────┴──────┤"
2570 PRINT"│
                    *8│"
2580 PRINT"└──────────────────────────────────────────────────────────────────────────────────────────
─────────────────────────────────────┘"
2590 COLOR 15,0
2600 LOCATE 23,2:PRINT "         Copyright (c) 1986, Bodner-Hutch
ins Inc., Houston, Texas      "
2610 COLOR 12,0
2620 LOCATE 1,5:PRINT BX1$
2630 LOCATE 2,5:PRINT BX2$
2640 LOCATE 3,5:PRINT BX3$;:COLOR 15,0
2650 LOCATE 9,2:PRINT A$(6)
2660 LOCATE 13,2:PRINT A$(7)
2670 LOCATE 17,2:PRINT A$(8)
2680 LOCATE 21,2:PRINT A$(9)
2690 IF NF<13 THEN 2770
2700 LN=9:K=6:J=13:GOSUB 3370
2710 IF NF<16 THEN 2770
2720 LN=13:K=7:J=16:GOSUB 3370
2730 IF NF<19 THEN 2770
2740 LN=17:K=8:J=19:GOSUB 3370
2750 IF NF<22 THEN 2770
2760 LN=21:K=9:J=22:GOSUB 3370
2770 IF SNF=0 THEN 3150
2780 COLOR 15,0
2790 CLS:LOCATE 5,1:PRINT "  Bodner-Hutchins Text Descriptor File
 Generator (Rev "+MREV$+") - Special Data":COLOR 0,FFC
2800 PRINT"┌──────────────────┬──────┬──────┬───┬─────┬──────────────────┬──────┬──────┬───┬─────────
──────┬──────┬─────┬───┬──────┬──────┐"
2810 PRINT"│SNM1              │FS1│FS2│V│DP│SNM2              │FS1│FS2│V│DP│SNM3
     │FS1│FS2│V│DP│TC│"
2820 PRINT"├──────────────────┴──────┴──────┴───┴─────┴──────────────────┴──────┴──────┴───┴─────────
──────┴──────┴─────┴───┴──────┴──────┤"
2830 PRINT"│
                    *9│"
2840 PRINT"├──────────────────┬──────┬──────┬───┬─────┬──────────────────┬──────┬──────┬───┬─────────
```

```
────────────────────────┤"
2850 PRINT"│SNM4        │FS1│FS2│V│DP│SNM5        │FS1│FS2│V│DP│SNM6
│FS1│FS2│V│DP│TC│"
2860 PRINT"├──────────────────────────────────────────────────────────────
────────────────────────┤"
2870 PRINT"│
                   *A│"
2880 PRINT"├──────────────────────────────────────────────────────────────
────────────────────────┤"
2890 PRINT"│SNM7        │FS1│FS2│V│DP│SNM8        │FS1│FS2│V│DP│SNM9
│FS1│FS2│V│DP│TC│"
2900 PRINT"├──────────────────────────────────────────────────────────────
────────────────────────┤"
2910 PRINT"│
                   *B│"
2920 PRINT"├──────────────────────────────────────────────────────────────
────────────────────────┤"
2930 PRINT"│SNM10       │FS1│FS2│V│DP│SNM11       │FS1│FS2│V│DP│SNM12
│FS1│FS2│V│DP│EF│"
2940 PRINT"├──────────────────────────────────────────────────────────────
────────────────────────┤"
2950 PRINT"│
                   FF│"
2960 PRINT"└──────────────────────────────────────────────────────────────
────────────────────────┘"
2970 COLOR 15,0
2980 LOCATE 23,2:PRINT "         Copyright (c) 1986, Bodner-Hutch
ins Inc., Houston, Texas         "
2990 COLOR 12,0
3000 LOCATE 1,5:PRINT BX1$
3010 LOCATE 2,5:PRINT BX2$
3020 LOCATE 3,5:PRINT BX3$;:COLOR 15,0
3030 LOCATE 9,2:PRINT A$(10)
3040 LOCATE 13,2:PRINT A$(11)
3050 LOCATE 17,2:PRINT A$(12)
3060 LOCATE 21,2:PRINT A$(13)
3070 NF=SNF:IF SNF =0 THEN 3150
3080 FLAG2=1:K=10:LN=9:J=1:GOSUB 3370
3090 IF SNF < 4 THEN 3150
3100 K=11:LN=13:J=4:GOSUB 3370
3110 IF SNF < 7 THEN 3150
3120 K=12:LN=17:J=7:GOSUB 3370
3130 IF SNF < 10 THEN 3150
3140 K=13:LN=21:J=10:GOSUB 3370
3150 COLOR 15,0:CLS:PRINT "         Bodner-Hutchins Text Descripto
r File Generator  (Rev "+MREV$+")          "
3160 PRINT"┌──────────────────────────────────────────────────────────────
────────────────────────┐"
3170 PRINT "│";:COLOR FFG,FFB:PRINT A$(1);:COLOR 15,0:PRINT "│"
3180 FOR I=2 TO 13:COLOR 15,0:A$(I)=LEFT$(A$(I)+C$,72)+B$(I):PRIN
T "│";:COLOR FFG,FFB:PRINT A$(I);:COLOR 15,0:PRINT "│":COLOR 15,0
:NEXT:COLOR 15,0
3190 PRINT"└──────────────────────────────────────────────────────────────
────────────────────────┘"
3200 COLOR 15,0:FILE$=Y$+".TDF"
```

```
3210 PRINT"        Data is being written to Text Descriptor File
[";:COLOR 0,15:PRINT FILE$;:COLOR 15,0:PRINT "]":PRINT
3220 PRINT"┌──────────────────────────────────────────────────
──────────────────┐"
3230 PRINT"│   This TDF, when used with its associated data file,
 can be processed by │"
3240 PRINT"│ any Descriptor File Processor (DFPxxx.EXE) to create
 native file formats.│"
3250 PRINT"└──────────────────────────────────────────────────
──────────────────┘"
3260 OPEN "O",#1,FILE$
3270 FOR I=1 TO 13:PRINT #1,A$(I):NEXT:CLOSE #1:CLOSE
3280 COLOR 0,0:SHELL "TDFDIR>NUL"
3290 COLOR 15,0:CLS:PRINT "                  Bodner-Hutchins Text
Descriptor File System                  "
3300 PRINT"───────────────────────────────────────────────────
─────────────────"
3310 IF Y$<>"Q" AND Y$<>"q" THEN 3330
3320 COLOR FFG,FFB:LOCATE 9,14:PRINT"Program terminated by user.
TDF generation aborted.":LOCATE 12,25:PRINT DTE$;:LOCATE 12,45:PR
INT TIME$;:COLOR 15,0:PRINT:GOTO 3340
3330 COLOR FFG,FFB:LOCATE 9,17:PRINT"Program terminated normally.
 TDF generated.":LOCATE 12,25:PRINT DTE$;:LOCATE 12,45:PRINT TIME
$;:COLOR 15,0:PRINT
3340 LOCATE 18,2:PRINT"─────────────────────────────────────
─────────────────────────"
3350 LOCATE 19,2:PRINT "         Copyright (c) 1986, Bodner-Hutch
ins Inc., Houston, Texas        "
3360 END
3370 REM *****************************************************
************
3380 REM * INQUIRY SUBROUTINE
          *
3390 REM *****************************************************
************
3400 REM
3410 H=19:GOSUB 4120:LOCATE 2,7:PRINT "Name of data field "+RIGHT
$(STR$(100+J),2)+":[          ]"
3420 LOCATE 2,30:LBL=2:LEB=29:LY=10:GOSUB 4200:IF YZ$>"" THEN 343
0
3421 IF FLAG2=0 THEN YZ$="FIELD_"+RIGHT$(STR$(100+J),2):GOTO 3430
3422 IF FLAG2=1 THEN YZ$="SPECL_"+RIGHT$(STR$(100+J),2)
3430 F1$=LEFT$(YZ$+"          ",10):T$=F1$:GOSUB 4130:F1$=T$:LOC
ATE LN,2:PRINT F1$;
3435 IF FLAG=1 THEN F2$="001":LOCATE LN,13:PRINT F2$;:GOTO 3470
3440 H=20:GOSUB 4120:LOCATE 2,7:PRINT "Starting column of field "
+RIGHT$(STR$(100+J),2)+" :[   ]"
3450 LOCATE 2,37:LBL=2:LEB=36:LY=3:GOSUB 4200:F2$=RIGHT$("000"+YZ
$,3):LOCATE LN,13:PRINT F2$;
3460 IF VAL(F2$)=0 AND F2$<>"000" THEN 3440
3470 H=21:GOSUB 4120:LOCATE 2,7:PRINT "Ending column of field   "
+RIGHT$(STR$(100+J),2)+" :[   ]"
3480 LOCATE 2,37:LBL=2:LEB=36:LY=3:GOSUB 4200:F3$=RIGHT$("000"+YZ
$,3):LOCATE LN,17:PRINT F3$;
3490 IF VAL(F3$)=0 AND F3$<>"000" THEN 3470
```

```
3500 H=22:GOSUB 4120:LOCATE 2,7:PRINT "Type of variable (FIDLC)
     [ ]"
3510 LOCATE 2,39:LBL=2:LEB=38:LY=1:GOSUB 4200:F4$=YZ$:LOCATE LN,2
1:PRINT F4$
3520 IF ASC(F4$)>96 THEN F4$=CHR$(ASC(F4$)-32)
3530 IF F4$<>"F" AND F4$<>"X" AND F4$<>"I" AND F4$<>"D" AND F4$<>
"L" AND F4$<>"C" THEN 3500
3560 LOCATE LN,21:PRINT F4$:F5$="NA":IF F4$<>"F" THEN 3620
3570 H=23:GOSUB 4120:LOCATE 2,7:PRINT "Number of decimals : [   ]
     "
3580 WD=VAL(F3$)-VAL(F2$)-1
3590 LOCATE 2,29:LBL=2:LEB=28:LY=3:GOSUB 4200:F5$=RIGHT$("00"+YZ$
,2):LOCATE LN,23:PRINT F5$;
3591 IF WD<1 THEN 3610
3600 IF VAL(F5$)>WD THEN PRINT CHR$(7);:F5$=""
3610 IF VAL(F5$)=0 AND F5$<>"00" THEN 3570
3620 IF NF<J+1 THEN 4040
3630 H=19:GOSUB 4120:LOCATE 2,7:PRINT "Name of data field "+RIGHT
$(STR$(100+J+1),2)+" [          ]"
3640 LOCATE 2,30:LBL=2:LEB=29:LY=10:GOSUB 4200:IF YZ$>"" THEN 365
0
3641 IF FLAG2=0 THEN YZ$="FIELD_"+RIGHT$(STR$(101+J),2):GOTO 3650
3642 IF FLAG2=1 THEN YZ$="SPECL_"+RIGHT$(STR$(101+J),2)
3650 F6$=LEFT$(YZ$+"          ",10):T$=F6$:GOSUB 4130:F6$=T$:LO
CATE LN,26:PRINT F6$;
3655 IF FLAG=1 THEN F7$="001":LOCATE LN,37:PRINT F7$;:GOTO 3690
3660 H=20:GOSUB 4120:LOCATE 2,7:PRINT "Starting column of field
"+RIGHT$(STR$(101+J),2)+" [   ]"
3670 LOCATE 2,37:LBL=2:LEB=36:LY=3:GOSUB 4200:F7$=RIGHT$("000"+YZ
$,3):LOCATE LN,37:PRINT F7$;
3680 IF VAL(F7$)=0 AND F7$<>"000" THEN 3660
3690 H=21:GOSUB 4120:LOCATE 2,7:PRINT "Ending column of field   "
+RIGHT$(STR$(101+J),2)+"  [   ]"
3700 LOCATE 2,37:LBL=2:LEB=36:LY=3:GOSUB 4200:F8$=RIGHT$("000"+YZ
$,3):LOCATE LN,41:PRINT F8$;
3710 IF VAL(F8$)=0 AND F8$<>"000" THEN 3690
3720 H=22:GOSUB 4120:LOCATE 2,7:PRINT "Type of variable (FIDLC)
     [ ]"
3730 LOCATE 2,39:LBL=2:LEB=38:LY=1:GOSUB 4200:FF4$=YZ$:LOCATE LN,
45:PRINT FF4$
3750 IF ASC(FF4$)>96 THEN FF4$=CHR$(ASC(FF4$)-32)
3760 IF FF4$<>"F" AND FF4$<>"I" AND FF4$<>"D" AND FF4$<>"L" AND F
F4$<>"C" THEN 3720
3770 LOCATE LN,45:PRINT FF4$:F9$="NA":IF FF4$<>"F" THEN 3830
3780 H=23:GOSUB 4120:LOCATE 2,7:PRINT "Number of decimals : [   ]
     "
3790 WD=VAL(F8$)-VAL(F7$)-1
3800 LOCATE 2,29:LBL=2:LEB=28:LY=2:GOSUB 4200:F9$=RIGHT$("00"+YZ$
,2):LOCATE LN,47:PRINT F9$;
3801 IF WD<1 THEN 3820
3810 IF VAL(F9$)>WD THEN PRINT CHR$(7);:F9$=""
3820 IF VAL(F9$)=0 AND F9$<>"00" THEN 3780
3830 IF NF<J+2 THEN 4040
3840 H=19:GOSUB 4120:LOCATE 2,7:PRINT "Name of data field "+RIGHT
$(STR$(100+J+2),2)+" [          ]"
```

```
3850 LOCATE 2,30:LBL=2:LEB=29:LY=10:GOSUB 4200:IF YZ$>"" THEN 386
0
3851 IF FLAG2=0 THEN YZ$="FIELD_"+RIGHT$(STR$(102+J),2):GOTO 3860
3852 IF FLAG2=1 THEN YZ$="SPECL_"+RIGHT$(STR$(102+J),2)
3860 F10$=LEFT$(YZ$+"          ",10):T$=F10$:GOSUB 4130:F10$=T$
:LOCATE LN,50:PRINT F10$;
3865 IF FLAG=1 THEN F11$="001":LOCATE LN,61:PRINT F11$;:GOTO 3900
3870 H=20:GOSUB 4120:LOCATE 2,7:PRINT "Starting column of field "
+RIGHT$(STR$(102+J),2)+"  [    ]"
3880 LOCATE 2,37:LBL=2:LEB=36:LY=3:GOSUB 4200:F11$=RIGHT$("000"+Y
Z$,3):LOCATE LN,61:PRINT F11$;
3890 IF VAL(F11$)=0 AND F11$<>"000" THEN 3870
3900 H=21:GOSUB 4120:LOCATE 2,7:PRINT "Ending column of field   "
+RIGHT$(STR$(102+J),2)+"  [    ]"
3910 LOCATE 2,37:LBL=2:LEB=36:LY=3:GOSUB 4200:F12$=RIGHT$("000"+Y
Z$,3):LOCATE LN,65:PRINT F12$;
3920 IF VAL(F12$)=0 AND F12$<>"000" THEN 3900
3930 H=22:GOSUB 4120:LOCATE 2,7:PRINT "Type of variable (FIDLC)
     [ ]"
3940 LOCATE 2,39:LBL=2:LEB=38:LY=1:GOSUB 4200:F13$=YZ$:LOCATE LN,
69:PRINT F13$
3960 IF ASC(F13$)>96 THEN F13$=CHR$(ASC(F13$)-32)
3970 IF F13$<>"F" AND F13$<>"I" AND F13$<>"D" AND F13$<>"L" AND F
13$<>"C" THEN 3930
3980 LOCATE LN,69:PRINT F13$:F14$="NA":IF F13$<>"F" THEN 4040
3990 H=23:GOSUB 4120:LOCATE 2,7:PRINT "Number of decimals : [    ]
     "
4000 WD=VAL(F12$)-VAL(F11$)-1
4010 LOCATE 2,29:LBL=2:LEB=28:LY=2:GOSUB 4200:F14$=RIGHT$("00"+YZ
$,2):LOCATE LN,71:PRINT F14$;
4011 IF WD<1 THEN 4030
4020 IF VAL(F14$)>WD THEN PRINT CHR$(7);:F14$=""
4030 IF VAL(F14$)=0 AND F14$<>"00" THEN 3990
4040 A$(K)=F1$+" "+F2$+" "+F3$+" "+F4$+" "+F5$+" "+F6$+" "+F7$+"
"+F8$
4050 A$(K)=A$(K)+" "+FF4$+" "+F9$+" "+F10$+" "+F11$+" "+F12$+" "+
F13$+" "+F14$
4060 F1$="":F2$="":F3$="":F4$="":F5$="":F6$="":F7$="":F8$="":F9$=
"":F10$="":F11$="":F12$="":F13$="":F14$="":F15$="":FF4$=""
4070 RETURN
4080 REM ****************************************
4090 REM * HELP LINE DISPLAY                    *
4100 REM ****************************************
4110 COLOR 15,0:LOCATE 1,1:PRINT H$(H):RETURN
4120 COLOR 15,0:LOCATE 23,1:PRINT H$(H):RETURN
4130 REM ****************************************
4140 REM * UPPERIZE STRINGS                     *
4150 REM ****************************************
4160 FOR I= 1 TO LEN(T$)
4170 IF ASC(MID$(T$,I,1))>=97 THEN T$=LEFT$(T$,I-1)+CHR$(ASC(MID$
(T$,I,1))-32)+RIGHT$(T$,LEN(T$)-I)
4180 NEXT
4190 RETURN
4200 REM ****************************************
4210 REM * ENTRY ROUTINE                        *
```

```
4220 REM ****************************************
4230 YZ$="":LOCATE 24,53:COLOR 15,0:PRINT"      Press Esc to Abor
t  ";
4240 IZ=1
4250 LOCATE LBL,LEB+IZ:COLOR 28,0:PRINT "_";:COLOR 12,0:F$(IZ)=IN
KEY$
4260 IF F$(IZ)="" THEN 4250
4265 IF LEN(F$(IZ))=2 THEN 4250
4270 IF ASC(F$(IZ))=8 AND IZ=1 THEN PRINT CHR$(7);:IZ=1:F$(IZ)=""
:GOTO 4250
4280 IF ASC(F$(IZ))=8 THEN LOCATE LBL,LEB+IZ:PRINT " ";:IZ=IZ-1:Y
Z$=LEFT$(YZ$,LEN(YZ$)-1):GOTO 4250
4290 IF ASC(F$(IZ))=13 THEN RETURN
4300 IF ASC(F$(IZ))=27 THEN Y$="Q":GOTO 3290
4310 LOCATE LBL,LEB+IZ:PRINT F$(IZ);:YZ$=YZ$+F$(IZ)
4320 IF IZ<LY THEN IZ=IZ+1:GOTO 4250
4340 YY$=INKEY$:IF YY$=""  THEN 4340
4350 IF ASC(YY$)=13 THEN RETURN
4355 IF ASC(YY$)=8 OR ASC(RIGHT$(YY$,1))=75 THEN YZ$=LEFT$(YZ$,LE
N(YZ$)-1):GOTO 4250
4360 GOTO 4340
```

```
10 REM ***************************************************************
**********
20 REM *
      *
30 REM *      DESCRIPTOR FILE EDITOR PROGRAM
      *
40 REM *
      *
50 REM * COPYRIGHT 1986 BODNER, HUTCHINS & ASSOCIATES, INC. REV 0
3/27/86  *
60 REM *
      *
70 REM ***************************************************************
**********
80 DIM A$(13),B$(13),F$(20),H$(30)
90 H$(1)="SOURCE DOCUMENT FILE NAME - ANY VALID DOS FILE NAME
         "
100 H$(2)="THE WIDTH OF THE LONGEST DATA LINE IN THE SOURCE FILE
          "
110 H$(3)="IF THE SOURCE FILE WRAPS AT END OF LINE THEN ANSWER N,
 IF NOT, ENTER Y  "
120 H$(4)="NORMALLY Y IF THERE IS A CARRIAGE RETURN
          "
130 H$(5)="IS THE SOURCE CONTINUOUS OR DOES IT BREAK AT END OF PA
GE  SKIP OVER PERF"
140 H$(6)="STANDARD 11 INCH PAGE IS 66 LINES. FOR OTHERS MULTIPLY
 PAGE LENGTH BY 6 "
150 H$(7)="THE STARTING LINE OF DATA THAT IS TO BE PROCESSED IN T
HE SOURCE FILE    "
160 H$(8)="THE LAST LINE OF DATA THAT IS TO BE PROCESSED IN THE S
OURCE FILE        "
170 H$(9)="IS THE SOURCE FILE VARIABLE LENGTH SEPARATED BY DELIME
TERS? IF SO, Y    "
180 H$(10)="TYPE THE FIRST DELIMETER CHARACTER (FOR EXAMPLE "+CHR
$(34)+" )                     "
190 H$(11)="TYPE THE SECOND DELIMETER CHARACTER (FOR EXAMPLE "+CH
R$(44)+" )                    "
200 H$(12)="TYPE THE THIRD DELIMETER CHARACTER (FOR EXAMPLE "+CHR
$(34)+" )                     "
210 H$(13)="THE SEQUENCE OF CHARACTERS THAT MARK A LINE TO BE IGN
ORED BY DFP          "
220 H$(14)="FIELDS DESIRED TO BE PROCESSED FROM SOURCE TO TARGET
FILE                 "
230 H$(15)="THE SEQUENCE OF CHARACTERS IDENTIFYING A LINE FOR SPE
CIAL PROCESSING    "
240 H$(16)="THE NUMBER OF LINES THAT THE SPECIAL DATA IS OFFSET F
ROM THE CODE LINE  "
250 H$(17)="THE STARTING COLUMN OF THE SPECIAL DATA LINE CODE IN
THE SOURCE FILE     "
260 H$(18)="NUMBER OF SPECIAL DATA FIELDS DESIRED TO BE PROCESSED
 TO THE TARGET      "
270 H$(19)="ENTER 1-10 ALPHANUMERIC CHARACTERS,NO SPACES ALLOWED,
USE UNDERLINE       "
280 H$(20)="ENTER THE STARTING COLUMN OF THE NAMED DATA FIELD
                    "
```

```
290 H$(21)="ENTER THE DESIRED END OF THE NAMED DATA FIELD.DEFINES
 WIDTH FOR TARGET  "
300 H$(22)="FLOATING POINT DECIMAL, INTEGER, DATE, LOGICAL, OR CH
ARACTER              "
310 H$(23)="NUMBER OF DIGITS DESIRED TO THE RIGHT OF THE DECIMAL
POINT                "
320 MN$="JanFebMarAprMayJunJulAugSepOctNovDec"
330 NN=VAL(LEFT$(DATE$,2))
340 DTE$=MID$(DATE$,4,2)+" "+MID$(MN$,((NN-1)*3)+1,3)+" "+RIGHT$(
DATE$,4)
350 FOR I= 1 TO 13:A$(I)="
                                             ":NEXT
360 A$(1)=A$(1)+"  "
370 C$=A$(1)
380 OPEN "I",#1,"CONFIG.TD"
390 INPUT #1,FFG
400 INPUT #1,FFB
410 INPUT #1,FFC
420 CLOSE #1
430 MREV$="1.80"
440 CMD$=COMMAND$
450 IF CMD$ ="" THEN 470
460 FL$=CMD$:GOTO 960
470 BX1$="┌────────────────────────────────────┐"
480 BX2$="│                                    │"
490 BX3$="└────────────────────────────────────┘"
500 FOR I=2 TO 10:B$(I)="*"+RIGHT$(STR$(I-1),1):NEXT
510 COLOR 15,0:CLS:PRINT "                 Bodner-Hutchins Text D
escriptor File System                "
520 PRINT"──────────────────────────────────────────────────────────
─────────────────────":COLOR FFG,FFB
530 LOCATE  7,20:PRINT BX1$
540 LOCATE  8,20:PRINT "│  Text Descriptor File Data Editor   │"
550 LOCATE  9,20:PRINT "├────────────────────────────────────┤"
560 LOCATE 10,20:PRINT "│  "+DTE$+"            "+TIME$+"  │"
570 LOCATE 11,20:PRINT "│                                    │"
580 LOCATE 12,20:PRINT "│            Version "+MREV$+"
 │"
590 LOCATE 13,20:PRINT BX2$
600 LOCATE 14,20:PRINT BX3$:COLOR 15,0:PRINT
610 LOCATE 22,2:PRINT"──────────────────────────────────────────
──────────────────────────────"
620 LOCATE 23,2:PRINT "         Copyright (c) 1986, Bodner-Hutchi
ns Inc., Houston, Texas      "
630 COLOR FFC,0:LOCATE 20,23:PRINT "Enter Q to quit and return to
 DOS"
640 COLOR FFB,0:FLAG=0
650 LOCATE 17,20:PRINT BX1$
660 LOCATE 18,20:PRINT BX2$
670 LOCATE 19,20:PRINT BX3$;
680 LOCATE 18,24:PRINT "Enter file name : [        ]"
690 FL$=""
700 FOR I= 1 TO 8
710 LOCATE 18,42+I:COLOR 28,0:PRINT "_";:COLOR 12,0:F$(I)=INKEY$
720 LOCATE 10,20:COLOR FFG,FFB:PRINT "│  "+DTE$+"            "+T
```

```
IME$+"  │":COLOR FFB,0
730 IF F$(I)="" THEN 710
740 IF LEN(F$(I))=2 THEN 710
750 IF ASC(F$(I))=8 AND I=1 THEN PRINT CHR$(7);:F$(I)="":I=1:GOTO
 710
760 IF ASC(F$(I))=8 THEN LOCATE 18,42+I:PRINT " ";:I=I-1:FL$=LEFT
$(FL$,LEN(FL$)-1):GOTO 710
770 IF ASC(F$(I))=13 THEN 800
780 LOCATE 18,42+I:PRINT F$(I);:FL$=FL$+F$(I)
790 NEXT
800 IF FL$="Q" OR FL$="q" THEN CLOSE:COLOR 15,0:CLS:END
810 IF LEN(FL$)>0 THEN 960
820 IF FLAG=1 THEN 690
830 OPEN "I",#1,"TDFDIR.TXT":COLOR 0,15:FLAG=1
840 LOCATE 3,60:PRINT"┌──────────┐"
850 LOCATE 4,60:PRINT"│ TDF Files │"
860 LOCATE 5,60:PRINT"├──────────┤"
870 IF EOF(1) THEN 940
880 INPUT #1,D$:D=D+1:IF D<5 OR VAL(LEFT$(D$,1))>0 THEN 870
890 LOCATE D+1,60:PRINT "│ "+LEFT$(D$,8)+"  │"
900 IF D<20 THEN 870
910 D=4:LOCATE 21,60:PRINT"└──────────┘":COLOR FFG,FFB:LOCATE 22
,55:PRINT"Press any key for more":COLOR 0,15:WD$=INKEY$:IF WD$=""
 THEN 910
920 COLOR 15,0:LOCATE 22,55:PRINT"──────────────────────":COLOR 0
,15
930 GOTO 870
940 CLOSE #1:LOCATE D+1,60:PRINT"└──────────┘":COLOR FFB,0
950 GOTO 690
960 ON ERROR GOTO 1000
970 CLOSE #1:OPEN "I",#1,LEFT$(FL$,8)+".TDF"
980 ON ERROR GOTO 0
990 GOTO 1010
1000 LOCATE 18,60:COLOR 15,0:PRINT CHR$(7)+"File not found!!":COL
OR FFB,0:RESUME 680
1010 FOR I=1 TO 13:INPUT #1,A$(I):A$(I)=RIGHT$(C$+A$(I),74):NEXT:
CLOSE #1
1020 FLAG=0:COLOR 15,0:CLS:PRINT "          Bodner-Hutchins Text
Descriptor File Data Editor   (Rev "+MREV$+")      "
1030 PRINT"┌──┬──────────────────────────────────────────────
──────────────────────────┐":COLOR FFG,FFB
1040 FOR I=1 TO 13:COLOR 15,0:PRINT "│"+RIGHT$(" "+STR$(I),2)+"│"
;:COLOR FFG,FFC:PRINT A$(I);:COLOR 15,0:PRINT"│":NEXT:COLOR 15,0
1050 PRINT"└──┴──────────────────────────────────────────────
──────────────────────────┘"
1060 COLOR 15,0
1070 FOR I=1 TO 13:B$(I)=A$(I):NEXT
1080 PRINT"           This is the data contained in Descriptor Fil
e [";:COLOR FFG,FFB:PRINT FL$+".TDF";:COLOR 15,0:PRINT "]"
1090 PRINT"  ┌──────────────────────────────────────────────────
──────────────────────┐"
1100 PRINT"  │  This program allows you to directly change the i
nformation in the     │"
1110 PRINT"  │ Text Descriptor File selected. A non-valid line nu
mber (0) ends Edit.  │"
```

```
1120 PRINT"  ├──────────────────────────────────────────────────────────
─────────────────────────┤"
1130 PRINT"  │
                         │"
1140 PRINT"  └──────────────────────────────────────────────────────────
─────────────────────────┘"
1150 LOCATE 24,2:PRINT "         Copyright (c) 1986, Bodner-Hut
chins Inc., Houston, Texas     ";
1160 C1$="":COLOR FFG,FFB:LOCATE 22,4:PRINT"  Please enter line n
umber you wish to change (1-13)  [  ]                  "
1170 DT$=LEFT$(DATE$,2)+"/"+MID$(DATE$,4,2)+"/"+RIGHT$(DATE$,2)
1180 COLOR FFG,FFB:C1$="":LOCATE 22,58:PRINT "[";:COLOR 28,0:PRIN
T "_";:COLOR FFG,FFB:PRINT" ]";:LOCATE 22,59:F$(1)=INKEY$:COLOR F
FG,0:LOCATE 17,1:PRINT DT$:LOCATE 17,72:PRINT TIME$:COLOR FFG,FFB
1190 IF F$(1)="" THEN 1180
1200 IF LEN(F$(1))>1 THEN 1180
1210 IF ASC(F$(1))=8 AND C1$="" THEN PRINT CHR$(7);:GOTO 1180
1220 IF VAL(F$(1))=0 THEN L=0:GOTO 1430
1230 LOCATE 22,59:PRINT F$(1);
1240 LOCATE 22,60:COLOR 28,0:PRINT "_";:COLOR FFG,FFB:F$(2)=INKEY
$:COLOR FFG,0:LOCATE 17,1:PRINT DT$:LOCATE 17,72:PRINT TIME$:COLO
R FFG,FFB:IF F$(2)="" THEN 1240
1250 IF LEN(F$(2))>1 THEN 1240
1260 IF ASC(F$(2))=8 THEN C1$="":GOTO 1180
1270 LOCATE 22,60:PRINT F$(2);:L=VAL(F$(1)+F$(2))
1280 IF L<0 OR L>13 THEN 1180
1290 IF L=0 THEN 1430
1300 COLOR 15,0:GOSUB 1660:COLOR FFG,FFB:LOCATE L+2,5:PRINT A$(L)
;
1310 LOCATE L+2,5:B$=A$(L):COLOR FFB,0:PRINT LEFT$(A$(L),1);:COLO
R FFG,FFB
1320 B1$=INKEY$:GOSUB 1820:IF B1$="" THEN 1320
1330 IF ASC(B1$)=27 THEN FLAG=1:GOTO 1510
1340 IF ASC(B1$)=8 AND POS(0)<=6 THEN PRINT CHR$(7);:GOTO 1320
1350 IF ASC(B1$)=13 THEN 1420
1360 EN=78:IF CSRLIN>3 THEN EN=75
1370 IF POS(0)>EN AND ASC(RIGHT$(B1$,1))=77 THEN PRINT CHR$(7);:G
OTO 1320
1380 IF ASC(B1$)=8 THEN C1$=LEFT$(C1$,LEN(C1$)-1):C2$=MID$(A$(L),
LEN(C1$)+1,1):LOCATE L+2,5:PRINT A$(L);:LOCATE L+2,5:PRINT C1$;:C
OLOR FFB,0:PRINT C2$;:COLOR FFG,FFB:GOTO 1320
1390 IF LEN(B1$)=2 THEN B1$=RIGHT$(B1$,1):GOSUB 1600:GOTO 1320
1400 C2$=MID$(A$(L),LEN(C1$)+2,1)
1410 LOCATE L+2,5:C1$=C1$+B1$:PRINT C1$;:COLOR FFB,0:PRINT C2$;:C
OLOR FFG,FFB:GOTO 1320
1420 A$(L)=C1$+RIGHT$(A$(L),LEN(A$(L))-LEN(C1$)):GOSUB 1760: GOTO
 1180
1430 COLOR FFG,FFB:LOCATE 22,4:PRINT"  Are you sure that you wish
 to save the changes (Y/N) [ ]           "
1440 LOCATE 22,60:INPUT "",Y$:IF Y$<>"Y" AND Y$<>"N" AND Y$<>"y"
AND Y$<>"n" THEN 1440
1450 IF Y$="n" OR Y$="N" THEN 1510
1460 FOR I=1 TO 13:IF A$(I)=B$(I) THEN 1480
1470 A$(I)=A$(I)+RIGHT$(B$(I),LEN(B$(I))-LEN(A$(I)))
1480 NEXT
```

```
1490 OPEN "O",#1,LEFT$(FL$,8)+".TDF"
1500 FOR I=1 TO 13:PRINT #1,A$(I):NEXT:CLOSE #1
1510 COLOR 15,0:CLS:PRINT "                    Bodner-Hutchins Text
Descriptor File System                    "
1520 PRINT"──────────────────────────────────────────────────────────────
──────────────────────"
1530 IF FLAG=1 THEN 1550
1540 COLOR FFG,FFB:LOCATE 9,17:PRINT"Program terminated normally.
 Edit completed.":LOCATE 12,25:PRINT DT$;:LOCATE 12,45:PRINT TIME
$;:COLOR 15,0:PRINT:GOTO 1560
1550$(1);
1550 COLOR FFG,FFB:LOCATE 9,17:PRINT"Program terminated by user.
Edit aborted.":LOCATE 12,25:PRINT DT$;:LOCATE 12,45:PRINT TIME$;:
COLOR 15,0:PRINT
1560 LOCATE 18,2:PRINT"──────────────────────────────────────────
──────────────────────────────────"
1570 LOCATE 19,2:PRINT "          Copyright (c) 1986, Bodner-Hutch
ins Inc., Houston, Texas        "
1580 END
1590 REM *******************************************
1600 IF (ASC(B1$)=8 OR ASC(B1$)=75) AND POS(0)<=6 THEN PRINT CHR$
(7);:RETURN
1610 IF ASC(B1$)=75 THEN C1$=LEFT$(C1$,LEN(C1$)-1):C2$=MID$(A$(L)
,LEN(C1$)+1,1):LOCATE L+2,5:PRINT A$(L);:LOCATE L+2,5:PRINT C1$;:
COLOR FFB,0:PRINT C2$;:COLOR FFG,FFB
1620 A$(L)=C1$+RIGHT$(A$(L),LEN(A$(L))-LEN(C1$))
1620 A$(L)=C1$+RIGHT$(A$(L),LEN(A$(L))-LEN(C1$))
1630 IF ASC(B1$)=77 THEN C1$=C1$+MID$(A$(L),LEN(C1$)+1,1):C2$=MID
$(A$(L),LEN(C1$)+1,1):LOCATE L+2,5:PRINT C1$;:COLOR FFB,0:PRINT C
2$;:COLOR FFG,FFB
1640 REM B0$=C1$+RIGHT$(B0$,LEN(B0$)-LEN(C1$))
1650 RETURN
1660 REM *************************************
1670 COLOR FFG,FFB:LOCATE 22,4:PRINT"  Make all desired changes a
nd press <Return> when done....          ":COLOR FFB,0
1680 IF L>1 THEN 1720
1690 LOCATE L,4:PRINT"┌──────────┬───┬─┬─┬─┬────┬────┬──┬─┬───┬───
┬───┬─────────┬──┬───────┬─┬───┬──┐";
1700 LOCATE L+1,4:PRINT"│FILENAME│LW.│C│L│F│LP.│SL.│EL.│D│DC1│DC2
│DC3│ILC......│NF│SDLC...│O│SCS│SN│";
1710 GOTO 1740
1720 LOCATE L,4:PRINT"┌──────────────┬───┬───┬─┬──┬──────────┬───┬
───┬─┬──┬──────────┬───┬───┬─┬──┐";
1730 LOCATE L+1,4:PRINT"│NM1          │FS1│FS2│V│DP│NM2         │FS1│F
S2│V│DP│NM3         │FS1│FS2│V│DP│TC│"
1740 LOCATE L+2,4:PRINT"│
                                      │";
1750 LOCATE L+3,4:PRINT"└────────────────────────────────────────
───────────────────────────┘";:RETURN
1760 COLOR 15,0:LOCATE 1,1:PRINT "              Bodner-Hutchins Text De
scriptor File Data Editor   (Rev "+MREV$+")                "
1770 PRINT"┌──┬─────────────────────────────────────────────────────
───────────────────────────┐":COLOR FFG,FFB
1780 FOR I=1 TO 13:COLOR 15,0:PRINT "│"+RIGHT$(" "+STR$(I),2)+"│"
;:COLOR FFG,FFC:PRINT A$(I);:COLOR 15,0:PRINT"│":NEXT:COLOR 15,0
```

```
1790 PRINT"└──┴──────────────────────────────────────────────────────────
──────────────────────────┘"
1800 COLOR FFG,FFB:LOCATE 22,4:PRINT"  Please enter line number y
ou wish to change (1-13)  [  ]                "
1810 RETURN
1820 Y0=POS(0):X0=CSRLIN
1830 IF Y0=Y AND X0=X THEN RETURN
1840 X=CSRLIN:Y=POS(0)
1850 IF X>3 THEN 2070
1860 H=18:IF Y<15 THEN H=1:GOTO 2030
1870 IF Y<19 THEN H=2:GOTO 2030
1880 IF Y<21 THEN H=3:GOTO 2030
1890 IF Y<23 THEN H=4:GOTO 2030
1900 IF Y<25 THEN H=5:GOTO 2030
1910 IF Y<29 THEN H=6:GOTO 2030
1920 IF Y<33 THEN H=7:GOTO 2030
1930 IF Y<37 THEN H=8:GOTO 2030
1940 IF Y<39 THEN H=9:GOTO 2030
1950 IF Y<43 THEN H=10:GOTO 2030
1960 IF Y<47 THEN H=11:GOTO 2030
1970 IF Y<51 THEN H=12:GOTO 2030
1980 IF Y<61 THEN H=13:GOTO 2030
1990 IF Y<64 THEN H=14:GOTO 2030
2000 IF Y<72 THEN H=15:GOTO 2030
2010 IF Y<74 THEN H=16:GOTO 2030
2020 IF Y<78 THEN H=17:GOTO 2030
2030 REM ****************************************
2040 REM * HELP LINE DISPLAY                    *
2050 REM ****************************************
2060 COLOR 0,15:LOCATE 22,4:PRINT H$(H):LOCATE X,Y:COLOR FFG,FFB:
RETURN
2070 H=23:IF Y<17 THEN H=19:GOTO 2030
2080 IF Y<21 THEN H=20:GOTO 2030
2090 IF Y<25 THEN H=21:GOTO 2030
2100 IF Y<27 THEN H=22:GOTO 2030
2110 IF Y<30 THEN H=23:GOTO 2030
2120 IF Y<41 THEN H=19:GOTO 2030
2130 IF Y<45 THEN H=20:GOTO 2030
2140 IF Y<49 THEN H=21:GOTO 2030
2150 IF Y<51 THEN H=22:GOTO 2030
2160 IF Y<54 THEN H=23:GOTO 2030
2170 IF Y<65 THEN H=19:GOTO 2030
2180 IF Y<69 THEN H=20:GOTO 2030
2190 IF Y<73 THEN H=21:GOTO 2030
2200 IF Y<75 THEN H=22:GOTO 2030
2210 GOTO 2000
```

```
10 REM ***********************************************************************
20 REM * Bodner-Hutchins Text Descriptor File System   DFPDBF.BAS
      *
30 REM ***********************************************************************
40 REM *      DESCRIPTOR FILE PROCESSOR PROGRAM FOR DBASE III
      *
50 REM *
      *
60 REM * COPYRIGHT 1986 BODNER, HUTCHINS & ASSOCIATES, INC. REV 0
4/14/86  *
70 REM *
      *
80 REM ***********************************************************************
90 DIM A$(13),B$(13),F0$(20),F1$(3,36),SC1(3,36),EC1(3,36),TP1$(3
,36),DP1(3,36),WDT(3,36)
100 DIM DB$(1024),DTA$(64),DTAF$(64),DTTP$(64),DTLN$(64),DTND$(64
),ADL$(36),W(36),TMP$(64)
110 C$="
                                                  "
120 OPEN "I",#1,"CONFIG.TD"
130 INPUT #1,FFG
140 INPUT #1,FFB
150 INPUT #1,FFC
160 CLOSE #1
170 MREV$="1.80"
180 BX1$="┌──────────────────────────────────────────────┐"
190 BX2$="│                                              │"
200 BX3$="└──────────────────────────────────────────────┘"
210 CMD$=COMMAND$
220 IF CMD$ ="" THEN 290
230 FOR I=1 TO LEN(CMD$):IF MID$(CMD$,I,1)=" " THEN 250
240 NEXT:FL$=CMD$:TP$="":GOTO 780
250 FL$=LEFT$(CMD$,I-1)
260 TP$=MID$(CMD$,I+1,LEN(CMD$)-I):IF TP$=" " OR TP$="" THEN 780
270 IF LEFT$(TP$,1)<>"\" AND MID$(TP$,2,1)<>":" THEN TP$="\"+TP$
280 GOTO 780
290 COLOR 15,0:CLS:PRINT "                 Bodner-Hutchins Text D
escriptor File System                      "
300 PRINT"────────────────────────────────────────────────────────────
─────────────────────":COLOR FFG,FFB
310 LOCATE  7,20:PRINT BX1$
320 LOCATE  8,20:PRINT "│    dBASE III (DBF) File Format         │"
330 LOCATE  9,20:PRINT "├────────────────────────────────────────┤"
340 LOCATE 10,20:PRINT "│     Descriptor File Processor          │"
350 LOCATE 11,20:PRINT "│         Version "+MREV$+"
│"
360 LOCATE 12,20:PRINT "│                                        │"
370 LOCATE 13,20:PRINT "│  "+DATE$+"                "+TIME$+"    │"
380 LOCATE 14,20:PRINT BX3$:COLOR 15,0
390 LOCATE 23,1:PRINT"────────────────────────────────────────────────
──────────────────────────────"
400 LOCATE 24,2:PRINT "       Copyright (c) 1986, Bodner-Hutchin
```

```
s Inc., Houston, Texas      ";
410 LOCATE 22,2:PRINT "     dBASE III & dBASE III Plus are tradem
arks of Ashton-Tate, Inc." ;
420 COLOR FFC,0:LOCATE 20,23:PRINT "Enter Q to quit and return to
 DOS"
430 COLOR 12,0:FLAG=0
440 LOCATE 17,20:PRINT BX1$
450 LOCATE 18,20:PRINT BX2$
460 LOCATE 19,20:PRINT BX3$;
470 LOCATE 18,24:PRINT "Enter file name : [         ]"
480 FL$=""
490 FOR I= 1 TO 8
500 LOCATE 18,42+I:COLOR 28,0:PRINT "_";:COLOR 12,0:F0$(I)=INKEY$
510 LOCATE 13,20:COLOR FFG,FFB:PRINT "|   "+DATE$+"              "
+TIME$+"   |":COLOR 12,0
520 IF F0$(I)="" THEN 500
530 IF ASC(F0$(I))=8 THEN LOCATE 18,42+I:PRINT " ";:I=I-1:FL$=LEF
T$(FL$,LEN(FL$)-1):GOTO 500
540 IF ASC(F0$(I))<33 AND ASC(F0$(I))<> 13 THEN 500
550 IF ASC(F0$(I))=13 THEN 580
560 LOCATE 18,42+I:PRINT F0$(I);:FL$=FL$+F0$(I)
570 NEXT
580 IF FL$="Q" OR FL$="q" THEN CLOSE:COLOR 15,0:CLS:END
590 IF LEN(FL$)>0 THEN 740
600 IF FLAG=1 THEN 480
610 OPEN "I",#1,"TDFDIR.TXT":COLOR 0,15:FLAG=1
620 LOCATE 3,60:PRINT"┌────────────┐"
630 LOCATE 4,60:PRINT"│ TDF Files  │"
640 LOCATE 5,60:PRINT"├────────────┤"
650 IF EOF(1) THEN 720
660 INPUT #1,D$:D=D+1:IF D<5 OR VAL(LEFT$(D$,1))>0 THEN 650
670 LOCATE D+1,60:PRINT "| "+LEFT$(D$,8)+"   |"
680 IF D<20 THEN 650
690 D=4:LOCATE 21,60:PRINT"└────────────┘":COLOR FFG,FFB:LOCATE 23
,55:PRINT"Press any key for more":COLOR 0,15:WD$=INKEY$:IF WD$=""
 THEN 690
700 COLOR 15,0:LOCATE 23,55:PRINT"──────────────────────":COLOR 0
,15
710 GOTO 650
720 CLOSE #1:LOCATE D+1,60:PRINT"└────────────┘":COLOR 12,0
730 GOTO 480
740 LOCATE 18,24:PRINT "Target Path [                ]"
750 LOCATE 18,37:INPUT "",TP$
760 IF LEN(TP$)=0 THEN 780
770 IF LEFT$(TP$,1)<>"\" AND MID$(TP$,2,1)<>":" THEN TP$="\"+TP$
780 ON ERROR GOTO 820
790 OPEN "I",#1,LEFT$(FL$,8)+".TDF"
800 ON ERROR GOTO 0
810 GOTO 830
820 LOCATE 19,60:COLOR 15,0:PRINT CHR$(7)+"File not found!!":COLO
R FFG,FFB:RESUME 290
830 FOR I=1 TO 13:INPUT #1,A$(I):A$(I)=RIGHT$(C$+A$(I),74):NEXT:C
LOSE #1
840 OPEN "O",#1,"DFP.OUT":PRINT #1,FL$:CLOSE #1
850 COLOR 15,0:CLS:PRINT "        Bodner-Hutchins Text Descriptor
```

```
 File Processor  (Rev "+MREV$+")            "
860 PRINT"┌──────────────────────────────────────────────────────────
──────────────────┐":COLOR FFG,FFC
870 FOR I=1 TO 13:COLOR 15,0:PRINT "│";:COLOR FFG,FFC:PRINT A$(I)
;:COLOR 15,0:PRINT "│":NEXT:COLOR 15,0
880 PRINT"└──────────────────────────────────────────────────────────
──────────────────┘"
890 COLOR 15,0
900 PRINT"      Data is being processed from Text Descriptor File
 [";:COLOR FFG,FFB:PRINT FL$;".TXT";:COLOR 15,0:PRINT "]"
910 PRINT"┌──────────────────────────────────────────────────────────
──────────────────┐"
920 PRINT"│    This TDF is being used by this DFP to convert the
associated ASCII    │"
930 PRINT"│  text file into a format directly useable by dBASE II
I & dBASE III Plus  │"
940 PRINT"├──────────────────────────────────────────────────────────
──────────────────┤"
950 PRINT"│
                    │"
960 PRINT"└──────────────────────────────────────────────────────────
──────────────────┘"
970 LOCATE 24,2:PRINT "       Copyright (c) 1986, Bodner-Hutchin
s Inc., Houston, Texas       ";
980 COLOR FFG,FFB:LOCATE 22,2:PRINT"       Now processing informa
tion from Text Descriptor File...          "
990 FM$=RIGHT$("        "+LEFT$(A$(1),8),8)+".TXT"
1000 LW=VAL(MID$(A$(1),10,3)):SL=VAL(MID$(A$(1),24,3)):EL=VAL(MID
$(A$(1),28,3)):LP=VAL(MID$(A$(1),20,3))
1010 NF=VAL(MID$(A$(1),56,3)):SNF=VAL(MID$(A$(1),73,3)):SCC=VAL(M
ID$(A$(1),69,3))
1020 LF$=MID$(A$(1),16,1):CR$=MID$(A$(1),14,1):DL$=MID$(A$(1),32,
1):OFS=VAL(MID$(A$(1),67,1))
1030 IF NF<=3 THEN NI=2
1040 IF NF>=4 AND NF<=6 THEN NI=3
1050 IF NF>=7 AND NF<=9 THEN NI=4
1060 IF NF>=10 AND NF<=12 THEN NI=5
1070 IF NF>=13 AND NF<=15 THEN NI=6
1080 IF NF>=16 AND NF<=18 THEN NI=7
1090 IF NF>=19 AND NF<=21 THEN NI=8
1100 IF NF>=22 AND NF<=24 THEN NI=9
1110 IF SNF<=3 THEN SNI=10
1120 IF SNF>=4 AND SNF<=6 THEN SNI=11
1130 IF SNF>=7 AND SNF<=9 THEN SNI=12
1140 IF SNF>=10 AND SNF<=12 THEN SNI=13
1150 FF$=MID$(A$(1),18,1):IC$=MID$(A$(1),46,8):SC$=MID$(A$(1),59,
7)
1160 FOR M=2 TO NI
1170 F1$(1,M-1)=MID$(A$(M),1,10):SC1(1,M-1)=VAL(MID$(A$(M),12,3))
:EC1(1,M-1)=VAL(MID$(A$(M),16,3)):TP1$(1,M-1)=MID$(A$(M),20,1):DP
1(1,M-1)=VAL(MID$(A$(M),22,2)):WDT(1,M-1)=EC1(1,M-1)-SC1(1,M-1)+1
1180 F1$(2,M-1)=MID$(A$(M),25,10):SC1(2,M-1)=VAL(MID$(A$(M),36,3)
):EC1(2,M-1)=VAL(MID$(A$(M),40,3)):TP1$(2,M-1)=MID$(A$(M),44,1):D
P1(2,M-1)=VAL(MID$(A$(M),46,2)):WDT(2,M-1)=EC1(2,M-1)-SC1(2,M-1)+
1
```

```
1190 F1$(3,M-1)=MID$(A$(M),49,10):SC1(3,M-1)=VAL(MID$(A$(M),60,3)
):EC1(3,M-1)=VAL(MID$(A$(M),64,3)):TP1$(3,M-1)=MID$(A$(M),68,1):D
P1(3,M-1)=VAL(MID$(A$(M),70,2)):WDT(3,M-1)=EC1(3,M-1)-SC1(3,M-1)+
1
1200 NEXT
1210 FOR M=10 TO SNI
1220 F1$(1,M-1)=MID$(A$(M),1,10):SC1(1,M-1)=VAL(MID$(A$(M),12,3))
:EC1(1,M-1)=VAL(MID$(A$(M),16,3)):TP1$(1,M-1)=MID$(A$(M),20,1):DP
1(1,M-1)=VAL(MID$(A$(M),22,2)):WDT(1,M-1)=EC1(1,M-1)-SC1(1,M-1)+1
1230 F1$(2,M-1)=MID$(A$(M),25,10):SC1(2,M-1)=VAL(MID$(A$(M),36,3)
):EC1(2,M-1)=VAL(MID$(A$(M),40,3)):TP1$(2,M-1)=MID$(A$(M),44,1):D
P1(2,M-1)=VAL(MID$(A$(M),46,2)):WDT(2,M-1)=EC1(2,M-1)-SC1(2,M-1)+
1
1240 F1$(3,M-1)=MID$(A$(M),49,10):SC1(3,M-1)=VAL(MID$(A$(M),60,3)
):EC1(3,M-1)=VAL(MID$(A$(M),64,3)):TP1$(3,M-1)=MID$(A$(M),68,1):D
P1(3,M-1)=VAL(MID$(A$(M),70,2)):WDT(3,M-1)=EC1(3,M-1)-SC1(3,M-1)+
1
1250 NEXT
1260 IF DL$<>"Y" THEN 1350
1270 W(1)=WDT(1,1):W(2)=WDT(2,1):W(3)=WDT(3,1)
1280 W(4)=WDT(1,2):W(5)=WDT(2,2):W(6)=WDT(3,2)
1290 W(7)=WDT(1,3):W(8)=WDT(2,3):W(9)=WDT(3,3)
1300 W(10)=WDT(1,4):W(11)=WDT(2,4):W(12)=WDT(3,4)
1310 W(13)=WDT(1,5):W(14)=WDT(2,5):W(15)=WDT(3,5)
1320 W(16)=WDT(1,6):W(17)=WDT(2,6):W(18)=WDT(3,6)
1330 W(19)=WDT(1,7):W(20)=WDT(2,7):W(21)=WDT(3,7)
1340 W(22)=WDT(1,8):W(23)=WDT(2,8):W(24)=WDT(3,8)
1350 COLOR FFG,FFB:LOCATE 22,2:PRINT"                   Now creating DB
F header ..........                       "
1360 GOSUB 2430
1370 FOR IJ=1 TO 36
1380 FOR II=1 TO 3:IF SC1(II,IJ)=0 THEN SC1(II,IJ)=1:WDT(II,IJ)=1
1390 NEXT:NEXT
1400 FOR H=3 TO LEN(SC$)
1410 IF MID$(SC$,H,2)="  " THEN 1430
1420 NEXT:GOTO 1440
1430 SC$=LEFT$(SC$,H-2)
1440 FOR H=3 TO LEN(IC$)
1450 IF MID$(IC$,H,2)="  " THEN 1470
1460 NEXT
1470 IC$=LEFT$(IC$,H-2)
1480 LN=0:FOR I= 1 TO NF:REM :IF DTTP$(I)="X" THEN 1485
1481 LN=LN+VAL(DTLN$(I))
1485 NEXT I:OP10$=""
1486 IF LN>255 THEN LNO=LN-255:LN=255:OP10$=SPACE$(LNO)
1487 OP1$=SPACE$(LN)
1490 FO$=LEFT$(FL$,8)+".OUT"
1500 OPEN "O",#2,FO$
1510 OPEN "I",#1,FM$
1520 IF DL$="Y" THEN 3250
1530 K=0:I=1
1540 IF EOF(1) THEN 1770
1541 IF CR$="Y" THEN LINE INPUT #1,F$:GOTO 1560
1550 F$=INPUT$(1,LW)
1560 K=K+1:IF LEFT$(F$,1)=CHR$(12) THEN K=0:LOCATE 22,4:PRINT "FO
```

```
RM FEED !!                                                  ":GOTO 1760
1570 IF LEFT$(F$,LEN(IC$))=IC$ THEN 1760
1580 IF SCC=0 THEN SCC=1
1590 IF MID$(F$,SCC,LEN(SC$))=SC$ OR LEFT$(F$,LEN(SC$))=SC$ THEN
GOSUB 2210:GOTO 1760
1600 IF LEN(F$)=0 THEN 1760
1610 J=1:LP1$=MID$(F$,SC1(1,J),WDT(1,J))
1620 LP2$=MID$(F$,SC1(2,J),WDT(2,J))
1630 LP3$=MID$(F$,SC1(3,J),WDT(3,J))
1640 OP$=LP1$:IF NF=>2 THEN OP$=OP$+LP2$
1650 IF NF=>3 THEN OP$=OP$+LP3$
1660 IF NF<=3 THEN 1740
1670 FOR J=2 TO NI-1
1680 LP1$=MID$(F$,SC1(1,J),WDT(1,J))
1690 LP2$=MID$(F$,SC1(2,J),WDT(2,J))
1700 LP3$=MID$(F$,SC1(3,J),WDT(3,J))
1710 OP$=OP$+LP1$:IF NF>(2+((J-1)*3)) THEN OP$=OP$+LP2$
1720 IF NF>(3+((J-1)*3)) THEN OP$=OP$+LP3$
1730 NEXT
1740 IF K>=SL AND K<=EL THEN PRINT #2,OP$:LOCATE 22,4:CNT=CNT+1:C
OLOR FFG,FFB:PRINT "Number Converted ";CNT;" ";LEFT$(MID$(F$,SC1(
1,1),WDT(1,1)),15);" ";LEFT$(MID$(F$,SC1(2,1),WDT(2,1)),15);" ";L
EFT$(MID$(F$,SC1(3,1),WDT(3,1)),15);
1750 IF K=LP THEN K=0:LOCATE 22,4:PRINT "PAGE BREAK!!       ":GOTO
 1760
1760 I=I+1:GOTO 1540
1770 CLOSE #1:CLOSE #2
1780 COLOR FFG,FFB:LOCATE 22,2:PRINT"       Loading second phase
processor for final conversion......                    "
1790 SHELL"DFPDBF2"
1800 COLOR 15,0:CLS:PRINT "       Bodner-Hutchins Text Descripto
r File Processor  (Rev "+MREV$+")                  "
1810 PRINT"┌─────────────────────────────────────────────────────
──────────────┐"
1820 PRINT"│Field Name   Start          End            Type
Decimals        Width │";
1830 PRINT"├─────────────────────────────────────────────────────
──────────────┤":COLOR FFG,FFB
1840 FOR J=1 TO NI-1
1850 COLOR 15,0:PRINT "│";:COLOR FFG,FFB:PRINT F1$(1,J),SC1(1,J),
EC1(1,J),TP1$(1,J),DP1(1,J);RIGHT$("                 "+STR$(WDT(1,
J)),15);" ";:COLOR 15,0:PRINT "│"
1860 IF F1$(2,J)="          " THEN 1900
1870 COLOR 15,0:PRINT "│";:COLOR FFG,FFB:PRINT F1$(2,J),SC1(2,J),
EC1(2,J),TP1$(2,J),DP1(2,J);RIGHT$("                 "+STR$(WDT(2,
J)),15);" ";:COLOR 15,0:PRINT "│"
1880 IF F1$(3,J)="          " THEN 1900
1890 COLOR 15,0:PRINT "│";:COLOR FFG,FFB:PRINT F1$(3,J),SC1(3,J),
EC1(3,J),TP1$(3,J),DP1(3,J);RIGHT$("                 "+STR$(WDT(3,
J)),15);" ";:COLOR 15,0:PRINT "│"
1900 NEXT J:COLOR 15,0
1910 IF SNF=0 THEN 2000
1920 PRINT"├─────────────────────────────────────────────────────
──────────────┤"
1930 COLOR FFG,FFB:FOR J=9 TO SNI-1
```

```
1940 COLOR 15,0:PRINT "|";:COLOR FFG,FFB:PRINT F1$(1,J),SC1(1,J),
EC1(1,J),TP1$(1,J),DP1(1,J);RIGHT$("                    "+STR$(WDT(1,
J)),15);" ";:COLOR 15,0:PRINT "|"
1950 IF F1$(2,J)="               " THEN 1990
1960 COLOR 15,0:PRINT "|";:COLOR FFG,FFB:PRINT F1$(2,J),SC1(2,J),
EC1(2,J),TP1$(2,J),DP1(2,J);RIGHT$("                    "+STR$(WDT(2,
J)),15);" ";:COLOR 15,0:PRINT "|"
1970 IF F1$(3,J)="               " THEN 1990
1980 COLOR 15,0:PRINT "|";:COLOR FFG,FFB:PRINT F1$(3,J),SC1(3,J),
EC1(3,J),TP1$(3,J),DP1(3,J);RIGHT$("                    "+STR$(WDT(3,
J)),15);" ";:COLOR 15,0:PRINT "|"
1990 NEXT J:COLOR 15,0
2000 PRINT"└──────────────────────────────────────────────────────────
──────────────────────┘"
2010 PRINT"        File structure as determined from the Text Desc
riptor File"
2020 LOCATE 19,1:COLOR FFG,FFC
2030 PRINT"┌──────────────────────────────────────────────────────────
──────────────────────┐"
2040 PRINT"|          This DFP has converted "+RIGHT$("    "+STR$(C
NT),5)+" data records from file "+RIGHT$("        "+FL$,8)+".TXT
 |"
2050 PRINT"|  and has created a DBF file with "+RIGHT$("    "+STR
$(NF+SNF),5)+" data fields in file "+RIGHT$("        "+FL$,8)+".D
BF  |"
2060 PRINT"└──────────────────────────────────────────────────────────
──────────────────────┘":COLOR 15,0
2070 PRINT "         Copyright (c) 1986, Bodner-Hutchins Inc., Hou
ston, Texas    ";
2080 ON ERROR GOTO 2120
2090 RMDIR TP$
2100 ON ERROR GOTO 0
2110 GOTO 2130
2120 IF ERR=76 THEN END
2130 CLOSE:IF TP$="" THEN END
2140 SH$="COPY "+FL$+".DBF "+TP$+">NUL"
2150 SHELL SH$
2160 SH$=FL$+".DBF"
2170 KILL SH$
2180 SH$=FL$+".OUT"
2190 KILL SH$
2200 END
2210 REM *****************************************************
************
2220 REM * SPECIAL CODE PROCESSOR
       *
2230 REM *
       *
2240 REM *****************************************************
************
2250 IF OFS=0 THEN 2270
2260 FOR O=1 TO OFS:LINE INPUT #1,F$:NEXT
2270 J=9:LP1$=MID$(F$,SC1(1,J),WDT(1,J))
2280 LP2$=MID$(F$,SC1(2,J),WDT(2,J))
2290 LP3$=MID$(F$,SC1(3,J),WDT(3,J))
```

```
2300 OP$=OP1$+OP10$+LP1$:IF SNF=>2 THEN OP$=OP$+LP2$
2310 IF SNF=>3 THEN OP$=OP$+LP3$
2320 IF SNF<=3 THEN 2410
2330 FOR J=10 TO SNI-1
2340 LP1$=MID$(F$,SC1(1,J),WDT(1,J))
2350 LP2$=MID$(F$,SC1(2,J),WDT(2,J))
2360 LP3$=MID$(F$,SC1(3,J),WDT(3,J))
2370 OP$=OP$+LP1$:IF SNF>(2+((J-9)*3)) THEN OP$=OP$+LP2$
2380 IF SNF>(3+((J-9)*3)) THEN OP$=OP$+LP3$
2390 NEXT
2400 COLOR FFG,FFB:LOCATE 22,2:PRINT"
                                                 "

2410 IF K>=SL AND K<=EL THEN PRINT #2,OP$:LOCATE 22,4:CNT=CNT+1:P
RINT "Special Line      ";CNT;" ";LEFT$(MID$(F$,SC1(1,9),WDT(1,9))
,10);" ";LEFT$(MID$(F$,SC1(2,9),WDT(2,9)),10);" ";LEFT$(MID$(F$,S
C1(3,9),WDT(3,9)),10)
2420 RETURN
2430 REM *********************************************************
************
2440 REM * CREATE DBASE DBF HEADER  FILE WITH NF AND SNF FIELDNAM
ES        *
2450 REM *
          *
2460 REM *********************************************************
************
2470 FOR I= 1 TO 64:DTLN$(I)="00":DTND$(I)="00":NEXT
2480 DB$(1)="03"
2490 DB$(2)=RIGHT$(DATE$,2)
2500 DB$(3)=LEFT$(DATE$,2)
2510 DB$(4)=MID$(DATE$,4,2)
2520 FOR I=5 TO 8:DB$(I)="00":NEXT
2530 FD$=LEFT$(FL$+"        ",8)+".DBF"
2540 FOR I= 1 TO NF STEP 3
2550 IF I=1 THEN KI=1:GOTO 2630
2560 IF I=4 THEN KI=2:GOTO 2630
2570 IF I=7 THEN KI=3:GOTO 2630
2580 IF I=10 THEN KI=4:GOTO 2630
2590 IF I=13 THEN KI=5:GOTO 2630
2600 IF I=16 THEN KI=6:GOTO 2630
2610 IF I=19 THEN KI=7:GOTO 2630
2620 IF I=22 THEN KI=8
2630 DTAF$(I)=F1$(1,KI):DTAF$(I+1)=F1$(2,KI):DTAF$(I+2)=F1$(3,KI)
2640 DTTP$(I)=TP1$(1,KI):DTTP$(I+1)=TP1$(2,KI):DTTP$(I+2)=TP1$(3,
KI)
2650 DTLN$(I)=STR$(WDT(1,KI)):DTLN$(I+1)=STR$(WDT(2,KI)):DTLN$(I+
2)=STR$(WDT(3,KI))
2660 IF DTTP$(I)="F" OR DTTP$(I)="I" THEN DTND$(I)=STR$(DP1(1,KI)
)
2670 IF DTTP$(I+1)="F" OR DTTP$(I+1)="I" THEN DTND$(I+1)=STR$(DP1
(2,KI))
2680 IF DTTP$(I+2)="F" OR DTTP$(I+2)="I" THEN DTND$(I+2)=STR$(DP1
(3,KI))
2690 NEXT I
2700 FOR I= 1 TO NF:IF DTTP$(I)="I" OR DTTP$(I)="F" THEN DTTP$(I)
="N"
```

```
2710 IF DTTP$(I)="D" THEN DTTP$(I)="C":DTLN$(I)="8"
2720 NEXT:M=I-1
2730 FOR I= 1 TO SNF STEP 3
2740 IF I=1 THEN KI=9:GOTO 2780
2750 IF I=4 THEN KI=10:GOTO 2780
2760 IF I=7 THEN KI=11:GOTO 2780
2770 IF I=10 THEN KI=12
2780 DTAF$(I+M)=F1$(1,KI):DTAF$(I+M+1)=F1$(2,KI):DTAF$(I+M+2)=F1$
(3,KI)
2790 DTTP$(I+M)=TP1$(1,KI):DTTP$(I+M+1)=TP1$(2,KI):DTTP$(I+M+2)=T
P1$(3,KI)
2800 DTLN$(I+M)=STR$(WDT(1,KI)):DTLN$(I+M+1)=STR$(WDT(2,KI)):DTLN
$(I+M+2)=STR$(WDT(3,KI))
2810 IF DTTP$(I+M)="F" OR DTTP$(I+M)="I" THEN DTND$(I+M)=STR$(DP1
(1,KI))
2820 IF DTTP$(I+M+1)="F" OR DTTP$(I+M+1)="I" THEN DTND$(I+M+1)=ST
R$(DP1(2,KI))
2830 IF DTTP$(I+M+2)="F" OR DTTP$(I+M+2)="I" THEN DTND$(I+M+2)=ST
R$(DP1(3,KI))
2840 NEXT I
2850 FOR I= 1 TO SNF:IF DTTP$(I+M)="I" OR DTTP$(I+M)="F" THEN DTT
P$(I+M)="N"
2860 IF DTTP$(I+M)="D" THEN DTTP$(I+M)="C":DTLN$(I+M)="8"
2870 NEXT
2880 LH=2+(32*(NF+NF+1)):LHH=INT(LH/256):LHL=LH-LHH*256
2890 DB$(9)=STR$(LHL)
2900 DB$(10)=STR$(LHH)
2910 FOR I=1 TO NF+SNF:NDATA=NDATA+VAL(DTLN$(I)):NEXT:NDATA=NDATA
+1
2920 NDH=INT(NDATA/256):NDL=NDATA-NDH*256
2930 DB$(11)=STR$(NDL):DB$(12)=STR$(NDH)
2940 FOR I=13 TO 32:DB$(I)="00":NEXT
2950 OPEN FD$ FOR OUTPUT AS #2
2960 FOR I=1 TO 32:PRINT #2,CHR$(VAL(DB$(I)));:NEXT
2970 FOR F=1 TO NF+SNF
2980 FOR L=1 TO 11:IF MID$(DTAF$(F),L,1)=" " THEN LK=L:GOTO 3000
2990 NEXT:LK=11
3000 FOR I=1 TO LK-1:DB$(I)=STR$(ASC(MID$(DTAF$(F),I,1))):NEXT
3010 FOR I=LK TO 11:DB$(I)="00":NEXT
3020 DB$(12)=STR$(ASC(DTTP$(F))):REM ASC OF TYPE
3030 DB$(13)=STR$(15+VAL(DTLN$(F-1)))
3040 DB$(14)="00"
3050 DB$(15)="00"
3060 DB$(16)="00"
3070 DB$(17)=DTLN$(F):REM ASC OF LENGTH
3080 DB$(18)="00":REM:IF DB$(12)<>"78" THEN 2610
3090 DB$(18)=DTND$(F):REM ASC OF NUMBER DEC
3100 FOR I=19 TO 32:DB$(I)="00":NEXT
3110 FOR I=1 TO 32:PRINT #2,CHR$(VAL(DB$(I)));:DB$(I)="00":NEXT
3120 NEXT F
3130 DB$(((SNF+NF+1)*32)+1)="13":DB$(((SNF+NF+1)*32)+2)="00"
3140 FOR I=((NF+SNF+1)*32)+1 TO ((SNF+NF+1)*32)+2:PRINT #2,CHR$(V
AL(DB$(I)));:NEXT
3150 CLOSE #2:RETURN
3160 OPEN FD$ FOR INPUT AS #2
```

```
3170 IF EOF(2) THEN 3220
3180 A=A+1
3190 DB$=INPUT$(1,#2)
3200 DB$(A)=RIGHT$("00"+HEX$(ASC(DB$)),2):IF ASC(DB$)=13 THEN 322
0
3210 GOTO 3170
3220  CLOSE #2:FOR I=1 TO A:PRINT DB$(I);" ";:IF INT(I/16)=I/16 T
HEN PRINT
3230  NEXT:PRINT
3240 RETURN
3350 REM ***********************************************************
**********
3260 REM * DELIMITED FILE PROCESSOR
         *
3270 REM *
         *
3280 REM ***********************************************************
**********
3290 CNT=0
3300 IF EOF(1) THEN 1770
3310 CNT=CNT+1:CNT2=0
3320 FOR I=1 TO NF
3330 INPUT #1,ADL$(I)
3331 REM:IF DTTP$(I)="X" THEN 3360
3332 ADL$(I)=LEFT$(ADL$(I)+C$,W(I))
3340 LOCATE 22,4:CNT2=CNT2+1:COLOR FFG,FFB:PRINT "Number Converte
";CNT;" Field # ";CNT2;" ";LEFT$(ADL$(I)+C$,30)
3350 PRINT #2,ADL$(I);
3360 NEXT:PRINT #2,""
3370 GOTO 3300
```

```
10 REM ***********************************************************
**********
20 REM *
       *
30 REM * DESCRIPTOR FILE PROCESSOR PROGRAM FOR DELIMITED FILE OUT
PUT        *
40 REM *
       *
50 REM * COPYRIGHT 1986 BODNER, HUTCHINS & ASSOCIATES, INC. REV 0
4/14/86    *
60 REM *
       *
70 REM ***********************************************************
**********
80 DIM A$(13),B$(13),F0$(13),F1$(3,36),SC1(3,36),EC1(3,36),TP1$(3
,36),DP1(3,36),WDT(3,36),ADL$(39),W(36)
90 C$="
                 "
100 OPEN "I",#1,"CONFIG.TD"
101 INPUT #1,FFG
102 INPUT #1,FFB
103 INPUT #1,FFC
104 CLOSE #1
105 MREV$="1.80"
120 BX1$="┌─────────────────────────────────────┐"
130 BX2$="│                                     │"
140 BX3$="└─────────────────────────────────────┘"
141 CMD$=COMMAND$
142 IF CMD$ ="" THEN 150
143 FOR I=1 TO LEN(CMD$):IF MID$(CMD$,I,1)=" " THEN 145
144 NEXT:FL$=CMD$:TP$="":GOTO 539
145 FL$=LEFT$(CMD$,I-1)
146 TP$=MID$(CMD$,I+1,LEN(CMD$)-I):IF TP$=" " OR TP$="" THEN 539
147 IF LEFT$(TP$,1)<>"\" AND MID$(TP$,2,1)<>":" THEN TP$="\"+TP$
148 GOTO 539
150 COLOR 15,0:CLS:PRINT "                 Bodner-Hutchins Text D
escriptor File System                 "
160 PRINT"────────────────────────────────────────────────────────
──────────────────────":COLOR FFG,FFB
170 LOCATE  7,20:PRINT BX1$
180 LOCATE  8,20:PRINT "│        Delimited File Format          │"
190 LOCATE  9,20:PRINT "├───────────────────────────────────────┤"
200 LOCATE 10,20:PRINT "│      Descriptor File Processor        │"
210 LOCATE 11,20:PRINT "│           Version "+MREV$+"
 │"
220 LOCATE 12,20:PRINT "│                                       │"
230 LOCATE 13,20:PRINT "│   "+DATE$+"           "+TIME$+"        │"
240 LOCATE 14,20:PRINT BX3$:COLOR 15,0
250 LOCATE 23,1:PRINT"────────────────────────────────────────
─────────────────────────────────"
260 LOCATE 24,2:PRINT "        Copyright (c) 1986, Bodner-Hutchin
s Inc., Houston, Texas       ";
261 COLOR FFC,0:LOCATE 20,23:PRINT "Enter Q to quit and return to
 DOS"
270 COLOR 12,0:FLAG=0
```

```
280 LOCATE 17,20:PRINT BX1$
290 LOCATE 18,20:PRINT BX2$
300 LOCATE 19,20:PRINT BX3$;
310 LOCATE 18,24:PRINT "Enter file name : [         ]"
320 FL$=""
330 FOR I= 1 TO 8
340 LOCATE 18,42+I:COLOR 28,0:PRINT "_";:COLOR 12,0:F0$(I)=INKEY$
350 LOCATE 13,20:COLOR FFG,FFB:PRINT "│  "+DATE$+"              "
+TIME$+"  │":COLOR 12,0
360 IF F0$(I)="" THEN 340
361 IF ASC(F0$(I))=8 THEN LOCATE 18,42+I:PRINT " ";:I=I-1:FL$=LEF
T$(FL$,LEN(FL$)-1):GOTO 340
365 IF ASC(F0$(I))<33 AND ASC(F0$(I))<> 13 THEN 340
370 IF ASC(F0$(I))=13 THEN 400
380 LOCATE 18,42+I:PRINT F0$(I);:FL$=FL$+F0$(I)
390 NEXT
400 IF FL$="Q" OR FL$="q" THEN CLOSE:COLOR 15,0:CLS:END
401 IF LEN(FL$)>0 THEN 530
410 IF FLAG=1 THEN 320
420 OPEN "I",#1,"TDFDIR.TXT":COLOR 0,15:FLAG=1
430 LOCATE 3,60:PRINT"┌───────────┐"
440 LOCATE 4,60:PRINT"│ TDF Files │"
450 LOCATE 5,60:PRINT"├───────────┤"
460 IF EOF(1) THEN 510
470 INPUT #1,D$:D=D+1:IF D<5 OR VAL(LEFT$(D$,1))>0 THEN 460
480 LOCATE D+1,60:PRINT "│ "+LEFT$(D$,8)+"  │"
490 IF D<20 THEN 460
491 D=4:LOCATE 21,60:PRINT"└───────────┘":COLOR FFG,FFB:LOCATE 23
,55:PRINT"Press any key for more":COLOR 0,15:WD$=INKEY$:IF WD$=""
 THEN 491
492 COLOR 15,0:LOCATE 23,55:PRINT"──────────────────────":COLOR 0
,15
500 GOTO 460
510 CLOSE #1:LOCATE D+1,60:PRINT"└───────────┘":COLOR 12,0
520 GOTO 320
530 LOCATE 18,24:PRINT "Target Path [                    ]"
531 LOCATE 18,37:INPUT "",TP$
532 IF LEN(TP$)=0 THEN 539
533 IF LEFT$(TP$,1)<>"\" AND MID$(TP$,2,1)<>":" THEN TP$="\"+TP$
539 ON ERROR GOTO 570
540 OPEN "I",#1,LEFT$(FL$,8)+".TDF"
550 ON ERROR GOTO 0
560 GOTO 580
570 LOCATE 21,60:PRINT CHR$(7)+"File not found!!":RESUME 310
580 FOR I=1 TO 13:INPUT #1,A$(I):A$(I)=RIGHT$(C$+A$(I),74):NEXT:C
LOSE #1
590 COLOR 15,0:CLS:PRINT "         Bodner-Hutchins Text Descriptor
 File Processor  (Rev "+MREV$+")            "
600 PRINT"┌──────────────────────────────────────────────────────
──────────────────┐":COLOR FFG,FFC
610 FOR I=1 TO 13:COLOR 15,0:PRINT "│";:COLOR FFG,FFC:PRINT A$(I)
;:COLOR 15,0:PRINT "│":NEXT:COLOR 15,0
620 PRINT"└──────────────────────────────────────────────────────
──────────────────┘"
630 COLOR 15,0
```

```
640 PRINT"      Data is being processed from Text Descriptor File
 [";:COLOR FFG,FFC:PRINT FL$;:PRINT ".TXT";:COLOR 15,0:PRINT "]"
650 PRINT"┌───────────────────────────────────────────────────────
──────────────────────┐"
660 PRINT"│     This TDF is being used by this DFP to convert the
associated ASCII     │"
670 PRINT"│ text file into a format useable by programs requiring
 Delimited formats   │"
680 PRINT"├───────────────────────────────────────────────────────
──────────────────────┤"
690 PRINT"│
                     │"
700 PRINT"└───────────────────────────────────────────────────────
──────────────────────┘"
710 COLOR FFG,FFC:LOCATE 22,2:PRINT"       Now processing informa
tion from Text Descriptor File...       "
711 FM$=RIGHT$("        "+LEFT$(A$(1),8),8)+".TXT"
720 LW=VAL(MID$(A$(1),10,3)):SL=VAL(MID$(A$(1),24,3)):EL=VAL(MID$
(A$(1),28,3)):LP=VAL(MID$(A$(1),20,3))
730 NF=VAL(MID$(A$(1),56,3)):SNF=VAL(MID$(A$(1),73,3)):SCC=VAL(MI
D$(A$(1),69,3))
740 LF$=MID$(A$(1),16,1):CR$=MID$(A$(1),14,1):DL$=MID$(A$(1),32,1
):OFS=VAL(MID$(A$(1),67,1))
750 DL1=34:DL2=44:DL3=34
760 IF NF<=3 THEN NI=2
770 IF NF>=4 AND NF<=6 THEN NI=3
780 IF NF>=7 AND NF<=9 THEN NI=4
790 IF NF>=10 AND NF<=12 THEN NI=5
800 IF NF>=13 AND NF<=15 THEN NI=6
810 IF NF>=16 AND NF<=18 THEN NI=7
820 IF NF>=19 AND NF<=21 THEN NI=8
830 IF NF>=22 AND NF<=24 THEN NI=9
840 IF SNF<=3 THEN SNI=10
850 IF SNF>=4 AND SNF<=6 THEN SNI=11
860 IF SNF>=7 AND SNF<=9 THEN SNI=12
870 IF SNF>=10 AND SNF<=12 THEN NI=13
880 FF$=MID$(A$(1),18,1):IC$=MID$(A$(1),46,8):SC$=MID$(A$(1),59,7
)
890 FOR M=2 TO NI
900 F1$(1,M-1)=MID$(A$(M),1,10):SC1(1,M-1)=VAL(MID$(A$(M),12,3)):
EC1(1,M-1)=VAL(MID$(A$(M),16,3)):TP1$(1,M-1)=MID$(A$(M),20,1):DP1
(1,M-1)=VAL(MID$(A$(M),22,2)):WDT(1,M-1)=EC1(1,M-1)-SC1(1,M-1)+1:
PW$=F1$(1,M-1)
910 GOSUB 2040:F1$(1,M-1)=LEFT$(F1$(1,M-1),NPK)
920 F1$(2,M-1)=MID$(A$(M),25,10):SC1(2,M-1)=VAL(MID$(A$(M),36,3))
:EC1(2,M-1)=VAL(MID$(A$(M),40,3)):TP1$(2,M-1)=MID$(A$(M),44,1):DP
1(2,M-1)=VAL(MID$(A$(M),46,2)):WDT(2,M-1)=EC1(2,M-1)-SC1(2,M-1)+1
:PW$=F1$(2,M-1)
930 GOSUB 2040:F1$(2,M-1)=LEFT$(F1$(2,M-1),NPK)
940 F1$(3,M-1)=MID$(A$(M),49,10):SC1(3,M-1)=VAL(MID$(A$(M),60,3))
:EC1(3,M-1)=VAL(MID$(A$(M),64,3)):TP1$(3,M-1)=MID$(A$(M),68,1):DP
1(3,M-1)=VAL(MID$(A$(M),70,2)):WDT(3,M-1)=EC1(3,M-1)-SC1(3,M-1)+1
:PW$=F1$(3,M-1)
950 GOSUB 2040:F1$(3,M-1)=LEFT$(F1$(3,M-1),NPK)
960 NEXT
```

```
970 FOR M=10 TO SNI
980 F1$(1,M-1)=MID$(A$(M),1,10):SC1(1,M-1)=VAL(MID$(A$(M),12,3)):
EC1(1,M-1)=VAL(MID$(A$(M),16,3)):TP1$(1,M-1)=MID$(A$(M),20,1):DP1
(1,M-1)=VAL(MID$(A$(M),22,2)):WDT(1,M-1)=EC1(1,M-1)-SC1(1,M-1)+1:
PW$=F1$(1,M-1)
990 GOSUB 2040:F1$(1,M-1)=LEFT$(F1$(1,M-1),NPK)
1000 F1$(2,M-1)=MID$(A$(M),25,10):SC1(2,M-1)=VAL(MID$(A$(M),36,3)
):EC1(2,M-1)=VAL(MID$(A$(M),40,3)):TP1$(2,M-1)=MID$(A$(M),44,1):D
P1(2,M-1)=VAL(MID$(A$(M),46,2)):WDT(2,M-1)=EC1(2,M-1)-SC1(2,M-1)+
1:PW$=F1$(2,M-1)
1010 GOSUB 2040:F1$(2,M-1)=LEFT$(F1$(2,M-1),NPK)
1020 F1$(3,M-1)=MID$(A$(M),49,10):SC1(3,M-1)=VAL(MID$(A$(M),60,3)
):EC1(3,M-1)=VAL(MID$(A$(M),64,3)):TP1$(3,M-1)=MID$(A$(M),68,1):D
P1(3,M-1)=VAL(MID$(A$(M),70,2)):WDT(3,M-1)=EC1(3,M-1)-SC1(3,M-1)+
1:PW$=F1$(3,M-1)
1030 GOSUB 2040:F1$(3,M-1)=LEFT$(F1$(3,M-1),NPK)
1040 NEXT
1050 IF DL$<>"Y" THEN 1140
1060 W(1)=WDT(1,1):W(2)=WDT(2,1):W(3)=WDT(3,1)
1070 W(4)=WDT(1,2):W(5)=WDT(2,2):W(6)=WDT(3,2)
1080 W(7)=WDT(1,3):W(8)=WDT(2,3):W(9)=WDT(3,3)
1090 W(10)=WDT(1,4):W(11)=WDT(2,4):W(12)=WDT(3,4)
1100 W(13)=WDT(1,5):W(14)=WDT(2,5):W(15)=WDT(3,5)
1110 W(16)=WDT(1,6):W(17)=WDT(2,6):W(18)=WDT(3,6)
1120 W(19)=WDT(1,7):W(20)=WDT(2,7):W(21)=WDT(3,7)
1130 W(22)=WDT(1,8):W(23)=WDT(2,8):W(24)=WDT(3,8)
1140 COLOR FFG,FFC:LOCATE 22,2:PRINT"            Now creating De
limited file.......                 "
1150 FOR IJ=1 TO 36
1160 FOR II=1 TO 3:IF SC1(II,IJ)=0 THEN SC1(II,IJ)=1:WDT(II,IJ)=1
1170 NEXT:NEXT
1180 FOR H=3 TO LEN(SC$)
1190 IF MID$(SC$,H,2)="  " THEN 1210
1200 NEXT:GOTO 1220
1210 SC$=LEFT$(SC$,H-2)
1220 FOR H=3 TO LEN(IC$)
1230 IF MID$(IC$,H,2)="  " THEN 1250
1240 NEXT:GOTO 1260
1250 IC$=LEFT$(IC$,H-2)
1260 IF DL1 >0 THEN DL1$=CHR$(DL1) ELSE DL1$=""
1270 IF DL2 >0 THEN DL2$=CHR$(DL2) ELSE DL2$=""
1280 IF DL3 >0 THEN DL3$=CHR$(DL3) ELSE DL3$=""
1290 DLC$=DL1$+DL2$+DL3$
1300 OP1$=DL3$+MID$(C$,SC1(1,1),WDT(1,1))+DLC$+MID$(C$,SC1(2,1),W
DT(2,1))+DLC$+MID$(C$,SC1(3,1),WDT(3,1))+DL1$+DL2$
1320 FO$=LEFT$(FL$,8)+".DAT"
1330 OPEN "O",#2,FO$
1340 OPEN "I",#1,FM$
1350 IF DL$="Y" THEN 2110
1360 K=0:I=1
1370 IF EOF(1) THEN 1600
1371 IF CR$="Y" THEN LINE INPUT #1,F$:GOTO 1390
1380 F$=INPUT$(1,LW)
1390 K=K+1:IF LEFT$(F$,1)=CHR$(12) THEN K=0:LOCATE 22,4:PRINT "FO
RM FEED !!     ":GOTO 1590
```

```
1400 IF LEFT$(F$,LEN(IC$))=IC$ THEN 1590
1410 IF SCC=0 THEN SCC=1
1420 IF MID$(F$,SCC,LEN(SC$))=SC$ OR LEFT$(F$,LEN(SC$))=SC$ THEN
GOSUB 1900:GOTO 1590
1430 IF LEN(F$)=0 THEN 1590
1440 J=1:LP1$=CHR$(34)+MID$(F$,SC1(1,J),WDT(1,J))+CHR$(34)
1450 LP2$=CHR$(34)+MID$(F$,SC1(2,J),WDT(2,J))+CHR$(34)
1460 LP3$=CHR$(34)+MID$(F$,SC1(3,J),WDT(3,J))+CHR$(34)
1470 OP$=LP1$:IF NF=>2 THEN OP$=OP$+","+LP2$
1480 IF NF=>3 THEN OP$=OP$+","+LP3$
1490 IF NF<=3 THEN 1570
1500 FOR J=2 TO NI-1
1510 LP1$=CHR$(34)+MID$(F$,SC1(1,J),WDT(1,J))+CHR$(34)
1520 LP2$=CHR$(34)+MID$(F$,SC1(2,J),WDT(2,J))+CHR$(34)
1530 LP3$=CHR$(34)+MID$(F$,SC1(3,J),WDT(3,J))+CHR$(34)
1540 OP$=OP$+","+LP1$:IF NF>(2+((J-1)*3)) THEN OP$=OP$+","+LP2$
1550 IF NF>(3+((J-1)*3)) THEN OP$=OP$+","+LP3$
1560 NEXT
1570 IF K>=SL AND K<=EL THEN PRINT #2,OP$:LOCATE 22,4:CNT=CNT+1:C
OLOR FFG,FFC:PRINT "Number Converted ";CNT;" ";LEFT$(MID$(F$,SC1(
1,1),WDT(1,1)),15);" ";LEFT$(MID$(F$,SC1(2,1),WDT(2,1)),15);" ";L
EFT$(MID$(F$,SC1(3,1),WDT(3,1)),15);
1580 IF K=LP THEN K=0:LOCATE 22,4:PRINT "PAGE BREAK!!       ":GOTO
 1590
1590 I=I+1:GOTO 1370
1600 CLOSE #1:CLOSE #2
1610 COLOR 15,0:CLS:PRINT "        Bodner-Hutchins Text Descripto
r File Processor  (Rev "+MREV$+")          "
1620 PRINT"┌──────────────────────────────────────────────────────
────────────────────┐"
1630 PRINT"│Field Name   Start          End           Type
Decimals        Width │";
1640 PRINT"├──────────────────────────────────────────────────────
────────────────────┤":COLOR FFG,FFB
1650 FOR J=1 TO NI-1
1660 COLOR 15,0:PRINT "│";:COLOR FFG,FFB:PRINT F1$(1,J),SC1(1,J),
EC1(1,J),TP1$(1,J),DP1(1,J);RIGHT$("                    "+STR$(WDT(1,
J)),15);" ";:COLOR 15,0:PRINT "│"
1670 IF F1$(2,J)="              " OR LEN(F1$(2,J))=0 THEN 1710
1680 COLOR 15,0:PRINT "│";:COLOR FFG,FFB:PRINT F1$(2,J),SC1(2,J),
EC1(2,J),TP1$(2,J),DP1(2,J);RIGHT$("                    "+STR$(WDT(2,
J)),15);" ";:COLOR 15,0:PRINT "│"
1690 IF F1$(3,J)="              " OR LEN(F1$(3,J))=0 THEN 1710
1700 COLOR 15,0:PRINT "│";:COLOR FFG,FFB:PRINT F1$(3,J),SC1(3,J),
EC1(3,J),TP1$(3,J),DP1(3,J);RIGHT$("                    "+STR$(WDT(3,
J)),15);" ";:COLOR 15,0:PRINT "│"
1710 NEXT J:COLOR 15,0
1720 IF SNF=0 THEN 1810
1730 PRINT"├──────────────────────────────────────────────────────
────────────────────┤"
1740 COLOR FFG,FFB:FOR J=9 TO SNI-1
1750 COLOR 15,0:PRINT "│";:COLOR FFG,FFB:PRINT F1$(1,J),SC1(1,J),
EC1(1,J),TP1$(1,J),DP1(1,J);RIGHT$("                    "+STR$(WDT(1,
J)),15);" ";:COLOR 15,0:PRINT "│"
1760 IF F1$(2,J)="              " OR LEN(F1$(2,J))=0 THEN 1800
```

```
1770 COLOR 15,0:PRINT "|";:COLOR FFG,FFB:PRINT F1$(2,J),SC1(2,J),
EC1(2,J),TP1$(2,J),DP1(2,J);RIGHT$("                    "+STR$(WDT(2,
J)),15);" ";:COLOR 15,0:PRINT "|"
1780 IF F1$(3,J)="               " OR LEN(F1$(3,J))=0 THEN 1800
1790 COLOR 15,0:PRINT "|";:COLOR FFG,FFB:PRINT F1$(3,J),SC1(3,J),
EC1(3,J),TP1$(3,J),DP1(3,J);RIGHT$("                    "+STR$(WDT(3,
J)),15);" ";:COLOR 15,0:PRINT "|"
1800 NEXT J:COLOR 15,0
1810 PRINT"└──────────────────────────────────────────────────────────
──────────────────────┘"
1820 PRINT"       File structure as determined from the Text Desc
riptor File"
1830 LOCATE 19,1:COLOR FFG,FFC
1840 PRINT"┌─────────────────────────────────────────────────────────
─────────────────────┐"
1850 PRINT"|       This DFP has converted "+RIGHT$("    "+STR$(C
NT),5)+" data records to file "+RIGHT$("        "+FL$,8)+".DAT
 |"
1860 PRINT"|        and has created a Delimited file with "+RIGHT
$("    "+STR$(NF+SNF),5)+" data fields.         |"
1870 PRINT"└──────────────────────────────────────────────────────────
──────────────────────┘":COLOR 15,0
1871 PRINT "        Copyright (c) 1986, Bodner-Hutchins Inc., Hou
ston, Texas    ";
1872 ON ERROR GOTO 1876
1873 RMDIR TP$
1874 ON ERROR GOTO 0
1875 GOTO 1881
1876 IF ERR=76 THEN END
1881 CLOSE:IF TP$="" THEN END
1882 SH$="COPY "+FL$+".OUT "+TP$+">NUL"
1883 SHELL SH$
1884 SH$="ERASE "+FL$+".OUT"
1885 SHELL SH$
1890 END
1900 REM ************************************************************
************
1910 REM * SPECIAL CODE PROCESSOR
         *
1920 REM *
         *
1930 REM ************************************************************
************
1940 IF OFS=0 THEN 1960
1950 FOR O=1 TO OFS:LINE INPUT #1,F$:NEXT
1960 J=9:LP1$=CHR$(34)+MID$(F$,SC1(1,J),WDT(1,J))+CHR$(34)
1962 LP2$=CHR$(34)+MID$(F$,SC1(2,J),WDT(2,J))+CHR$(34)
1963 LP3$=CHR$(34)+MID$(F$,SC1(3,J),WDT(3,J))+CHR$(34)
1964 OP$=OP1$+LP1$:IF SNF=>2 THEN OP$=OP$+LP2$
1965 IF SNF=>3 THEN OP$=OP$+LP3$
1966 IF SNF<=3 THEN 2020
1967 FOR J=10 TO SNI-1
1968 LP1$=CHR$(34)+MID$(F$,SC1(1,J),WDT(1,J))+CHR$(34)
1969 LP2$=CHR$(34)+MID$(F$,SC1(2,J),WDT(2,J))+CHR$(34)
1970 LP3$=CHR$(34)+MID$(F$,SC1(3,J),WDT(3,J))+CHR$(34)
```

```
1974 OP$=OP$+LP1$:IF SNF>(2+((J-9)*3)) THEN OP$=OP$+LP2$
1975 IF SNF>(3+((J-9)*3)) THEN OP$=OP$+LP3$
2000 NEXT
2010 COLOR FFG,FFB:LOCATE 22,2:PRINT"
                                                "
2020 IF K>=SL AND K<=EL THEN PRINT #2,OP$:LOCATE 22,4:CNT=CNT+1:P
RINT "Special Line     ";CNT;" ";LEFT$(MID$(F$,SC1(1,9),WDT(1,9))
,10);" ";LEFT$(MID$(F$,SC1(2,9),WDT(2,9)),10);" ";LEFT$(MID$(F$,S
C1(3,9),WDT(3,9)),10)
2030 RETURN
2040 REM *********************************************************
************
2050 REM * FIELD PACKER
           *
2060 REM *
           *
2070 REM *********************************************************
************
2080 FOR Q=1 TO LEN(PW$):IF MID$(PW$,Q,1)=" " THEN NPK=Q-1:RETURN
2090 NEXT:NPK=Q
2100 RETURN
2110 REM *********************************************************
************
2120 REM * DELIMITED FILE PROCESSOR
           *
2130 REM *
           *
2140 REM *********************************************************
************
2150 CNT=0
2160 IF EOF(1) THEN 1600
2170 CNT=CNT+1:CNT2=0
2180 FOR I=1 TO NF
2190 INPUT #1,ADL$(I):ADL$(I)=LEFT$(ADL$(I)+C$,W(I))
2200 LOCATE 22,4:CNT2=CNT2+1:COLOR FFG,FFB:PRINT "Number Converte
d ";CNT;" Field # ";CNT2;" ";LEFT$(ADL$(I)+C$,30)
2210 IF I>1 THEN PRINT #2,DL2$;
2220 PRINT #2,DL1$+ADL$(I)+DL3$;
2230 NEXT:PRINT #2,""
2240 GOTO 2160
```

```
10 REM ************************************************************
**********
20 REM *
       *
30 REM * DESCRIPTOR FILE PROCESSOR PROGRAM FOR LOTUS 1-2-3
       *
40 REM *
       *
50 REM * COPYRIGHT 1986 BODNER, HUTCHINS & ASSOCIATES, INC. REV 0
4/14/86  *
60 REM *
       *
70 REM ************************************************************
**********
80 DIM A$(13),B$(13),F0$(13),F1$(3,36),SC1(3,36),EC1(3,36),TP1$(3
,36),DP1(3,36),WDT(3,36),W(36),ADL$(36),TP$(36)
90 C$="
                  "
100 OPEN "I",#1,"CONFIG.TD"
101 INPUT #1,FFG
102 INPUT #1,FFB
103 INPUT #1,FFC
104 CLOSE #1
105 MREV$="1.80"
110 BX1$="┌────────────────────────────────────────┐"
120 BX2$="│                                        │"
130 BX3$="└────────────────────────────────────────┘"
131 CMD$=COMMAND$
132 IF CMD$ ="" THEN 149
133 FOR I=1 TO LEN(CMD$):IF MID$(CMD$,I,1)=" " THEN 135
134 NEXT:FL$=CMD$:TP$="":GOTO 479
135 FL$=LEFT$(CMD$,I-1)
136 TP$=MID$(CMD$,I+1,LEN(CMD$)-I):IF TP$=" " OR TP$="" THEN 479
137 IF LEFT$(TP$,1)<>"\" AND MID$(TP$,2,1)<>":" THEN TP$="\"+TP$
138 FOR I=1 TO LEN(TP$):IF MID$(TP$,I,1)=" " THEN 140
139 NEXT:FTP$="":GOTO 479
140 FTP$=MID$(TP$,I+1,LEN(TP$)-I)
141 TP$=LEFT$(TP$,I-1)
148 GOTO 479
149 COLOR 15,0:CLS:PRINT "                    Bodner-Hutchins Text D
escriptor File System                "
150 PRINT"────────────────────────────────────────────────────────────
─────────────────────────":COLOR FFG,FFB
160 LOCATE  7,20:PRINT BX1$
170 LOCATE  8,20:PRINT "│       LOTUS 1-2-3 (PRN) File           │"
180 LOCATE  9,20:PRINT "├────────────────────────────────────────┤"
190 LOCATE 10,20:PRINT "│      Descriptor File Processor         │"
200 LOCATE 11,20:PRINT "│            Version "+MREV$+"
│"
210 LOCATE 12,20:PRINT "│                                        │"
220 LOCATE 13,20:PRINT "│   "+DATE$+"              "+TIME$+"    │"
230 LOCATE 14,20:PRINT BX3$:COLOR 15,0
240 LOCATE 23,1:PRINT"────────────────────────────────────────────
───────────────────────────────────"
250 LOCATE 24,2:PRINT "         Copyright (c) 1986, Bodner-Hutchin
```

```
s Inc., Houston, Texas      ";
260 LOCATE 22,2:PRINT "        1-2-3 is a trademark of Lotus Deve
lopment Corporation"
261 COLOR FFC,0:LOCATE 20,23:PRINT "Enter Q to quit and return to
 DOS"
270 COLOR 12,0:FLAG=0
280 LOCATE 17,20:PRINT BX1$
290 LOCATE 18,20:PRINT BX2$
300 LOCATE 19,20:PRINT BX3$;
310 LOCATE 18,24:PRINT "Enter file name : [        ]"
320 FL$=""
321 FOR I= 1 TO 8
322 LOCATE 18,42+I:COLOR 28,0:PRINT "_";:COLOR 12,0:F0$(I)=INKEY$
323 LOCATE 13,20:COLOR FFG,FFB:PRINT "|   "+DATE$+"               "
+TIME$+"  |":COLOR 12,0
324 IF F0$(I)="" THEN 322
325 IF ASC(F0$(I))=8 THEN LOCATE 18,42+I:PRINT " ";:I=I-1:FL$=LEF
T$(FL$,LEN(FL$)-1):GOTO 322
326 IF ASC(F0$(I))<33 AND ASC(F0$(I))<> 13 THEN 322
327 IF ASC(F0$(I))=13 THEN 330
328 LOCATE 18,42+I:PRINT F0$(I);:FL$=FL$+F0$(I)
329 NEXT
330 IF FL$="Q" OR FL$="q" THEN CLOSE:COLOR 15,0:CLS:END
331 IF LEN(FL$)>0 THEN 470
340 IF FLAG=1 THEN 320
360 OPEN "I",#1,"TDFDIR.TXT":COLOR 0,15:FLAG=1
370 LOCATE 3,60:PRINT"┌───────────┐"
380 LOCATE 4,60:PRINT"│ TDF Files │"
390 LOCATE 5,60:PRINT"├───────────┤"
400 IF EOF(1) THEN 450
410 INPUT #1,D$:D=D+1:IF D<5 OR VAL(LEFT$(D$,1))>0 THEN 400
420 LOCATE D+1,60:PRINT "| "+LEFT$(D$,8)+"  |"
430 IF D<20 THEN 400
431 D=4:LOCATE 21,60:PRINT"└───────────┘":COLOR FFG,FFB:LOCATE 23
,55:PRINT"Press any key for more":COLOR 0,15:WD$=INKEY$:IF WD$=""
 THEN 431
432 COLOR 15,0:LOCATE 23,55:PRINT"──────────────────────":COLOR 0
,15
440 GOTO 400
450 CLOSE #1:LOCATE D+1,60:PRINT"└───────────┘":COLOR 12,0
460 GOTO 320
470 LOCATE 18,24:PRINT "Target Path [                 ]"
471 LOCATE 18,37:INPUT "",TP$
472 IF LEN(TP$)=0 THEN 479
473 IF LEFT$(TP$,1)<>"\" AND MID$(TP$,2,1)<>":" THEN TP$="\"+TP$
479 ON ERROR GOTO 510
480 OPEN "I",#1,LEFT$(FL$,8)+".TDF"
481 INPUT #1,A$(1)
482 FM$=RIGHT$("        "+LEFT$(A$(1),8),8)+".TXT"
483 CLOSE #1
484 OPEN "I",#1,FM$
485 CLOSE #1
486 OPEN "I",#1,LEFT$(FL$,8)+".TDF"
490 ON ERROR GOTO 0
500 GOTO 520
```

```
510 LOCATE 21,60:PRINT CHR$(7)+"File not found!!":RESUME 310
520 FOR I=1 TO 13:INPUT #1,A$(I):A$(I)=RIGHT$(C$+A$(I),74):NEXT:C
LOSE #1
540 COLOR 15,0:CLS:PRINT "        Bodner-Hutchins Text Descriptor
 File Processor  (Rev "+MREV$+")              "
550 PRINT"┌──────────────────────────────────────────────────────
──────────────────────┐":COLOR FFG,FFB
560 FOR I=1 TO 13:COLOR 15,0:PRINT "│";:COLOR FFG,FFC:PRINT A$(I)
;:COLOR 15,0:PRINT "│":NEXT:COLOR 15,0
570 PRINT"└──────────────────────────────────────────────────────
──────────────────────┘"
580 COLOR 15
590 PRINT"      Data is being processed from Text Descriptor File
 [";:COLOR FFG,FFB:PRINT FL$;:PRINT ".TXT";:COLOR 15,0:PRINT "]"
600 PRINT"┌──────────────────────────────────────────────────────
──────────────────────┐"
610 PRINT"│    This TDF is being used by this DFP to convert the
associated ASCII     │"
620 PRINT"│   text file into a format directly useable by Lotus D
evelopment 1-2-3.    │"
630 PRINT"├──────────────────────────────────────────────────────
──────────────────────┤"
640 PRINT"│
                     │"
650 PRINT"└──────────────────────────────────────────────────────
──────────────────────┘"
660 COLOR FFG,FFB:LOCATE 22,2:PRINT"        Now processing informa
tion from Text Descriptor File...        "
670 FM$=RIGHT$("        "+LEFT$(A$(1),8),8)+".TXT"
680 LW=VAL(MID$(A$(1),10,3)):SL=VAL(MID$(A$(1),24,3)):EL=VAL(MID$
(A$(1),28,3)):LP=VAL(MID$(A$(1),20,3))
690 NF=VAL(MID$(A$(1),56,3)):SNF=VAL(MID$(A$(1),73,3)):SCC=VAL(MI
D$(A$(1),69,3))
700 LF$=MID$(A$(1),16,1):CR$=MID$(A$(1),14,1):DL$=MID$(A$(1),32,1
):OFS=VAL(MID$(A$(1),67,1))
710 DL1=34:DL2=44:DL3=34
720 IF NF<=3 THEN NI=2
730 IF NF>=4 AND NF<=6 THEN NI=3
740 IF NF>=7 AND NF<=9 THEN NI=4
750 IF NF>=10 AND NF<=12 THEN NI=5
760 IF NF>=13 AND NF<=15 THEN NI=6
770 IF NF>=16 AND NF<=18 THEN NI=7
780 IF NF>=19 AND NF<=21 THEN NI=8
790 IF NF>=22 AND NF<=24 THEN NI=9
800 IF SNF<=3 THEN SNI=10
810 IF SNF>=4 AND SNF<=6 THEN SNI=11
820 IF SNF>=7 AND SNF<=9 THEN SNI=12
830 IF SNF>=10 AND SNF<=12 THEN NI=13
840 FF$=MID$(A$(1),18,1):IC$=MID$(A$(1),46,8):SC$=MID$(A$(1),59,7
)
850 FOR M=2 TO NI
860 F1$(1,M-1)=MID$(A$(M),1,10):SC1(1,M-1)=VAL(MID$(A$(M),12,3)):
EC1(1,M-1)=VAL(MID$(A$(M),16,3)):TP1$(1,M-1)=MID$(A$(M),20,1):DP1
(1,M-1)=VAL(MID$(A$(M),22,2)):WDT(1,M-1)=EC1(1,M-1)-SC1(1,M-1)+1:
PW$=F1$(1,M-1)
```

```
870 GOSUB 2140:F1$(1,M-1)=LEFT$(F1$(1,M-1),NPK)
880 F1$(2,M-1)=MID$(A$(M),25,10):SC1(2,M-1)=VAL(MID$(A$(M),36,3))
:EC1(2,M-1)=VAL(MID$(A$(M),40,3)):TP1$(2,M-1)=MID$(A$(M),44,1):DP
1(2,M-1)=VAL(MID$(A$(M),46,2)):WDT(2,M-1)=EC1(2,M-1)-SC1(2,M-1)+1
:PW$=F1$(2,M-1)
890 GOSUB 2140:F1$(2,M-1)=LEFT$(F1$(2,M-1),NPK)
900 F1$(3,M-1)=MID$(A$(M),49,10):SC1(3,M-1)=VAL(MID$(A$(M),60,3))
:EC1(3,M-1)=VAL(MID$(A$(M),64,3)):TP1$(3,M-1)=MID$(A$(M),68,1):DP
1(3,M-1)=VAL(MID$(A$(M),70,2)):WDT(3,M-1)=EC1(3,M-1)-SC1(3,M-1)+1
:PW$=F1$(3,M-1)
910 GOSUB 2140:F1$(3,M-1)=LEFT$(F1$(3,M-1),NPK)
920 NEXT
930 FOR M=10 TO SNI
940 F1$(1,M-1)=MID$(A$(M),1,10):SC1(1,M-1)=VAL(MID$(A$(M),12,3)):
EC1(1,M-1)=VAL(MID$(A$(M),16,3)):TP1$(1,M-1)=MID$(A$(M),20,1):DP1
(1,M-1)=VAL(MID$(A$(M),22,2)):WDT(1,M-1)=EC1(1,M-1)-SC1(1,M-1)+1:
PW$=F1$(1,M-1)
950 GOSUB 2140:F1$(1,M-1)=LEFT$(F1$(1,M-1),NPK)
960 F1$(2,M-1)=MID$(A$(M),25,10):SC1(2,M-1)=VAL(MID$(A$(M),36,3))
:EC1(2,M-1)=VAL(MID$(A$(M),40,3)):TP1$(2,M-1)=MID$(A$(M),44,1):DP
1(2,M-1)=VAL(MID$(A$(M),46,2)):WDT(2,M-1)=EC1(2,M-1)-SC1(2,M-1)+1
:PW$=F1$(2,M-1)
970 GOSUB 2140:F1$(2,M-1)=LEFT$(F1$(2,M-1),NPK)
980 F1$(3,M-1)=MID$(A$(M),49,10):SC1(3,M-1)=VAL(MID$(A$(M),60,3))
:EC1(3,M-1)=VAL(MID$(A$(M),64,3)):TP1$(3,M-1)=MID$(A$(M),68,1):DP
1(3,M-1)=VAL(MID$(A$(M),70,2)):WDT(3,M-1)=EC1(3,M-1)-SC1(3,M-1)+1
:PW$=F1$(3,M-1)
990 GOSUB 2140:F1$(3,M-1)=LEFT$(F1$(3,M-1),NPK)
1000 NEXT
1001 IF DL$<>"Y" THEN 1020
1002 W(1)=WDT(1,1):W(2)=WDT(2,1):W(3)=WDT(3,1)
1003 W(4)=WDT(1,2):W(5)=WDT(2,2):W(6)=WDT(3,2)
1004 W(7)=WDT(1,3):W(8)=WDT(2,3):W(9)=WDT(3,3)
1005 W(10)=WDT(1,4):W(11)=WDT(2,4):W(12)=WDT(3,4)
1006 W(13)=WDT(1,5):W(14)=WDT(2,5):W(15)=WDT(3,5)
1007 W(16)=WDT(1,6):W(17)=WDT(2,6):W(18)=WDT(3,6)
1008 W(19)=WDT(1,7):W(20)=WDT(2,7):W(21)=WDT(3,7)
1009 W(22)=WDT(1,8):W(23)=WDT(2,8):W(24)=WDT(3,8)
1012 TP$(1)= TP1$(1,1):TP$(2)=TP1$(2,1): TP$(3)=TP1$(3,1)
1013 TP$(4)= TP1$(1,2):TP$(5)=TP1$(2,2): TP$(6)=TP1$(3,2)
1014 TP$(7)= TP1$(1,3):TP$(8)=TP1$(2,3): TP$(9)=TP1$(3,3)
1015 TP$(10)=TP1$(1,4):TP$(11)=TP1$(2,4):TP$(12)=TP1$(3,4)
1016 TP$(13)=TP1$(1,5):TP$(14)=TP1$(2,5):TP$(15)=TP1$(3,5)
1017 TP$(16)=TP1$(1,6):TP$(17)=TP1$(2,6):TP$(18)=TP1$(3,6)
1018 TP$(19)=TP1$(1,7):TP$(20)=TP1$(2,7):TP$(21)=TP1$(3,7)
1019 TP$(22)=TP1$(1,8):TP$(23)=TP1$(2,8):TP$(24)=TP1$(3,8)
1020 COLOR FFG,FFB:LOCATE 22,2:PRINT"                Now creating (P
RN) file for import into 1-2-3                "
1030 GOSUB 1980
1040 FOR IJ=1 TO 36
1050 FOR II=1 TO 3:IF SC1(II,IJ)=0 THEN SC1(II,IJ)=1:WDT(II,IJ)=1
1060 NEXT:NEXT
1070 FOR H=3 TO LEN(SC$)
1080 IF MID$(SC$,H,2)="  " THEN 1100
1090 NEXT:GOTO 1110
```

```
1100 SC$=LEFT$(SC$,H-2)
1110 FOR H=3 TO LEN(IC$)
1120 IF MID$(IC$,H,2)="  " THEN 1140
1130 NEXT:GOTO 1150
1140 IC$=LEFT$(IC$,H-2)
1150 DL1$=CHR$(DL1)
1160 DL2$=CHR$(DL2)
1170 DL3$=CHR$(DL3)
1180 DLC$=DL1$+DL2$+DL3$
1190 OP1$=DL3$+MID$(C$,SC1(1,1),WDT(1,1))+DLC$+MID$(C$,SC1(2,1),W
DT(2,1))+DLC$+MID$(C$,SC1(3,1),WDT(3,1))+DL1$+DL2$
1200 IF FTP$<>"" THEN FO$=LEFT$(FTP$,8)+".PRN":GOTO 1211
1210 FO$=LEFT$(FL$,8)+".PRN"
1211 FOO$=CHR$(34)+"---------------------------------------------
-"+CHR$(34)
1212 FO1$=CHR$(34)+"  This data has been processed by DFPLTS.EXE"
+CHR$(34)
1213 FO2$=CHR$(34)+"using a BODNER-HUTCHINS Text Descriptor File"
+CHR$(34)
1214 FO4$=CHR$(34)+"  This conversion was done at "+TIME$+CHR$(34
)
1215 FO5$=CHR$(34)+"on "+DATE$+" from file "+FM$+CHR$(34)
1216 FO6$=CHR$(34)+" "+CHR$(34)
1220 OPEN "O",#2,FO$
1221 IF MID$(A$(1),68,1)="X" THEN 1282
1222 PRINT #2,FO6$
1230 PRINT #2,FOO$
1231 PRINT #2,FO1$
1240 PRINT #2,FO2$
1241 PRINT #2,FOO$
1250 PRINT #2,FO4$
1251 PRINT #2,FO5$
1252 PRINT #2,FOO$
1253 PRINT #2,FO6$
1260 PRINT #2,CHR$(34)+W1$+CHR$(34)
1270 PRINT #2,W$
1280 PRINT #2,CHR$(34)+W1$+CHR$(34)
1282 LOCATE 22,2:PRINT"
                             "
1290 OPEN "I",#1,FM$
1291 IF DL$="Y" THEN 3000
1300 K=0:I=1
1310 IF EOF(1) THEN 1520
1311 IF CR$="Y" THEN LINE INPUT #1,F$:GOTO 1330
1320 F$=INPUT$(1,LW)
1330 K=K+1:IF LEFT$(F$,1)=CHR$(12) THEN K=0:LOCATE 22,4:PRINT "FO
RM FEED !!      ":GOTO 1510
1340 IF LEFT$(F$,LEN(IC$))=IC$ THEN 1510
1350 IF SCC=0 THEN SCC=1
1360 IF MID$(F$,SCC,LEN(SC$))=SC$ OR LEFT$(F$,LEN(SC$))=SC$ THEN
GOSUB 1840:GOTO 1510
1370 IF LEN(F$)=0 THEN 1510
1430 FOR J=1 TO NI-1
1431 LP1$=CHR$(34)+MID$(F$,SC1(1,J),WDT(1,J))+CHR$(34)
1432 LP2$=CHR$(34)+MID$(F$,SC1(2,J),WDT(2,J))+CHR$(34)
```

```
1433 LP3$=CHR$(34)+MID$(F$,SC1(3,J),WDT(3,J))+CHR$(34)
1440 IF TP1$(1,J)="F" OR TP1$(1,J)="I" THEN LP1$=STR$(VAL(MID$(F$
,SC1(1,J),WDT(1,J)))):IF LEFT$(LP1$,1)=" " THEN LP1$=RIGHT$(LP1$,
LEN(LP1$)-1)
1450 IF TP1$(2,J)="F" OR TP1$(2,J)="I" THEN LP2$=STR$(VAL(MID$(F$
,SC1(2,J),WDT(2,J)))):IF LEFT$(LP2$,1)=" " THEN LP2$=RIGHT$(LP2$,
LEN(LP2$)-1)
1460 IF TP1$(3,J)="F" OR TP1$(3,J)="I" THEN LP3$=STR$(VAL(MID$(F$
,SC1(3,J),WDT(3,J)))):IF LEFT$(LP3$,1)=" " THEN LP3$=RIGHT$(LP3$,
LEN(LP3$)-1)
1461 IF J=1 THEN OP$=LP1$ ELSE OP$=OP$+","+LP1$
1462 IF NF=>(2+((J-1)*3)) THEN OP$=OP$+","+LP2$
1470 IF NF=>(3+((J-1)*3)) THEN OP$=OP$+","+LP3$
1480 NEXT
1490 IF K>=SL AND K<=EL THEN PRINT #2,OP$:LOCATE 22,4:CNT=CNT+1:C
OLOR FFG,FFB:PRINT "Number Converted ";CNT;" ";LEFT$(MID$(F$,SC1(
1,1),WDT(1,1)),15);" ";LEFT$(MID$(F$,SC1(2,1),WDT(2,1)),15);" ";L
EFT$(MID$(F$,SC1(3,1),WDT(3,1)),15);
1500 IF K=LP THEN K=0:LOCATE 22,4:PRINT "PAGE BREAK!!       ":GOTO
 1510
1510 I=I+1:GOTO 1310
1520 CLOSE #1:CLOSE #2
1540 COLOR 15,0:CLS:PRINT "       Bodner-Hutchins Text Descripto
r File Processor  (Rev "+MREV$+")           "
1550 PRINT"┌─────────────────────────────────────────────────────
──────────────────┐"
1560 PRINT"│Field Name   Start          End            Type
Decimals       Width │";
1570 PRINT"├─────────────────────────────────────────────────────
──────────────────┤":COLOR FFG,FFB
1580 FOR J=1 TO NI-1
1590 COLOR 15,0:PRINT "│";:COLOR FFG,FFB:PRINT F1$(1,J),SC1(1,J),
EC1(1,J),TP1$(1,J),DP1(1,J);RIGHT$("                  "+STR$(WDT(1,
J)),15);" ";:COLOR 15,0:PRINT "│"
1600 IF F1$(2,J)="            " OR LEN(F1$(2,J))=0 THEN 1640
1610 COLOR 15,0:PRINT "│";:COLOR FFG,FFB:PRINT F1$(2,J),SC1(2,J),
EC1(2,J),TP1$(2,J),DP1(2,J);RIGHT$("                  "+STR$(WDT(2,
J)),15);" ";:COLOR 15,0:PRINT "│"
1620 IF F1$(3,J)="            " OR LEN(F1$(3,J))=0 THEN 1640
1630 COLOR 15,0:PRINT "│";:COLOR FFG,FFB:PRINT F1$(3,J),SC1(3,J),
EC1(3,J),TP1$(3,J),DP1(3,J);RIGHT$("                  "+STR$(WDT(3,
J)),15);" ";:COLOR 15,0:PRINT "│"
1640 NEXT J:COLOR 15,0
1650 IF SNF=0 THEN 1740
1660 PRINT"├─────────────────────────────────────────────────────
──────────────────┤"
1670 COLOR FFG,FFB:FOR J=9 TO SNI-1
1680 COLOR 15,0:PRINT "│";:COLOR FFG,FFB:PRINT F1$(1,J),SC1(1,J),
EC1(1,J),TP1$(1,J),DP1(1,J);RIGHT$("                  "+STR$(WDT(1,
J)),15);" ";:COLOR 15,0:PRINT "│"
1690 IF F1$(2,J)="            " OR LEN(F1$(2,J))=0 THEN 1730
1700 COLOR 15,0:PRINT "│";:COLOR FFG,FFB:PRINT F1$(2,J),SC1(2,J),
EC1(2,J),TP1$(2,J),DP1(2,J);RIGHT$("                  "+STR$(WDT(2,
J)),15);" ";:COLOR 15,0:PRINT "│"
1710 IF F1$(3,J)="            " OR LEN(F1$(3,J))=0 THEN 1730
```

```
1720 COLOR 15,0:PRINT "│";:COLOR FFG,FFB:PRINT F1$(3,J),SC1(3,J),
EC1(3,J),TP1$(3,J),DP1(3,J);RIGHT$("                    "+STR$(WDT(3,
J)),15);" ";:COLOR 15,0:PRINT "│"
1730 NEXT J:COLOR 15,0
1740 PRINT"└──────────────────────────────────────────────────────────
───────────────┘"
1750 PRINT"       File structure as determined from the Text Desc
riptor File"
1751 IF NF+SNF< 18 THEN 1760
1752 COLOR 15,0:LOCATE 1,1:PRINT "       Bodner-Hutchins Text De
scriptor File Processor  (Rev "+MREV$+")            "
1753 PRINT"┌──────────────────────────────────────────────────────────
───────────────┐"
1754 PRINT"│Field Name   Start          End           Type
Decimals        Width │";
1755 PRINT"├──────────────────────────────────────────────────────────
───────────────┤":COLOR FFG,FFB
1760 LOCATE 19,1:COLOR FFG,FFC
1770 PRINT"┌──────────────────────────────────────────────────────────
───────────────┐"
1780 PRINT"│         This DFP has converted "+RIGHT$("    "+STR$(C
NT),5)+" data records and has created          │"
1790 PRINT"│         a 1-2-3 file with "+RIGHT$("    "+STR$(NF+SNF
),5)+" data fields in file "+LEFT$(FO$+"            ",12)+"
   │"
1800 PRINT"└──────────────────────────────────────────────────────────
───────────────┘":COLOR 15,0
1810 PRINT "       Copyright (c) 1986, Bodner-Hutchins Inc., Hou
ston, Texas    ";
1811 ON ERROR GOTO 1819
1812 RMDIR TP$
1813 ON ERROR GOTO 0
1814 GOTO 1820
1819 IF ERR=76 THEN END
1820 IF TP$="" THEN END
1821 SH$="COPY "+FO$+" "+TP$+">NUL"
1822 SHELL SH$
1823 SH$=FO$
1824 KILL SH$
1830 END
1840 REM *********************************************************
************
1850 REM * SPECIAL CODE PROCESSOR
        *
1860 REM *
        *
1870 REM *********************************************************
************
1880 IF OFS=0 THEN 1920
1890 FOR O=1 TO OFS:LINE INPUT #1,F$:NEXT
1920 FOR J=9 TO SNI-1
1921 LP1$=CHR$(34)+MID$(F$,SC1(1,J),WDT(1,J))+CHR$(34)
1922 LP2$=CHR$(34)+MID$(F$,SC1(2,J),WDT(2,J))+CHR$(34)
1923 LP3$=CHR$(34)+MID$(F$,SC1(3,J),WDT(3,J))+CHR$(34)
1924 IF TP1$(1,J)="F" OR TP1$(1,J)="I" THEN LP1$=STR$(VAL(MID$(F$
```

```
,SC1(1,J),WDT(1,J)))):IF LEFT$(LP1$,1)=" " THEN LP1$=RIGHT$(LP1$,
LEN(LP1$)-1)
1925 IF TP1$(2,J)="F" OR TP1$(2,J)="I" THEN LP2$=STR$(VAL(MID$(F$
,SC1(2,J),WDT(2,J)))):IF LEFT$(LP2$,1)=" " THEN LP2$=RIGHT$(LP2$,
LEN(LP2$)-1)
1926 IF TP1$(3,J)="F" OR TP1$(3,J)="I" THEN LP3$=STR$(VAL(MID$(F$
,SC1(3,J),WDT(3,J)))):IF LEFT$(LP3$,1)=" " THEN LP3$=RIGHT$(LP3$,
LEN(LP3$)-1)
1927 IF J=9 THEN OP$=OP1$+LP1$ ELSE OP$=OP$+","+LP1$
1928 IF SNF=>(2+((J-9)*3)) THEN OP$=OP$+","+LP2$
1929 IF SNF=>(3+((J-9)*3)) THEN OP$=OP$+","+LP3$
1940 NEXT
1950 COLOR FFG,FFB:LOCATE 22,2:PRINT"
                                                                  "
1960 IF K>=SL AND K<=EL THEN PRINT #2,OP$:LOCATE 22,4:CNT=CNT+1:P
RINT "Special Line     ";CNT;" ";LEFT$(MID$(F$,SC1(1,9),WDT(1,9))
,10);" ";LEFT$(MID$(F$,SC1(2,9),WDT(2,9)),10);" ";LEFT$(MID$(F$,S
C1(3,9),WDT(3,9)),10)
1970 RETURN
1980 REM *****************************************************
************
1990 REM * CREATE LOTUS 1-2-3 PRN FILE WITH NF AND SNF FIELDNAMES
         *
2000 REM *
         *
2010 REM *****************************************************
************
2020 FO$=LEFT$(FL$,8)+".PRN":W$=""
2030 FOR W=1 TO NI-1:W$=W$+CHR$(34)+F1$(1,W)+CHR$(34):IF LEN(F1$(
2,W))>0 THEN W$=W$+","+CHR$(34)+F1$(2,W)+CHR$(34)
2040 IF LEN(F1$(3,W))>0 THEN W$=W$+","+CHR$(34)+F1$(3,W)+CHR$(34)
+","
2050 NEXT
2060 IF SNF=0 THEN 2100
2070 FOR W=9 TO SNI-1:W$=W$+CHR$(34)+F1$(1,W)+CHR$(34):IF LEN(F1$
(2,W))>0 THEN W$=W$+","+CHR$(34)+F1$(2,W)+CHR$(34)
2080 IF LEN(F1$(3,W))>0 THEN W$=W$+","+CHR$(34)+F1$(3,W)+CHR$(34)
+","
2090 NEXT
2100 IF RIGHT$(W$,1)="," THEN W$=LEFT$(W$,LEN(W$)-1)
2110 W1$="":FOR W=1 TO 253:W1$=W1$+"=":NEXT
2120 W1$=LEFT$(W1$,LEN(W$))
2130 RETURN
2140 REM *****************************************************
************
2150 REM * FIELD PACKER
         *
2160 REM *
         *
2170 REM *****************************************************
************
2180 FOR Q=1 TO LEN(PW$):IF MID$(PW$,Q,1)=" " THEN NPK=Q-1:RETURN
2190 NEXT:NPK=Q
2200 RETURN
3000 REM *****************************************************
```

```
************
3010 REM * DELIMITED FILE PROCESSOR
         *
3020 REM *
         *
3030 REM ********************************************************
************
3035 CNT=0
3040 IF EOF(1) THEN 1520
3050 CNT=CNT+1:CNT2=0
4030 FOR I=1 TO NF
4040 INPUT #1,ADL$(I):ADL$(I)=LEFT$(ADL$(I)+C$,W(I))
4045 LOCATE 22,4:CNT2=CNT2+1:COLOR FFG,FFB:PRINT "Number Converte
d ";CNT;" Field # ";CNT2;" ";LEFT$(ADL$(I)+C$,30)
4046 IF I>1 THEN PRINT #2,DL2$;
4047 IF TP$(I)="F" OR TP$(I)="I" THEN ADL$(I)=STR$(VAL(ADL$(I))):
ADL$(I)=RIGHT$(ADL$(I),LEN(ADL$(I))-1):PRINT #2,ADL$(I);:GOTO 406
0
4050 PRINT #2,DL1$+ADL$(I)+DL3$;
4060 NEXT:PRINT #2,""
4070 GOTO 3040
```

```
10 REM ***********************************************************
**********
20 REM *
       *
30 REM * DESCRIPTOR FILE PROCESSOR PROGRAM FOR MULTIMATE
       *
40 REM *
       *
50 REM * COPYRIGHT 1986 BODNER, HUTCHINS & ASSOCIATES, INC. REV 0
4/14/86   *
60 REM *
       *
70 REM ***********************************************************
**********
80 DIM A$(13),B$(13),F0$(13),F1$(3,36),SC1(3,36),EC1(3,36),TP1$(3
,36),DP1(3,36),WDT(3,36),ADL$(39),W(36)
90 C$="
                    "
100 OPEN "I",#1,"CONFIG.TD"
101 INPUT #1,FFG
102 INPUT #1,FFB
103 INPUT #1,FFC
104 CLOSE #1
105 MREV$="1.80"
110 BX1$="┌────────────────────────────────────┐"
120 BX2$="│                                    │"
130 BX3$="└────────────────────────────────────┘"
131 CMD$=COMMAND$
132 IF CMD$ ="" THEN 140
133 FOR I=1 TO LEN(CMD$):IF MID$(CMD$,I,1)=" " THEN 135
134 NEXT:FL$=CMD$:TP$="":GOTO 479
135 FL$=LEFT$(CMD$,I-1)
136 TP$=MID$(CMD$,I+1,LEN(CMD$)-I):IF TP$=" " OR TP$="" THEN 479
137 IF LEFT$(TP$,1)<>"\" AND MID$(TP$,2,1)<>":" THEN TP$="\"+TP$
138 GOTO 479
140 COLOR 15,0:CLS:PRINT "                 Bodner-Hutchins Text D
escriptor File System                  "
150 PRINT"────────────────────────────────────────────────────────────
─────────────────────":COLOR FFG,FFB
160 LOCATE  7,20:PRINT BX1$
170 LOCATE  8,20:PRINT "│        MultiMate Merge File          │"
180 LOCATE  9,20:PRINT "├──────────────────────────────────────┤"
190 LOCATE 10,20:PRINT "│      Descriptor File Processor       │"
200 LOCATE 11,20:PRINT "│            Version "+MREV$+"
 │"
210 LOCATE 12,20:PRINT "│                                      │"
220 LOCATE 13,20:PRINT "│   "+DATE$+"              "+TIME$+"   │"
230 LOCATE 14,20:PRINT BX3$:COLOR 15,0
240 LOCATE 23,1:PRINT"────────────────────────────────────────────────
─────────────────────────────"
250 LOCATE 24,2:PRINT "          Copyright (c) 1986, Bodner-Hutch
ins Inc., Houston, Texas        ";
260 LOCATE 22,2:PRINT "                  MultiMate is a trademark o
f Ashton-Tate, Inc." ;
261 COLOR FFC,0:LOCATE 20,23:PRINT "Enter Q to quit and return to
```

```
 DOS"
270 COLOR 12,0:FLAG=0
280 LOCATE 17,20:PRINT BX1$
290 LOCATE 18,20:PRINT BX2$
300 LOCATE 19,20:PRINT BX3$;
310 LOCATE 18,24:PRINT "Enter file name : [        ]"
320 FL$=""
321 FOR I= 1 TO 8
322 LOCATE 18,42+I:COLOR 28,0:PRINT "_";:COLOR 12,0:F0$(I)=INKEY$
323 LOCATE 13,20:COLOR FFG,FFB:PRINT "│   "+DATE$+"                  "
+TIME$+"   │":COLOR 12,0
324 IF F0$(I)="" THEN 322
325 IF ASC(F0$(I))=8 THEN LOCATE 18,42+I:PRINT " ";:I=I-1:FL$=LEF
T$(FL$,LEN(FL$)-1):GOTO 322
326 IF ASC(F0$(I))<33 AND ASC(F0$(I))<> 13 THEN 322
327 IF ASC(F0$(I))=13 THEN 330
328 LOCATE 18,42+I:PRINT F0$(I);:FL$=FL$+F0$(I)
329 NEXT
330 IF FL$="Q" OR FL$="q" THEN CLOSE:COLOR 15,0:CLS:END
331 IF LEN(FL$)>0 THEN 470
340 IF FLAG=1 THEN 320
360 OPEN "I",#1,"TDFDIR.TXT":COLOR 0,15:FLAG=1
370 LOCATE 3,60:PRINT"┌───────────┐"
380 LOCATE 4,60:PRINT"│ TDF Files │"
390 LOCATE 5,60:PRINT"├───────────┤"
400 IF EOF(1) THEN 450
410 INPUT #1,D$:D=D+1:IF D<5 OR VAL(LEFT$(D$,1))>0 THEN 400
420 LOCATE D+1,60:PRINT "│ "+LEFT$(D$,8)+"  │"
430 IF D<20 THEN 400
431 D=4:LOCATE 21,60:PRINT"└───────────┘":COLOR FFG,FFB:LOCATE 23
,55:PRINT"Press any key for more":COLOR 0,15:WD$=INKEY$:IF WD$=""
 THEN 431
432 COLOR 15,0:LOCATE 23,55:PRINT"──────────────────────":COLOR 0
,15
440 GOTO 400
450 CLOSE #1:LOCATE D+1,60:PRINT"└───────────┘":COLOR 12,0
460 GOTO 320
470 LOCATE 18,24:PRINT "Target Path [              ]"
471 LOCATE 18,37:INPUT "",TP$
472 IF LEN(TP$)=0 THEN 479
473 IF LEFT$(TP$,1)<>"\" AND MID$(TP$,2,1)<>":" THEN TP$="\"+TP$
479 ON ERROR GOTO 510
480 OPEN "I",#1,LEFT$(FL$,8)+".TDF"
490 ON ERROR GOTO 0
500 GOTO 520
510 LOCATE 21,60:PRINT CHR$(7)+"File not found!!":RESUME 310
520 FOR I=1 TO 13:INPUT #1,A$(I):A$(I)=RIGHT$(C$+A$(I),74):NEXT:C
LOSE #1
540 COLOR 15,0:CLS:PRINT "        Bodner-Hutchins Text Descriptor
 File Processor  (Rev "+MREV$+")          "
550 PRINT"┌──────────────────────────────────────────────────────
─────────────────┐":COLOR FFG,FFC
560 FOR I=1 TO 13:COLOR 15,0:PRINT "│";:COLOR FFG,FFC:PRINT A$(I)
;:COLOR 15,0:PRINT "│":NEXT:COLOR 15,0
570 PRINT"└──────────────────────────────────────────────────────
```

```
─────────────────────────────┘"
580 COLOR 15,0
590 PRINT"      Data is being processed from Text Descriptor File
 [";:COLOR FFG,FFB:PRINT FL$;:PRINT ".TXT";:COLOR 15,0:PRINT "]"
600 PRINT"┌──────────────────────────────────────────────────────────
─────────────────────────────┐"
610 PRINT"│    This TDF is being used by this DFP to convert the
associated ASCII          │"
620 PRINT"│   text file into a format directly useable by MultiMa
te Merge Utility.         │"
630 PRINT"├──────────────────────────────────────────────────────────
─────────────────────────────┤"
640 PRINT"│
                          │"
650 PRINT"└──────────────────────────────────────────────────────────
─────────────────────────────┘"
660 COLOR FFG,FFB:LOCATE 22,2:PRINT"        Now processing informa
tion from Text Descriptor File...         "
670 FM$=RIGHT$("        "+LEFT$(A$(1),8),8)+".TXT"
680 LW=VAL(MID$(A$(1),10,3)):SL=VAL(MID$(A$(1),24,3)):EL=VAL(MID$
(A$(1),28,3)):LP=VAL(MID$(A$(1),20,3))
690 NF=VAL(MID$(A$(1),56,3)):SNF=VAL(MID$(A$(1),73,3)):SCC=VAL(MI
D$(A$(1),69,3))
700 LF$=MID$(A$(1),16,1):CR$=MID$(A$(1),14,1):DL$=MID$(A$(1),32,1
):OFS=VAL(MID$(A$(1),67,1))
710 DL1=34:DL2=44:DL3=34
720 IF NF<=3 THEN NI=2
730 IF NF>=4 AND NF<=6 THEN NI=3
740 IF NF>=7 AND NF<=9 THEN NI=4
750 IF NF>=10 AND NF<=12 THEN NI=5
760 IF NF>=13 AND NF<=15 THEN NI=6
770 IF NF>=16 AND NF<=18 THEN NI=7
780 IF NF>=19 AND NF<=21 THEN NI=8
790 IF NF>=22 AND NF<=24 THEN NI=9
800 IF SNF<=3 THEN SNI=10
810 IF SNF>=4 AND SNF<=6 THEN SNI=11
820 IF SNF>=7 AND SNF<=9 THEN SNI=12
830 IF SNF>=10 AND SNF<=12 THEN NI=13
840 FF$=MID$(A$(1),18,1):IC$=MID$(A$(1),46,8):SC$=MID$(A$(1),59,7
)
850 FOR M=2 TO NI
860 F1$(1,M-1)=MID$(A$(M),1,10):SC1(1,M-1)=VAL(MID$(A$(M),12,3)):
EC1(1,M-1)=VAL(MID$(A$(M),16,3)):TP1$(1,M-1)=MID$(A$(M),20,1):DP1
(1,M-1)=VAL(MID$(A$(M),22,2)):WDT(1,M-1)=EC1(1,M-1)-SC1(1,M-1)+1:
PW$=F1$(1,M-1)
870 GOSUB 2040:F1$(1,M-1)=LEFT$(F1$(1,M-1),NPK)
880 F1$(2,M-1)=MID$(A$(M),25,10):SC1(2,M-1)=VAL(MID$(A$(M),36,3))
:EC1(2,M-1)=VAL(MID$(A$(M),40,3)):TP1$(2,M-1)=MID$(A$(M),44,1):DP
1(2,M-1)=VAL(MID$(A$(M),46,2)):WDT(2,M-1)=EC1(2,M-1)-SC1(2,M-1)+1
:PW$=F1$(2,M-1)
890 GOSUB 2040:F1$(2,M-1)=LEFT$(F1$(2,M-1),NPK)
900 F1$(3,M-1)=MID$(A$(M),49,10):SC1(3,M-1)=VAL(MID$(A$(M),60,3))
:EC1(3,M-1)=VAL(MID$(A$(M),64,3)):TP1$(3,M-1)=MID$(A$(M),68,1):DP
1(3,M-1)=VAL(MID$(A$(M),70,2)):WDT(3,M-1)=EC1(3,M-1)-SC1(3,M-1)+1
:PW$=F1$(3,M-1)
```

```
910 GOSUB 2040:F1$(3,M-1)=LEFT$(F1$(3,M-1),NPK)
920 NEXT
930 FOR M=10 TO SNI
940 F1$(1,M-1)=MID$(A$(M),1,10):SC1(1,M-1)=VAL(MID$(A$(M),12,3)):
EC1(1,M-1)=VAL(MID$(A$(M),16,3)):TP1$(1,M-1)=MID$(A$(M),20,1):DP1
(1,M-1)=VAL(MID$(A$(M),22,2)):WDT(1,M-1)=EC1(1,M-1)-SC1(1,M-1)+1:
PW$=F1$(1,M-1)
950 GOSUB 2040:F1$(1,M-1)=LEFT$(F1$(1,M-1),NPK)
960 F1$(2,M-1)=MID$(A$(M),25,10):SC1(2,M-1)=VAL(MID$(A$(M),36,3))
:EC1(2,M-1)=VAL(MID$(A$(M),40,3)):TP1$(2,M-1)=MID$(A$(M),44,1):DP
1(2,M-1)=VAL(MID$(A$(M),46,2)):WDT(2,M-1)=EC1(2,M-1)-SC1(2,M-1)+1
:PW$=F1$(2,M-1)
970 GOSUB 2040:F1$(2,M-1)=LEFT$(F1$(2,M-1),NPK)
980 F1$(3,M-1)=MID$(A$(M),49,10):SC1(3,M-1)=VAL(MID$(A$(M),60,3))
:EC1(3,M-1)=VAL(MID$(A$(M),64,3)):TP1$(3,M-1)=MID$(A$(M),68,1):DP
1(3,M-1)=VAL(MID$(A$(M),70,2)):WDT(3,M-1)=EC1(3,M-1)-SC1(3,M-1)+1
:PW$=F1$(3,M-1)
990 GOSUB 2040:F1$(3,M-1)=LEFT$(F1$(3,M-1),NPK)
1000 NEXT
1001 IF DL$<>"Y" THEN 1010
1002 W(1)=WDT(1,1):W(2)=WDT(2,1):W(3)=WDT(3,1)
1003 W(4)=WDT(1,2):W(5)=WDT(2,2):W(6)=WDT(3,2)
1004 W(7)=WDT(1,3):W(8)=WDT(2,3):W(9)=WDT(3,3)
1005 W(10)=WDT(1,4):W(11)=WDT(2,4):W(12)=WDT(3,4)
1006 W(13)=WDT(1,5):W(14)=WDT(2,5):W(15)=WDT(3,5)
1007 W(16)=WDT(1,6):W(17)=WDT(2,6):W(18)=WDT(3,6)
1008 W(19)=WDT(1,7):W(20)=WDT(2,7):W(21)=WDT(3,7)
1009 W(22)=WDT(1,8):W(23)=WDT(2,8):W(24)=WDT(3,8)
1010 COLOR FFG,FFB:LOCATE 22,2:PRINT"                Now creating Do
cument file........                          "
1020 GOSUB 1850
1030 FOR IJ=1 TO 36
1040 FOR II=1 TO 3:IF SC1(II,IJ)=0 THEN SC1(II,IJ)=1:WDT(II,IJ)=1
1050 NEXT:NEXT
1060 FOR H=3 TO LEN(SC$)
1070 IF MID$(SC$,H,2)="  " THEN 1090
1080 NEXT:GOTO 1100
1090 SC$=LEFT$(SC$,H-2)
1100 FOR H=3 TO LEN(IC$)
1110 IF MID$(IC$,H,2)="  " THEN 1130
1120 NEXT:GOTO 1140
1130 IC$=LEFT$(IC$,H-2)
1140 IF DL1 >0 THEN DL1$=CHR$(DL1) ELSE DL1$=""
1150 IF DL2 >0 THEN DL2$=CHR$(DL2) ELSE DL2$=""
1160 IF DL3 >0 THEN DL3$=CHR$(DL3) ELSE DL3$=""
1170 DLC$=DL1$+DL2$+DL3$
1180 OP1$=DL3$+MID$(C$,SC1(1,1),WDT(1,1))+DLC$+MID$(C$,SC1(2,1),W
DT(2,1))+DLC$+MID$(C$,SC1(3,1),WDT(3,1))+DL1$
1200 FO$=LEFT$(FL$,8)+".DAT"
1210 OPEN "O",#2,FO$
1220 OPEN "I",#1,FM$
1225 IF DL$="Y" THEN 3000
1230 K=0:I=1
1240 IF EOF(1) THEN 1390
1241 IF CR$="Y" THEN LINE INPUT #1,F$:GOTO 1260
```

```
1250 F$=INPUT$(1,LW)
1260 K=K+1:IF LEFT$(F$,1)=CHR$(12) THEN K=0:LOCATE 22,4:PRINT "FO
RM FEED !!      ":GOTO 1380
1270 IF LEFT$(F$,LEN(IC$))=IC$ THEN 1380
1280 IF SCC=0 THEN SCC=1
1290 IF MID$(F$,SCC,LEN(SC$))=SC$ OR LEFT$(F$,LEN(SC$))=SC$ THEN
GOSUB 1710:GOTO 1380
1300 IF LEN(F$)=0 THEN 1380
1301 J=1:LP1$=CHR$(34)+MID$(F$,SC1(1,J),WDT(1,J))+CHR$(34)
1302 LP2$=CHR$(34)+MID$(F$,SC1(2,J),WDT(2,J))+CHR$(34)
1303 LP3$=CHR$(34)+MID$(F$,SC1(3,J),WDT(3,J))+CHR$(34)
1304 OP$=LP1$:IF NF=>2 THEN OP$=OP$+","+LP2$
1305 IF NF=>3 THEN OP$=OP$+","+LP3$
1306 IF NF<=3 THEN 1360
1307 FOR J=2 TO NI-1
1308 LP1$=CHR$(34)+MID$(F$,SC1(1,J),WDT(1,J))+CHR$(34)
1309 LP2$=CHR$(34)+MID$(F$,SC1(2,J),WDT(2,J))+CHR$(34)
1310 LP3$=CHR$(34)+MID$(F$,SC1(3,J),WDT(3,J))+CHR$(34)
1311 OP$=OP$+","+LP1$:IF NF>(2+((J-1)*3)) THEN OP$=OP$+","+LP2$
1312 IF NF>(3+((J-1)*3)) THEN OP$=OP$+","+LP3$
1313 NEXT
1360 IF K>=SL AND K<=EL THEN PRINT #2,OP$:LOCATE 22,4:CNT=CNT+1:C
OLOR FFG,FFB:PRINT "Number Converted ";CNT;" ";LEFT$(MID$(F$,SC1(
1,1),WDT(1,1)),15);" ";LEFT$(MID$(F$,SC1(2,1),WDT(2,1)),15);" ";L
EFT$(MID$(F$,SC1(3,1),WDT(3,1)),15);
1370 IF K=LP THEN K=0:LOCATE 22,4:PRINT "PAGE BREAK!!       ":GOTO
 1380
1380 I=I+1:GOTO 1240
1390 CLOSE #1:CLOSE #2
1410 COLOR 15,0:CLS:PRINT "        Bodner-Hutchins Text Descripto
r File Processor  (Rev "+MREV$+")         "
1420 PRINT"┌──────────────────────────────────────────────────────
─────────────────────┐"
1430 PRINT"│Field Name   Start          End           Type
Decimals        Width │";
1440 PRINT"├──────────────────────────────────────────────────────
─────────────────────┤":COLOR FFG,FFB
1450 FOR J=1 TO NI-1
1460 COLOR 15,0:PRINT "│";:COLOR FFG,FFB:PRINT F1$(1,J),SC1(1,J),
EC1(1,J),TP1$(1,J),DP1(1,J);RIGHT$("                "+STR$(WDT(1,
J)),15);" ";:COLOR 15,0:PRINT "│"
1470 IF F1$(2,J)="              " OR LEN(F1$(2,J))=0 THEN 1510
1480 COLOR 15,0:PRINT "│";:COLOR FFG,FFB:PRINT F1$(2,J),SC1(2,J),
EC1(2,J),TP1$(2,J),DP1(2,J);RIGHT$("                "+STR$(WDT(2,
J)),15);" ";:COLOR 15,0:PRINT "│"
1490 IF F1$(3,J)="              " OR LEN(F1$(3,J))=0 THEN 1510
1500 COLOR 15,0:PRINT "│";:COLOR FFG,FFB:PRINT F1$(3,J),SC1(3,J),
EC1(3,J),TP1$(3,J),DP1(3,J);RIGHT$("                "+STR$(WDT(3,
J)),15);" ";:COLOR 15,0:PRINT "│"
1510 NEXT J:COLOR 15,0
1520 IF SNF=0 THEN 1610
1530 PRINT"├──────────────────────────────────────────────────────
─────────────────────┤"
1540 COLOR FFG,FFB:FOR J=9 TO SNI-1
1550 COLOR 15,0:PRINT "│";:COLOR FFG,FFB:PRINT F1$(1,J),SC1(1,J),
```

```
EC1(1,J),TP1$(1,J),DP1(1,J);RIGHT$("                    "+STR$(WDT(1,
J)),15);" ";:COLOR 15,0:PRINT "|"
1560 IF F1$(2,J)="              " OR LEN(F1$(2,J))=0 THEN 1600
1570 COLOR 15,0:PRINT "|";:COLOR FFG,FFB:PRINT F1$(2,J),SC1(2,J),
EC1(2,J),TP1$(2,J),DP1(2,J);RIGHT$("                    "+STR$(WDT(2,
J)),15);" ";:COLOR 15,0:PRINT "|"
1580 IF F1$(3,J)="              " OR LEN(F1$(3,J))=0 THEN 1600
1590 COLOR 15,0:PRINT "|";:COLOR FFG,FFB:PRINT F1$(3,J),SC1(3,J),
EC1(3,J),TP1$(3,J),DP1(3,J);RIGHT$("                    "+STR$(WDT(3,
J)),15);" ";:COLOR 15,0:PRINT "|"
1600 NEXT J:COLOR 15,0
1610 PRINT"└──────────────────────────────────────────────────
──────────────────────────┘"
1620 PRINT"       File structure as determined from the Text Desc
riptor File"
1630 LOCATE 19,1:COLOR FFG,FFC
1640 PRINT"┌──────────────────────────────────────────────────
──────────────────────────┐"
1650 PRINT"|         This DFP has converted "+RIGHT$("    "+STR$(C
NT),5)+" data records to file "+RIGHT$("        "+FL$,8)+".DAT
 |"
1660 PRINT"|  and has created a MultiMate file with "+RIGHT$("
 "+STR$(NF+SNF),5)+" data fields in "+RIGHT$("        "+FL$,8)+".
DOC |"
1670 PRINT"└──────────────────────────────────────────────────
──────────────────────────┘":COLOR 15,0
1671 PRINT "         Copyright (c) 1986, Bodner-Hutchins Inc., Hou
ston, Texas    ";
1672 ON ERROR GOTO 1676
1673 RMDIR TP$
1674 ON ERROR GOTO 0
1675 GOTO 1680
1676 IF ERR=76 THEN END
1680 CLOSE:IF TP$="" THEN END
1681 SH$="COPY "+FL$+".DOC "+TP$+">NUL"
1682 SHELL SH$
1683 SH$="COPY "+FL$+".DAT "+TP$+">NUL"
1684 SHELL SH$
1685 SH$="ERASE "+FL$+".DAT"
1686 SHELL SH$
1687 SH$="ERASE "+FL$+".DOC"
1688 SHELL SH$
1700 END
1710 REM ****************************************************
************
1720 REM * SPECIAL CODE PROCESSOR
       *
1730 REM *
       *
1740 REM ****************************************************
************
1750 IF OFS=0 THEN 1761
1760 FOR O=1 TO OFS:LINE INPUT #1,F$:NEXT
1761 J=9:IF TP1$(1,J)="F" OR TP1$(1,J)="I" THEN LP1$=MID$(F$,SC1(
1,J),WDT(1,J)) ELSE LP1$=CHR$(34)+MID$(F$,SC1(1,J),WDT(1,J))+CHR$
```

```
(34)
1762 IF TP1$(2,J)="F" OR TP1$(2,J)="I" THEN LP2$=MID$(F$,SC1(2,J)
,WDT(2,J)) ELSE LP2$=CHR$(34)+MID$(F$,SC1(2,J),WDT(2,J))+CHR$(34)
1763 IF TP1$(3,J)="F" OR TP1$(3,J)="I" THEN LP3$=MID$(F$,SC1(3,J)
,WDT(3,J)) ELSE LP3$=CHR$(34)+MID$(F$,SC1(3,J),WDT(3,J))+CHR$(34)
1764 OP$=OP1$+LP1$:IF SNF=>2 THEN OP$=OP$+LP2$
1765 IF SNF=>3 THEN OP$=OP$+LP3$
1766 IF SNF<=3 THEN 1830
1767 FOR J=10 TO SNI-1
1768 IF TP1$(1,J)="F" OR TP1$(1,J)="I" THEN LP1$=MID$(F$,SC1(1,J)
,WDT(1,J)) ELSE LP1$=CHR$(34)+MID$(F$,SC1(1,J),WDT(1,J))+CHR$(34)
1769 IF TP1$(2,J)="F" OR TP1$(2,J)="I" THEN LP2$=MID$(F$,SC1(2,J)
,WDT(2,J)) ELSE LP2$=CHR$(34)+MID$(F$,SC1(2,J),WDT(2,J))+CHR$(34)
1770 IF TP1$(3,J)="F" OR TP1$(3,J)="I" THEN LP3$=MID$(F$,SC1(3,J)
,WDT(3,J)) ELSE LP3$=CHR$(34)+MID$(F$,SC1(3,J),WDT(3,J))+CHR$(34)
1774 OP$=OP$+LP1$:IF SNF>(2+((J-9)*3)) THEN OP$=OP$+LP2$
1775 IF SNF>(3+((J-9)*3)) THEN OP$=OP$+LP3$
1810 NEXT
1820 COLOR FFG,FFB:LOCATE 22,2:PRINT"
                                                     "
1830 IF K>=SL AND K<=EL THEN PRINT #2,OP$:LOCATE 22,4:CNT=CNT+1:P
RINT "Special Line     ";CNT;" ";LEFT$(MID$(F$,SC1(1,9),WDT(1,9))
,10);" ";LEFT$(MID$(F$,SC1(2,9),WDT(2,9)),10);" ";LEFT$(MID$(F$,S
C1(3,9),WDT(3,9)),10)
1840 RETURN
1850 REM *****************************************************
************
1860 REM * CREATE MAILMERGE DOCUMENT FILE WITH NF AND SNF FIELDNA
MES         *
1870 REM *
            *
1880 REM *****************************************************
************
1890 MM$=LEFT$(FL$,8)+".DOC":FO$=LEFT$(FL$,8)+".DAT":S$=CHR$(195)
1900 OPEN "O",#1,MM$
1905 GOSUB 5000: REM DOC FILE
1910 PRINT #1,S$+"DEFINE"+S$;CHR$(174);
1911 PRINT #1,"FILE TYPE SEQUENTIAL";CHR$(174);
1920 FOR W= 1 TO NI-1:PRINT #1,"FIELD NAME "+F1$(1,W);CHR$(174);:
IF LEN(F1$(2,W))>0 THEN PRINT #1,"FIELD NAME "+F1$(2,W);CHR$(174)
;
1930 IF LEN(F1$(3,W))>0 THEN PRINT #1,"FIELD NAME "+F1$(3,W);CHR$
(174);
1940 NEXT
1950 IF SNF=0 THEN 1990
1960 FOR W= 9 TO SNI-1:PRINT #1,"FIELD NAME "+F1$(1,W);CHR$(174);
:IF LEN(F1$(2,W))>0 THEN PRINT #1,"FIELD NAME "+F1$(2,W);CHR$(174
);
1970 IF LEN(F1$(3,W))>0 THEN PRINT #1,"FIELD NAME "+F1$(3,W);CHR$
(174);
1980 NEXT
1990 PRINT #1,S$+"END DEFINE"+S$;CHR$(174);
2000 PRINT #1,CHR$(174);
2010 PRINT #1,CHR$(174);
2020 PRINT #1,CHR$(174);
```

```
2021 PRINT #1,S$+F1$(1,1)+S$;CHR$(174);
2025 FOR W=1 TO 1900:PRINT #1," ";:NEXT
2030 CLOSE #1:RETURN
2040 REM ***********************************************************
************
2050 REM * FIELD PACKER
         *
2060 REM *
         *
2070 REM ***********************************************************
************
2080 FOR Q=1 TO LEN(PW$):IF MID$(PW$,Q,1)=" " THEN NPK=Q-1:RETURN
2090 NEXT:NPK=Q
2100 RETURN
3000 REM ***********************************************************
************
3010 REM * DELIMITED FILE PROCESSOR
         *
3020 REM *
         *
3030 REM ***********************************************************
************
3035 CNT=0
3040 IF EOF(1) THEN 1390
3050 CNT=CNT+1:CNT2=0
4030 FOR I=1 TO NF
4040 INPUT #1,ADL$(I):ADL$(I)=LEFT$(ADL$(I)+C$,W(I))
4045 LOCATE 22,4:CNT2=CNT2+1:COLOR FFG,FFB:PRINT "Number Converte
d ";CNT;" Field # ";CNT2;" ";LEFT$(ADL$(I)+C$,30)
4046 IF I>1 THEN PRINT #2,DL2$;
4050 PRINT #2,DL1$+ADL$(I)+DL3$;
4060 NEXT:PRINT #2,""
4070 GOTO 3040
5000 REM ***********************************************************
************
5001 REM * DOCUMENT FILE HEADER
         *
5002 REM *
         *
5010 REM ***********************************************************
************
5020 DF$=LEFT$(FL$+"                    ",20):I=0
5021 DA$=LEFT$(DATE$,2)+"/"+MID$(DATE$,4,2)+"/"+MID$(DATE$,9,2):D
A$=DA$+DA$
5030 OPEN "I",3,"BASE.DOC"
5050 J=1
5080 IF EOF(3) THEN 5190
5090 I=I+1
5100 A$=INPUT$(1,#3)
5101 IF I>=405 AND I<421 THEN A$=MID$(DA$,I-404,1)
5110 IF I<=20 THEN A$=MID$(DF$,I,1)
5120 J=J+1
5130 PRINT #1,CHR$(ASC(A$));
5160 IF I<1103 THEN 5080
5190 CLOSE #3:RETURN
```

```
294A:0100  65 6E 76 65 6C 6F 70 65-20 20 20 20 20 20 20 20   envelope
294A:0110  20 20 20 20 00 00 00 00-00 00 00 00 00 00 00 00       ............
294A:0120  00 00 00 00 00 00 00 00-00 00 00 00 00 00 00 00   ................
294A:0130  00 00 00 00 00 00 00 00-00 00 00 00 00 00 00 00   ................
294A:0140  00 00 00 00 00 00 00 00-00 00 00 00 00 00 00 00   ................
294A:0150  00 00 00 00 00 00 00 00-00 00 00 00 00 00 00 00   ................
294A:0160  00 00 00 00 00 00 00 00-00 00 00 00 00 00 00 00   ................
294A:0170  00 00 00 00 00 00 00 00-00 00 00 00 00 00 00 00   ................
294A:0180  00 00 00 00 00 00 00 00-00 00 00 00 00 00 00 00   ................
294A:0190  00 00 00 00 00 00 00 00-00 00 00 00 00 00 00 00   ................
294A:01A0  00 00 00 00 00 00 00 00-00 00 00 00 00 00 00 00   ................
294A:01B0  00 00 00 00 00 00 00 00-00 00 00 00 00 00 00 00   ................
294A:01C0  00 00 00 00 00 00 00 00-00 00 00 00 00 00 00 00   ................
294A:01D0  00 00 00 00 00 00 00 00-00 00 00 00 00 00 00 00   ................
294A:01E0  00 00 00 00 00 00 00 00-00 00 00 00 00 00 00 00   ................
294A:01F0  00 00 00 00 00 00 00 00-00 00 00 00 00 00 00 00   ................
294A:0120  00 00 00 00 00 00 00 00-00 00 00 00 00 00 00 00   ................
294A:0130  00 00 00 00 00 00 00 00-00 00 00 00 00 00 00 00   ................
294A:0140  00 00 00 00 00 00 00 00-00 00 00 00 00 00 00 00   ................
294A:0150  00 00 00 00 00 00 00 00-00 00 00 00 00 00 00 00   ................
294A:0160  00 00 00 00 00 00 00 00-00 00 00 00 00 00 00 00   ................
294A:0170  00 00 00 00 00 00 00 00-00 00 00 00 00 00 00 00   ................
294A:0180  00 00 00 00 00 00 00 00-00 00 00 00 00 00 00 00   ................
294A:0190  00 00 00 00 00 00 00 00-00 00 00 00 00 00 00 00   ................
294A:01A0  00 00 00 00 00 00 00 00-00 00 00 00 00 00 00 00   ................
294A:01B0  00 00 00 00 00 00 00 00-00 00 00 00 00 00 00 00   ................
294A:01C0  00 00 00 00 00 00 00 00-00 00 00 00 00 00 00 00   ................
294A:01D0  00 00 00 00 00 00 00 00-00 00 00 00 00 00 00 00   ................
294A:01E0  00 00 00 00 00 00 00 00-00 00 00 00 00 00 00 00   ................
294A:01F0  00 00 00 00 00 00 00 00-00 00 00 00 00 00 00 00   ................
294A:0200  00 00 00 00 00 00 00 00-00 00 00 00 00 00 00 00   ................
294A:0210  00 00 00 00 00 00 00 00-00 00 00 00 00 00 00 00   ................
294A:0220  00 00 00 00 00 00 00 00-00 00 00 00 00 00 00 00   ................
294A:0230  00 00 00 00 00 00 00 00-00 00 00 00 00 00 00 00   ................
294A:0240  00 00 00 00 00 00 00 00-00 00 00 00 00 00 00 00   ................
294A:0250  00 00 00 00 00 00 00 00-00 00 00 00 00 00 00 00   ................
294A:0260  00 00 00 00 00 00 00 00-00 00 00 00 00 00 00 00   ................
294A:0270  00 00 00 00 00 00 00 00-00 00 00 00 00 00 00 00   ................
294A:0280  00 00 00 00 00 00 00 00-00 00 00 00 00 00 00 00   ................
294A:0290  00 00 00 00 30 38 2F 30-38 2F 38 35 30 33 2F 32   ....08/08/8503/2
294A:02A0  31 2F 38 36 00 00 1E 00-01 00 01 00 01 00 01 00   1/86............
294A:02B0  01 00 42 00 01 00 00 00-04 00 54 54 59 43 52 4C   ..B.......TTYCRL
294A:02C0  46 20 06 08 00 50 00 00-00 20 20 20 20 20 20 20   F ...P...
294A:02D0  20 00 00 00 00 00 00 00-15 00 00 00 4A 02 00 00    ...........J...
294A:02E0  2E 00 00 37 20 20 20 20-20 20 20 20 44 00 00 00   ...7        D...
294A:02F0  00 00 00 00 00 00 00 00-00 00 00 01 01 00 01 00   ................
```

Fig. B-1. DOS DEBUG Memory drop of BASE.DOC file used by DFPMMT.BAS.

```
10 REM ****************************************************************
**********
20 REM *
    *
30 REM * DESCRIPTOR FILE PROCESSOR PROGRAM SDF
    *
40 REM *
    *
50 REM * COPYRIGHT 1986 BODNER, HUTCHINS & ASSOCIATES, INC. REV 0
4/14/86  *
60 REM *
    *
70 REM ****************************************************************
**********
80 DIM A$(13),B$(13),F0$(13),F1$(3,36),SC1(3,36),EC1(3,36),TP1$(3
,36),DP1(3,36),WDT(3,36),ADL$(36),W(36),S1(3,36)
90 C$="
          "
100 OPEN "I",#1,"CONFIG.TD"
110 INPUT #1,FFG
120 INPUT #1,FFB
130 INPUT #1,FFC
140 CLOSE #1
150 MREV$="1.80"
160 BX1$="┌────────────────────────────────────┐"
170 BX2$="│                                    │"
180 BX3$="└────────────────────────────────────┘"
190 CMD$=COMMAND$
200 IF CMD$ ="" THEN 270
210 FOR I=1 TO LEN(CMD$):IF MID$(CMD$,I,1)=" " THEN 230
220 NEXT:FL$=CMD$:TP$="":GOTO 750
230 FL$=LEFT$(CMD$,I-1)
240 TP$=MID$(CMD$,I+1,LEN(CMD$)-I):IF TP$=" " OR TP$="" THEN 750
250 IF LEFT$(TP$,1)<>"\" AND MID$(TP$,2,1)<>":" THEN TP$="\"+TP$
260 GOTO 750
270 COLOR 15,0:CLS:PRINT "                   Bodner-Hutchins Text D
escriptor File System                          "
280 PRINT"────────────────────────────────────────────────────────────
───────────────────":COLOR FFG,FFB
290 LOCATE  7,20:PRINT BX1$
300 LOCATE  8,20:PRINT "│     Standard Data Format (SDF)      │"
310 LOCATE  9,20:PRINT "├────────────────────────────────────┤"
320 LOCATE 10,20:PRINT "│     Descriptor File Processor       │"
330 LOCATE 11,20:PRINT "│          Version "+MREV$+"
│"
340 LOCATE 12,20:PRINT "│                                    │"
350 LOCATE 13,20:PRINT "│  "+DATE$+"               "+TIME$+"  │"
360 LOCATE 14,20:PRINT BX3$:COLOR 15,0
370 LOCATE 22,1:PRINT"────────────────────────────────────────────
───────────────────────────────────"
380 LOCATE 23,2:PRINT "         Copyright (c) 1986, Bodner-Hutchin
s Inc., Houston, Texas       ";
390 COLOR FFC,0:LOCATE 20,23:PRINT "Enter Q to quit and return to
 DOS"
400 COLOR 12,0:FLAG=0
```

```
410 LOCATE 17,20:PRINT BX1$
420 LOCATE 18,20:PRINT BX2$
430 LOCATE 19,20:PRINT BX3$;
440 LOCATE 18,24:PRINT "Enter file name : [        ]"
450 FL$=""
460 FOR I= 1 TO 8
470 LOCATE 18,42+I:COLOR 28,0:PRINT "_";:COLOR 12,0:FO$(I)=INKEY$
480 LOCATE 13,20:COLOR FFG,FFB:PRINT "│  "+DATE$+"                        "
+TIME$+"  │":COLOR 12,0
490 IF FO$(I)="" THEN 470
500 IF ASC(FO$(I))=8 THEN LOCATE 18,42+I:PRINT " ";:I=I-1:FL$=LEF
T$(FL$,LEN(FL$)-1):GOTO 470
510 IF ASC(FO$(I))<33 AND ASC(FO$(I))<> 13 THEN 470
520 IF ASC(FO$(I))=13 THEN 550
530 LOCATE 18,42+I:PRINT FO$(I);:FL$=FL$+FO$(I)
540 NEXT
550 IF FL$="Q" OR FL$="q" THEN CLOSE:COLOR 15,0:CLS:END
560 IF LEN(FL$)>0 THEN 710
570 IF FLAG=1 THEN 450
580 OPEN "I",#1,"TDFDIR.TXT":COLOR 0,15:FLAG=1
590 LOCATE 3,60:PRINT"┌───────────┐"
600 LOCATE 4,60:PRINT"│ TDF Files │"
610 LOCATE 5,60:PRINT"├───────────┤"
620 IF EOF(1) THEN 690
630 INPUT #1,D$:D=D+1:IF D<5 OR VAL(LEFT$(D$,1))>0 THEN 620
640 LOCATE D+1,60:PRINT "│ "+LEFT$(D$,8)+"  │"
650 IF D<20 THEN 620
660 D=4:LOCATE 21,60:PRINT"└───────────┘":COLOR FFG,FFB:LOCATE 23
,55:PRINT"Press any key for more":COLOR 0,15:WD$=INKEY$:IF WD$=""
 THEN 660
670 COLOR 15,0:LOCATE 23,55:PRINT"──────────────────────":COLOR 0
,15
680 GOTO 620
690 CLOSE #1:LOCATE D+1,60:PRINT"└───────────┘":COLOR 12,0
700 GOTO 450
710 LOCATE 18,24:PRINT "Target Path [               ]"
720 LOCATE 18,37:INPUT "",TP$
730 IF LEN(TP$)=0 THEN 750
740 IF LEFT$(TP$,1)<>"\" AND MID$(TP$,2,1)<>":" THEN TP$="\"+TP$
750 ON ERROR GOTO 790
760 OPEN "I",#1,LEFT$(FL$,8)+".TDF"
770 ON ERROR GOTO 0
780 GOTO 800
790 LOCATE 18,60:PRINT CHR$(7)+"File not found!!":RESUME 440
800 FOR I=1 TO 13:INPUT #1,A$(I):A$(I)=RIGHT$(C$+A$(I),74):NEXT:C
LOSE #1
810 COLOR 15,0:CLS:PRINT "           Bodner-Hutchins Text Descriptor
 File Generator  (Rev "+MREV$+")           "
820 PRINT"┌──────────────────────────────────────────────────────────
──────────────────┐":COLOR FFG,FFC
830 FOR I=1 TO 13:COLOR 15,0:PRINT "│";:COLOR FFG,FFC:PRINT A$(I)
;:COLOR 15,0:PRINT "│":NEXT:COLOR 15,0
840 PRINT"└──────────────────────────────────────────────────────────
──────────────────┘"
850 COLOR 15,0
```

```
860 PRINT"      Data is being processed from Text Descriptor File
 [";:COLOR FFG,FFC:PRINT FL$;:COLOR 15,0:PRINT "]"
870 PRINT"┌──────────────────────────────────────────────────────────
──────────────────┐"
880 PRINT"│    This TDF is being used by this DFP to convert the
associated ASCII │"
890 PRINT"│  text file into a Standard Data Format (SDF) used by
many applications. │"
900 PRINT"├──────────────────────────────────────────────────────────
──────────────────┤"
910 PRINT"│
                 │"
920 PRINT"└──────────────────────────────────────────────────────────
──────────────────┘"
930 COLOR FFG,FFB:LOCATE 22,2:PRINT"
                                                                  "
940 FM$=RIGHT$("        "+LEFT$(A$(1),8),8)+".TXT"
950 LW=VAL(MID$(A$(1),10,3)):SL=VAL(MID$(A$(1),24,3)):EL=VAL(MID$
(A$(1),28,3)):LP=VAL(MID$(A$(1),20,3))
960 NF=VAL(MID$(A$(1),56,3)):SNF=VAL(MID$(A$(1),73,3)):SCC=VAL(MI
D$(A$(1),69,3))
970 LF$=MID$(A$(1),16,1):CR$=MID$(A$(1),14,1):DL$=MID$(A$(1),32,1
):OFS=VAL(MID$(A$(1),67,1))
980 DL1=VAL(MID$(A$(1),34,3)):DL2=VAL(MID$(A$(1),38,3)):DL3=VAL(M
ID$(A$(1),42,3))
990 IF NF<=3 THEN NI=2
1000 IF NF>=4 AND NF<=6 THEN NI=3
1010 IF NF>=7 AND NF<=9 THEN NI=4
1020 IF NF>=10 AND NF<=12 THEN NI=5
1030 IF NF>=13 AND NF<=15 THEN NI=6
1040 IF NF>=16 AND NF<=18 THEN NI=7
1050 IF NF>=19 AND NF<=21 THEN NI=8
1060 IF NF>=22 AND NF<=24 THEN NI=9
1070 IF SNF<=3 THEN SNI=10
1080 IF SNF>=4 AND SNF<=6 THEN SNI=11
1090 IF SNF>=7 AND SNF<=9 THEN SNI=12
1100 IF SNF>-10 AND SNF<=12 THEN NI=13
1110 FF$=MID$(A$(1),18,1):IC$=MID$(A$(1),46,8):SC$=MID$(A$(1),59,
7)
1120 FOR M=2 TO NI
1130 F1$(1,M-1)=MID$(A$(M),1,10):SC1(1,M-1)=VAL(MID$(A$(M),12,3))
:EC1(1,M-1)=VAL(MID$(A$(M),16,3)):TP1$(1,M-1)=MID$(A$(M),20,1):DP
1(1,M-1)=VAL(MID$(A$(M),22,2)):WDT(1,M-1)=EC1(1,M-1)-SC1(1,M-1)+1
1140 F1$(2,M-1)=MID$(A$(M),25,10):SC1(2,M-1)=VAL(MID$(A$(M),36,3)
):EC1(2,M-1)=VAL(MID$(A$(M),40,3)):TP1$(2,M-1)=MID$(A$(M),44,1):D
P1(2,M-1)=VAL(MID$(A$(M),46,2)):WDT(2,M-1)=EC1(2,M-1)-SC1(2,M-1)+
1
1150 F1$(3,M-1)=MID$(A$(M),49,10):SC1(3,M-1)=VAL(MID$(A$(M),60,3)
):EC1(3,M-1)=VAL(MID$(A$(M),64,3)):TP1$(3,M-1)=MID$(A$(M),68,1):D
P1(3,M-1)=VAL(MID$(A$(M),70,2)):WDT(3,M-1)=EC1(3,M-1)-SC1(3,M-1)+
1
1160 NEXT
1170 FOR M=10 TO SNI
1180 F1$(1,M-1)=MID$(A$(M),1,10):SC1(1,M-1)=VAL(MID$(A$(M),12,3))
:EC1(1,M-1)=VAL(MID$(A$(M),16,3)):TP1$(1,M-1)=MID$(A$(M),20,1):DP
```

```
1(1,M-1)=VAL(MID$(A$(M),22,2)):WDT(1,M-1)=EC1(1,M-1)-SC1(1,M-1)+1
1190 F1$(2,M-1)=MID$(A$(M),25,10):SC1(2,M-1)=VAL(MID$(A$(M),36,3)
):EC1(2,M-1)=VAL(MID$(A$(M),40,3)):TP1$(2,M-1)=MID$(A$(M),44,1):D
P1(2,M-1)=VAL(MID$(A$(M),46,2)):WDT(2,M-1)=EC1(2,M-1)-SC1(2,M-1)+
1
1200 F1$(3,M-1)=MID$(A$(M),49,10):SC1(3,M-1)=VAL(MID$(A$(M),60,3)
):EC1(3,M-1)=VAL(MID$(A$(M),64,3)):TP1$(3,M-1)=MID$(A$(M),68,1):D
P1(3,M-1)=VAL(MID$(A$(M),70,2)):WDT(3,M-1)=EC1(3,M-1)-SC1(3,M-1)+
1
1210 NEXT
1220 IF DL$<>"Y" THEN 1310
1230 W(1)=WDT(1,1):W(2)=WDT(2,1):W(3)=WDT(3,1)
1240 W(4)=WDT(1,2):W(5)=WDT(2,2):W(6)=WDT(3,2)
1250 W(7)=WDT(1,3):W(8)=WDT(2,3):W(9)=WDT(3,3)
1260 W(10)=WDT(1,4):W(11)=WDT(2,4):W(12)=WDT(3,4)
1270 W(13)=WDT(1,5):W(14)=WDT(2,5):W(15)=WDT(3,5)
1280 W(16)=WDT(1,6):W(17)=WDT(2,6):W(18)=WDT(3,6)
1290 W(19)=WDT(1,7):W(20)=WDT(2,7):W(21)=WDT(3,7)
1300 W(22)=WDT(1,8):W(23)=WDT(2,8):W(24)=WDT(3,8)
1310 FOR IJ=1 TO 36
1320 FOR II=1 TO 3:IF SC1(II,IJ)=0 THEN SC1(II,IJ)=1:WDT(II,IJ)=1
1330 NEXT:NEXT
1340 FOR H=3 TO LEN(SC$)
1350 IF MID$(SC$,H,2)="  " THEN 1370
1360 NEXT:GOTO 1380
1370 SC$=LEFT$(SC$,H-2)
1380 FOR H=3 TO LEN(IC$)
1390 IF MID$(IC$,H,2)="  " THEN 1410
1400 NEXT:GOTO 1420
1410 IC$=LEFT$(IC$,H-2)
1420 DL1$=""
1430 DL2$=""
1440 DL3$=""
1450 DLC$=""
1460 OP1$=MID$(C$,SC1(1,1),WDT(1,1))+MID$(C$,SC1(2,1),WDT(2,1))+M
ID$(C$,SC1(3,1),WDT(3,1))
1470 FO$=LEFT$("NEW_"+FL$,8)+".TXT"
1480 OPEN "O",#2,FO$
1490 OPEN "I",#1,FM$
1500 IF DL$="Y" THEN 2380
1510 K=0:I=1
1520 IF EOF(1) THEN 1760
1530 IF CR$="Y" THEN LINE INPUT #1,F$:GOTO 1550
1540 F$=INPUT$(1,LW)
1550 K=K+1:IF LEFT$(F$,1)=CHR$(12) THEN K=0:LOCATE 22,4:PRINT "FO
RM FEED !!      ":GOTO 1750
1560 IF LEFT$(F$,LEN(IC$))=IC$ THEN 1750
1570 IF SCC=0 THEN SCC=1
1580 IF MID$(F$,SCC,LEN(SC$))=SC$ OR LEFT$(F$,LEN(SC$))=SC$ THEN
GOSUB 2160:GOTO 1750
1590 IF LEN(F$)=0 THEN 1750
1600 J=1:LP1$=MID$(F$,SC1(1,J),WDT(1,J))
1610 LP2$=MID$(F$,SC1(2,J),WDT(2,J))
1620 LP3$=MID$(F$,SC1(3,J),WDT(3,J))
1630 OP$=LP1$:IF NF=>2 THEN OP$=OP$+LP2$
```

```
1640 IF NF=>3 THEN OP$=OP$+LP3$
1650 IF NF<=3 THEN 1730
1660 FOR J=2 TO NI-1
1670 LP1$=MID$(F$,SC1(1,J),WDT(1,J))
1680 LP2$=MID$(F$,SC1(2,J),WDT(2,J))
1690 LP3$=MID$(F$,SC1(3,J),WDT(3,J))
1700 OP$=OP$+LP1$:IF NF>(2+((J-1)*3)) THEN OP$=OP$+LP2$
1710 IF NF>(3+((J-1)*3)) THEN OP$=OP$+LP3$
1720 NEXT
1730 IF K>=SL AND K<=EL THEN PRINT #2,OP$:LOCATE 22,4:CNT=CNT+1:C
OLOR FFG,FFB:PRINT "Number Converted ";CNT;" ";LEFT$(MID$(F$,SC1(
1,1),WDT(1,1)),15);" ";LEFT$(MID$(F$,SC1(2,1),WDT(2,1)),15);" ";L
EFT$(MID$(F$,SC1(3,1),WDT(3,1)),15);
1740 IF K=LP THEN K=0:LOCATE 22,4:PRINT "PAGE BREAK!!      ":GOTO
 1750
1750 I=I+1:GOTO 1520
1760 CLOSE #1:CLOSE #2
1770 COLOR 15,0:CLS:PRINT "       Bodner-Hutchins Text Descripto
r File Generator  (Rev "+MREV$+")                "
1780 PRINT"┌──────────────────────────────────────────────────────
──────────────┐"
1790 PRINT"│Field Name   Start          End            Type
Decimals       Width │";
1800 PRINT"├──────────────────────────────────────────────────────
──────────────┤":COLOR FFG,FFB
1810 FOR J=1 TO NI-1
1820 COLOR 15,0:PRINT "│";:COLOR FFG,FFB:PRINT F1$(1,J),SC1(1,J),
EC1(1,J),TP1$(1,J),DP1(1,J);RIGHT$("                   "+STR$(WDT(1,
J)),15);" ";:COLOR 15,0:PRINT "│"
1830 IF F1$(2,J)="            " OR LEN(F1$(2,J))=0 THEN 1870
1840 COLOR 15,0:PRINT "│";:COLOR FFG,FFB:PRINT F1$(2,J),SC1(2,J),
EC1(2,J),TP1$(2,J),DP1(2,J);RIGHT$("                   "+STR$(WDT(2,
J)),15);" ";:COLOR 15,0:PRINT "│"
1850 IF F1$(3,J)="            " OR LEN(F1$(3,J))=0 THEN 1870
1860 COLOR 15,0:PRINT "│";:COLOR FFG,FFB:PRINT F1$(3,J),SC1(3,J),
EC1(3,J),TP1$(3,J),DP1(3,J);RIGHT$("                   "+STR$(WDT(3,
J)),15);" ";:COLOR 15,0:PRINT "│"
1870 NEXT J:COLOR 15,0
1880 IF SNF=0 THEN 1970
1890 PRINT"├──────────────────────────────────────────────────────
──────────────┤"
1900 COLOR FFG,FFB:FOR J=9 TO SNI-1
1910 COLOR 15,0:PRINT "│";:COLOR FFG,FFB:PRINT F1$(1,J),SC1(1,J),
EC1(1,J),TP1$(1,J),DP1(1,J);RIGHT$("                   "+STR$(WDT(1,
J)),15);" ";:COLOR 15,0:PRINT "│"
1920 IF F1$(2,J)="            " OR LEN(F1$(2,J))=0 THEN 1960
1930 COLOR 15,0:PRINT "│";:COLOR FFG,FFB:PRINT F1$(2,J),SC1(2,J),
EC1(2,J),TP1$(2,J),DP1(2,J);RIGHT$("                   "+STR$(WDT(2,
J)),15);" ";:COLOR 15,0:PRINT "│"
1940 IF F1$(3,J)="            " OR LEN(F1$(3,J))=0 THEN 1960
1950 COLOR 15,0:PRINT "│";:COLOR FFG,FFB:PRINT F1$(3,J),SC1(3,J),
EC1(3,J),TP1$(3,J),DP1(3,J);RIGHT$("                   "+STR$(WDT(3,
J)),15);" ";:COLOR 15,0:PRINT "│"
1960 NEXT J:COLOR 15,0
1970 PRINT"└──────────────────────────────────────────────────────
```

```
──────────────────────────┘"
1980 PRINT"       File structure as determined from the Text Desc
riptor File"
1990 LOCATE 19,1:COLOR FFG,FFC
2000 PRINT"┌──────────────────────────────────────────────────────
──────────────────────────┐"
2010 PRINT"│          This DFP has converted "+RIGHT$("     "+STR$(C
NT),5)+" data records to file "+FO$+"     │"
2020 PRINT"└──────────────────────────────────────────────────────
──────────────────────────┘":COLOR 15,0
2030 PRINT "          Copyright (c) 1986, Bodner-Hutchins Inc., Hou
ston, Texas     ";
2040 ON ERROR GOTO 2080
2050 RMDIR TP$
2060 ON ERROR GOTO 0
2070 GOTO 2090
2080 IF ERR=76 THEN CLOSE:GOTO 2510
2090 CLOSE:IF TP$="" THEN 2510
2100 SH$="COPY "+FO$+TP$+">NUL"
2110 SHELL SH$
2120 SH$="ERASE "+FO$
2130 SHELL SH$
2140 GOTO 2510
2150 END
2160 REM *******************************************************
************
2170 REM * SPECIAL CODE PROCESSOR
           *
2180 REM *
           *
2190 REM *******************************************************
************
2200 IF OFS=0 THEN 2220
2210 FOR O=1 TO OFS:LINE INPUT #1,F$:NEXT
2220 J=9:LP1$=MID$(F$,SC1(1,J),WDT(1,J))
2230 LP2$=MID$(F$,SC1(2,J),WDT(2,J))
2240 LP3$=MID$(F$,SC1(3,J),WDT(3,J))
2250 OP$=OP1$+LP1$:IF SNF=>2 THEN OP$=OP$+LP2$
2260 IF SNF=>3 THEN OP$=OP$+LP3$
2270 IF SNF<=3 THEN 2360
2280 FOR J=10 TO SNI-1
2290 LP1$=MID$(F$,SC1(1,J),WDT(1,J))
2300 LP2$=MID$(F$,SC1(2,J),WDT(2,J))
2310 LP3$=MID$(F$,SC1(3,J),WDT(3,J))
2320 OP$=OP$+LP1$:IF SNF>(2+((J-9)*3)) THEN OP$=OP$+LP2$
2330 IF SNF>(3+((J-9)*3)) THEN OP$=OP$+LP3$
2340 NEXT
2350 COLOR FFG,FFB:LOCATE 22,2:PRINT"
                                                          "
2360 IF K>=SL AND K<=EL THEN PRINT #2,OP$:LOCATE 22,4:CNT=CNT+1:P
RINT "Special Line     ";CNT;" ";LEFT$(MID$(F$,SC1(1,9),WDT(1,9))
,10);" ";LEFT$(MID$(F$,SC1(2,9),WDT(2,9)),10);" ";LEFT$(MID$(F$,S
C1(3,9),WDT(3,9)),10)
2370 RETURN
2380 REM *******************************************************
```

```
************
2390 REM * DELIMITED FILE PROCESSOR
          *
2400 REM *
          *
2410 REM *********************************************************
************
2420 CNT=0
2430 IF EOF(1) THEN 1760
2440 CNT=CNT+1:CNT2=0
2450 FOR I=1 TO NF
2460 INPUT #1,ADL$(I):ADL$(I)=LEFT$(ADL$(I)+C$,W(I))
2470 LOCATE 22,4:CNT2=CNT2+1:COLOR FFG,FFB:PRINT "Number Converte
d ";CNT;" Field # ";CNT2;" ";LEFT$(ADL$(I)+C$,30)
2480 PRINT #2,ADL$(I);
2490 NEXT:PRINT #2,""
2500 GOTO 2430
2510 REM *********************************************************
************
2520 REM * AUTOTDF MAKER
          *
2530 REM *
          *
2540 REM *********************************************************
************
2550 WD=0:S1=1:FOR J=1 TO NI-1
2560 S1(1,J)=S1+WD:WD=WD+WDT(1,J)
2570 IF F1$(2,J)="               " OR LEN(F1$(2,J))=0 THEN 2610
2580 S1(2,J)=S1+WD:WD=WD+WDT(2,J)
2590 IF F1$(3,J)="               " OR LEN(F1$(3,J))=0 THEN 2610
2600 S1(3,J)=S1+WD:WD=WD+WDT(3,J)
2610 NEXT J
2620 FT$=LEFT$(FO$+"               ",8)+" "+RIGHT$(STR$(1000+WD),3)+"
Y Y Y 066 001 066 N 000 000 000 .             "
2630 LX1$=RIGHT$(STR$(100+NF),2)+" .          0 000 00"
2640 A$(1)=FT$+LX1$
2650 FOR J=1 TO NI-1
2660 A$(J+1)=F1$(1,J)+" "+RIGHT$(STR$(1000+S1(1,J)),3)+" "+RIGHT$
(STR$(1000+S1(1,J)-1+WDT(1,J)),3)+" "+TP1$(1,J)+" "+RIGHT$(STR$(1
00+DP1(1,J)),2)+" "
2670 IF F1$(2,J)="               " OR LEN(F1$(2,J))=0 THEN 2710
2680 A$(J+1)=A$(J+1)+F1$(2,J)+" "+RIGHT$(STR$(1000+S1(2,J)),3)+"
"+RIGHT$(STR$(1000+S1(2,J)-1+WDT(2,J)),3)+" "+TP1$(2,J)+" "+RIGHT
$(STR$(100+DP1(2,J)),2)+" "
2690 IF F1$(3,J)="               " THEN 2710
2691 IF LEN(F1$(3,J))=0 THEN 2710
2700 A$(J+1)=A$(J+1)+F1$(3,J)+" "+RIGHT$(STR$(1000+S1(3,J)),3)+"
"+RIGHT$(STR$(1000+S1(3,J)-1+WDT(3,J)),3)+" "+TP1$(3,J)+" "+RIGHT
$(STR$(100+DP1(3,J)),2)+" "
2710 NEXT J
2720 B$(11)="*A"
2730 B$(12)="*B"
2740 B$(13)="FF"
2750 FOR J=2 TO 10:B$(J)="*"+RIGHT$(STR$(J-1),1):NEXT
2760 CLOSE #1:OPEN "O",#1,LEFT$("NEW_"+FL$,8)+".TDF"
```

```
2770 PRINT #1,A$(1):FOR J=2 TO 13:PRINT #1,LEFT$(A$(J)+C$,72)+B$(
J):NEXT:CLOSE #1
2780 LOCATE 19,1:COLOR FFG,FFC
2790 PRINT"┌──────────────────────────────────────────────────────────
──────────────────────┐"
2800 PRINT"│  A TDF has been created so that you can use "+FO$+"
with other DFPs │"
2810 PRINT"└──────────────────────────────────────────────────────────
──────────────────────┘":COLOR 15,0
2820 PRINT "        Copyright (c) 1986, Bodner-Hutchins Inc., Hou
ston, Texas    ";
2830 END
```

```
10 REM ***********************************************************
**********
20 REM *
       *
30 REM * DESCRIPTOR FILE PROCESSOR PROGRAM FOR WORDSTAR/MAILMERGE
       *
40 REM *
       *
50 REM * COPYRIGHT 1986 BODNER, HUTCHINS & ASSOCIATES, INC. REV 0
4/14/86  *
60 REM *
       *
70 REM ***********************************************************
**********
80 DIM A$(13),B$(13),F0$(13),F1$(3,36),SC1(3,36),EC1(3,36),TP1$(3
,36),DP1(3,36),WDT(3,36),ADL$(39),W(36)
90 C$="
                   "
100 OPEN "I",#1,"CONFIG.TD"
101 INPUT #1,FFG
102 INPUT #1,FFB
103 INPUT #1,FFC
104 CLOSE #1
105 MREV$="1.80"
110 BX1$="┌──────────────────────────────────────┐"
120 BX2$="│                                      │"
130 BX3$="└──────────────────────────────────────┘"
131 CMD$=COMMAND$
132 IF CMD$ ="" THEN 140
133 FOR I=1 TO LEN(CMD$):IF MID$(CMD$,I,1)=" " THEN 135
134 NEXT:FL$=CMD$:TP$="":GOTO 479
135 FL$=LEFT$(CMD$,I-1)
136 TP$=MID$(CMD$,I+1,LEN(CMD$)-I):IF TP$=" " OR TP$="" THEN 479
137 IF LEFT$(TP$,1)<>"\" AND MID$(TP$,2,1)<>":" THEN TP$="\"+TP$
138 GOTO 479
140 COLOR 15,0:CLS:PRINT "                    Bodner-Hutchins Text D
escriptor File System                   "
150 PRINT"────────────────────────────────────────────────────────────
──────────────────────":COLOR FFG,FFB
160 LOCATE  7,20:PRINT BX1$
170 LOCATE  8,20:PRINT "│          WordStar/MailMerge          │"
180 LOCATE  9,20:PRINT "├──────────────────────────────────────┤"
190 LOCATE 10,20:PRINT "│      Descriptor File Processor       │"
200 LOCATE 11,20:PRINT "│           Version "+MREV$+"
  │"
210 LOCATE 12,20:PRINT "│                                      │"
220 LOCATE 13,20:PRINT "│  "+DATE$+"              "+TIME$+"   │"
230 LOCATE 14,20:PRINT BX3$:COLOR 15,0
240 LOCATE 23,1:PRINT"─────────────────────────────────────────────
─────────────────────────────"
250 LOCATE 24,2:PRINT "        Copyright (c) 1986, Bodner-Hutchin
s Inc., Houston, Texas      ";
260 LOCATE 22,2:PRINT "  WordStar & MailMerge are trademarks of
MicroPro International, Inc." ;
261 COLOR FFC,0:LOCATE 20,23:PRINT "Enter Q to quit and return to
```

```
 DOS"
270 COLOR 12,0:FLAG=0
280 LOCATE 17,20:PRINT BX1$
290 LOCATE 18,20:PRINT BX2$
300 LOCATE 19,20:PRINT BX3$;
310 LOCATE 18,24:PRINT "Enter file name : [        ]"
320 FL$=""
321 FOR I= 1 TO 8
322 LOCATE 18,42+I:COLOR 28,0:PRINT "_";:COLOR 12,0:F0$(I)=INKEY$
323 LOCATE 13,20:COLOR FFG,FFB:PRINT "│  "+DATE$+"                 "
+TIME$+"  │":COLOR 12,0
324 IF F0$(I)="" THEN 322
325 IF ASC(F0$(I))=8 THEN LOCATE 18,42+I:PRINT " ";:I=I-1:FL$=LEF
T$(FL$,LEN(FL$)-1):GOTO 322
326 IF ASC(F0$(I))<33 AND ASC(F0$(I))<> 13 THEN 322
327 IF ASC(F0$(I))=13 THEN 330
328 LOCATE 18,42+I:PRINT F0$(I);:FL$=FL$+F0$(I)
329 NEXT
330 IF FL$="Q" OR FL$="q" THEN CLOSE:COLOR 15,0:CLS:END
331 IF LEN(FL$)>0 THEN 470
340 IF FLAG=1 THEN 320
360 OPEN "I",#1,"TDFDIR.TXT":COLOR 0,15:FLAG=1
370 LOCATE 3,60:PRINT"┌───────────┐"
380 LOCATE 4,60:PRINT"│ TDF Files │"
390 LOCATE 5,60:PRINT"├───────────┤"
400 IF EOF(1) THEN 450
410 INPUT #1,D$:D=D+1:IF D<5 OR VAL(LEFT$(D$,1))>0 THEN 400
420 LOCATE D+1,60:PRINT "│ "+LEFT$(D$,8)+"  │"
430 IF D<20 THEN 400
431 D=4:LOCATE 21,60:PRINT"└───────────┘":COLOR FFG,FFB:LOCATE 23
,55:PRINT"Press any key for more":COLOR 0,15:WD$=INKEY$:IF WD$=""
 THEN 431
432 COLOR 15,0:LOCATE 23,55:PRINT"──────────────────────":COLOR 0
,15
440 GOTO 400
450 CLOSE #1:LOCATE D+1,60:PRINT"└───────────┘":COLOR 12,0
460 GOTO 320
470 LOCATE 18,24:PRINT "Target Path [                 ]"
471 LOCATE 18,37:INPUT "",TP$
472 IF LEN(TP$)=0 THEN 479
473 IF LEFT$(TP$,1)<>"\" AND MID$(TP$,2,1)<>":" THEN TP$="\"+TP$
479 ON ERROR GOTO 510
480 OPEN "I",#1,LEFT$(FL$,8)+".TDF"
490 ON ERROR GOTO 0
500 GOTO 520
510 LOCATE 21,60:PRINT CHR$(7)+"File not found!!":RESUME 310
520 FOR I=1 TO 13:INPUT #1,A$(I):A$(I)=RIGHT$(C$+A$(I),74):NEXT:C
LOSE #1
540 COLOR 15,0:CLS:PRINT "        Bodner-Hutchins Text Descriptor
 File Processor  (Rev "+MREV$+")          "
550 PRINT"┌───────────────────────────────────────────────────────
──────────────────┐":COLOR FFG,FFB
560 FOR I=1 TO 13:COLOR 15,0:PRINT "│";:COLOR FFG,FFC:PRINT A$(I)
;:COLOR 15,0:PRINT "│":NEXT:COLOR 15,0
570 PRINT"└───────────────────────────────────────────────────────
```

```
─────────────────────────┘"
580 COLOR 15,0
590 PRINT"      Data is being processed from Text Descriptor File
 [";:COLOR FFG,FFB:PRINT FL$;:PRINT ".TXT";:COLOR 15,0:PRINT "]"
600 PRINT"┌─────────────────────────────────────────────────────
─────────────────────────┐"
610 PRINT"│    This TDF is being used by this DFP to convert the
associated ASCII     │"
620 PRINT"│   text file into a format directly useable by WordSta
r and MailMerge.     │"
630 PRINT"├─────────────────────────────────────────────────────
─────────────────────────┤"
640 PRINT"│
                     │"
650 PRINT"└─────────────────────────────────────────────────────
─────────────────────────┘"
660 COLOR FFG,FFB:LOCATE 22,2:PRINT"       Now processing informa
tion from Text Descriptor File...          "
670 FM$=RIGHT$("        "+LEFT$(A$(1),8),8)+".TXT"
680 LW=VAL(MID$(A$(1),10,3)):SL=VAL(MID$(A$(1),24,3)):EL=VAL(MID$
(A$(1),28,3)):LP=VAL(MID$(A$(1),20,3))
690 NF=VAL(MID$(A$(1),56,3)):SNF=VAL(MID$(A$(1),73,3)):SCC=VAL(MI
D$(A$(1),69,3))
700 LF$=MID$(A$(1),16,1):CR$=MID$(A$(1),14,1):DL$=MID$(A$(1),32,1
):OFS=VAL(MID$(A$(1),67,1))
710 DL1=34:DL2=44:DL3=34
720 IF NF<=3 THEN NI=2
730 IF NF>=4 AND NF<=6 THEN NI=3
740 IF NF>=7 AND NF<=9 THEN NI=4
750 IF NF>=10 AND NF<=12 THEN NI=5
760 IF NF>=13 AND NF<=15 THEN NI=6
770 IF NF>=16 AND NF<=18 THEN NI=7
780 IF NF>=19 AND NF<=21 THEN NI=8
790 IF NF>=22 AND NF<=24 THEN NI=9
800 IF SNF<=3 THEN SNI=10
810 IF SNF>=4 AND SNF<=6 THEN SNI=11
820 IF SNF>=7 AND SNF<=9 THEN SNI=12
830 IF SNF>=10 AND SNF<=12 THEN NI=13
840 FF$=MID$(A$(1),18,1):IC$=MID$(A$(1),46,8):SC$=MID$(A$(1),59,7
)
850 FOR M=2 TO NI
860 F1$(1,M-1)=MID$(A$(M),1,10):SC1(1,M-1)=VAL(MID$(A$(M),12,3)):
EC1(1,M-1)=VAL(MID$(A$(M),16,3)):TP1$(1,M-1)=MID$(A$(M),20,1):DP1
(1,M-1)=VAL(MID$(A$(M),22,2)):WDT(1,M-1)=EC1(1,M-1)-SC1(1,M-1)+1:
PW$=F1$(1,M-1)
870 GOSUB 2060:F1$(1,M-1)=LEFT$(F1$(1,M-1),NPK)
880 F1$(2,M-1)=MID$(A$(M),25,10):SC1(2,M-1)=VAL(MID$(A$(M),36,3))
:EC1(2,M-1)=VAL(MID$(A$(M),40,3)):TP1$(2,M-1)=MID$(A$(M),44,1):DP
1(2,M-1)=VAL(MID$(A$(M),46,2)):WDT(2,M-1)=EC1(2,M-1)-SC1(2,M-1)+1
:PW$=F1$(2,M-1)
890 GOSUB 2060:F1$(2,M-1)=LEFT$(F1$(2,M-1),NPK)
900 F1$(3,M-1)=MID$(A$(M),49,10):SC1(3,M-1)=VAL(MID$(A$(M),60,3))
:EC1(3,M-1)=VAL(MID$(A$(M),64,3)):TP1$(3,M-1)=MID$(A$(M),68,1):DP
1(3,M-1)=VAL(MID$(A$(M),70,2)):WDT(3,M-1)=EC1(3,M-1)-SC1(3,M-1)+1
:PW$=F1$(3,M-1)
```

```
910 GOSUB 2060:F1$(3,M-1)=LEFT$(F1$(3,M-1),NPK)
920 NEXT
930 FOR M=10 TO SNI
940 F1$(1,M-1)=MID$(A$(M),1,10):SC1(1,M-1)=VAL(MID$(A$(M),12,3)):
EC1(1,M-1)=VAL(MID$(A$(M),16,3)):TP1$(1,M-1)=MID$(A$(M),20,1):DP1
(1,M-1)=VAL(MID$(A$(M),22,2)):WDT(1,M-1)=EC1(1,M-1)-SC1(1,M-1)+1:
PW$=F1$(1,M-1)
950 GOSUB 2060:F1$(1,M-1)=LEFT$(F1$(1,M-1),NPK)
960 F1$(2,M-1)=MID$(A$(M),25,10):SC1(2,M-1)=VAL(MID$(A$(M),36,3))
:EC1(2,M-1)=VAL(MID$(A$(M),40,3)):TP1$(2,M-1)=MID$(A$(M),44,1):DP
1(2,M-1)=VAL(MID$(A$(M),46,2)):WDT(2,M-1)=EC1(2,M-1)-SC1(2,M-1)+1
:PW$=F1$(2,M-1)
970 GOSUB 2060:F1$(2,M-1)=LEFT$(F1$(2,M-1),NPK)
980 F1$(3,M-1)=MID$(A$(M),49,10):SC1(3,M-1)=VAL(MID$(A$(M),60,3))
:EC1(3,M-1)=VAL(MID$(A$(M),64,3)):TP1$(3,M-1)=MID$(A$(M),68,1):DP
1(3,M-1)=VAL(MID$(A$(M),70,2)):WDT(3,M-1)=EC1(3,M-1)-SC1(3,M-1)+1
:PW$=F1$(3,M-1)
990 GOSUB 2060:F1$(3,M-1)=LEFT$(F1$(3,M-1),NPK)
1000 NEXT
1001 IF DL$<>"Y" THEN 1010
1002 W(1)=WDT(1,1):W(2)=WDT(2,1):W(3)=WDT(3,1)
1003 W(4)=WDT(1,2):W(5)=WDT(2,2):W(6)=WDT(3,2)
1004 W(7)=WDT(1,3):W(8)=WDT(2,3):W(9)=WDT(3,3)
1005 W(10)=WDT(1,4):W(11)=WDT(2,4):W(12)=WDT(3,4)
1006 W(13)=WDT(1,5):W(14)=WDT(2,5):W(15)=WDT(3,5)
1007 W(16)=WDT(1,6):W(17)=WDT(2,6):W(18)=WDT(3,6)
1008 W(19)=WDT(1,7):W(20)=WDT(2,7):W(21)=WDT(3,7)
1009 W(22)=WDT(1,8):W(23)=WDT(2,8):W(24)=WDT(3,8)
1010 COLOR FFG,FFB:LOCATE 22,2:PRINT"                Now creating Do
cument file........                    "
1020 GOSUB 1850
1030 FOR IJ=1 TO 36
1040 FOR II=1 TO 3:IF SC1(II,IJ)=0 THEN SC1(II,IJ)=1:WDT(II,IJ)=1
1050 NEXT:NEXT
1060 FOR H=3 TO LEN(SC$)
1070 IF MID$(SC$,H,2)="  " THEN 1090
1080 NEXT:GOTO 1100
1090 SC$=LEFT$(SC$,H-2)
1100 FOR H=3 TO LEN(IC$)
1110 IF MID$(IC$,H,2)="  " THEN 1130
1120 NEXT:GOTO 1140
1130 IC$=LEFT$(IC$,H-2)
1140 IF DL1 >0 THEN DL1$=CHR$(DL1) ELSE DL1$=""
1150 IF DL2 >0 THEN DL2$=CHR$(DL2) ELSE DL2$=""
1160 IF DL3 >0 THEN DL3$=CHR$(DL3) ELSE DL3$=""
1170 DLC$=DL1$+DL2$+DL3$
1180 OP1$=DL3$+MID$(C$,SC1(1,1),WDT(1,1))+DLC$+MID$(C$,SC1(2,1),W
DT(2,1))+DLC$+MID$(C$,SC1(3,1),WDT(3,1))+DL1$
1200 FO$=LEFT$(FL$,8)+".DAT"
1210 OPEN "O",#2,FO$
1220 OPEN "I",#1,FM$
1225 IF DL$="Y" THEN 3000
1230 K=0:I=1
1240 IF EOF(1) THEN 1390
1241 IF CR$="Y" THEN LINE INPUT #1,F$:GOTO 1260
```

```
1250 F$=INPUT$(1,LW)
1260 K=K+1:IF LEFT$(F$,1)=CHR$(12) THEN K=0:LOCATE 22,4:PRINT "FO
RM FEED !!      ":GOTO 1380
1270 IF LEFT$(F$,LEN(IC$))=IC$ THEN 1380
1280 IF SCC=0 THEN SCC=1
1290 IF MID$(F$,SCC,LEN(SC$))=SC$ OR LEFT$(F$,LEN(SC$))=SC$ THEN
GOSUB 1710:GOTO 1380
1300 IF LEN(F$)=0 THEN 1380
1301 J=1:LP1$=CHR$(34)+MID$(F$,SC1(1,J),WDT(1,J))+CHR$(34)
1302 LP2$=CHR$(34)+MID$(F$,SC1(2,J),WDT(2,J))+CHR$(34)
1303 LP3$=CHR$(34)+MID$(F$,SC1(3,J),WDT(3,J))+CHR$(34)
1304 OP$=LP1$:IF NF=>2 THEN OP$=OP$+","+LP2$
1305 IF NF=>3 THEN OP$=OP$+","+LP3$
1306 IF NF<=3 THEN 1360
1307 FOR J=2 TO NI-1
1308 LP1$=CHR$(34)+MID$(F$,SC1(1,J),WDT(1,J))+CHR$(34)
1309 LP2$=CHR$(34)+MID$(F$,SC1(2,J),WDT(2,J))+CHR$(34)
1310 LP3$=CHR$(34)+MID$(F$,SC1(3,J),WDT(3,J))+CHR$(34)
1311 OP$=OP$+","+LP1$:IF NF>(2+((J-1)*3)) THEN OP$=OP$+","+LP2$
1312 IF NF>(3+((J-1)*3)) THEN OP$=OP$+","+LP3$
1313 NEXT
1360 IF K>=SL AND K<=EL THEN PRINT #2,OP$:LOCATE 22,4:CNT=CNT+1:C
OLOR FFG,FFB:PRINT "Number Converted ";CNT;" ";LEFT$(MID$(F$,SC1(
1,1),WDT(1,1)),15);" ";LEFT$(MID$(F$,SC1(2,1),WDT(2,1)),15);" ";L
EFT$(MID$(F$,SC1(3,1),WDT(3,1)),15);
1370 IF K=LP THEN K=0:LOCATE 22,4:PRINT "PAGE BREAK!!       ":GOTO
 1380
1380 I=I+1:GOTO 1240
1390 CLOSE #1:CLOSE #2
1410 COLOR 15,0:CLS:PRINT "        Bodner-Hutchins Text Descripto
r File Processor  (Rev "+MREV$+")          "
1420 PRINT"┌──────────────────────────────────────────────────
─────────────────┐"
1430 PRINT"│Field Name   Start         End           Type
Decimals       Width │";
1440 PRINT"├──────────────────────────────────────────────────
─────────────────┤":COLOR FFG,FFB
1450 FOR J=1 TO NI-1
1460 COLOR 15,0:PRINT "│";:COLOR FFG,FFB:PRINT F1$(1,J),SC1(1,J),
EC1(1,J),TP1$(1,J),DP1(1,J);RIGHT$("                "+STR$(WDT(1,
J)),15);" ";:COLOR 15,0:PRINT "│"
1470 IF F1$(2,J)="            " OR LEN(F1$(2,J))=0 THEN 1510
1480 COLOR 15,0:PRINT "│";:COLOR FFG,FFB:PRINT F1$(2,J),SC1(2,J),
EC1(2,J),TP1$(2,J),DP1(2,J);RIGHT$("                "+STR$(WDT(2,
J)),15);" ";:COLOR 15,0:PRINT "│"
1490 IF F1$(3,J)="            " OR LEN(F1$(3,J))=0 THEN 1510
1500 COLOR 15,0:PRINT "│";:COLOR FFG,FFB:PRINT F1$(3,J),SC1(3,J),
EC1(3,J),TP1$(3,J),DP1(3,J);RIGHT$("                "+STR$(WDT(3,
J)),15);" ";:COLOR 15,0:PRINT "│"
1510 NEXT J:COLOR 15,0
1520 IF SNF=0 THEN 1610
1530 PRINT"├──────────────────────────────────────────────────
─────────────────┤"
1540 COLOR FFG,FFB:FOR J=9 TO SNI-1
1550 COLOR 15,0:PRINT "│";:COLOR FFG,FFB:PRINT F1$(1,J),SC1(1,J),
```

```
EC1(1,J),TP1$(1,J),DP1(1,J);RIGHT$("                    "+STR$(WDT(1,
J)),15);" ";:COLOR 15,0:PRINT "|"
1560 IF F1$(2,J)="            " OR LEN(F1$(2,J))=0 THEN 1600
1570 COLOR 15,0:PRINT "|";:COLOR FFG,FFB:PRINT F1$(2,J),SC1(2,J),
EC1(2,J),TP1$(2,J),DP1(2,J);RIGHT$("                    "+STR$(WDT(2,
J)),15);" ";:COLOR 15,0:PRINT "|"
1580 IF F1$(3,J)="            " OR LEN(F1$(3,J))=0 THEN 1600
1590 COLOR 15,0:PRINT "|";:COLOR FFG,FFB:PRINT F1$(3,J),SC1(3,J),
EC1(3,J),TP1$(3,J),DP1(3,J);RIGHT$("                    "+STR$(WDT(3,
J)),15);" ";:COLOR 15,0:PRINT "|"
1600 NEXT J:COLOR 15,0
1610 PRINT"└──────────────────────────────────────────────────────────
──────────────────┘"
1620 PRINT"       File structure as determined from the Text Desc
riptor File"
1630 LOCATE 19,1:COLOR FFG,FFC
1640 PRINT"┌──────────────────────────────────────────────────────────
──────────────────┐"
1650 PRINT"|       This DFP has converted "+RIGHT$("     "+STR$(C
NT),5)+" data records to file "+RIGHT$("        "+FL$,8)+".DAT
|"
1660 PRINT"|   and has created a WS file with "+RIGHT$("    "+STR
$(NF+SNF),5)+" data fields in file "+RIGHT$("        "+FL$,8)+".D
OC  |"
1670 PRINT"└──────────────────────────────────────────────────────────
──────────────────┘":COLOR 15,0
1671 PRINT "          Copyright (c) 1986, Bodner-Hutchins Inc., Hou
ston, Texas     ";
1672 ON ERROR GOTO 1679
1673 RMDIR TP$
1674 ON ERROR GOTO 0
1675 GOTO 1680
1679 IF ERR=76 THEN END
1680 IF TP$="" THEN END
1681 SH$="COPY "+FL$+".DOC "+TP$+">NUL"
1682 SHELL SH$
1683 SH$="COPY "+FL$+".DAT "+TP$+">NUL"
1684 SHELL SH$
1685 SH$=FL$+".DAT"
1686 KILL SH$
1687 SH$=FL$+".DOC"
1688 KILL SH$
1700 END
1710 REM *************************************************************
************
1720 REM * SPECIAL CODE PROCESSOR
         *
1730 REM *
         *
1740 REM *************************************************************
************
1750 IF OFS=0 THEN 1761
1760 FOR O=1 TO OFS:LINE INPUT #1,F$:NEXT
1761 J=9:LP1$=CHR$(34)+MID$(F$,SC1(1,J),WDT(1,J))+CHR$(34)
1762 LP2$=CHR$(34)+MID$(F$,SC1(2,J),WDT(2,J))+CHR$(34)
```

```
1763 LP3$=CHR$(34)+MID$(F$,SC1(3,J),WDT(3,J))+CHR$(34)
1764 OP$=OP1$+LP1$:IF SNF=>2 THEN OP$=OP$+LP2$
1765 IF SNF=>3 THEN OP$=OP$+LP3$
1766 IF SNF<=3 THEN 1830
1767 FOR J=10 TO SNI-1
1768 LP1$=CHR$(34)+MID$(F$,SC1(1,J),WDT(1,J))+CHR$(34)
1769 LP2$=CHR$(34)+MID$(F$,SC1(2,J),WDT(2,J))+CHR$(34)
1770 LP3$=CHR$(34)+MID$(F$,SC1(3,J),WDT(3,J))+CHR$(34)
1774 OP$=OP$+LP1$:IF SNF>(2+((J-9)*3)) THEN OP$=OP$+LP2$
1775 IF SNF>(3+((J-9)*3)) THEN OP$=OP$+LP3$
1810 NEXT
1820 COLOR FFG,FFB:LOCATE 22,2:PRINT"
                                                                  "
1830 IF K>=SL AND K<=EL THEN PRINT #2,OP$:LOCATE 22,4:CNT=CNT+1:P
RINT "Special Line     ";CNT;" ";LEFT$(MID$(F$,SC1(1,9),WDT(1,9))
,10);" ";LEFT$(MID$(F$,SC1(2,9),WDT(2,9)),10);" ";LEFT$(MID$(F$,S
C1(3,9),WDT(3,9)),10)
1840 RETURN
1850 REM *****************************************************
************
1860 REM * CREATE WORDSTAR DOCUMENT FILE WITH NF AND SNF FIELDNAM
ES          *
1870 REM *
            *
1880 REM *****************************************************
************
1890 WS$=LEFT$(FL$,8)+".DOC":FO$=LEFT$(FL$,8)+".DAT":W1$="#######
###"
1900 OPEN "O",#1,WS$
1910 FOR W=1 TO NI-1:W$=W$+F1$(1,W):WA$=WA$+"&"+F1$(1,W)+"& ":IF
LEN(F1$(2,W))>0 THEN W$=W$+","+F1$(2,W):WA$=WA$+"&"+F1$(2,W)+"& "
1920 IF LEN(F1$(3,W))>0 THEN W$=W$+","+F1$(3,W)+",":WA$=WA$+"&"+F
1$(3,W)+"& "
1930 NEXT
1940 IF SNF=0 THEN 1980
1950 FOR W=9 TO SNI-1:W$=W$+F1$(1,W):WA$=WA$+"&"+F1$(1,W)+"& ":IF
 LEN(F1$(2,W))>0 THEN W$=W$+","+F1$(2,W):WA$=WA$+"&"+F1$(2,W)+"&
"
1960 IF LEN(F1$(3,W))>0 THEN W$=W$+","+F1$(3,W)+",":WA$=WA$+"&"+F
1$(3,W)+"& "
1970 NEXT
1980 PRINT #1,".OP"
1990 PRINT #1,".DF "+FO$
2000 PRINT #1,".RV "+W$
2010 PRINT #1," "
2020 PRINT #1,WA$
2030 PRINT #1," "
2040 PRINT #1,".PA"
2050 CLOSE #1:RETURN
2060 REM *****************************************************
************
2070 REM * FIELD PACKER
            *
2080 REM *
            *
```

```
2090 REM ******************************************************
************
2100 FOR Q=1 TO LEN(PW$):IF MID$(PW$,Q,1)=" " THEN NPK=Q-1:RETURN
2110 NEXT:NPK=Q
2120 RETURN
3000 REM ******************************************************
************
3010 REM * DELIMITED FILE PROCESSOR
         *
3020 REM *
         *
3030 REM ******************************************************
************
3035 CNT=0
3040 IF EOF(1) THEN 1390
3050 CNT=CNT+1:CNT2=0
4030 FOR I=1 TO NF
4040 INPUT #1,ADL$(I):ADL$(I)=LEFT$(ADL$(I)+C$,W(I))
4045 LOCATE 22,4:CNT2=CNT2+1:COLOR FFG,FFB:PRINT "Number Converte
d ";CNT;" Field # ";CNT2;" ";LEFT$(ADL$(I)+C$,30)
4046 IF I>1 THEN PRINT #2,DL2$;
4050 PRINT #2,DL1$+ADL$(I)+DL3$;
4060 NEXT:PRINT #2,""
4070 GOTO 3040
```

```
* ---------------------------------------------------------------
-------------
*
* Program:              DFPDBF2.PRG
* System:               Descriptor File Processor for dBase III
* Programmer:           Michael Simon Bodner
* Written:              03/12/86
* Revised By:           Michael Simon Bodner
* Revision Date:        03/12/86
*
* ---------------------------------------------------------------
-------------
*
* Comments:             This is the part 2 of the dfp for dbase
*
* ---------------------------------------------------------------
-------------
*
* Calls:
*
* ---------------------------------------------------------------
-------------
SET TALK OFF
SET SAFETY OFF
PUBLIC CLIPPER
IF CLIPPER
EXTERNAL ISCOLOR,ISPRINTER
IF ISCOLOR()
   SET COLOR to GR+/R,R/
ELSE
   SET COLOR to W/ , /W
ENDIF ISCOLOR
ENDIF CLIPPER
PUBLIC MDATA,MFILE
USE DFP
ZAP
APPEND FROM DFP.OUT SDF
MDATA=DATA
@ 21,1 SAY SPACE(73)
@ 21,5 SAY ' Now placing converted data into dBase file '+trim('&
MDATA')+'.DBF ......'
MFILE=(TRIM('&MDATA')+'.OUT')
USE &MDATA
ZAP
APPEND FROM &MFILE SDF
USE
```

Index

Edited by Marianne Krcma

So that TAB BOOKS Inc. can better fill your reading needs . . .

please take a moment to complete and return this card. We appreciate your comments and suggestions.

1. I am interested in books on the following subjects:

- ☐ automotive
- ☐ aviation
- ☐ business
- ☐ computer, hobby
- ☐ computer, professional
- ☐ electronics, hobby
- ☐ electronics, professional
- ☐ finance
- ☐ how to, do-it-yourself
- ☐ engineering (specify): ____________
- ☐ other (specify) ____________
- ☐ other (specify) ____________

2. I own/use a computer:

- ☐ IBM ____________
- ☐ Apple ____________
- ☐ Commodore ____________
- ☐ Macintosh ____________
- ☐ ATARI ____________
- ☐ AMIGA ____________
- ☐ Other (specify) ____________

3. This card came from TAB book (specify title and/or number):

____

4. I purchase books:

- ☐ from general bookstores
- ☐ from technical bookstores
- ☐ from college bookstores
- ☐ through the mail
- ☐ by telephone
- ☐ by electronic mail
- ☐ other (specify) ____________

Comments ____________

____

____

Name ____________

Company ____________

Address ____________

City ____________

State ____________ Zip ____________